British Birds

British birds –
their fascinating stories

Geoff Green

Published by Geoff Green

Kindle direct publishing

Dedication

Many thanks to my wife, Shirley and my family who have been so very supportive and encouraging during the writing of this book and for their patience whilst absorbed watching birds over the years.

TABLE OF CONTENTS:

ON BEING A BIRD 1

Feathers 2

Legs, feet and toes 13

Beaks and bills 17

Metabolic rate 24

Size matters 25

Sexual differences 27

UP, UP AND AWAY 30

Designed for flight 31

The mechanics of flying 34

Flight patterns 38

Migration 41

Preparing for migration 44

Finding their way 46

Flocking 53

SINGING LIKE A LARK 57

Songs and calls 58

How do they do it? 62

Why birds sing and call 65

Variations on a theme 68

MATES, MATING AND BREEDING 71

Breeding relationships 72

Courtship 75

Sex 79

Nesting 81

Eggs 85

SENSE AND SENSIBILITY 95

Sight 96

Sound 104

Touch 107

Taste...108

Smell...109

Magnetism...109

Eating...110

Drinking..113

Sleeping...113

Intelligence 114

Emotions 118

Imprinting 120

POPULATIONS...122

Measuring populations...123

Extrinsic factors 127

Intrinsic factors 130

Life expectancy 131

Habitat change 132

Climate change..134

Hunting 135

Human exploitation...137

Conservation..144

Counting and tracking..155

ORDER! ORDER!..160

How many? 161

Defining a species..161

History of taxonomy 163

Current classification...167

What's in a name?...173

Myth, magic and fact..182

SPECIES ACCOUNTS...184

Geese, swans, ducks and mergansers 187

Grouse, quails, pheasants and partridge 202

Grebes...207

Pigeons and doves..210

Cuckoos 216

Nightjars and swifts 219

Cranes, rails, crakes and gallinules 223

Waders, plovers, gulls, terns and guillemots 229

Divers 260

Shearwaters and petrels 263

Gannets, cormorants and shags 267

Herons, egrets and bitterns 271

Hawks, eagles, buzzards, kites and ospreys 276

Owls 287

Kingfishers 297

Woodpeckers and wrynecks 300

Falcons and kestrels 306

Parrots 312

Passeriformes 312

Collective nouns 389

APPENDICES 395

Appendix 1 Zoological terms 395

Appendix 2 Record breakers 404

Appendix 3 Phrases and idioms 408

REFERENCES 411

BIBLIOGRAPHY 411

INDEX 416

PREFACE

Human beings have been intrigued by birds for millennia and continue to be so today. We have been beguiled by their lives, behaviour, song and by flight. This closeness is reflected in our relationships with birds, some of which have been mutually beneficial others have been (and continue to be) exploitative.

The aim of this book is to explore this fascinating world of birds, particularly British birds. The first four chapters examine how birds live. The topics explored include flight, unravelling the mystery of migration, how birds breed through the wonderful process of egg production and also the marvel of bird song. In addition the senses birds use are explored as well as the remarkable intelligence of some birds. Following this is a review of the factors affecting bird populations including human exploitation and conservation stories, plus the current status of bird species in the UK.

The next chapter moves on to explain the way in which birds are organised into orders, familes, genus and species. The final chapter gives species' accounts for 235 of the more common Britsh birds. Here, for each species, is a broad range of information on the names given to birds (local, formal and scientific) plus their derivation and meaning, often providing valuable insights. Alongside this are any myths, tales, lore, stories or superstitions for many birds as well as references in literature or music, (set in boxes) often revealing the close relationship humans have had with birds over millennia.

The book includes tables of data, graphs, drawings and over 50 line drawings by the author.

Enjoy this book as it opens up the wonderful, fascinating and often mysterious lives of British birds.

CHAPTER ONE

ON BEING A BIRD

Any discussion about birds needs to start with a clear, unambiguous definition of what a bird is. Thankfully that is easy – feathers. All birds have feathers; no other animal has feathers. Therefore feathers are the unique defining characteristic of all birds. That merely distinguishes a bird from all other animals. To fully understand what it is to be a bird we need to identify the key features of a bird. The list below is a set of features which characterises birds:

- **Winged** – the vast majority of birds have wings and can fly or swim or have the remains of what once were wings.

- **Bipedal** – all birds have two legs.

- **Warm blooded** – birds have a system to maintain their own body temperature i.e. they are endothermic. This includes a four chambered heart.

- **Vertebrates** – birds are classed as vertebrates (in the phylum Chordata) along with fish, amphibians, reptiles and mammals. Hence birds have a back bone and skeleton.

- **Hard shelled eggs** – birds reproduce by laying eggs.

- **Beak** – for feeding and other purposes but they lack teeth.

- **Pneumatic bones** – most of the bones of many birds have a unique hollow structure linked to the respiratory system.

Each of these key features requires some elaboration:

Feathers

Feathers play a central role in the life of a bird, performing several vital functions:

Enabling flight	Providing insulation
Water proofing	Attracting a mate
Providing camouflage	Detecting prey
Enabling swimming	Assisting with buoyancy
Cleaning	Communicating
Defending	Generating sound

A feather is comprised of a central shaft, called the rachis, with barbs either side. The rachis is hollow and made of keratin (the same chemical as human nails). Barbs branch out from the rachis at 45^0 and barbules (when present) branch off the barbs at 90^0 and have small hooks at the end. In some feathers the barbs are loose e.g. for insulation. In others they lock together using barbules, hooking the barbs in place e.g. on wing feathers. The body end of the shaft is the quill. Recent research has found that barbules are spaced within 8 to 16 micrometers of one another in all birds, from the hummingbird to the condor, suggesting that the spacing remains constant, despite size differences and this is an important property for flight. The same research found that the underside of a feather can capture air for lift, while the top of the feather can block air out when gravity needs to take over.

Feathers start with a growth through the skin; a tip pushes out and ejects the old feather. The barbs are formed at this stage but remain encased in a sheath. When the feather reaches its full length the sheath falls off to reveal the barbs (and barbules, if present). Once feathers have grown and emerged from their protective sheath, they are comprised of dead cells, having no blood supply and no nerves (except filoplumes).

Feather maintenance is a vital activity for birds. That is why birds bathe and spend a significant amount of time preening. For the vast majority of birds flight feathers are only replaced by moulting once a year and body feathers twice a year (less frequently for large birds) so feathers must be maintained in top condition. Flight efficiency requires feathers to be in the best possible condition. During the winter birds rely on their feathers to keep them warm. In the breeding season many male birds (and some female birds) need their plumage to be at its best to attract a mate.

Preening restores feathers back into their correct place. With flight feathers preening locks the barbules back around the barbs to keep the vanes together (or air will pass through the feathers and reduce flight efficiency). Down feathers need fluffing back up to maintain their insulation properties. Bristles need cleaning to ensure they maintain their sensitivity. Preening also removes the empty sheath that once wrapped the newly emerged feathers during moulting. Woodpigeon's feathers are attached weakly compared to other birds, so that in the event of a strike from a bird of prey, like a Peregrine, the feathers fall out easily and the bird escapes with its life. This is known as fright moult. This explains why sometimes you come across a pile of feathers with no obvious sign of a carcass or blood. A Woodpigeon might have escaped with its life from the claws or sharp beak of a predator and be left with a bald patch.

Bathing helps keep the feathers clean and free from parasites. Birds suffer from a range of parasites which live off feathers, debris or blood. The categories of parasite include flies, lice, mites, fleas and ticks. To alleviate the detrimental effect of these parasites birds preen and bathe. Feather deterioration is one of the reasons that birds eventually have to moult. Some birds, like the Jay, use ants to rid their feathers and bodies of parasites. They squeeze the ants so they eject formic acid onto their bodies to kill the parasites. Other birds have dust baths, again to rid their feathers of parasites. Also some birds lie prostrate on the ground and spread out their wings to sun their feathers. Sunning also has the effect of converting preen oil into vitamin D. It is also easier to remove parasites from warm feathers, plus parasites are more likely to move when warm. In cold weather birds fluff up their feathers to increase insulation and water proofing.

Feathers are also vital to keeping birds water proofed. To do this many birds apply a waxy secretion to their feathers from a gland accessed from the cloaca, the rear vent. Birds use their beaks to stroke this oil onto their feathers to maintain water proofing. This oil also has antibacterial properties. Oddly the edges of the Cormorant's wing feathers are not water proof hence the need for Cormorants to sit with their wings out stretched to dry them after an underwater foray. Birds in the heron family do not have a preen gland. Instead they have powder feathers on their breast which they use to rid their other feathers of the slime from catching slippery fish and to assist with water proofing. The barbs of these feathers break up into a powder. The use of feathers to attract a mate is dealt with in Chapter 4 Mates, mating and breeding.

Camouflage is an important feature of many birds. The vast majority of birds are acutely aware of the possibility of becoming a predator's meal. So the feathers of many birds are cryptically coloured to minimise the chance of being spotted. The cryptic colour of female Nightjar is so good it is possible to approach the bird within a few metres when it is sat on the nest. The male's similar colouration (the only difference between the sexes are the white dots on the male's wing tip and tail) provides excellent camouflage as it sits lengthways on a tree branch; incidentally the only bird to sit lengthways – other birds sit across a branch in order to perch. Other birds with excellent camouflage are the Snow Bunting and the Ptarmigan. The latter bird moults into feather colours that match its winter white, snowy environment and then moults in spring into brown colours to blend into its heather environment. Some birds are coloured to provide camouflage whilst hunting. Several seabirds, like the auks, have underside colouration which blends in with the sky, so that potential prey items cannot see a bird eying up its next meal in the sea below.

Birds use feather wear to their advantage. In some species as the feathers wear they reveal a new colouration. The Snow Bunting's body feathers change from white to black as they wear, going from a camouflage colouration in winter to an attractive black and white mixture, used to attract a mate at the start of the breeding season. This might be a reason why the Snow Bunting only needs to moult once a year. Similarly, Starling's feathers wear from their speckled winter plumage to an iridescent black in spring; quite a transformation. Oddly the Starling only moults once a year, after breeding. These changes in colouration as the seasons change can create challenges for bird identification in the field.

Occasionally birds utilise feathers to generate sound. The Snipe produces a drumming sound during its stoop display flight. The outer tail feathers twist out at a wide angle and produce a characteristic sound. The Woodcock generates a sound with its flight feathers during its roding display flight. The three outer primary feathers are stiffened and emarginated, producing a sound when flapped rapidly.

Types of feather

1- Contour feather

Contour - these feathers have a fluffy base with tips that are more structured with barbs, which helps with water proofing. They are the main feathers that cover a bird's body. Their colouring can provide camouflage. In some species, like the Long-eared Owl, contour feathers can be used for displays of aggression. A typical song bird is covered with about 2 500 contour feathers.

2 - Wing feather

Wing - called remiges, are largely made of barbs and barbules that lock together to form two vanes, one either side of the central shaft, enabling the wing to push air during flight (rather than pass through it). The barbs are asymmetrically arranged either side of the rachis giving a forward facing vane that is narrower than the rear facing vane; being a very clever adaptation that is essential to efficient flight. Primary flight feathers can pivot in their follicle so they can twist between the up beat and the down beat when flying.

Primary flight feathers are also anchored to bone with ligaments; all other feathers are not anchored in this way, except the two central tail feathers. This gives the strength necessary for flight and enables the feathers to be accurately positioned. Primary feathers have tapered ends. In some birds the vane narrows towards the tip (on the forward vane) and this is called emargination. Primary feathers are numbered inner to outer. Secondary flight feathers do not twist in the manner of the primary flight feathers and the vanes are usually the same width each side of the rachis. Secondary feathers have rounded or squared ends and are numbered outer to inner. Secondary flight feathers act as an aerofoil to provide lift in flight.

Tail - called rectrices, again are made up of barbs and barbules, like wing feathers. Each vane is arranged symmetrically either side of the rachis in the central tail feathers and asymmetrically on the outer feathers. Tail feathers are numbered inner to outer. The central two tail feathers are anchored to bone. In the Woodpecker and Treecreeper families the tail feathers are strengthened to enable the bird to brace themselves against a vertical tree trunk whilst feeding. Tail feathers help some birds steer whilst flying. The rear display plumage of some male birds, such as a peacock, is not comprised of tail feathers but of feathers attached to the body above the tail.

Semi-plume - these feathers possess a rachis but have no hooks on their barbules and lack the structure of a vane. They provide an insulating layer of feathers.

3 - Semi-plume feather

Down - these feathers do not have a rachis and are made up of fluffy flexible barbs. Their loose structure traps heat. Down is used to provide insulation and is more prevalent in ducks than song birds. Some fledglings (mainly altricial young) are covered in down at birth and moult into contour feathers as they mature.

4 - Down feather

Bristles - a simple rachis often used to protect the eyes and face. In some species, like the Nightjar, the facial bristles assist in catching their aerial moth prey.

Filoplumes - a simple rachis with a few barbs at the end of the shaft. Filoplumes are only found with other feathers. They have nerve endings which are used to keep other feathers in place or to adjust them e.g. flight feathers.

In most birds feathers are not evenly distributed over the whole body. Instead the feathers are arranged in patches with some areas of skin only having down or semi-plume feathers and no contour feathers. The areas of skin where contour feathers occur is called pterylae and bare areas apteria. The arrangement of these feathered areas varies across orders and families. For example, water birds have a more comprehensive coverage of feathers to ensure they remain insulated against cold water.

5 - Filoplume

Owls have adaptations their wing feathers to ensure they fly silently towards unsuspecting prey. They have soft feather projections on their wings, combs along the leading edge, downy filaments on the upper surface and fringed tips to the trailing edge. All to achieve silent flight!

How birds' feathers are coloured

Colours are formed in two different ways; either from pigments or from light refraction caused by the structure of the feather and in some cases a combination of both.

Pigmentation

Pigments are coloured substances that can be found in both plants and animals. The colouration created by pigments is independent of the structure of the feather. Pigment colours are produced by the pigment absorbing all the wavelengths of white light except for the observed colour. Pigment colouration in birds derives from three groups - carotenoids, melanins and porphyrins:

- o **Carotenoids** - are derived from plants that are part of a bird's diet and produce yellow and orange colours.

- o **Melanins** - are synthesised and produce colours from black to reddish browns and pale yellows. Feathers that contain melanin are stronger and more resistant to wear. Feathers without any pigmentation are the weakest of all. In some birds, like the gulls, the wing tips are black which strengthens them against excessive wear.

- o **Porphyrins** - are made by the liver and produce pink, brown, red and green colours. They fluoresce when exposed to ultra-violet light.

Structural colours are produced as light is refracted by the proteins in the feather:

- o **Iridescence**- these colours are produced by the refraction of light passing through the feather's barbules. Refraction works like a prism, splitting the light into its component colours. As the viewing angle changes, the refracted light becomes visible as an iridescent display. An example of iridescence is the bright turquoise feather colour of the Kingfisher. When viewed in low light these feathers appear brown. The colour seen varies with the viewing angle.

- o **Non-iridescence** - tiny air pockets in the barbs of feathers scatter incoming light, resulting in a specific colour. Blue colours in feathers are almost always produced in this manner where the blue wavelength of light is refracted and the remaining colours are absorbed by a layer of melanin.

- o **Ultraviolet** - the feathers of many species also reflect light in the ultraviolet range. Many birds' eyes can detect a wider spectrum of light than humans', including ultraviolet wavelengths. For example, the blue cap of a Blue Tit reflects ultra violet wavelengths of light which the female can see but we can't. The more prominent the blue cap the more attractive the male.

Abnormalities

Occasionally birds can be seen with abnormal feathering. A number of conditions might cause this:

- o **Leucism** - pale or white patches caused genetically.
- o **Melanism** - unnaturally dark feathers due to an excess of the dark pigment, melanin.
- o **Albinism** - all the feathers are pale or white plus the bird has red or pink eyes and legs. A genetic condition causing a lack of pigmentation.

The wonder of feathers is well summarised by Colin Tudge in his book *Consider the birds* "All in all, the individual bones and skeleton as a whole is a supreme exercise in civil engineering. But the key to the whole design lies in one of nature's most ingenious inventions. Feathers".

Numbers of feathers

The table below gives some examples of the number of primary, secondary flight and tail feathers:

8

Table 1 - Numbers of feathers

Bird species	Primary	Secondary	Tail
Ducks, Geese, Swans.	11	15-24	12-24
Woodpeckers	10	11	12
Owls	10	11-19	12
Pigeons	10	11-15	12
Sandpipers	10	11	12
Gulls and Terns	11	11	12
Falcons	10	16	12-14
Passerines	9-10	9-11	12

The total number of feathers on a bird varies. A typical song bird will have 1500 – 3000 feathers making up about 6% of their body mass. A small hummingbird has only about 900 feathers whilst the Mute Swan has 20 000 feathers, with the majority on its long neck.

Moulting

As we noted earlier feathers are made up of dead cells with no blood supply or nerves and are incapable of regeneration. Given the hectic and energetic life style of most birds, feathers get damaged; they fall out, wear out or are affected by parasites. To regain a set of feathers in full working order it is necessary for birds to lose their old feathers and replace them with new ones in a process called moulting. Moulting is not exclusive to birds: cats, dogs, snakes, lizards, crabs and frogs all moult.

What triggers off moulting is not fully understood. Environmental factors play a part as do hormones. Clearly birds avoid moulting during the breeding season and they will only moult when this has the least impact on their survival. Needless to say different species of bird have developed variations to the general theme of moulting.

The process of moulting commences when a new feather begins to push through the follicle of an existing feather. As the new feather emerges it pushes out the old feather. The new feather structure (as described earlier) is wrapped in a sheath and when the rachis reaches its final length the blood supply is cut off and the sheath falls away to reveal the new feather.

Generally (there are always exceptions) moulting occurs in an orderly fashion. Flight feathers are replaced in matched pairs, often starting with the primary feathers, to minimise the reduction in flight efficiency. In the passerine order of birds flight feather moult starts with the inner most primary first, moving outwards, the tertials commence their moult about half way through the replacement of the primary feathers, followed by the secondary flight feathers, inner to outer. Whilst moulting its flight feathers the bird moults its body feathers.

Tail feathers are usually moulted inner to outer in pairs. Woodpecker and Treecreepers, who use their tail feathers to balance vertically on a tree trunk, moult their tail feathers in matched pairs starting with the second inner most feathers to ensure it can still feed on trees trunks whilst moulting.

Most birds (with several exceptions) undertake a full moult (wings and body feathers) in late summer after breeding is completed and a further partial moult (body feathers only) in spring prior to breeding. Moulting requires a lot of energy to manufacture a large number of new feathers. Also birds during moult are at greater risk of predation as they are less mobile. Also during moult birds are less water proof and have less insulation. Some birds, like the Snow Bunting and Starling, only moult once a year. The Long-tailed Duck moults three times a year.

Some species undergo a catastrophic moult whereby all the feathers are replaced simultaneously. For those species that do this, like the Shelduck and Goosander, they need a safe haven to moult where the risk of predation is minimal. Male Shelduck fly off to safe havens where large numbers gather to moult. Divers moult all their flight feathers at once and are flightless for 2 weeks. Ducks typically moult after breeding into a dull eclipse plumage before moulting again soon afterwards into full breeding plumage. Male ducks moult all their flight feathers at once, making them vulnerable to predation. The dull eclipse plumage makes the male less vulnerable to predation whilst it moults its flight feathers. Once these are replaced the bird moults again to restore its colourful breeding plumage. The female duck moults later after her young have become independent. Puffins moult all their wing feathers at once in winter. The bird has a high wing loading so losing just a few wing feathers at a time would render the bird flightless anyway. Hence, losing its wing feathers all at once shortens the moult period and is a lower risk strategy.

Migration is a challenge. Some species undertake a full moult prior to their journey; others undertake a partial moult prior to leaving and complete their moult on arrival at their feeding grounds, whilst others leave moulting until they have reached their migratory destination. The ability to fly efficiently, with new feathers, has to be balanced against the considerable energy required for moulting. Unusually the Willow Warbler undertakes a full moult twice a year; once on its breeding grounds and once on its wintering grounds. The Golden Plover undergoes a full moult on its northerly breeding grounds before migrating south. Both sexes of Knot congregate on the Waddensee during their northerly migratory flight to moult into their colourful breeding plumage. The Common Sandpiper undertakes a full moult whilst on its western sub-Sahara resting grounds. Oystercatchers breeding in Iceland undergo a full moult before migrating to the UK for the winter. Cranes don't moult their wing feathers until they reach maturity at age 3 - 4 years old.

Larger birds, such as the Golden Eagle, can take two years to complete a full moult whilst small birds can complete a moult in 4 weeks. Also larger birds, as they mature, moult into intermediate plumages. So for example, a Herring Gull only attains its full adult plumage at the age of four. Determining the age of sub-adult birds provide a challenge in the field. Some features are easy to spot, so if there is a terminal black band on the tail of a Herring Gull, it is an immature bird. The width of this band decreases with each moult. However, a bird in sub-adult plumage does not mean it cannot breed. Birds in immature plumage might have reached sexual maturity. Some young birds undergo a partial moult, such as the Robin. A juvenile in first plumage has a spotted breast; they then moult into the familiar red-breasted adult plumage.

Female birds (and some males) lose the feathers on their belly to create a brood patch which they use to keep their eggs at the optimum temperature to develop and hatch successfully. It is known that in some birds, like the Swallow, the brood patch is used to count the number of eggs laid, so she stops laying eggs when the right clutch size is reached. The Razorbill has two brood patches for one egg, heating two sides of the egg whilst brooding. The Herring Gull has three brood patches to brood its three eggs. On average the Goldcrest lays 10 eggs but only 2 or 3 eggs are in contact with the brood patch. The other eggs are warmed by the female's legs whose blood supply increases to a temperature of 41^0 C.

Visual displays

Birds often perform displays involving the use of feathers and to signal information to other birds of the same or different species. Displays fulfil a number of functions:

Courtship	Aggression	Begging
Greeting	Subordination	Defence
Alarm		

These displays are visual signals involving body postures, plumage displays including head, body, wing and tail feathers, use of the beak and legs and various movements. Displays are social communication between birds – to the same species or other species, between males and females or to birds of the same sex. See the Section on Courtship in Chapter 4. Courtship displays can include allopreening, touching beaks, presenting food and dancing. Threat displays are used to defend territory, mate, nest, chicks or food. A response to a threat display can be a submissive posture where the bird turns away, drops to the ground, pulls its head into its shoulders or crouches.

Some examples of displays include:

- Ruff and Black Grouse displaying at a lek to attract a female.
- Male and female Great Crested Grebes performing an elaborate courtship display.
- Male Kingfishers showing off their plumage to a prospective mate (usually with a fish in his beak).
- Male Dunnocks lowering their bodies and shimmering their wing feathers to attract a mate.
- Male and female Crane performing their ritualised dance.
- Male duck stretching its wing feathers to display its colourful speculum.
- Male and female Gannets greeting each other on a cliff top after a winter apart at sea.
- Swans spreading their feathers to warn off an intruder.
- Hatchlings engaging in begging displays to be the preferred recipient of a tasty morsel.

Flight

The primary purpose of wings is flight but some birds' wings are vestigial and they are now unable to fly. Of the approximately 60 species of birds (out of a total of about 10 000) that cannot fly, most are in a completely separate group. Later, in the Chapter Order! Order! we will look in detail at how birds are classified. At the top level birds are in a class of their own, called Aves. Immediately beneath this are two sub-classes – Paleognathes and Neognathes. The difference is based on the structure of the jaw, with –nathes meaning jaw. The Paleognathes (old jaws) include the ostriches, rheas, emus, cassowaries and kiwis; all flightless birds. As a result there are anatomical differences, such as the absence of a keel bone (required to hold the flight muscles). Some of the current non-fliers were capable of flight at one time and have now lost that ability. The Kiwi is an example. This bird, endemic to New Zealand, had no reason to fly and so its wings shrank and are now useless. Sadly this has caused its demise as the bird was for a long time at the top of the food chain until humans introduced predators (such as rodents and mustalids) that now threaten the existence of this flightless bird. Most other birds can fly and are classed as Neognathes. One clear exception to this is the penguins that are specialised swimming birds that cannot fly. All British birds are in the sub-class Neognathe. As flight is so important to birds, this will be dealt with in detail in the next Chapter Up Up and away.

Legs, feet and toes

Most birds are classified as digitigrade animals, meaning they walk on their toes, rather than the whole foot. Birds use their legs, feet and toes for many different functions including:

Walking	Running	Climbing
Swimming	Steering underwater	Perching
Carrying	Landing	Feeding
Catching prey	Killing prey	Holding
Scratching	Cradling eggs	Turning eggs
Heating eggs	Courtship	Building nests
Preening	Heat loss regulation	

Anatomically the legs which you can see on most birds are the equivalent of the human foot, ankle and toes. The knee joint remains hidden on nearly all birds. The joint that you often do see is the equivalent of our ankle.

Avian feet, like beaks, tell us a great deal about the taxonomic relationships, behaviour and ecology of birds. More than half of the species of birds are passerines, birds characterised largely by their feet. Foot structure varies among the other major taxonomic groups.

These differences are related to the life-styles of the birds:

- Passerines have feet with four separate toes, three of them directed forward and one (the first or inner toe, the equivalent of our big toe called the hallux) directed backwards. All four passerine toes join the leg at the same level to aid walking and perching.
- Swifts have strong claws for clinging to vertical surfaces. Some swifts have all four toes pointing forward.
- Kingfishers have the middle and outer toes fused for part of their length which helps excavating their nest tunnels.
- The woodpeckers have two toes pointed forward and two backward which aids clinging to tree trunks.
- Birds of prey' toes are highly separated. They have powerful feet with grasping strong, sharp, highly curved claws and roughened pads on the undersides to better grasp prey.
- The fish-eating Osprey has a reversible toe so it catches prey with two toes facing forwards and two back and then switches to three forward facing toes when perched. It also has spines on the pads on the soles of its toes for grasping slippery fish.
- Owls can turn their fourth (outer) toe either forwards or backwards.
- Ducks, swans and geese have completely webbed feet.
- Birds that spend a lot of time walking tend to have flat feet with a reduced backward-pointing toe.

- Shorebirds that walk on soft surfaces have some webbing between the toes.
- Water birds and shorebirds have three toes pointed forward but the hind toe is often reduced and raised so that it joins the tarsus above the level of the other toes and loses contact with the ground.
- Game birds, which scratch a great deal, have blunt, thick claws attached to powerful legs.
- Ptarmigans, which walk on snow, have heavily feathered, insulated feet that function as snowshoes.
- Ravens in the Arctic have thicker, horny, insulating soles on their feet that are up to six times thicker than tropical Ravens'.
- Birds with bare legs, especially those with webbed feet, like gulls, avoid heat loss from their extremities by circulatory adaptations (see below).

Below is a diagram of the common toe arrangements in birds:

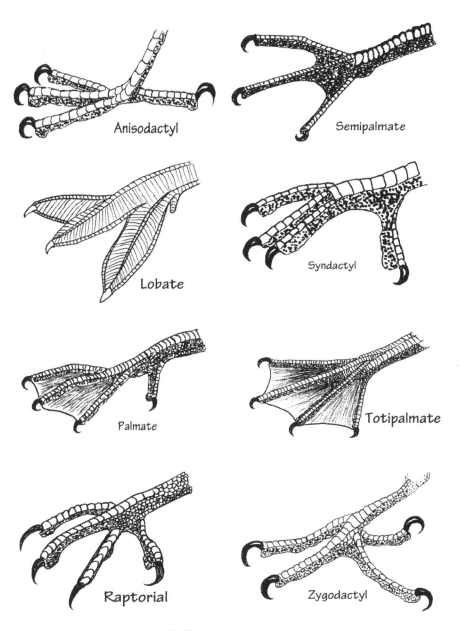

6 - Toe arrangements

Table 2 - Toe arrangements

Arrangement:	Typical species:
Anisodactyl	Perching birds - Passeriformes.
Lobate	Grebes, coots, phalaropes.
Palmate	Ducks, geese, gulls, terns, divers
Raptorial	Falcons; hawks; eagles; harriers.
Semipalmate	Waders, herons, grouse.
Syndactyl	Kingfishers.
Totipalmate	Cormorants, gannets.
Zygodactyl	Woodpeckers, owls.

All birds have claws at the end of the toes. The claws are typically curved and the radius of curvature tends to be greater in larger birds. Some species (including nightjars, herons and owls) have comb-like serrations on the claw of the middle toe, possibly used in scratch preening.

Most birds have four toes and are numbered, with the hind toe (the hallux) numbered 1 and then the other toes 2 – 4 inner to outer. Toes 2 to 4 have 2, 3 and 4 phalanges (toe bones) respectively. Ostriches have only two toes and rheas and emu have three.

Being able to grasp and hold is an essential function of a bird's foot. Passerine birds are commonly known as perching birds. These birds have a system of tendons in their feet that lock the toes automatically to grasp whatever they are perched on. Flexor tendons in the rear of the leg run from the underside of the toes to the leg muscles. As the leg bends under the weight of the bird the tendons pull and cause the toes to grasp. This is an involuntary reflex, not requiring any control by the bird, so these birds are able to sleep whilst perched. Eagles have an exceptionally strong grasp and kill their prey with their talons, as do all hawks. To ensure that they do not lose their grip on a prey item, the tendons from their talons run in a sheath with a ratchet mechanism acting to lock its talons as its prey tries to escape.

The arteries and veins intertwine in the legs, so heat can be transferred using a counter-current exchange from arteries back to veins before reaching the feet. In this mechanism the warm blood from the artery heats up the cool blood returning to the heart in the veins from the feet. The feet get cooler blood but enough to keep the cells alive. Some birds like gulls, herons, ducks and geese can regulate their temperature through their feet this way. Without this mechanism birds would gradually melt the ice they are standing on (and possibly get trapped in the ice). Also the heart would have cope with very cool blood being returned from the cold feet. Gulls can open a valve to turn back the bloodstream above the foot and constrict blood flow to the foot. This reduces heat loss by more than 90 percent. In gulls, the temperature of the base of the leg can be 32° C, while that of the foot could near to 0° C. Most birds have few nerves and blood vessels in their feet.

Bird's legs are covered in keratin scales, which are replaced through a moulting process. In most birds the scales overlap each other; an arrangement called scutullate feet. In other birds, like the falcons, the scales are organised as plates; an arrangement called reticulate. Foot colour changes over the seasons, for example, a Puffin's feet fade from a bright red colour in the breeding season to yellow in the non-breeding season. Nocturnal Nightjar's use their claws to catch their moth prey and transfer their catch to their mouth using serrations on their middle toe.

Eggs

The fascinating story of the egg as a means of reproduction is dealt with in Chapter 4 Mates, mating and breeding.

Beaks and bills

The beak is one of the defining characteristics of birds and it has acquired a spectacular and diverse range of functions:

Eating	Preening	Manipulating	Probing
Killing	Grasping	Climbing	Carrying
Scratching	Fighting	Digging	Courting
Nest building	Feeding young	Regurgitation	

Birds have no teeth, hence the expression 'rare as hen's teeth'. If they had teeth they would require a heavier jaw and large muscles. Such a bird would have a centre of gravity nearer its head (rather than where it needs to be at the mid-point of the wings) rendering it unable to fly. In order to fly a bird's forelimbs have been fully utilised for flight and as a result the beak has taken on many additional functions.

The beak is comprised of two mandibles covered in a horny layer of keratin. This layer tends to be thicker near the tip, where the most wear occurs. In most birds the horny sheath exfoliates and is continuously replenished from underneath. Sometimes the sheath develops bright colours for use in courtship and is subsequently shed. For example, the breeding Puffin has a highly coloured beak which changes to a dull appearance after its colourful scales peel off at the end of the breeding season. The edges of the beak in some birds are sharpened for cutting, in others serrated for grasping and are soft except for the harder tip. In the majority of birds the upper mandible is fixed with the lower mandible carrying out all the work, being attached to a strong muscle. The Puffin's beak is hinged in such a way that the upper and lower mandibles remain parallel, so the bird can accumulate a large number of its favourite food, the sand eel. Also the interior of the Puffin's beak is lined with spines that prevent its prey from escaping whilst they catch more food. The words bill and beak are synonymous.

Birds have adapted to gleaning food from a very wide range of sources hence their appearance in virtually every type of environment and nearly all regions of the world. This diversity has given rise to a very wide range of beak sizes and shapes. The range of food types includes:

- o **Carnivores** - birds that feed on meat. They have strong, hooked beaks securely attached to the skull with the upper part protruding over the lower. They use the beak to tear and pull the flesh off their prey. Birds of prey are an example.

- o **Granivores** – birds that feed mainly on seeds. They have short, robust beaks that end in a conical shape, allowing them to break seeds. Finches are an example.

- o **Frugivores** – birds that specialise in eating fruit, which they open to obtain the pulp or seeds. They usually have a short, curved beak with a specialised tip for extracting the edible part of the seeds. The lower mandible is flat and sharp, for splitting hard fruits. These are the only birds capable of moving the upper part of the beak independently. This allows them to exert more force to break seeds and fruit.

- o **Insectivores** – birds that eat insects of all kinds. Some birds that hunt insects in the air do so with their mouths open having a short, wide and flat beak and often a large gape. For example, Swallow and Swift. Nightjars have a bristle-fringed, wide gape that scoops insects up during their nocturnal aerial feeding forays. Other birds catch insects from the ground. These birds have short, straight, thin beaks, such as the Robin and the warblers. Others pierce the bark of the trees to remove larvae and have straight, strong beaks to penetrate the bark, such the woodpeckers and Nuthatch.

- o **Piscivores** - birds that feed on fish. In most cases these birds have large, strong beaks with a curved tip or serrated ridges to prevent their prey from escaping. This group includes birds like the gulls, tubenoses, cormorants and sawtooths.

- o **Omnivores** – birds that eat anything! These birds have large beaks enabling them to tackle a wide range of food. Examples include the crow family.

- o **Vegetarian** – birds with a predominantly vegetable diet. Beaks are usually broad at the base enabling them to nibble their food. Geese and dabbling ducks are examples.

- o **Coniferous** – feeding on the seeds of conifer cones. Beaks are specialised to pry open cones and then to extract the seeds. Crossbills are an example.

- o **Kleptoparastites** - birds with a varied diet, depending on what they can steal. Beaks tend to be strong to wrench food from other birds. Examples include the skuas but many other birds are opportunistic parasitic feeders e.g. the Black-headed Gull that harries Lapwing.

- o **Waders** - these birds have slender beaks of various lengths, adapted to searching for invertebrates under the water whilst keeping their heads out of the water. The tips of these birds' beaks are touch sensitive in order to detect prey. The sandpipers and godwits are examples.

- o **Filter feeders** - these birds have wide, flat beaks. These beaks have a filtering system whereby the bird removes the water and separates out the organisms on which these birds feed. Some ducks are in this group.

Below are drawings of a variety of birds' beaks:

Tern
Piscivorous - catches fish on surface of water.

Red-breasted Merganser
Piscivore - with serrated bill edge to secure fish prey

Chaffinch
Granivorous - eats small seeds

Raven
Scavenger

Wren
Insectivorous
Bill for insects, worms etc..

Great Spotted Woodpecker
Insectivorous and chisel boring bill

Kestrel
Carnivore - bird of prey - tearing meat.

Puffin
Piscivorous

Avocet
Scything - sweeps bill to catch invertebrates

Little Owl
Carnivore

7 - Beak patterns

These beaks just represent some UK birds. In other parts of the world there are even more spectacular examples of beaks, such as toucans, flamingos, skimmers and pelicans. The spectacular Toco Toucan's beak makes up over 50% of its body surface area!

The **gape** is the interior of the bird's open mouth. The gapes of juvenile altricial birds are often brightly coloured, sometimes with contrasting spots or other patterns and may be an indication of their health, fitness and competitive ability. Based on this, the parents decide how to distribute food among the chicks in the nest. Some birds have wide gapes enabling them to swallow large prey whole e.g. owls and herons. Aerial insectivores, like the swifts, swallows and martins have wide gapes for catching their prey.

The **tomia** are the cutting edges of the two mandibles. These range from rounded to slightly sharp. Granivorous birds, for example, have ridges on their tomia, which helps the bird to slice through a seed's outer hull. Most falcons have a sharp projection along the upper mandible, with a corresponding notch on the lower mandible. They use this to fatally sever their prey's vertebrae. The shrikes have one or more of these sharp projections. The mergansers have sawtooth serrations along their tomia, which help them to keep hold of their slippery, wriggling prey. Other birds have tomia lined with bunches of short bristles along their entire length. Most of these species are insectivores. Several ducks eat by drawing in water through the tip of their beak and expel it through the sides of the beak. As it does so the fine plates, called lamellae, on the side of the beak, traps their food.

The tips of some bird's beaks have sensitive nerve endings. Waders typically can feel for their invertebrate prey deep in mud. These nerves detect prey by touch, vibration or pressure changes. The Woodcock has a long beak with a very sensitive tip, which it uses to probe into soft ground to find its worm prey. The tips of some birds' beaks are able to move in order to catch prey. This phenomenon is called rhynchokinesis. Buffon the 18th century naturalist wrote "the tip is rather flesh than horn and appears to be susceptible to a sort of touch, calculated for detecting prey in the mire".

Most species of birds have external **nares** (nostrils) located on their beak. The nares are two holes that link to the respiratory system. In most bird species, the nares are located towards the base of the upper mandible. Strangely the Kiwi's nares are located at the tip of their beaks to help locate their prey by smell. Cormorants and gannets have no external nares as water would enter when they dived. Instead they breathe through their mouths. Usually nares are uncovered but in some species they are covered with feathers, including grouse, ptarmigans, crows and woodpeckers. The feathers over a ptarmigan's nostrils help to warm the air it inhales, whilst those on a woodpecker help to keep wood chips from clogging its nasal passages.

Some birds including raptors and owls have a waxy structure called a **cere** (from the Latin cera, meaning wax) covering the base of the beak. The cere is typically bare and often brightly coloured. In raptors, the cere is a sexual signal which indicates the quality of a bird as a mate. The brightness of the orange of a Montagu's Harrier's cere correlates to its body mass and physical condition.

All birds in the family Anatidae (ducks, geese and swans) have a plate of hard horny tissue at the tip of the beak. This structure sometimes spans the entire width of the beak and forms a hook at the end of the beak. This is used in feeding on vegetation.

A number of insectivorous birds have **rictal bristles** around the base of the beak. They may function as a net to capture flying prey e.g. Swift. Also they may prevent particles from striking the eyes.

Variations – the beaks of some species vary by sex and season:

- o   In some species the size and proportions of the beak vary between males and females. For example, females of nearly all shorebirds have longer beaks than males. Female Avocets have beaks which are slightly more upturned than those of males, thought to be associated with turning its eggs on the nest with the beak curvature matching those of her eggs. The female Curlew has a longer beak than the male allowing the sexes to access different food.
- o   Males of the larger gull species have bigger, stouter beaks than those of females and juveniles have smaller, more slender beaks.
- o   The beaks of closely related birds vary in size and shape to enable the different species to focus on eating a specific food. This enables birds to live and thrive in the same area because they are not all competing for the same (sometimes scarce) food source. An example of this is the finches, with each species having a different beak shape or size. The Greenfinch has a general purpose beak that enables it to eat a range of seeds. The Goldfinch has a longer, thinner beak that is suited to its thistle and teasel diet. The Bullfinch as a shorter, stouter beak that helps it peel fruit buds for the seeds. The Hawfinch has a massive beak and is capable of cracking cherry and damson seeds. The Hawfinch is capable of exerting a force of 50 kg not bad for a bird weighing 50 g. Another example of this is the crossbills. The Scottish Crossbill feeds on pine seeds whilst the Crossbill feeds on spruce seeds. Waders have a range of beak lengths from the short beak of the plovers, through to the medium length Dunlin beak to the longer beaked Godwits. This enables each of these species to live together in winter on mud flats as they each probe to a different depth to find their food.
- o   A number of birds (usually winter seed eaters like the finches and tits) change to an insect diet in summer to feed their young and in

doing so their beaks change shape and size. The Great Tit's beak becomes longer and narrower in summer.

- o The tip of an Oystercatcher's beak changes shape depending on the type of food it eats and the manner in which it opens its shell fish food. One technique is to hammer the mollusc open with a short, blunt beak or use the chisel-shaped beak. Birds can have a longer, pointed beak by which they feed on invertebrates under the ground. As food sources change so can the beak shape and this takes 2 – 3 weeks. The bird's beaks grow at about 0.4 mm a day to recover wear and tear.
- o Blackcaps that winter in Britain have longer, narrower beaks than those wintering in Spain, with research indicating this is as a result of using our garden bird feeders.
- o The beak of the Puffin is photo-luminescent meaning that the beak glows in the dark enabling the chick to locate its parent in the dark nest burrow.

Some species, including storks, cranes and some owls, clap their beaks as a form of communication, especially as part of a courtship display. Gannets engage in billing by raising their beaks high and clattering them against each other. Puffins also use their beaks in courtship when they meet after being apart for the winter. Beaks are used by birds not just for preening themselves, as part of their feather hygiene regime but a number of species engage in allopreening. Partners who preen each other serves two purposes. One is to preen the parts of the partner's body they cannot reach and second is to strengthen the pair bond and maintain social monogamy, prevalent in most bird species. Birds are often seen stroking their flight feathers with their beak to re-align the barbs in the primary feathers to improve flight efficiency.

Many birds use their beaks in defence and attack if they get into disputes over territory or mates. If you visit a tern colony and get too close to a nest, the adults will attack aggressively, flying at the intruder's head with its beak. Likewise, skuas will do the same. If woodland birds discover a sleeping Tawny Owl they will attack the owl and use their beaks to inflict injury on the owl until it moves away. In defending their territory birds will use their beaks in a fight, to peck or bite an intruder. Falcons use their beaks to kill prey.

Bones

Birds have a strong skeletal framework made up of bones, many of which are fused together. Also most bones are hollow and the pneumatic structure is linked to the respiratory system. The hollow bones are very strong for their weight but are not much lighter than the equivalent mammalian bones. Rigidity is important for the skeleton to be able to withstand the considerable forces generated when flying. This is especially true of the thorax and pelvis. The skeleton accounts for about 5% of a bird's weight. In species which feed under water their bones are solid as they need the weight to swim with ease.

Metabolic rate

Birds live energetic lives requiring a high metabolic rate. Their high energy activities include:

Flying	Migrating	Evading predators
Chasing prey	Swimming	Diving
Walking	High altitude flying	Moulting
Courtship	Nest building	Egg production
Egg laying	Incubation	Feeding young
Defending territory	Singing	
Thermo regulation		

Flight requires high levels of energy, with some birds perpetually in flight, like the Swift. Other birds prefer to swim and dive, such as ducks, divers (and in the extreme the penguins) which again requires high levels of energy as does powering the comparatively large flight muscles. For example, a Woodpigeon's pectoral muscles account for 40% of its weight. A further additional weight is the need for a large keel bone to hold the large pectoral muscles in place. A pigeon in flight consumes ten times the energy of the bird at rest. Some birds, such as ducks, spend more time swimming which requires 3 to 4 times the energy compared to when at rest.
A bird's high metabolic rate is achieved by:

o **Rapid and efficient digestion of food** - to generate energy quickly. Many birds have a large oesophagus which can be used to store food or ingest large items of food. For example, owls ingest rodents whole and cormorants take whole fish. Several birds have a crop where they can store food, for example, the Woodpigeon can store quantities of seed and the Jay up to eight acorns. Many birds have a gizzard which grinds food into an easily digestible size. The gizzard often contains grit or small stones to assist in this process. See the Section Eating in Chapter 5 for more detail on a bird's digestive system.

o **Highly efficient respiratory system** - to supply sufficient oxygen for high energy activities. Bird's lungs are not especially large but birds have a number of large air sacs in various parts of their body cavity which are involved in respiration. In addition many bones are pneumatic with the hollow area linked to the respiratory system. Birds do not have a diaphragm but air is inhaled and exhaled through the action of muscles on the air sacs. Birds have a four chambered heart but it is anatomically different from mammals to ensure sufficient oxygenated blood is supplied to the very large flight muscles. Smaller birds (with their higher metabolic rate) have proportionally larger hearts and a faster heart beat. Rest heart beats vary from 345 / min in a Carrion Crow, to 460 in a House Sparrow to 615 in a hummingbird.

Respiratory cycle:

- First inhalation - air passes down the trachea and splits by the syrinx into each lung. →
- Most of the inhaled air by-passes the lungs and enters the abdominal air sacs with the abdomen expanding to pull air in. →
- First exhalation – the abdomen contracts and the air passes into the lungs for the exchange of oxygen and carbon dioxide. →
- Second inhalation – the air from the lungs passes into the anterior air sacs. →
- Second exhalation – the anterior air sacs contract and the spent air passes into the trachea and to the atmosphere.

- **Reducing heat loss** - birds have various strategies for reducing heat loss in order to control their metabolic rate. Birds can fluff out their feathers to trap insulating air, reducing heat loss by a third. Some species have a denser winter plumage. Birds also stand on one foot and tuck their heads into their bodies to reduce heat loss. Some birds huddle together to reduce heat loss, such as Wrens and Pied Wagtails. A small huddle of three Long-tailed Tits reduces heat loss by 39%. Heat loss is greater at the extremities. Some birds, like gulls, have a complex heat exchange system in their legs and head to reduce heat loss. Heat exchangers are comprised of arteries and veins that split into small blood vessels, with heat exchanged between the two in this area. In this way a gull's foot blood supply can be cooled to about 4^0 C, reducing heat loss in this area. The air sacs are also thought to assist in cooling. As air flows over the moist air sacs, the moisture evaporates which cools that area of the body. Some birds engage in gular flapping i.e. they open their mouth and flap the skin on their neck, to help with cooling.

Size matters

The table below demonstrates the range of sizes of a number of UK birds:

Table 3 – Species size variations

SPECIES	LENGTH (cm)	WING SPAN (cm)
Canada Goose	95	168
Mute Swan	152	223
Mallard	58	90
Ptarmigan	35	57
Great Crested Grebe	48	88
Woodpigeon	41	78
Coot	37	75
Lapwing	30	84
Herring Gull	60	144
Arctic Tern	34	80
Great Northern Diver	80	137
Cormorant	90	145
Grey Heron	94	185
Golden Eagle	82	212
Sparrowhawk	33	62
Tawny Owl	38	99
Raven	64	135
Great Tit	14	24
Goldcrest	9	14
Willow Warbler	11	19
Robin	14	21
Song Thrush	23	34
Chaffinch	14	26

From: (1)

It is worth noting that the size of individual birds of the same sex and species vary. Guide book data for a species might show weight in a range e.g. male Sparrowhawk 151 g +/- 16 g and female 266 g +/- 41 g. Hence the largest male might weigh 167 g and smallest female 225 g The same pertains for body and wing span dimensions with a male Sparrowhawk's body length varying between 29 – 34 cm and the female's 35 – 41 cm and the male's wing span 58 – 65 cm and the female's 67 – 80 cm.

Sexual differences

Another avian characteristic is that the males and females of some species differ either in colouration or size, or both. This phenomenon is called sexual dimorphism.

Colouration - where there is a difference in colouration between the sexes, it is frequently the male that is the more brightly coloured as it is the male that needs to attract a mate. Females are able to differentiate between competing males through visual attraction. The downside is a brightly coloured male makes it more susceptible to predation. On the other hand the female often remains cryptically coloured so that, particularly when sitting on her nest brooding, she is camouflaged. Providing the male successfully attracts a mate and has offspring, being brightly coloured is a successful breeding strategy. Colouration often takes the form of bright feathers but can include wattles (brightly coloured bare skin on the chin or head), crests and tails (technically tail feathers, such as the Peacock's, are not on the tail, they are attached to the end of the body). Also beak and leg colours change seasonally. Often beaks are more brightly coloured in the breeding season. For example, the male Mute Swan's beak develops a prominent black knob in the breeding season as well as a brighter coloured beak, hence the name cob. Similarly the male Shelduck's beak develops a large red knob in the breeding season.

Usually juveniles are the same the colour as the female which confers camouflage and a reduced risk of predation. In some species the male's non-breeding plumage is cryptic and similar or identical to the female. Some males are polymorphic i.e. there is a significant variation in colouration between individuals. Ruffs are an example of this where there is intense competition for the attention of a female. In a lek the males strut their individual plumages in order to attract a female and mate with her. Some male Ruffs have a duller plumage and are relegated to the perimeter of the lek and are less likely to mate. In a number of species the male and female are identical throughout the year e.g. the Wren and Robin. About 70% of passerines are sexually monochromatic i.e. males and females have the same colouration.

Reverse dimorphism occurs in some species. The female Dotterel and phalaropes are brightly coloured (and they also sing) with the males being much duller. The females attract a mate and then, after laying her eggs, leave the male to brood and care for the chicks. This is not laziness on the female's part; after laying her first brood she then mates with another male and brings up a second brood, saving valuable time in what is a short breeding season for these northerly breeding birds.

Size - in some species males are bigger than females, some are the same size and in yet other species the female is bigger. The general rule is that in polygynous species, where males compete for females, males tend to be larger than females. The male Ruff is larger than the female; the male's wingspan is 57 cm and he weighs 180 g whilst the smaller female's wingspan is 47 cm and she weighs 110 g. In polyandrous species, where the females compete for males, the female is larger. Sometimes the size difference is subtle. In the Swallow the male's two outermost tail feathers are longer than the females and this is used to select a mate. Size sexual dimorphism frequently occurs in birds of prey, with the females being considerably larger than the males. The female is able to kill much larger prey than the male so between them they have a wider range of potential prey.

Below is a table of the weight differences between sexes for a number species:

Table 4 – Species weight differences between sexes

SPECIES:	WEIGHT g		
	Male:	Female:	DIFF %:
Canada Goose	4270	3670	116
Mute Swan	10750	8540	126
Mallard	1270	1130	112
Ptarmigan	500	400	125
Great Crested Grebe	1100	1100	-
Woodpigeon	528	489	108
Coot	810	690	117
Lapwing	250	250	-
Herring Gull	1200	850	140
Arctic Tern	110	110	-
Great Northern Diver	4000	4000	-
Cormorant	2500	2100	119
Grey Heron	1500	1500	-
Golden Eagle	3700	5300	70
Sparrowhawk	150	266	57

	WEIGHT g		
SPECIES:	Male:	Female:	DIFF %:
Tawny Owl	400	500	80
Raven	1300	1100	118
Great Tit	18	18	-
Goldcrest	6	6	-
Willow Warbler	9	9	-
Robin	18	18	-
Song Thrush	77	71	108
Chaffinch	22	22	-

DIFF % = Male weight as % of female weight.

Ref. (1)

Historically sexual dimorphism created some confusion with identification. The appearance of male and female harriers is significantly different. The males are a light grey colour and the females are much darker with a prominent white band at the top of the tail, hence the name ringtail. That led to the male Hen Harrier and the male Montagu's Harrier being identified as the male and female of a species and the respective females as the pair of a separate species. It was Montagu who realised that this was wrong made the correct identification that we have now for both species. Similarly, the male and female Mallard were once thought to be separate species. Contradictorily, in species where the sexes are identical, historically some species were linked to another species to make the male / female pair. Famously the Robin was the male to the Wren as the female. Hence the names cock robin and Jenny wren. This was enshrined in folk tales and verse. See the entries for the Robin and Wren later in Chapter 8 Species accounts. The plumage of juvenile birds is sometimes significantly different from the adult plumage to the extent that in some species the juvenile was thought to be a separate species e.g. juvenile Kittiwakes that have a strong black and white patterning not present in the adults.

CHAPTER TWO

UP, UP AND AWAY

For millennia human beings have pondered and marvelled at bird flight. The Psalmist in Psalm 55 writes "I said 'Oh, that I had the wings of a dove, I would fly away and be at rest.'" written when the author was surrounded by his enemies. The desire to escape is encapsulated in a bird's flight. Leonardo da Vinci (1452 – 1519) made extensive studies of birds and flight, producing over 500 sketches in 18 folios. Whilst he enumerated some very detailed requirements for flight when he constructed flying machines to test these ideas they failed to work. In the 19th century Otto Lilienthal (1848 – 1896) made a detailed study of how the White Stork flew. Based on this he derived the aerodynamic properties required for flight. He was the first person to make repeated successful flights in a heavier-than-air glider, managing to fly for 250 m. The Wright brothers studied birds' wings in detail, especially the wing tips, which enable a bird to turn in flight. Utilising these design features they were able to make their historical first controlled, sustained, powered flight in 1903. The actress, Hedy Lamarr (1914 – 2000), was a keen inventor and helped change the design of wings to improve aircraft speed by studying and analysing the wing design of fast flying birds.

Designed for flight

If an aeronautical design engineer were given a brief to design an animal that flew it would require several vital innovations and a vivid imagination. The first and over-riding criteria would be lightness. Flight requires enormous effort to provide sufficient lift and propulsion. To contain the necessary muscle structure within a practicable size the whole animal has to be exceptionally light. Birds have achieved lightness in the following ways:

- o **A lightweight skeleton** - avian bones have a thin-walled, honey-combed structure which is particularly strong. This bone structure is linked to the respiratory system and a series of air sacs. Birds also have fewer bones with a number fused together making a light, strong structure. The major deviation from this is the need for a large, strong keel bone to support the large flight muscles. Attached to this is the wish bone that acts as a spring during flapping flight.

- o **A system of large air sacs** - within the skeleton a series of air sacs help reduce a bird's overall weight along with improving the efficiency of the respiratory system. A bird's respiratory system makes up 20% of a bird's body volume compared to 5% in mammals.

- o **No teeth or bony tail** - if birds had either teeth or a bony tail, their centre of gravity would shift forward or rearwards which would be disastrous for flight. The centre of gravity needs to be located by the wings; anywhere else and a bird could not sustain level flight. As a result of having no teeth the digestive system often includes a crop to store unmasticated food and frequently a gizzard to grind food (often using small stones) prior to digestion.

- **Minimum of water** - bird's bodies contain very little dense water. Whilst water is essential to a bird's life, the water content of a bird's body is very low. The kidneys extract nitrogenous waste as uric acid rather than urine. This is combined with faeces as semi-solid waste excreted through the cloaca. Birds have no need for bladders and their liver is comparatively small. Also birds do not have sweat glands.

- **Gonads** - female birds have only one ovary. Outside the breeding season this shrinks in size. Also a male's testes shrink to a very small size. The gonads are re-generated to working size only at the start of the next breeding season. The Woodpigeon is an exception to this.

Another essential requirement for efficient flight is the need for the centre of gravity to be centralised at a point in the body near the mid-point of the wings. The main muscles for flight and leg movement are contained in the body rather than on the limbs themselves. This assists with locating the centre of gravity at the mid-point of the flight muscle (pectoral muscle).

Aircraft pilots under sudden acceleration or deceleration can suffer blackouts or haemorrhaging. Some birds, like swifts and hawks, which suddenly accelerate or decelerate, have a thin area on their skull to reduce these potential problems.

Whilst flying has many advantages it comes with some serious restrictions. The main one is size. Simple physics dictates that there is a limit to the size of a bird that can fly. If you take a small bird, say a Wren, at 10 cm long, then double its length to equal that of a Starling, at 20 cm, the volume of the bird has increased by eight times. All that extra weight has to be supported in flight by wings whose surface area has only increased fourfold. Consequently even with its proportionally bigger wings a Starling's wings (all other factors being equal) have to carry twice the weight of a Wren's wings. This increases the wing loading of the larger bird (expressed as x grams per cm²). A further doubling in size, to say a Chough, 40 cm long, means the volume to be supported by the wings increases eight times (from the Starling) and sixty-four times that of the Wren. But the surface area of the wings to support that extra weight has only increased by four times to be sixteen times greater than that of the Wren. Without taking the example any further it is easy to see that there has to be limit to how large a flying bird can be. The wing loading of the largest flying birds reaches the limits of the strength of the avian skeleton and the power of the musculature.

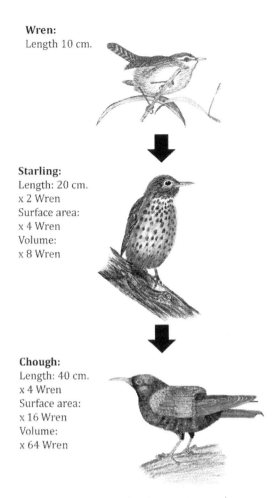

Wren:
Length 10 cm.

Starling:
Length: 20 cm.
x 2 Wren
Surface area:
x 4 Wren
Volume:
x 8 Wren

Chough:
Length: 40 cm.
x 4 Wren
Surface area:
x 16 Wren
Volume:
x 64 Wren

8 - Wing loading ratios

An added complication is that larger wings require much stronger, larger wing muscles to power flight. Muscle power increases with the surface area of the muscle (not its volume) so the Starling's flight muscle power increases to four times that of the Wren but has to provide power to lift a bird eight times heavier. Hence, when you get to a bird the size of a Mute Swan with a body length of 80 cm a wing span of 2.4 m. and weighing 11.8 kg, the limits of flight are being reached. The Mute Swan is the largest flying British bird. The largest flying bird in the world is the Kori Bustard weighing 18 kg. The bird with the longest wing span is the Wandering Albatross with a span of 3.1 m. weighing a mere 11.9 kg. It is not surprising that the world's largest bird, the Ostrich, weighing in at 120 kg, cannot fly.

Whilst this increase in size is a limiting factor for flying, it does have a positive benefit. With larger birds the surface area to volume ratio is lower than in smaller birds so larger birds lose less body heat and can survive cold weather better.

The mechanics of flying

Bird flight is analogous to aircraft flight. Both require lift for height and thrust for motion.

- o **Lift** - the crucial design feature for lift is the shape of the cross section of the wing, which has to be asymmetric, with the underside flatter than the longer, rounded upper side. As air flows over the two wing surfaces the air speed is lower on the underside than the upper as it has a shorter distance to travel. According to Bernoulli's principle pressure falls with an increase in the speed of fluids. Hence there is a comparatively higher pressure on the underside, producing lift. A greater angle between the air flow and wing increases lift (up to a limit, after which the bird would stall). A rounded leading edge assists with lift. As air passes over the wings it produces drag which is a force that pulls against the forward thrust. After the air has passed over the wing vortices are created behind the wing, which are swirls of rotating air. In birds the secondary feathers generate lift.

The diagram below gives a simplified view of the forces at work:

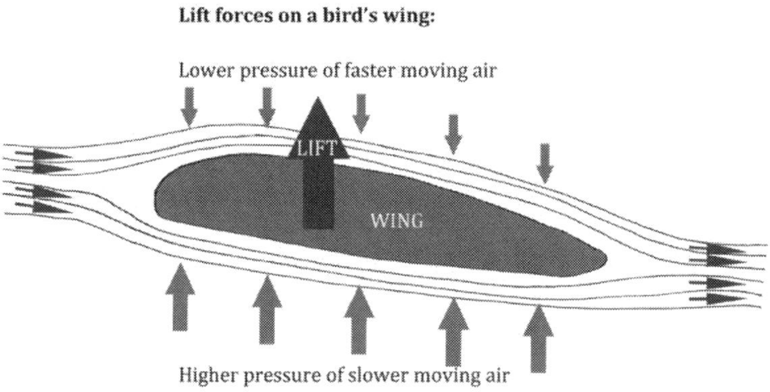

Lift forces on a bird's wing:

Lower pressure of faster moving air

LIFT

WING

Higher pressure of slower moving air

9 - Wing lift forces

- o **Thrust** - required for forward motion and is generated by the primary feathers of the flapping wings. On the down beat the wings create thrust and push the bird forward. The vanes of the primary feathers are asymmetric with the forward vane being narrower than the rearward vane. This ingenious design feature ensures that on the downward stroke the feathers are flattened together to move the air and generate thrust whilst on the upward stroke the feathers turn and open allowing air to pass through.

Otherwise the two strokes (up and down) would cancel each other out.

The diagram below shows these forces (simplified) on a flying Swallow:

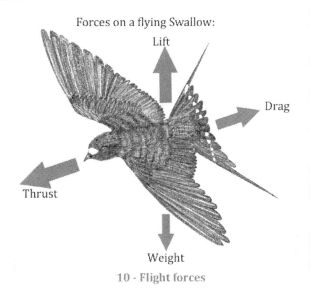

Forces on a flying Swallow:

Lift

Drag

Thrust

Weight

10 - Flight forces

Wing design - as with other characteristics wings vary in shape and relative size between species to best suit a bird's environment and way of life.

Wing shapes are assessed using two parameters:

o **Aspect ratio** - provides a measure of the shape of the wing. Aspect ratio is calculated as the wing span squared divided by the wing area. Short, stubby wings have a low aspect ratio and long, narrow wings a high ratio. Aspect ratio measures aerodynamic efficiency. A high aspect ratio wing generates lower drag and hence is more efficient. The down side is that long wings have to be strong and hence heavier. Also manoeuvrability is reduced with longer wings, which is crucial to some birds e.g. living in a woodland environment and chasing prey.

o **Wing loading** - measures the weight bearing of the wing. This is calculated as the bird's weight divided by the wing area. Birds with proportionally smaller wings have a higher wing loading. The range of wing loading in birds is 1 to 20 kg / m² whilst a jumbo jet wing loading is 730 kg / m².

The table below gives the wing design data for a diverse range of birds:

Table 5 - Typical wing loadings

Species:	Weight (g):	Aspect ratio:	Wing loading (N / m²)
Barn Owl	280	6.7	19
Barnacle Goose	1150	10.1	98
Blue Tit	10	6.8	17
Buzzard	1000	5.8	33
Common Tern	120	13.2	25
Dunlin	45	8.6	30
Gannet	2820	13.2	118
Goldcrest	6	4.8	13
Great-crested Grebe	890	10.6	144
Grey Heron	1320	7.8	40
Grey Partridge	350	6.3	94
Herring Gull	1000	10	50
Kingfisher	320	6.9	32
Moorhen	310	6.7	69
Red-throated Diver	960	12.2	106
Sparrowhawk	190	6.5	28
Swallow	22	8	16

Wing shape is important as it provides the bird with the type of flight that best matches its life style. Shape is a trade-off between speed, energy use and manoeuvrability. There are basically four wing shapes:

o **Elliptical** – a curving tapered wing pattern with a small, rounded tip. These wings have a low aspect ratio and are useful for manoeuvring in confined spaces, like woodland. The shape also enables a quick take off which is useful in escaping predators. Examples of birds possessing this shape are many non-migratory passerines and game birds.

o **Short and pointed** – high speed wings with a high wing loading and rapid wing beats. Peregrine are an example of this where the bird only flies in short, high speed bursts to catch its prey. Ducks also possess this wing shape.

- o **Long and thin** – high aspect ratio wings with a low wing loading. Useful for slower flight. Wind hoverers, like the Kestrel, have this wing shape, as does the Nightjar and the terns. Many seabirds that use active soaring (see below) also have this wing pattern as well as waders, Swallow, martins and Swift.

- o **Long and broad** – useful for passive soaring. Many birds of prey (except the hawks) possess this wing shape.

Below are typical silhouettes of four wing shapes:

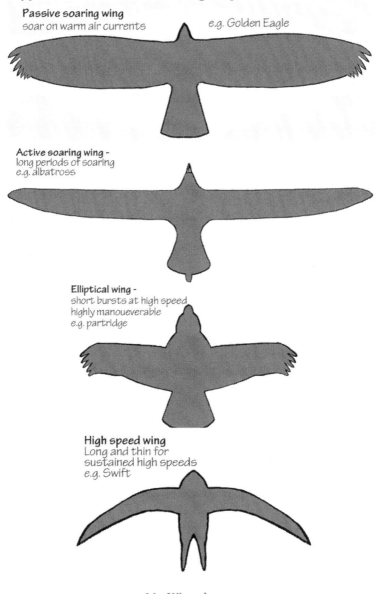

11 - Wing shapes

Flight patterns

Whilst flight has many advantages the energy requirements for flight are very high. Flapping flight is very energy intensive and birds have developed various means of reducing the energy required:

o **Gliding** - a low energy mode of flight with the wings out-stretched and stationary. To maintain speed and overcome drag the bird gradually has to lose height. The glide ratio (the ratio of forward distance travelled to downward fall) varies between 10:1 and 15:1 for birds of prey. Gliding is energy efficient and uses about 2.2x of rest energy whilst flapping flight uses 10 – 15x of rest energy. Birds with a high wing loading cannot glide easily but need to constantly flap e.g. Puffin.

o **Soaring** - birds use air currents to assist with gaining height and flying. Soaring reduces heart rate by up to 40% and flight speeds are almost doubled. There are two types of soaring:

o **Passive** – using up-currents of warm air. Typically eagles and buzzards use thermals to soar and gain height followed by gliding. These birds have comparatively broad wings with a low wing loading. Often their primaries are emarginated (separated wing tips) to assist with manoeuvrability, lower drag and reduce the production of vortices. Soaring Golden Eagles can gain height at a rate of 3 to 5 m / sec with very little horizontal movement.

o **Active** – using the vertical movements of air caused by waves or geographical features, like cliffs or woods. Marine birds often use active soaring as a flight pattern. They use the upward movement of air at the front of a wave to soar up and then proceed to glide until they need to restore their height again by soaring. Gulls and Fulmar also use this technique often catching the wind diverted by cliffs. These birds have longer, thinner wings that have a high aspect ratio.

o **Hovering** - a flight with zero air speed and is a high energy sapping mode of flight. Hummingbirds are the masters of this technique but have to feed continuously to maintain their energy levels. The hummingbirds have highly specialised, complex modifications to their wing joints enabling their wings to articulate and produce equilibrium between forward and backward flight motion.

o **Wind hovering** - this is also flight with zero air speed. Here the bird uses the wind's force to exactly balance their forward wing flapping force. Kestrel, terns and Storm Petrel employ this technique when looking for food. Again this is a high energy mode of flight and has to be balanced with the success of capturing food.

o **V formation** - some birds fly in a V formation which is an energy efficient means of flying. The birds behind the leader utilise the vortices produced by the bird in front. By placing themselves in exactly the right position the following birds can gain up-lift from the swirling air. The birds also need to coordinate their wing flaps to gain any advantage. However, the leader has to swop over from time to time as the front bird cannot benefit from any vortices. Geese, ducks and swans typically fly in a V formation.

- o **Undulating flight** - a gliding descent followed by flapping to regain height.

- o **Bounding flight** - a period of flapping followed by a period of flight with folded wings. Often used by birds with a low aspect ratio and high wing loading, such as the passerines, woodpeckers and kingfisher.

- o **Ground effect** - by flying close to a flat surface induced drag can be reduced. Ducks and Cormorant fly low over water as an efficient method of flying.

- o **Swimming** - for a number of birds wings have a dual purpose – flying and swimming. Some birds swim using just their legs e.g. some ducks, others use only their wings e.g. auks and some use both wings and feet e.g. Eider and Common Scoter. For those that swim using their wings the wing shape has to be a compromise between flight and swimming. Several species have solid bones which help reduce buoyancy and assists in remaining under water. The supreme swimming birds are the penguins who have largely adapted to life under the ocean. Emperor Penguin have been recorded diving to 565 m and remaining under water for 32 minutes.

Albatross have perfected the technique of active soaring and although they are large, heavy birds they can fly around oceans for many days and weeks. Storm Petrels, being pelagic, long distance fliers use a variety of techniques to make flight more efficient. They aid their flight by means of flap-glides, where bursts of flapping are followed by a period of gliding; the amount of flapping depending on the strength of the wind and the choppiness of the water.

By attaching flight-recorders to Andean Condors researchers were able to log the bird's wingbeats. The bird, which can weigh up to 15 kg, is the world's heaviest soaring bird. This research found that the bird flaps its wings for just 1% of its flight time and more than 75% of the bird's flapping was associated with take-off. Once in the sky condors can sustain soaring for long periods of time with one bird managing to fly for five hours without flapping, covering around 172 km .

The Kestrel is the only British bird of prey to systematically wind hover and is able to keep its eye almost motionless as it beats its wings into the wind. Whilst hovering the bird's eyes hardly move (max. 6 mm) and it does this by moving its head back and forth to conserve energy by gliding for a short time rather than flapping all the time. Kestrels can only maintain hovering for about 3 hours a day to maintain a balance between energy intake and expenditure. Hovering pays off for the Kestrel, which needs at least four voles (or similar animals) per day increasing to 8 a day whilst breeding.

Migration

Migration is defined as the seasonal movement from breeding areas to resting grounds. Migratory flights are referred to as outward and return migration. Migration should not be seen as a single event but more a continuous activity (except when birds are breeding). Birds that migrate to the UK for winter or to resting grounds far away often continue to move round from location to location, determined by food supply and weather. Migration also takes on many forms (see below). In the UK far more birds migrate here for winter (estimated 16 m) than do in summer (estimated 5 m).

Migratory journeys are undertaken by insects, fish and mammals as well as birds but more species of bird migrate and cover greater distances than any other group. The fundamental reason for migrating is to secure an adequate food supply. Insectivorous birds breeding during the UK summer must migrate to the southern hemisphere as there is insufficient insect food in the UK during winter, particularly airborne insects. The advantages of flying to the northern hemisphere for summer are the longer hours of daylight in which to feed young and the abundance of food. The expansive tundra, boreal forests and taiga which waders, ducks, geese and swans migrate to provides a comparatively predator-free environment. This is particularly important for ground-nesting birds, which in the UK would have to contend with predators such as foxes, weasels, rats, polecats and hedgehogs. In the far north the constant daylight promotes rapid growth of fresh vegetation, providing ample food for herbivorous birds such as geese and habitats for insects which in turn provide food for insectivorous birds, like many breeding waders. Similarly seabirds need to move as their food supply is often seasonal. In the Arctic seas during winter there are very few fish and only a few or no hours of daylight for feeding.

Another reason for migrating is that temperature extremes might force a bird species to move. Whilst birds can endure low temperatures there are limits to this endurance. Similarly birds are affected by high temperatures and move if necessary.

As with any survival strategy there are risks and benefits. All the risks of undertaking a migratory journey, often of several thousand kilometres, through or over inhospitable terrain, not being sure where the next meal might come from, subject to extreme weather plus being exposed to predation along with the high levels of energy required needs to be balanced against staying in a region where there is little food, few hours of daylight and extreme weather. For many species migration is a successful survival strategy. Migratory birds appear to be successful as they lay fewer eggs and generally only have one brood. Using this breeding strategy many species still maintain a stable population. Resident birds tend to have several, larger broods. Not all birds in the population of a species migrate. Swallows breeding in the UK migrate but those in southern Europe do not.

The phenomenon of migration was realised as long ago as the 6th century BC. In the Bible Job wrote "Does the hawk take flight by your wisdom and spread its wings towards the south?" and at around the same time Jeremiah wrote "Even the stork in the sky knows her appointed seasons and the dove, the swift and the thrush observe the time of their migration". Homer, writing in the *Iliad*, said of the Trojan armies "like Cranes which flee from the coming winter and sudden rain" so he knew about migrating birds as did Aristotle who also noted that cranes made journeys "to the end of the world". Another fanciful explanation given by Aristotle and others was that some species transmogrified i.e. became another species during winter. He thought the Cuckoo became a Sparrowhawk (they have similar flight profiles) and Redstarts became Robins. Willughby in the 17th century was unsure what happened to the Cuckoo, thinking it might enter a state of torpor or fly off to sunnier climes.

In terms of developing an understanding of migration it is surprising that it took until the 19th century for migration to be fully accepted as a phenomenon. Prior to this time various people, including some highly respected observers and scientists, came up with some colourful suggestions for the fact that some birds were not seen in certain seasons. For example, Gilbert White wrote "..at least many of the swallow kind do not leave us in winter but lay themselves up like insects or bats, in a torpid state .... as bats do" i.e. in a state of hibernation. In Cornwall a recent belief was that the bird spent the winter in disused mine shafts. Incidentally, only one species of bird hibernates (the Poorwill, a relative of the Nightjar)! Gilbert White's brother, John, saw migration first hand in Gibraltar, in the 1750's and informed his brother of these observations. But still migration remained unsolved. Another tale was that Swallows sank into mud in autumn and rose again the next year. In the 16th century the myth was that they hibernated in mud and fishermen were able to catch and revive them by holding them to a fire. A Royal Society investigation in 1660's confirmed this! For more detail on the Swallow and Sand Martin see the species entries in Chapter 8. Other more fanciful tales were that birds, like the Woodcock, flew to the moon for the winter! Similarly birds only seen in winter, such as the Barnacle Goose, gave rise to strange stories of where they went in summer. One documented story is that the bird morphed into a barnacle, attached itself to a rope and hid under the water until the following winter! Hence the name. For more detail see the species account in Chapter 8. One of the first published, accurate statements of migration was by Thomas Bewick in 1798 stating "they (Swallows) leave us when this country can no longer furnish them with a supply of their proper and natural food ...". Spot on! In a remarkable insight into bird migration the Icelandic Bishop of Skalholt said of geese in the 17th century "I speak of fowl which come from abroad; t'out the winter they do not dwell amongst us... every autumn they make for neighbouring countries of England and Scotland...".

True migratory flights exhibit some of the following characteristics:

- **Leap frog migration** - some birds of the same species that breed further north migrate further south than the other more southerly breeding populations, e.g. Ringed Plover, Blackcap and Swift.

- **Intermittent migration** - where one group of a species migrates to a different area than another group. For example, fledgling Starlings migrate to a different area than their parents.

- **Duration** – where outward migration from the breeding area is significantly slower than the return flight.

- **Loop migration** –the route of migration changes between the outward flight and the return flight, e.g. Lesser Whitethroat returns to the UK by a more easterly route.

- **Direction** - varies between populations of the same species, so Scandinavian birds take a different route than UK birds to their African resting grounds.

- **Partial** - only a proportion of the population migrate, such as the Robin and Blackbird.

- **Differential** - birds of the same species migrate different distances. For example, where males migrate a shorter distance than females so they can return to the breeding ground earlier and establish their breeding territory.

- **Philopatry** - the majority of bird species demonstrate this phenomenon i.e. they return to same place each year. This includes migration to breeding areas and back to resting areas. Exceptions include Redwing and Brambling, both winter migrants to the UK from Scandinavia, with individuals flying to a different area each winter.

- **Natal fidelity** - the majority of juveniles demonstrate this characteristic by returning to their place of birth after the return migration. One of the marvels of migration is that fledglings are able to fly to their resting area, often without any help from their parents and then undertake a return flight to the precise location of their birth. Sometimes the return flight is made after several years, returning to breed only when they have reached sexual maturity.

The majority of long distance migratory birds that are normally diurnal undertake nocturnal migratory flights. There are several reasons for this:

43

- Predation - fewer predators at night. Most birds of prey cannot migrate at night as they rely on daytime up-draughts of warm air on which to soar and glide.

- Feeding - migrants can feed during the day to stock up on energy for the next leg of their energy sapping flight.

- Energy - birds save energy by flying in the cool night air when wind speeds are lower. Birds need to reach an equilibrium between heating up (flying consumes high levels of energy) and cooling in the night air. They also need to avoid dehydration by flying in the cooler air. Birds are better adapted to breathing in thin air and do not suffer from hypoxia - oxygen deficiency in thin air. Flying at altitude also requires less energy where air resistance is lower. Typically small birds fly at about 1000 m. Research, using tracking technology, discovered that some migrants fly at high altitudes, much higher than previously thought. Great Reed Warblers were tracked as they migrated and they flew at almost 4 000 m. They were noted flying at their highest altitude whilst flying over the Mediterranean Sea and the Sahara desert.

- Navigation - birds can use stars as a compass.

Like many small birds the Blackcap migrates at night to benefit from the cooler air, enabling them to conserve water. Their ideal air temperature for flying is 10⁰ C which can be attained at about 1000 m at night but would require flying at a height of 3000 m during the day.

Preparing for migration

Migratory birds show altered behaviour when the time approaches for migration. Birds use a variety of environmental cues to determine when to migrate. One of the most prominent is day length. The activity pattern of birds and their behaviour throughout the day is referred to as their circadian rhythm (circa meaning around and diem meaning day). For most birds their main periods of activity coincide with daylight and they rest at night. In spring, the longer days and shorter nights signal that it is time to prepare for migration. Birds become restless, called zugunruhe (from the German - migration restlessness) beating their wings at a high frequency and orientating themselves in the direction of their migratory flight. In autumn the shortening length of day triggers off zugunruhe again as birds detect small changes in the length of day; this is called photoperiodicity. Experiments have established that this behaviour is innate. In fact it is the brain that detects the changing light levels as the season's change that provides the trigger, not the light falling on the eye. In one investigation into migration a hand-reared Knot, which could not fly, continued to show all the signs of migratory behaviour, including putting on weight (from 130 g to 190

g) and moulting, leading to the conclusion that migratory behaviour is innate. In many species the young migrate without help from their parents, for example, Puffins and Swallows and of course the Cuckoo who never sees its parents! Migratory birds have smaller brains (brains consume a lot of energy) possibly because these birds do not need to learn to migrate as the behaviour is innate, hence the smaller brain. About 355 species of bird migrate each year from Europe to Africa. In one experiment to determine if migration was a heritable characteristic, Blackcaps from the Canaries and Europe were inter-bred. The resulting hybrid offspring migrated to an intermediate area, proving that migratory instinct is inherited.

To prepare for the rigours of migration birds alter their diets as hyperphagia kicks in. They eat large amounts of food, putting on considerable weight; as much as a 50% increase in weight in the form of fat. Fat is energy rich and yields twice as much energy and water compared to carbohydrates or protein. Birds lose water in flight and this is replenished because burning fat as fuel produces water as a by-product. Many birds alter their diet from insects to berries to gain this weight at a time when insect numbers are falling. Migrants can acquire 10% of their fat-free body weight per day and can accumulate sufficient fat for their journey in 2 weeks' eating. The Swift increases its weight from 43 g to 54 g in readiness for migrating. The Curlew Sandpiper increases its weight from 53 g to 80 g with the 27 g of fat providing enough energy for a journey of 3 200 km. With larger birds this is limited by the need to keep weight to the maximum required to maintain the ability to fly e.g. storks, geese and swans have to limit their weight increase. Birds have to make sure they have the right amount of body fat. Too much causes overheating; too little and they run out of fuel. They also have to contend with overheating. The core body temperature of birds in flight has been recorded as high as 44^0 C against the norm of 40^0 C. Birds that feed off aerial insects like swifts, swallows and martins do not need to add much weight or fat as they can feed en-route.

Birds necessarily have to moult. However, migrants have a variety of moult patterns. Some moult before migrating, some undertake a partial moult, migrate and complete their moult on arrival and others moult only on arrival at their resting grounds. The Blackcap moults here before migrating whilst its close relative the Garden Warbler moults on arrival at its resting grounds in sub-Saharan Africa. For more detail on moulting refer to the Section on Moulting in Chapter 1.

The Bar-tailed Godwit holds the world record for the longest known non-stop flight of any bird, flying from New Zealand to the Yellow Sea in China, a distance of over 11 000 km, taking 8 days. Another New Zealand bird flew over 11 000 km to Alaska. Like many birds the Godwit builds up huge fat reserves to make such a long flight. To make room for the fat and to keep its flying weight down it absorbs part of its tissues (like the liver and kidney) and then restores these to full functioning weight at the end of its flight. This process is known as auto cannibalism.

Finding their way

Birds have three compass systems enabling them to maintain a constant direction using an external reference system:

- o **Sun** - using highly complex calculations birds are able to fly in a preferred compass direction if they can detect sunlight, even through a small gap in the clouds. They cannot take a bearing if the sky is completely covered.

- o **Stars** - birds can read the pattern of stars in the sky, using the North Star as a reference point (in the northern hemisphere).

- o **Magnetic** - birds are able to detect the earth's magnetic field.

Orientation is comprised of compass orientation i.e. directional and goal orientation i.e. destination location. When birds orientate to a compass bearing using the sun they have to make some highly complex calculations. The sun's horizontal movement (the azimuth) varies with the time of day. The sun appears to move slower at the start and end of the day and fastest at mid-day. Also the compass direction of the rising and setting sun varies with time of year and is only exactly east and west twice a year at the equinox. Every day the azimuth reaches its peak at noon, always exactly south.

It is clear that birds can set a compass bearing and orientate using a sighting of the sun, even if this is merely sunlight seen through a gap in the clouds. They are able to calculate the position of the sun using polarised light. Light waves from the sun vibrate in all planes at right angles to the direction of travel. Reflected light, such as that reflected through a gap in the clouds, vibrates only in one plane i.e. it is polarised. A bird's eye detects this polarisation and can compute the position of the sun from this.

A bird's sun compass calculation is linked to the bird's circadian rhythm. In an experiment pigeons were exposed to artificial day light with an amended light and dark cycle. This reset the birds' circadian rhythm. When the birds were released on a sunny day they flew off in the wrong direction for homing to their resting place by miscalculating the required compass orientation.

Birds use the fact that the earth's magnetic field is at 90^0 at the poles and 0^0 at the equator. From this they can calculate the correct orientation for their journey by measuring the direction of the magnetic field at their current location. Also the magnetic field is weaker at the equator, so birds might be able to measure the strength of the magnetic field at their present location and compute an orientation from this.

For **goal orientation** it is thought that birds are able to memorise geographical features and use this to home in on a specific location. Many birds return to exactly the same area year after year, including the previous year's fledglings that must have some memory of the location. For example, Swallows are highly philopatric (highly attached to their place of birth). It seems they must memorise local landscape features to locate their birthplace. Homing pigeons need to have seen the geographical features of their home location if they are to make a successful return journey.

A key component essential to successful migration is having the ability to orientate accurately during all stages of the journey. Several experiments have been conducted to establish how birds orientate and to understand some of the mysteries of migration.

Caged fledgling Blackcaps were observed facing in a set direction coinciding with their migratory orientation, providing they could see the night sky. The cage was then placed in a planetarium and the birds continued to face in their south-easterly migratory orientation. The projected sky was then rotated but the birds continued to face in the 'new' south-east orientation. The night sky was changed to project the sky at a place on their migratory route which required a different orientation for the outward flight. Once again the birds faced in the correct new orientation for their flight from that place having interpreted a completely new night sky. When shown the night sky of their destination they fell asleep!

In a German experiment with migratory caged Robins, the birds could not see the sky (to orientate by) but on commencing their fluttering (indicating their readiness to migrate) the birds moved to the SW of the cage. When the cage was isolated from any magnetic fields the birds no longer orientated in a specific direction. When the direction of the magnetic field was altered the birds changed their orientation accordingly.

The Arctic Tern undertakes one of the longest migratory journeys of any bird, indeed of any animal, flying from one polar region to the other and back several times in its lifetime. Terns breeding in Canada fly east to Greenland to be joined by birds nesting there. They fly onwards to Iceland to be joined by more birds and then fly south to West Africa where there split to fly either to Brazil or the Falkland Islands before arriving in Antarctic.

Experiments were conducted on caged Starlings to determine if they could learn to orientate and how fixed that learning is. A bird cage was placed in the centre of a table whose outer edge rotated and on which 12 lidded boxes were placed and with a rotating wall round the edge, allowing the bird to see only sky. The bird was then taught to look for food only in the box set in a fixed direction e.g. east, with other boxes empty. The walls were then rotated and the bird allowed out of its cage. The bird always went to the food box in the compass direction it had been trained to move i.e. east. If there was no food in the box the bird did not try to find food in the other boxes in a different orientation. It was noted that on release from its cage the bird looked up at the sky. When the sky was fully cloudy the birds could not orientate. This confirmed that Starlings are able to take a compass bearing from the sky.

In another experiment with Starlings, a group of adults and fledglings ready for migration were taken a distance south from their breeding grounds and released. The adults were able to migrate to their intended resting grounds but the fledglings flew in a compass direction as if they had flown from their breeding grounds but on a parallel line shifted south and landed up overwintering in Spain. The next spring they flew back to their birth place. Next autumn they returned to Spain and not to the traditional resting area of their parents. The adults must have had both an internal compass and map. A compass on its own would not have led them to their previous resting place. The fledglings only had a compass to direct them to their resting area (their flight taking them on a displaced path) but must have had a compass and map to locate their breeding area. Their first flight to Spain had been imprinted and changed their migratory flight behaviour the following year.

The Manx Shearwater is a long distant migrant that breeds on islands in the UK and Ireland, leaving our shores for the coast off Brazil and Argentina; a journey of 9 000 km. The birds nest in rabbit holes and both male and female take turns to incubate the one egg and feed the fledgling. The off-duty bird goes off on a 6 day feeding journey which early in the season involves flying to the Bay of Biscay fishing for young sardines. In an experiment adults just about to leave on a food journey were caged and taken to various locations including Cambridge, Venice and the Swiss Alps. The birds were released and all of them were able to orientate onto a direct route back to their nesting site. Even though the Shearwater is a pelagic bird it flew overland on its direct return journey.

The Wheatear makes one of the longest migratory journeys of any passerine bird from Sub-Saharan Africa in spring to the Northern Hemisphere including northern and central Asia, Europe, Greenland, Alaska and parts of Canada. Birds of the Greenland race, *leucorhoa*, make one of the longest transoceanic crossings of any passerine. In spring most migrate along a route (commonly used by waders and waterfowl) from Africa via continental Europe, the British Isles and Iceland to Greenland. However, autumn sightings from ships suggest that some birds cross the North Atlantic directly from Canada and Greenland to southwest Europe, a distance of up to 2 500 km. Miniature tracking devices have recently shown that the northern wheatear has one of the longest migratory flights known – 15 000 km, from sub-Saharan Africa to their Arctic breeding grounds, flying on average, 290 km per day.

Ospreys have been tracked whilst migrating and travel about 430 km a day. In autumn the birds stop off to refuel and take their time whereas in spring they return to the UK in about 20 days, stopping off to refuel for about 4 days. Woodcock migrate in stages to and from their Russian breeding grounds. Experiments show that the decision to continue their journey is based on weather conditions. Tagged birds did not migrate when temperatures were around zero but most migrated when the temperature rose to 11^0 C. They also tended to wait for a tailwind to assist them. Migrants fitted with geolocators were recorded as flying at almost 4 000 m, which is much higher than had previously been thought. In another experiment 25 Swallows were fitted with geolocators. These revealed that pairs of Swallows sometimes stay together for the duration of their migratory journey.

Remarkably many young birds leave their nesting area and migrate without the help of their parents. Frequently parents feed their young until they are big and strong enough to fly and then they will leave the nesting area before the young to commence their migratory journey. In some instances the female leaves before the male, such as with the Dunlin and Phalarope. The young of many species migrate independently of their parents. These youngsters spend a season on their southerly resting grounds and are then able to migrate back to the exact same spot they were raised in. Puffin chicks are left in the burrow nest by their parents and leave at night (to avoid predation) and fly off seemingly in random directions. Puffin chicks do not seem to have an innate sense of where to fly to but spend their time wandering round the oceans for 2 to 3 years before breeding. Adult Dunlins migrate from their breeding area before their young (the females first then the males), arrive at their winter feeding grounds and find the best places to feed. The young use a different migratory route. Remarkably the young are faithful to their natal area and will return to breed the following spring and nest within 20 m of their birth place. Before leaving the UK Dunlin increase their weight at a rate of 0.6 g per day from around 53 g to 75 g to provide the fuel resources needed for their flight north.

Another species which has been successfully tracked for several years is the Cuckoo. The BTO have been tracking Cuckoo migratory journeys since 2011. One male was tracked for 3 years, travelling 47 000 km, spending 47% of his time in the Congo, 38% on migration and only 15% in the UK. Interactive maps on the BTO web site track the journeys of the Cuckoos in real time giving a much greater insight into their routes, stopping off points and wintering quarters. Geese and swan species tend to migrate in family groups, assisting one another as they make their long distance flights.

Most birds of prey have to select a migratory route which minimises the length of sea crossing. Birds of prey fly by soaring and gliding. To do this they need warm air that rises from land (not sea) to soar and gain height and then make progress by gliding rather than constantly flapping their wings, as many other birds do. This also restricts their movement to the warmer parts of the day and they cannot move very far at night. That is why vast numbers of birds of prey congregate on Gibraltar to make the short sea crossing to North Africa to continue their journey. An exception to this is the Osprey. Although a bird of prey Osprey do not habitually glide and soar but use their wings in a flapping motion hence it can fly over water. Ospreys migrating from the UK fly over the Mediterranean rather than fly to a narrow crossing such as Gibraltar. Smaller birds that are normally diurnal become nocturnal whilst migrating, to avoid becoming an easy meal for a bird of prey.

A further factor in migration that has been discovered is the influence of the lunar cycle, with research demonstrating the influence of the lunar cycle on movement activity and migration tactics in the Nightjar. Using GPS data the movements of 39 birds were logged. They found that the daily foraging activity more than doubled during moon-lit nights and this resulted in a clear cycle in the intensity of migratory movements, with up to 100% of the birds migrating following full-moon periods.

Migrants tend to have more rounded wings than resident birds. This shape causes less air resistance, with rounded, shorter wings assisting manoeuvrability. In migratory passerines the length of the wing tip makes up 40% of the wing length compared to only 20% in residents. Migrants have larger pectoral muscles (up to 35% of body mass) and adaptations to the muscle fibre to assist using oxygen efficiently. Migrants do not suffer from hypoxia (oxygen deficiency at high altitudes) and their haemoglobin is modified to assist high altitude flying. The highest recorded flying bird is a Ruppell's Griffon Vulture seen flying at over 11 000 m.

When birds are ready to migrate they do not all leave at once and arrive at the same time, but arrival and departure dates vary. The table below shows therange of arrival and departure dates for a range of species in Devon:

Table 6 - Arrival and departure dates

SPECIES	ARRIVAL		DEPARTURE	
	Mean earliest	Extreme earliest	Mean latest	Extreme latest
Osprey	3 April	12 Feb	10 Oct	6 Dec
Sandwich Tern	17 Feb	5 Jan	14 Nov	29 Dec
Cuckoo	2 April	5 Feb	4 Sept	10 Dec
Nightjar	1 May	2 April	18 Sept	18 Oct
Swift	17 April	9 March	9 Oct	16 Dec
Swallow	17 March	31 Jan	24 Nov	29 Dec

SPECIES	ARRIVAL		DEPARTURE	
	Mean earliest	Extreme earliest	Mean latest	Extreme latest
Whitethroat	6 April	14 March	19 Oct	26 Dec
Spotted Flycatcher	15 April	9 Feb	21 Oct	20 Nov
Fieldfare	6 Oct	29 July	18 April	7 June

Ref. (2)

Smell is also used by some birds to navigate. In an experiment with Manx Shearwaters several groups of birds were taken from their breeding area in the UK and one group was taken to Boston USA. On release the birds flew off in the direction of their breeding area across a featureless ocean. Some birds had their sense of smell disabled and became disorientated, unable to navigate home.

Another study with shearwaters demonstrated that olfactory information is used to navigate at sea. The birds were split into three groups. One group had their sense of smell impaired; a second was subject to magnetic disruption and a control group had a normal sense of smell. The birds' movements at sea were then tracked using GPS loggers. All three groups successfully navigated to the foraging grounds and found food. However, on the return journey those with an impaired sense of smell showed significantly different orientation behaviour from the other two groups. Instead of being well-orientated towards home when they were out of sight of land, the birds embarked on straight but poorly orientated flights across the ocean. Their orientation improved when approaching land, suggesting that the birds consult an olfactory map when out of sight of land but are subsequently able to find their way using familiar landscape features.

Birds generally are able to orientate in a preferred direction, not just migrants. Homing pigeons have an excellent sense of direction but do not migrate. Non-migratory birds that are displaced from their breeding grounds can quickly find their way back.

Homing pigeons are descended from the Rock Dove, which is a non-migratory bird. Homing behaviour is not the same as migratory behaviour. Pigeons need to see the sun to return home. In an experiment newly bred birds were allowed to see the sky and the horizon but were not allowed to see their surroundings. When taken 160 km away, they were able, on their first flight, to find their way back home. Another set of birds were only allowed to see the sky from their cage and when released were unable to find their way back home. This indicates that the birds need to use the horizon as a reference point in their calculations which uses the sun's location to direct them home.

The calculation is complex and involves the bird knowing the altitude and speed of the sun's travel across the sky at home and where it is currently placed to compute the required direction of travel.

Homing pigeons have been used for millennia to carry messages, including by the Romans and the Phoenicians. One tale is that Rothschild's bank used pigeons to carry the news of Napoleon's defeat at Waterloo, to gain an advantage on investments. Also Reuter's news service started with the use of pigeons to carry messages. In WW2 the Americans had 54 000 birds in their Pigeon Service!

Care needs to be taken when observing birds in different seasons not to categorise a UK species as either a migrant or non-migrant. For example, the UK population of the common Blackbird is sedentary. However, the Blackbird you see in winter could well be a migrant from Europe. Similarly for the Chaffinch which migrates from Scandinavia. Notably more females than males arrive here, as the males stay nearer home so they can return to their breeding territory early, before the returning females. Blackcaps are another example where the birds we see in summer in the UK migrate to Africa and continental birds, in increasing numbers, migrate to the UK for winter. Research has shown that these birds are attracted by and rely on our bird feeders. Also as the effects of climate change have greater impact birds will change their migratory strategy. For some birds their survival strategy might change as it becomes feasible to stay and survive the UK winter and no longer subject themselves to the risks of migration. Some UK breeding birds, like the Lapwing, migrate south in harsh winters and return to their natal area to breed again. Birds breeding in southern England may migrate to the south of France and Iberia.

Birds also exhibit focused movements other than migration. These include:

- **Dispersal** - juveniles move from their natal area which leads to lower competition and less inter-breeding with siblings. Female and juvenile Great Tits and Black-headed Gulls both exhibit dispersal movement. Males tend to stay on territory. Another example is where birds form large roosts in winter, such as the Starling and then disperse during the day to feed.

- **Irruptions** - an irregular invasion into other areas often caused by food shortage or overcrowding. Often the species involved rely on a limited range of food which varies in abundance year to year. Some northerly breeding birds move to the UK. For example, in some years Waxwing and Brambling from Fennoscandia fly here in large numbers if their local food supply fails or is limited. Waxwings are berry eaters and Brambling feed off beech mast. These foods are abundant in some years and scarce in others. When in short supply the birds migrate to the UK.

- o **Nomadic** - regular extensive movement with the bird having no specific breeding area, for example Crossbills who seek out conifer forests with ripening cones.

- o **Escape** - from extreme weather giving rise to movements of birds from the continent to the UK in winter. Ducks will move from frozen water and birds of prey away from snow blizzards. European birds move in large numbers to the UK if the winter on the continent turns severe. Bearded Tits are normally sedentary but in severe winters will move in flocks to better reed bed feeding areas.

- o **Spreading** - leading to a change in distribution. This is being observed more frequently as a result of climate change. The distribution of Puffin has changed recently. The bird eats sand eels which prefer cooler water and they are now found in more northerly waters. So the Puffin's distribution has shifted north vacating its southerly breeding areas. The Collared Dove spread its breeding range from Europe into and across the UK over a period of years. Red Kite are spreading to many areas of the UK from their re-introduction area in the Chilterns.

- o **Moulting** - some birds fly to an area where they undergo a catastrophic moult, such as the Shelduck and Goosander.

- o **Altitudinal** - in bad winter weather some birds move to lower altitudes e.g. the Dipper when upland streams are frozen. Kingfishers make similar movement.

Flocking

Why birds flock

One key aspect of bird behaviour that humans have observed and been fascinated by is when birds flock. So much so that for many birds there are a number of collective nouns, such as a charm of Goldfinch or a parliament of Rooks. The Starling is a bird notable for the size of its winter roost flocks, called murmerations. These nouns are fully listed at the end of Chapter 8. Some birds are highly gregarious and flock in huge numbers. Large numbers gather at dusk to settle in trees and bushes to feel secure. Waders are a group of birds which often gather in huge flocks. As they feed on the vast open spaces of estuaries they are vulnerable to predation, so they flock to minimise this risk. One of the most spectacular bird-watching sights is to see a huge flock of Knot take to the air and swirl round, making fantastic shapes as they wheel up, round and down. The record for flock size in Europe probably goes to the Brambling with one flock estimated at 7 million birds! Flying birds seem to work in unison and never collide with each other. Research has established that birds in a flock also fly faster, possibly gaining from the vortices generated by the birds in front, in the same way that geese do when flying in a V formation. One scientist worked out that any one bird needs to be able to keep check on the position of their nearest seven neighbours in order to avert collisions. Flocks maintain order when all the individuals obey the same set of rules as the other birds, especially in responding to the movements of near neighbours. Order does not depend on the size of the flock as order is maintained within a small number of birds. In some species (though not all) it is thought that white wing bars assist birds in following the bird in front and avoiding collisions. However, the Black-tailed Godwit does have a white wing bar but its close relative the Bar-tailed Godwit does not. Of course, many other species of animal, insect and fish display flocking behaviour e.g. herds of animals, swarms of insects and shoals of fish.

Birds gather together in large groups for a number of reasons:

- **Foraging** – many birds in winter gather in sometimes spectacular numbers to feed together. Geese, ducks and waders commonly do this.

- **Protection from predators** – birds which gather or fly in large numbers present a picture of confusion for a predator, which finds it hard to pick up one individual in a fast moving flock. This is referred to as the dilution principle.

- **Communal breeding** – several species gather in flocks to breed. Seabirds typically breed in huge numbers on cliffs. Rooks build nests together in trees, as does the Fieldfare.

- **Aerodynamics** – geese and swans fly in a V formation that reduces the energy required for long distance migratory flights (except for the lead bird, with birds swopping round the lead).

- **Families** – some birds, like female Shelduck, form large family groupings with chicks of several families joining together, again for safety in numbers.

- **Warmth** – in winter several birds flock at night, forming roosts, to reduce heat loss in cold weather. Pied Wagtails, Wrens and Long-tailed Tits are examples.

Smaller birds are always on the alert for a predatory bird looking for a tasty meal. A flock confuses the potential predator who finds it difficult to pick off one from amongst a swirling mass of birds. Within flocks of thrush and other ground feeding birds, individuals take turns to look up for potential danger and then alert the whole group. This means that the majority of birds can concentrate on eating. When alerted they all fly off in a flock to comparative safety e.g. to a nearby tree. Other birds will collectively mob a predator.

For similar reasons of security some birds nest colonially. A common example of this are Rooks who form large rookeries in tall trees. The largest recorded UK rookery was 6 700 nests at Hatton Castle, Aberdeenshire and the largest recorded Rook roost in the UK was 65 000 birds in Scotland. By nesting together their young are more secure against predators. Again individuals alert the group to a threat and will collectively attack a marauding predator. Some birds form mixed feeding flocks in woodland areas thereby providing more pairs of eyes to act as an early warning system against a predator attack. Uniquely amongst the thrushes the Fieldfare is a colonial tree nester at its Scandinavian breeding grounds. In an experiment it was noted that the breeding productivity of Merlins which nested with Fieldfare was double the average. Fieldfares see off predators by mobbing the intruder and defecating on them which can incapacitate the bird. The bird has a different alarm call for ground predators and aerial predators. Sometimes shrikes and falcons nest in the same trees, affording the birds' mutual protection.

During severe cold weather birds flock to stay warm. For example, Wrens huddle together to keep warm, Pied Wagtails gather in large flocks, often in trees in town centres, Starlings form massive roosts and Long-tailed Tits often have a favourite branch to gather on at night. Herons are very much solitary birds but they can sometimes be seen standing huddled together in cold weather to keep warm.

In a few species of birds, males gather in groups to attract a mate. This behaviour has been noted for Black Grouse, Red Grouse and Ruff. Black Grouse gather in leks during autumn, when no females are present, possibly to establish territory. All these birds gather in leks in spring to attract a female and mate. By utilising this behaviour the males are making themselves visible to a greater number of females thus increasing their chances of successfully mating.

Geese and Swans (amongst other birds) undertake their migratory flights in family flocks. Typically they fly in a V formation which is aerodynamically efficient. This group behaviour also ensures that the juveniles are guided to the feeding ground or roost destination and can learn from the adults. The V formation also enhances communication and coordination within the group. Gulls also fly in a V formation when flying to their roost. However, they only do this in relatively calm conditions. If it is windy they don't fly in formation, possibly because the wind interrupts the air vortices used in the V formation flight.

Some birds flock to find food. A shoal of mackerel will quickly attract the attention of a flock of Gannets. The bird associates with other animals, such as dolphins, to identify where the shoals of fish are and for the dolphins to chase the fish towards the water's surface. Adult Gannets will lead feeding forays, with the young following the adults, often in large mixed flocks. This behaviour improves hunting efficiency and navigation and helps the young to learn hunting skills. In winter members of the tit family will form flocks to forage for food, which can often be scarce.

In a rather bizarre method of feeding, Great White Pelicans flock in large number on the Danube delta. The birds take to the air to locate flocks of feeding Cormorants. They land in the middle of the Cormorants. The pelicans then harass the birds until they give up their fish prey. Pelicans cannot dive and would not be able to feast on these fish without stealing them.

It is not unusual for birds to form mixed flocks. High tide roosts on estuaries are often comprised of several species, often presenting birdwatchers with an interesting identification challenge. Lapwings traditionally mix with Golden Plovers in fields left fallow for the winter.

As with any set of behaviours there are advantages and disadvantages and birds will obviously choose the behaviour that on balance improves their chance of survival and successful breeding. The disadvantages of flocking include the greater risk of spreading disease. When a large number of birds flock together in close proximity, any diseased bird can infect its neighbour.

Birds that flock also present a greater visible presence to a potential predator. Whilst the overall chance of an individual bird being caught is lower, predators can see a flock easily. Often a predator will look for a weak individual to pick off. A Peregrine hunting a flock of small ducks or waders will look for a weaker bird which cannot stay within the close confines of the flock. The bird of prey can then catch this individual with comparative ease. The Woodpigeon forages for food in large flocks, with the stronger birds feeding near the centre with the weaker birds on the perimeter on the look-out for predators, like the Peregrine.

Another form of flocking behaviour occurs with the chicks of some species who gather together to form a crèche. Some species of goose and duck form large crèches. For example, Canada Geese chicks form crèches of up to 100. As chicks of these species are precocial they are developed enough almost immediately after hatching to feed themselves. Other species whose young form into crèches include Eider, Goosander, Long-tailed Duck, Red-breasted Merganser, Sandwich Tern and Shelduck. Supervision of the crèche (when it occurs) is usually by a small number of female guardians whose role is to alert the crèche to an intruder or predator. The chicks form into these larger groups to lose themselves in a crowd and reduce the risk of predation (dilution principle) as with flocks of adults.

CHAPTER THREE

SINGING LIKE A LARK

Songs and calls

One of the major reasons why human beings are attracted to birds is because they sing; the other major attraction is flight. In Chapter 8 Species accounts, there are many examples of bird's local names deriving from their song. For example, the local names for the Mistle Thrush are based on its song and call such as horse thrush, where the cry is said to sound like a horse neighing; rattle thrush; screech thrush from its alarm call; shrill cock and squawking thrush. A significant number of formal names are onomatopoeic, like Cuckoo and Chiffchaff. We are aware of the presence of birds by their song (and their calls). For millennia humans have found bird song both attractive and beguiling:

- Human beings link bird song with emotions, such as the cooing of doves being associated with love.
- We mark the seasons by bird song, such as hearing the Cuckoo in spring. Delius commemorated this in his 1912 composition *On hearing the first Cuckoo in spring*.
- Aristotle investigated animal sounds and stated that bird voices were different from other animals "Certain species of birds above all animals and next after man, possess the faculty of uttering articulate sounds". He concluded that birds possessed higher level language skills but not to the level of human beings.
- Lucretius in the 1st century BC wrote "Through all the woods they heard the charming noise, Of chirping birds and tried to frame their voice and imitate. Thus birds instructed man and taught him songs before his art began" claiming that birds are the basis for our rich culture of music.
- A Chinese proverb states 'A bird does not sing because it has an answer. It sings because it has a song'.
- Kant writing in the 18th century wondered why we never tire of listening to bird song whereas if humans endlessly repeated a few notes we'd get fed up.
- When we wish to compliment someone's singing we use the expression 'sing like a bird' or 'sing like a lark', implying birds set the gold standard for singing.
- Bird song appears in many myths, for example the one associated with the Golden Plover's cry which is said to be the souls of the Jews who were doomed to wander for crucifying Jesus.

Over the millennia very many writers, poets and composers have written about the wonder of bird song, describing the song in words and the emotional impact it has on us. Many have tried to represent the sound of bird songs and calls in words or music:

- John Clare transcribed the iconic **Nightingale**'s song into words – "'chew-chew chew-chew' and higher still, 'cheer-cheer cheer-cheer' more loud and shrill 'cheer-up, cheer-up, cheer-up' – and dropped". Izak Walton wrote "it breathes such sweet music out of her little instrumental throat that it might make mankind think miracles had not ceased". Shakespeare wrote in *Romeo and Juliet* "It is not yet near day; it was the nightingale and not the lark that pierc'd the fearful hollow of thine ear. Nightly she sings on your pomegranate tree; believe me, love, it was the nightingale".
- The **Turtle Dove** is another well known bird, referred to by Solomon in the Bible "For lo, the winter is past, and the rain is over --- the time for the singing of birds is come, and the voice of the turtle is heard in our land". Other ancient writings refer to doves, through to Shakespeare and to modern times for example songwriter Buddy Holly.
- The **Skylark** is another wonderful songster much written about. Ralph Vaughan Williams in his orchestral work, *The Lark Ascending,* represented the bird's song in music. Shakespeare included this in a sonnet "Haply I think on thee ... like to the lark at the break of day arising, from the sullen earth, sings hymns at heaven's gate". George Meredith wrote a long poem called *The Lark Ascending* which includes the words "He rises and begins to round; He drops the silver chain of sound..." along with Shelley, Tennyson, Browning and Blake who all wrote about the Skylark.
- Wordsworth was charmed by the **Wren**'s song, writing "So sweetly 'mid the gloom the invisible bird; Sang to herself, that there I could have made; my dwelling place, and lived for ever there; To hear such music".
- **Owls** get a mention in *Henry VI* with Henry saying to the Duke of Gloucester "the owl shriek'd at thy birth - an evil sign" and in *Love's Labour's Lost* "When blood is nipped and ways be foul, then mightly sings the staring owl, Tu-who, Tu-whit, tu-who – a merry note".
- Another songster with a reputation is the **Song Thrush**. For Browning the bird was a reminder of home and wrote in *Home thoughts from abroad* "That's the wise thrush; he sings his song twice over, lest you should think he could never recapture the first fine careless rapture". Thomas Hardy also wrote about the bird in *The darkling Thrush* - "I leant upon the coppice gate, When frost was spectre grey, And winter's dregs made desolate, The weakening eye of the day... At once a voice arose among, the blackened twigs overhead, In a full-hearted evensong, of joy illimited". Another piece of evidence of the emotional attachment we have with birds is seen with the early settlers to Australia and New Zealand. They took Song Thrush with them so the bird's song could remind them of the home country. The

bird is now common in New Zealand but it failed to establish in Australia.

- o   Father Kircher (1602 – 1680) wrote an important book on musicology. One of his books, *Musurgia Universalis,* contains the musical notation for a range of bird songs, including the Cuckoo, Nightingale and Quail. A little later Rameau (1683 – 1764) wrote harpsichord music which included a suite entitled *Le rappel des oiseaux* (The conference of birds).

- o   Messiaen, the composer, specialised in translating bird song into musical notation. In 1940, whilst serving in the French army, he listened to bird song using this to write a clarinet piece for a colleague to play. Later, when a prisoner of war, he continued to write music based on bird song which was played at a concert in the Stalag where he was incarcerated. He composed a piece for the flute entitled *Le merle noir* (Blackbird). He eventually produced a seven volume compilation of music based on bird song, *Catalogue d'oiseaux*.

- o   Other composers have incorporated bird song into their compositions. Vivaldi used finch song in one of his flute concertos. Beethoven famously used bird song in his 6th Symphony, the Pastoral, using the songs of the Cuckoo, Quail and Yellowhammer in the second movement. Mozart kept a Starling as a pet and it is thought he used the bird's mimicry song to write his so called joke pieces. Handel wrote an organ concerto entitled *The Cuckoo and Nightingale*.

- o   The Catalan region of Spain has a traditional song called *The song of birds* made famous by Casal's cello version. The song represents the joy of nature for Jesus' birth saying "the little birds sing. They go to celebrate Him, With their delicate voices". A range of birds appear such as the Linnet, Nightingale, Woodlark and Wren.

Later in Chapter 8 Species accounts there are several more quotations and references to bird song.

Bird guide books often give a word representation of a bird's song. For example, the Chaffinch's song is represented in one as 'zitt- zitt- zitt- zitt- zitt- sett- sett- sett-chatt-chitteridia'. Not easy to translate such complex music into mere words!

Inevitably, as with much human behaviour, there is a dark side to our associations with bird song. To satisfy a desire to listen to bird song, it became the practice in the 18th and 19th centuries to keep caged birds in houses. Finches in particular (Goldfinch, Linnet, Bullfinch) were caged to provide song. Added to this there was the cruel practice of blinding birds, based on the false supposition of making them sing better. Another cruel practice was to split or cut the tongues of caged birds, again supposedly to make them sing better. Chaffinches were sold for 50 shillings (a small fortune then). Singing competitions were held. In the wild Bullfinch do not sing but have the remarkable facility to be taught to sing complex songs accurately. Turner observed this in the 16th century observing "It is the readiest bird to learn, and imitates a pipe very closely with its voice". In Germany schools were set up to train Bullfinch, which were then sold. Bullfinch can learn two or three tunes very well and pitch perfect! Up until the 19th century birds were traded at a high price. If kept in captivity the birds will imprint on their human trainers and owners, forming a pair bond with a human in the absence of another bird. Also Bullfinch reared by a canary adopted the canary's song, as did their off-spring. Siskin were also kept as cage birds. When bred in the same cage as canaries (who are also in the finch family) the Siskin sang the canaries song! Thankfully the practice of keeping caged birds disappeared in the late 19th century.

Song is defined as a sound that serves to communicate with other members of the same species. Birds also make calls. The distinction between songs and calls is arbitrary.

- o **Songs** - tend to be long, complex vocalisations produced (mainly) by the male often before and during the breeding season. Many species have variations to their song. A song is made up of distinct phrases which can be made up of several units (or syllables) occurring in a particular pattern. We'll look at this in more detail later. Not all birds sing. Birds in the order Passeriformes are marked out as song birds, except for the corvid and sparrow families, which do not sing. Birds from other orders can sing (but not all and others not very well). Some groups have almost no song at all, such as the storks, pelicans and vultures.

- o **Calls** - are shorter, simpler vocalisations produced by both sexes and are produced in specific contexts related to functions such as flight and alarm. Calls tend to be fixed, with little variation.

Birds sing in the frequency range 500 Hz to 6 KHz, with the top of the range being lower than human hearing at 15 KHz. However, birds can discriminate song variations far better than we can. When we listen to bird song there appears to be little difference between individuals but the birds themselves can identify the slight variations between each male's song. Males are able to detect the minor differences between individual's songs and through this become aware of the presence of rivals and any new intruders to their territory. When competing males are all vying for the attention of a female at the start of the breeding season, the female can tell the difference between the individual songs, as she wishes to pick out the male with the best song, as this indicates a stronger, healthier male to father her chicks. Experiments have shown that diseased birds do not sing as well and are less attractive to females. Being able to hold territory indicates a male bird is fit and strong. Singing is directed at optimising breeding success. Many males continue to sing after the first brood has hatched because the male still has a strong motivation to guard against an intruding, non-mated male coming into his territory and mating with his female. Also the female might chose to mate with another male and singing is geared to prevent this by re-enforcing the pair bond.

Guillemots breed on closely packed cliffs, sometimes in large numbers but as a returning adult flies back into the nest area it can differentiate the call of its own chick amongst the cacophony of the site. In fact the situation is even more intriguing. As the chick in the egg starts to emerge (by piercing the shell) it emits a sound. The parents listen to this, memorise the unique sound and then use it to recognise its chick amongst all the others.

The Nightjar makes a very distinctive churring song, emitting about 30 notes per second in a song that can last for 9 minutes. Gilbert White was staying in a hermitage when a Nightjar arrived and he recorded "we were struck with wonder to find the organs of that little animal, when put in motion, gave a sensible vibration to the whole building".

Bird song can be very loud, even to the point of irritation. The Corncrake calls loudly at 105 dB (the loudness of human conversation is about 70 dB) both night and day. The Corncrake has protected itself against hearing damage from its own sound with an internal reflex mechanism in its ear. The Capercaillie similarly has a flap over its ears to prevent damage from the loudness of its own sounds. Birds in urban environments sing louder than their rural counterparts to combat background sounds. Bitterns sing both very loudly and at a low frequency of 200 Hz to be heard hidden in their reed bed home. At the other end of the scale the Goldcrest sings at 9 KHz, possibly out of the hearing range of some other birds.

The greatest intensity of singing, particularly in the breeding season, is around dawn. Why birds sing with greater intensity at dawn is not clear. It could be that foraging for food then is more difficult whereas other birds can hear the singing, both rival males and potential mates. Also, bird song might be better heard at that time and for an individual's songs to be identified, plus sound travels further in the cooler morning air. The timing of the dawn chorus varies with the level of cloud cover, with lower overnight temperatures and stronger winds all lowering the intensity of singing. Certain species commence their dawn chorus earlier than others. The Blackbird is often first, followed by the Robin, then the Wren and warblers.

How do they do it?

The means by which birds generate their sounds is significantly different from how we as humans generate sound. Birds have a larynx (to ensure food does not pass into the lungs) but unlike humans it has no function in producing sound. Instead birds have a syrinx that is located further down the trachea at the point where the trachea splits in two for air to enter the lungs. Syrinx means twin flute in Greek, a name that comes from the Greek tale of the god Pan. The daughter of the river god, Ladon, was turned into a reed with her body becoming a hollow stem, from which pan pipes are made. The syrinx has thin walls that vibrate like the skin of a drum, with muscles tensing and relaxing to vary the pitch of the sound. Also membranes can constrict the passage of air through the bronchial tubes. The syrinx can produce two separate frequencies at the same time (humans cannot). Birds are able to move seamlessly between high and low notes by switching sides of the syrinx and without taking breath. The syrinx is almost 100% efficient in converting the energy of the air passing through into sound hence the ability of such small creatures to sing so loudly. Some passerine birds have as many as five pairs of muscles acting on the syrinx producing the highly complex sounds we hear. The respiratory muscles also add to this, these being linked to the air sacs that provide air for sound production. Birds in non-passerine orders rely on two main muscles to produce sound hence their songs are less complex. The whistle sounds of some birds, like ducks, are generated using a separate mechanism. In some birds the trachea is enlarged to modify or amplify the sound. The Crane and Bittern have a particularly long trachea which helps them to produce their deep, low frequency sound.

Young birds learn their species song by listening and memorising the species song they hear whilst a fledgling. Birds at an early age have the ability to generate song but it takes time and much practice to become an accomplished songster. In one experiment young Chaffinch chicks were reared in a sound proof cage, to prevent them hearing any sounds that they could learn and reproduce. In time all they could produce was a very simple song, unlike the adult song. This is called a sub-song and is innate i.e. it is inherited and not learned. If these isolated young birds are then played the adult song, they are able to learn and sing it. In the wild young birds learn song from adults. Song is learned in year 1 and the bird can then fully recollect it in year 2 and for small birds that might be their only breeding season. The most productive time for learning song is age 2 weeks to 14 weeks, after which the bird just extends its repertoire. In some species if the young bird fails to learn its song within a prescribed time limit, it is unable to do so later in life, whereas in other species learning can take place in later life.

Someone hypothesised about the song of the Wren, which is distinctive, loud, at 90 dB and lasts for about 7 seconds, out of its short 18 month life. The question was: if we scaled the Wren up to Pavarotti's size what would this avian Pavarotti have sounded like? Pavarotti would need to sing for over 5 minutes without taking breath and far exceed 90 dB in loudness! The Wren sings at a very high pitch; about the top note on a piano. Here's a calculation: each distinct phrase of a Wren's song consists of about 100 notes; it sings about 5 phrases a minute equalling 30 000 notes / hour and about 100 000 notes a day if it sings for about 3 / 4 hours a day and it sings for 120 days / year giving 12 million notes a year!! One measurement taken of Wren song during a day in the breeding season recorded 280 strophes sung between 3.45 and 4.20 am; 60 strophes between 12.55 and 13.30 and none 21.45 – 22.20. It pays to get up with the lark (or the Wren) to hear the full dawn chorus!

High frequency sound travels the greatest distance when unobstructed whilst low frequency sound travels further through dense vegetation. Hence the low boom of a Bittern is designed to cut through its reed bed surroundings. The whistle of a Goldeneye can be heard over a kilometre away.

In a few species that exhibit reverse sexual dimporphism (the female is larger and / or more colourful) it is the female that sings e.g. Dotterel and the phalaropes.

In fact bird song is more complex than our ears are able to detect and only when recordings of bird song are converted into a sonogram can the full complexity of the song be appreciated. Sonograms are a graph of frequency against time giving a visual representation of the sounds produced by the song. Some examples are given overleaf:

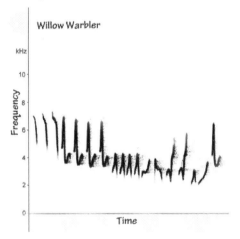

Willow Warbler's song

This is a simple chart showing a clear frequency range, with one strophe distinctly followed by another.

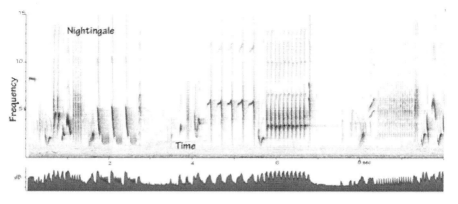

Nightingale's song

This shows the complex song of the Nightingale. The left axis is frequency and the small graph underneath is the amplitude in dB. The sonogram demonstrates the wide frequency range, complexity and dynamics of its song.

An experiment on female canaries demonstrated that they were stimulated into being ready to copulate when they heard the male's 2-note trill which is repeated 17 times a second. The trill is a high note followed by a low note and only the complex avian syrinx can produce this song (not the simple human larynx).

Why birds sing and call

The chief purpose of bird song is to establish and maintain territory and then to attract a mate. Most birds only sing for a portion of the year during a period associated with breeding. Singing is triggered by day length and hormone production. During the non-breeding season the male's testes shrink (to save weight) as its hormone levels change. As the days lengthen in spring hormone levels change and the testes grow back. The area of the brain associated with song also shrinks and expands in the same manner. This led to the discovery that in fact new neurons can form in the brain. With a few exceptions only the male of the species sings. Female Robins sing in late autumn probably to defend their territory but cease as the breeding season approaches. The key to successful breeding for many birds is the possession of a defended territory (some birds, like Rooks, are communal breeders but even then nests are defended against intruders). To defend territory male birds sing. This is their first line of defence and requires the least energy. If an intruder persists the defender will sing louder and with aggression and then might move closer to confront the intruder. Only as a last resort will the defender use physical aggression. In singing the male is also trying to attract a female with the richness of his song, trying to be better than any rivals. In an experiment with Hoopoe it was established that the length of the first strophe in its song was directly correlated to its reproductive success. Males with a longer strophe attracted more females, produced more fledglings and were able to provision more food than rivals with a shorter song.

In an experiment with wild Great Tits, the male's territory song was recorded. The birds were then removed from the territory. Speakers then played the recorded song in one area of the territory, a simple song in another area and nothing in a third area. Other males then occupied the territories where no song was played and kept out of the areas where the original male song was played. They recognised the need to keep out! In a further variation the experimenters played a range of song repertoires in these territories. Males kept out of the territories where the complex songs were played.

Securing a mate is not always solely about song. In some species nest site selection and building is the attraction. The male Wren builds multiple nests and shows these to a prospective female. She will then decide which if any nest is suitable for her chicks.

Birds have a range of calls used for a variety of purposes including:

- o Attracting a mate
- o Forming bonds
- o Claiming territory
- o Defending territory
- o Identifying individuals in a colony or flock
- o Warning of predators
- o Expressing distress when frightened
- o Begging for food by hatchlings and fledglings
- o Contacting other birds in flocks
- o Contacting mates
- o Staying together with flight calls, especially whilst migrating

Calls are short, repetitive and specifically related to a function. Calls are a means of communication both within and between species (singing is species specific). Alert calls are used by many birds to draw attention to the presence of a predator and maybe recognised by many species at once. Mobbing calls are a call to arms to eject a potential predator from an area, for example when a roosting Tawny Owl is spotted. When the presence of a predator is detected birds in the area birds will mob it to force it to leave. Corvids also do the same in the air with Buzzards. Passerines have up to 20 distinct calls, with birds in other orders having fewer. Location calls are made between bonded males and females and also by chicks and fledglings to parents. The male Bullfinch does not sing in the wild but can be heard emitting a gentle contact call to his partner (this species is strictly sexually monogamous) to ensure they remain together. In an experiment in 1955 a sonogram was used to record the calls of Chaffinch. In all twelve distinct calls were identified:

Flight	Social
Injury	Aggression
Three alarm calls	Three courtship calls
Begging call by nestling	Begging call by fledgling

Overleaf are two contrasting sonograms. The first is a sonogram of the Blackbird's song – showing a complex pattern of frequencies over a protracted period. The second is a sonogram of the Blackbird's call – showing a much simpler pattern which is repeated over short periods of time.

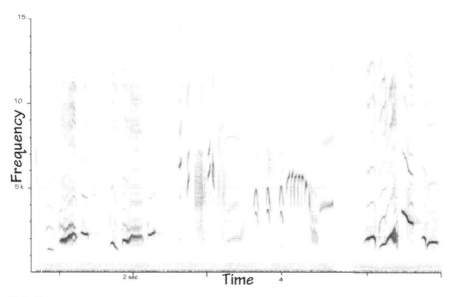

Blackbird's song

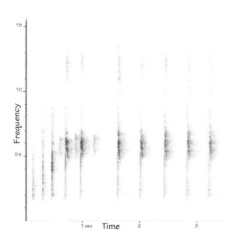

Blackbird's call

Some schools of thought believe that bird song is solely functional and is an activity directed at breeding success and survival. This derives from a belief that all bird behaviour is driven by reproductive success. All behaviour is purposeful and nothing is done merely for the sake of it or solely for pleasure. Others believe that bird song is associated with enjoyment and pleasure. Darwin wrote "Nothing is more common than for animals to take pleasure in practicing whatever instinct they follow at other times for real good". David Rothenburg in his interesting book, *Why birds sing*, gives an answer: "for the same reason we sing – because we can. Because we love to inhabit the pure realm of sound. Because we must sing. No explanation will erase the eternal need to sing". The writer of Ecclesiastes wrote about the power of bird song "Curse not the king ... for a bird of the air will carry the voice, and that which has wings shall tell the matter". Birds singing outside of the breeding season are, according to some writers, expressing well being. They sing because they can, not because they must. Others suggest that singing then is an opportunity to practice their song and to add variations to their song repertoire. Certainly juveniles do practice singing and adult birds extend their repertoire to perfect what is an essential function in a bird's life.

Variations on a theme

Some bird's song patterns are constant whilst other species have many variations on a theme. The Great Tit (a frustrating bird to identify from its song) has a wide repertoire of songs. A male will sing one phrase several times and then switch to another variation. One explanation is that this strategy confuses other males into thinking there are several male Great Tits in a territory. The Blackbird has up to 100 phrases it can call on to sing. The Song Thrush also has a similar number of phrases he uses, with the usual pattern of singing the same phrase twice or three times and then moving onto the next phrase. Older males have a larger range of phrases which is more attractive to a female. Male Sedge Warblers are masters of building up variations on a theme. He starts with some basic phrases and then develops a range of variations which are unique to the individual bird. Experiments have shown that the male with the most complex song paired with females sooner than males with a simpler song. On the other hand (at least to our ears) all individuals of species like the Wren, Chiffchaff and Chaffinch sing the same song.

Dialects amongst birds are well established. Local populations develop their own specific variation of the species' song to create an identifiable dialect. Individuals in a local population can discern an intruder singing with a different dialect. Scientists are not sure why birds do this; it could be to retain a local gene pool, which might develop into a sub-species. Females are known to select mates from the local population not an intruder. Skylarks have local dialects. In Norway scientists identified clear local dialects in Redwing populations. If male Redwings moved to a new district they found it impossible to attract a mate. In one extraordinary project the dialects of UK and New Zealand Yellowhammers were compared. As was the case with many animals, emigrants to New Zealand took some reminders of the home country, including Yellowhammers (possibly for their song). The birds settled so well they spread and grew in number, eventually becoming a pest. The project compared the recorded songs of UK birds with those of New Zealand birds. Yellowhammers are known to have local dialects. The expectation was that the UK birds would have retained a greater number of dialects than those in New Zealand. The opposite turned out to be the case. The New Zealand birds had retained a full range of UK dialects having thrived there but possibly UK dialects have been lost here due to a large decline in bird numbers. Scientists in Poland investigated the song of the male Cuckoo. They found that Cuckoos which lived in a locality were able to distinguish the song of an unfamiliar stranger from another area. Locals were aggressive to strangers but tolerated each other.

A number of birds have the power of mimicry. They hear a range of sounds in their environment and then reproduce them, sometimes with amazing accuracy. Starlings are good mimics and reproduce other birds' songs as well as environmental sounds, such as traffic noise and 'phone rings. Their song is partially made up of mimicry. The longer and more complex a male's song is, the greater the chance of successfully mating, being a rule that applies to many birds. However, the master mimic has to be the Marsh Warbler. The song of this rare UK summer migrant is wholly made up of mimicry of other birds' songs. A Belgian woman scientist, Francoise Dowsett-Lemaire, studied the bird's song in detail. She established that the Marsh Warbler could mimic most birds in its locality. Then the research became mysterious; this mimicry of European bird song only accounted for about half of the warbler's song. The mystery was finally solved when Dowsett-Lemaire made a trip to East Africa (being an expert on African birds) and discovered that the other half of the warbler's song was made up of mimicry of bird song heard in its winter quarters. So the bird was able to memorise song from its wintering quarters (plus some birds it met on its migratory journey) as well as those it heard on its summer breeding grounds in Europe. It takes the bird 30 minutes to sing through its whole repertoire. Her research identified mimicry from a staggering total of 100 European birds and a similar number of African birds. Oddly, her research showed that the female Marsh Warbler is not wholly impressed with this marvel and selects its mate on the basis of the best nest site the males make available for her.

Duetting, where the male song provokes a song response from the female, occurs in a few species. Tawny Owls are an example, where the tu-wit hoot is made by the female and the to-woo is the male's response. Hence, the much used 'to-wit to-woo' is in fact both the male and female combining as a duet. Swifts have been observed duetting when a bird returns to the nest after a feeding foray.

The Great Spotted and Lesser Spotted Woodpeckers use drumming to establish territory and attract a mate. The Barn Owl's wings emit a quiet, low frequency sound at 1 KHz, whereas its rodent prey squeaks at 8 KHz, so the Owl is still able to hear its prey.

Birds also make sounds other than calls and song. Some birds make mechanical sounds. For example, the male Snipe generates a drumming sound from its outer tail feathers as part of its courtship display. Birds, such as the Puffin and Guillemot, clap their mandibles together as part of their pair bonding display, especially when they meet again after being apart during the non-breeding season. Cranes clap their mandibles as part of their elaborate courtship display. Wing clapping is practised by Woodpigeons and Nightjar. Swans, geese and pheasants all emit a flight noise with their wings.

Two non-British species, the oilbirds and the cave swifts, use echo location (in the manner of bats) to navigate in their dark environment.

CHAPTER FOUR

MATES, MATING AND BREEDING

Breeding relationships

The drive to reproduce is fundamental to the continued existence of all life forms, including birds. For birds, breeding is highly complex, involving a wide range of behaviours, with many differences across various orders and families. All birds reproduce by laying eggs. Beyond that there is a great variety of means employed to achieve the goal of reproductive success.

For most birds in the temperate zone breeding is a seasonal activity. We often use the phrase 'in the breeding season' and for the UK that is in spring. With the vast majority of birds both males and females are only able to breed during this period. Outside of the breeding season most species' sexual organs shrink and don't function. This saves weight; vital for flying. The Woodpigeon is an exception to this general rule and they are capable of reproducing at any time of the year. Crossbills have a breeding season that is linked to the availability of its cone seed food rather than terrestrial seasons, so they can breed at different times of the year.

As the breeding season approaches:

- Day light hours increase as do temperatures.
- A greater range of food is available, especially insect prey and invertebrate prey.
- Hormone levels rise causing sex organs to re-activate so the male can produce sperm and sing and for the female to ovulate.
- Territory is established with many birds. Often the male will establish territory by singing with great vigour.
- Partial moult of the body feathers just before the breeding season gives the males particularly a resplendent full set of clean, colourful feathers.
- Migratory journeys end around this time. Birds return from their winter quarters to their summer, breeding area. For others they leave their UK winter resting grounds to fly north to their breeding area. For some species this might be a long distance journey, for others a shorter, local journey. Migratory journeys were discussed in detail in the Section on Migration in Chapter 2.

The trigger for commencing breeding activities is the increase in light levels which occurs as the days lengthen in spring, being similar to the trigger for migratory activity. This leads to a change in hormone levels and the male and female sex organs re-grow to a functioning size. In the male House Sparrow the testes are the size of a pin head outside the breeding season and re-grow to the size of a baked bean. In male birds the portion of the brain associated with song expands enabling the male to sing. The breaking leaf buds on the beech tree is a trigger for the Blue Tit to commence breeding activities, as they crucially need to time the birth of their chicks with the emergence of caterpillar food. Also, warmer evening temperatures trigger off nest building.

In the 1930's a Dutch researcher, Damsté, experimented with artificially altering normal spring behaviour in Greenfinches. In spring he reduced the light levels the birds were kept in and he noticed the gonads shrank and sperm production stopped. In autumn he increased the light levels and the reverse occurred, plus the birds began to sing. Other experiments identified that it was light levels on the skull which made the difference, not light on the eyes. This in turn triggers the release of hormones that cause the gonads to re-activate for the birds to reach breeding condition. The bird's internal clock is also involved in this process. Lack carried out experiments on Great Tits and found that the bird timed egg laying to coincide with the emergence of its caterpillar food. Somehow the birds predicted this several weeks in advance; lay too early and the caterpillars would not be out, too late and they would be all gone. The ability to do this is inherited.

The type of relationship between males and females can be split into:

- o **Socially monogamous relationships** - where the male and female form a pair bond for at least the duration of the breeding season with both males and females fully involved in parenting. About 92% of bird species practice social monogamy as this is frequently the most efficient means of successfully producing the next generation of the species.

- o **Sexually monogamous relationships** - where the pair have sex only with each other, to the exclusion of all others. Sexual monogamy is relatively rare in birds. When speaking of avian sexual monogamy there is the danger of anthropomorphism; of imputing human behaviour and moral values onto birds. Birds are solely concerned with their reproductive success. Birds employ whatever strategy is required to secure their highest level of succession; with birds the strategies employed vary a great deal.

Males maintain a socially monogamous relationship by defending the female from intruders. This involves frequent copulation with his mate to ensure that all the off-spring which he will help to bring up are his. The male will defend the eggs against predation, hence the often angry scenes on close-packed nesting cliff colonies. In some species one parent is absent for several days, feeding at sea, such as the Manx Shearwater. With these species the other mate has to remain to incubate the egg (or eggs). Monogamy might be for one season or for a lifetime. Experiments have shown that breeding success is higher if pairs stay together but pairs divorce if breeding success rates are low. The divorce rate for successful pairs of Manx Shearwater is 5% whereas it is 27% for unsuccessful pairs. With Kittiwake, pairs that remain together fledge 17% more chicks. About 80% of bird species are socially monogamous, compared to about 3% for mammals. This is not surprising as the avian breeding strategy requires the energy and attention of both parents to successfully rear chicks. Exceptions do occur, notably amongst the duck family, where the male has little or nothing to do with helping rear his family.

The forms of mating system in birds are:

Table 7 - Mating systems

Mating system:	Relationship:	Care of young:
Monogamy	One F with one M	Both
Polygyny	Many F with one M	Female
Polyandry	One F with many M	Male
Polygynandry	Many F with many M	Both

Monogamy - a pair might be sexually monogamous for a breeding season or until they split up or for life. Sexual monogamy is practiced for example, by the Mute Swan which is a high fidelity species. They pair for life and remain together during the non-breeding season. The longer they remain together (and Mute Swans live on average for 10 years) the better the pair are at raising young to adulthood. If a pair is poor at raising young, then the pair bond might be broken. Pairs of Gannets are faithful to each other. They part after the breeding season to spend most of their life at sea and re-connect at the start of the next breeding season. A strong pair bond is established again with an energetic courtship display – see the next Section on Courtship. It pays for the species to be highly efficient. The pair needs to establish the rights to their nesting site (they return to the same spot on the crowded cliff breeding site) and to lay their eggs at just the right time. Too early and the egg perishes, too late and there isn't sufficient time for the chick to mature. Puffins also exhibit high fidelity and like the Gannet an adult pair part company after breeding. They re-establish their bond the following spring, with a courtship display involving their colourful beaks. Divorce does occur with about 7% of pairs, especially where breeding success was low in the previous season. A divorced male will only move a short distance (in one study 1.7 m) to set up a new nest. Bereaved male Puffins will move further (4 m) to set up a new nest. The Bullfinch is a sexually monogamous species, so much so that males produce less sperm and have smaller testes, as they don't mate as often as polygamous birds. Bullfinch mate for life and remain together throughout the year, seldom parting company. The male and female are both active in raising young.

Polygyny - is prevalent in avian relationships. The word means many women. Males are strongly driven to mate with as many females as possible to ensure that their genetic line continues. If the quality of territory held by males varies (in terms of providing good nesting sites and an ample supply of food for the young) the male holding the best territory will attract several females, which leads to polygyny. The male provides little help with nesting or care of the young. Mallard ducks are an example of polygyny. Based on DNA studies up to 50% of a brood of Mallard have different fathers. However, this is complicated by the practice of egg dumping by other females; not uncommon in duck species. Having a mix of genes ensures that a weakness in the DNA is not compounded and thus increases the off-spring's chance of survival. The male Pied Flycatcher (a summer migrant to the UK) arrives early to secure its territory, as do many migrants. It selects a suitable tree nest-hole and then sets about attracting a female. After his partner lays her eggs he then flies off and tries to make a second home, select a new nest site and attract another female. This suits the male, as he has more progeny and it suits a second female if that secures her having some chicks.

Polyandry - the relationship of one female with many males is rare amongst bird species, occurring in less than 1% of species. Often this relationship is associated with reverse sexual dimorphism, where the female takes the lead for breeding, is the most colourful one, who sings and holds territory. The female selects the male and after mating the female lays the eggs in a nest, leaving the male to incubate the eggs and feed the chicks. After laying her eggs the female goes off and finds another male and repeats the procedure. The female won't see her off-spring before migrating and the male leaves the chicks at an early stage, before they can fly. In migratory species the young have to find their own way to their resting grounds. An example of this is seen with the Dotterel, phalaropes and Sanderling.

Polygynandry - the relationship of many males with many females is another rare mating system. In this system many males defend a single territory and the females are separated around this area. Sometimes the male might help a female. The older, more dominant females get more help from the males resulting in a higher breeding success. Polygynandry is practiced by the Dunnock, where two or three males are in a group relationship with two or three females. Dunnocks have found this form of relationship to be the most successful way to maximise breeding success. Male Dunnocks have enlarged testicles and a large supply of sperm as they engage in sperm competition with other males. The female selects a male and approaches him for a copulation that lasts about 1 second. However, Dunnocks might mate 30 times a day.

Courtship

Courtship in birds is highly variable, including some highly flamboyant and sometimes bizarre behaviour. The wide variety of song and use of plumage displays seen in bird courtship ensures that pairs of a species mate together and it helps avoid confusion and mis-pairing with other species. Courtship also helps the male and female synchronise their reproductive cycles. This ensures that the sex organs re-grow and are fully functioning ready for the breeding season. Courtship behaviour includes:

Singing	Displaying	Dancing
Allopreening	Strutting	Aerobatics
Feeding	Nest building	Chasing
Stroking beaks	Clapping beaks	Posturing
Flight displays		

Many male birds sing (especially passerines) and this was discussed fully in Chapter 3. In some species the male is responsible for securing territory (the primary function of song), providing a nest site and ensuring an adequate food supply. Singing is also aimed at attracting a female and repelling other males. In some less musical species the birds use a call rather than a more musical song. In some species displaying is a male only activity seen in its extreme form in lek displays (see below) whilst other species perform a mutual display, like the Great Crested Grebe (again, see below).

A **courtship display** helps the female to select the most suitable male partner, as the one with the best set of genes to pass on to their young and who can ensure a high level of breeding success. Often this involves the striking features of the male's plumage. In some species displaying is taken to extremes, like the Peacock. In many bird species the male has more colourful feathers and often these are larger, such as the Pheasant. Whilst it is clear that large, colourful displays are attractive it does come at a considerable cost to the male. He has to expend significant amounts of energy on growing these display feathers and these feathers might also be an encumbrance and put the male in danger. Darwin classified this process as sexual selection (as opposed to natural selection), whereby the female selects a male on the basis of these characters. He suggested that on balance it must pay the male to have these costly display feathers in order to secure mating with a female and ensure his genetic line continues. The Redshank engages in a courtship display with the male chasing around the female and the birds tilting forward in a posture. Unmated males also indulge in a display flight to attract a mate. Male Swallows have longer outer tail feathers than the female and it is the males with the longer streamers that attract a mate. In an experiment the tail feathers of some male Swallows were artificially lengthened. This improved the mating performance of these males. Those with shorter tails were less successful. Male Goldeneyes display by throwing their head right back, kicking their legs out and emitting a whistle.   The courtship display of the harriers includes a flambouyant aerial display by the male and a food pass where the male flies above the female, realeasing a tasty morsel and she turns upside down to dexterously catch the item.

The **leks** associated with Ruffs and Black Grouse are a specific and extravagant form of courtship display. The word lek derives from the

Swedish meaning to play. Males may spend a considerable time displaying at the lek with no female in attendance. After the female has mated the males may well move onto another lek to try their luck there. Females are able to breed over a long period so males have a greater chance of mating. The female does not get any help after mating. The young are born precocial, so can look after themselves soon after hatching. Male Ruff are considerably larger than the female. The male's cloacal organ is also comparatively large, being a feature of birds that have to compete to mate. The males' breeding plumage is characterised by the colourful, unique ruff of neck feathers, head tufts and bright bare patches of skin on its face. For the females a brighter plumage indicates a healthier, stronger male with fewer parasites. The brightly coloured males are called territorial males who stake out a small patch on the lek and engage in a vigorous display ritual. Matters are complicated by the fact that some males are dowdier, with their ruff being pale coloured. They are called satellite males, standing on the outer edge of the lek. They are opportunistic maters, running to a female whilst the other males are not looking! Yet another set of males are smaller and do not grow any distinctive plumage. They attend the outer regions of a lek and again hope to sneak in and mate whilst the other males are not looking. These males have very large testes. Castrated males do not grow their distinctive ruff, demonstrating that the growth of these feathers is hormonal. Black Grouse commence their leks in the autumn with no females in attendance. They just need to practice and refine their skills ready for mating in spring. Lekking includes emitting a loud grunt to add to the display of feathers.

One of the most elegant and sophisticated **courtship dances** is that of the Great Crested Grebe. The male and female, who have identical flamboyant breeding plumage, start their display by croaking at one another, followed by an underwater swim. On returning to the surface they raise their colourful head plumes, spread their wings and then shake their heads, moving their necks up and down. One bird then goes off paddling its feet on the surface of the water. Finally, they dive for some weed and present this in an elaborate display to their potential mate. As if this is not enough, mating can only take place out of the water (they cannot mate in the water as ducks can). To do this they build a special raft as a love nest for mating (eggs are laid on a different raft). What a magnificent and original routine to secure a mate! Cranes undertake an elaborate display that includes elements of dancing, leaping, beak stroking and emitting loud trumpeting sounds. Some birds have brightly coloured wattles such as the game birds e.g. the Red Grouse whose size of wattle is proportional to its testosterone levels. Several duck species have a brightly coloured speculum on their wings. Males preen their wing feathers to reveal these feathers to attract a female. Herons also clash their beaks together during their courtship display. The Avocets' mating ceremony involves dipping their beak in water, preening the mate's breast, with the male moving round the female.

Courtship feeding is performed by some species. It assists the female in assessing how well the male can provision food for her whilst she broods their eggs and chicks. The male tern feeds the female prior to and during incubation. A male bringing more food leads to a larger clutch size. A female Blue Tit receives about 40% of her food from the male. The female Osprey remains on the nest throughout the breeding season and is fed by the male, as are their chicks.

A number of seabirds form a life-long pair bond including the Gannet, Puffin, Guillemot, Razorbill, Kittiwake, Manx Shearwater and Fulmar. These birds typically nest on remote cliff sites, some with only a minimal amount of space on a shelf for a nest. Whilst space is at a premium the cliffs are near to rich sources of food to see the pair through the breeding season. These species typically spend the non-breeding season way out at sea, with the Manx Shearwater for example making a long distance, oceanic migratory journey to South America. When the bird's internal clock signals the start of the breeding season remarkably pairs return to the exact same site they left 9 months previously. They then have the task of looking for their mate again in a large flock of birds. When they do find each other the pair undertake an elaborate display, which re-establishes the pair bond. With many species this involves displays of affection, such as stroking their beaks together and showy displays using their wings. With the Puffins, their beaks return to full colour again after having moulted their colour platelets the previous autumn into a plain colour. The pair then returns to their nest site and establish their nest burrow prior to laying their one egg.

A male Peregrine will display his prowess using an aerial display with the female judging how well that male might be at catching prey. Snipe also undertake an aerial display over the nest area that incorporates creating a sound from its outer tail feathers. Woodpeckers use drumming to delineate territory and to attract a female. In experiments where drumming has been recorded and the sonogram analysed, it is clear that each male has a specific drum beat which females are able to recognise and differentiate between competing males. Woodpeckers also touch beaks as part of their courtship ritual.

Courtship for the Wren involves the male building a series of about 5 nests, called cock nests, singing to attract a female, showing her the nests and then letting her choose the most suitable nest in which to lay their eggs. Warblers such as the Blackcap, Garden Warbler, Lesser Whitethroat, Whitethroat and Dartford Warbler all do this as part of their courtship. Male Redshank make up to 15 scrapes with the female selecting one for a nest. Herons display at their tree nest where they have no immediate enemies.

Courtship with many species incorporates allopreening, whereby the male and female preen each other. The word allo means other. This important function serves two main purposes. The first is the benefit from preening, to rid their mate of parasites that they cannot reach. Doing this also reduces the risk of parasitic infection of their young. The second is to establish and re-enforce the pair bond. Allopreening is performed with sensitivity. Although bird's beaks are made of horny material the tips are full of touch sensors. Highly social birds tend to spend considerable time allopreening, especially those that nest in densely packed colonies. Some parents also allopreen with their chicks.

Male birds hold territory during the breeding season to ensure the provision of food for their mate and off-spring and secondly to secure a nest site for the female's eggs and to protect the young (especially in species where hatchlings are altricial i.e. are unable to look after themselves). Outside the breeding season territory might still be held for feeding and roosting. Territory ensures space is used efficiently. The area held can be very small, like in sea-bird colonies (Guillemots breed at a density of 70 per m^2.) to a back garden through to the vast area held as territory by a Golden Eagle (as much 200 km^2.). An area can become saturated with breeding territories leaving some pairs of birds unable to breed.

Sex

Male birds have a paired set of testes, which grow to functioning size at the start of the breeding season, expanding by about 100 times. Female birds have a single oviduct (with the exception of some birds of prey). Again, the oviduct grows at the start of the breeding season, up to 50 times larger than its non-breeding size. After copulation females can store sperm in tubules in the lower part of the oviduct. When the female ovulates sperm is issued from this store and travels up the oviduct to fertilise the ova. Some birds, like the petrels, can store sperm for up to 2 months. This is vital, as males and females do not always remain with each other and timing is all important when laying an egg. For example, the female Cuckoo has to vigilantly watch her host's nest and time her egg production so that she lays her egg at exactly the right time. She may not have the opportunity to mate with a male at the exact time required.

Human males have two sex chromosomes in their DNA – X and Y. A human sperm contains either an X or a Y chromosome. In human female' ova both chromosomes are type X. If a sperm containing a Y chromosome fertilises an ova, the resulting embryo is male i.e. possesses X and Y chromosomes. If a sperm containing an X chromosome fertilises an ova, the resulting embryo is female i.e. possesses only X chromosomes. In birds the chromosomes are labelled Z and W. Avian males have only the Z chromosome so all sperm contains just the Z chromosome. Females possess both the Z and W chromosomes. If the male sperm fertilises an ova containing a Z chromosome, the resulting embryo is male i.e. possesses only Z chromosomes. If a sperm fertilises an ova containing a W chromosome, the resulting embryo is female i.e. possesses both Z and W chromosomes. The sex of offspring is entirely random so all females lay an equal number of male and female eggs (in the long term).

Both sexes of most birds utilise the cloaca for copulation, a vent located at the rear, underside of the bird. The cloaca has several functions. It is used to excrete waste from the digestive system, to access the preen gland and it is here the female lays its eggs and from which the male ejects his sperm. This arrangement saves weight by having one multi-purpose gland rather than several separate ones. In preparation for the breeding season the cloaca swells and protrudes slightly (more in males than females). Copulation takes place by the male and female connecting their cloaca, often only for a second or two. However, the record for the lengthiest known copulation goes to the Aquatic Warbler which mates for a full 30 minutes. The females are very elusive so the male has to make very sure that he implants his sperm in the female. He might not get another chance! In a small number of species, notably in swans, ducks and geese, the birds copulate in water so the males have a penis to prevent the sperm being washed away.

Infidelity often occurs in the avian world. Once again fidelity is a human construct that governs the moral behaviour between individuals. As humans we have a sense of what is right and wrong. The behaviour of male and female birds is driven by sexual selection operating at the level of the individual bird (not the species). Most female birds are promiscuous and even females in species that are sexually monogamous will indulge in extra-pair copulations. This behaviour drives the male to regularly have sex with his mate to ensure his paternity of the eggs the female lays. This race by males to ensure that his line continues (as opposed to any other male) is called sperm competition. In some species this is exemplified by the males being larger and more colourful. Where sperm competition is the highest the males have large testes. Ruff demonstrate this where the most colourful and extravagant male is given the opportunity to mate to the exclusion of other males competing at the lek. In some monogamous species, like the Bullfinch, sperm competition is low where the testes are comparatively small and the cloacal protuberance is virtually non-existent.

Some species, like the Great Crested Grebe, Cormorant and Shag also practice reverse mounting, where the female mounts the male. This phenomenon is not fully understood. There is no evidence that copulation takes place. One theory is that it re-enforces the pair bond as part of courtship, as these reverse mountings tend to occur early on in courtship.

During incubation the hormone prolactin is released which reduces the bird's levels of sex hormones. In some species, like the Nightingale, the male bird stops singing at this time. Remarkably, if a clutch is lost or destroyed, the male commences singing again. For the vast majority of species, once the breeding season is over the sex organs shrink (to save weight) and, in males, the area of the brain associated with singing shrinks.

Nesting

The variety of nests constructed by birds is diverse:

- o **Domed nest** - Wren, Long-tailed Tit, Magpie, Dipper and House Martin. Domed nests help keep predators at bay and the eggs warm, giving protection from inclement weather. These can be elaborate constructions built with many different materials.

- o **Excavated hole** – such as the Woodpeckers, who locate their tree-hole nest on the side of the tree away from the prevailing wind. After excavating a hole little else is added to make the nest.

- o **Burrows** – Puffin and Manx Shearwater excavate a tunnel into the ground with a small nest chamber at the end. Puffins also excavate a small ante-chamber for the chick to defecate in to keep the main chamber clean and pest free. Kingfisher and Sand Martin excavate a tunnel in a sandy bank with a small chamber at the end for the eggs and chicks.

- o **Platform** - made of twigs and vegetation, used by ducks, swans, geese and grebes.

- o **Open, cup-shaped** - made of small twigs, vegetation and lined with soft, insulating materials. Used by many small birds, such as the Robin.

- o **Tree cavity** - adapt a natural cavity in a tree. Used by Treecrepper, tits, Nuthatch, Smew and Goldeneye.

- o **Tree nests** - large twig constructions, often added to year on year, used by species such as the Eagle, Osprey, Sparrowhawk, Goshawk and the corvids.

- o **Scrape** - birds like terns and Ringed Plover lays their eggs on a pebble beach in a simple scrape, with the eggs cryptically coloured for camouflage.

- o **No nest** - some birds make virtually no nest like the Guillemot, which lays its egg on bare rock. Owls find a suitable cavity but do not build any nest.

The Long-tailed Tit's nest is a wonder of avian engineering. Their nests are enclosed, elongated structures woven from moss, lichen, spider silk and plant material. Towards the top, the nest has an entrance hole and a soft lining containing more than 2 000 feathers. As the chicks grow larger the structure expands to create more space. The nests are commonly located low in the woodland shrub layer, suspended among the forks of suitable branches. Once hatched, youngsters are cared for by the parents and sometimes by other members of the flock whose own breeding attempts have failed. If the nest fails the adults will assist with bringing up the young of another pair. As Long-tailed Tits stay in family groups it is likely this assistance is given by an aunt and uncle of the young. The explanation for this behaviour (which might be seen as altruistic) is that the aunt and uncle are helping to maintain the hereditary line. The young fledge within 3 weeks of hatching and remain with the parents' flock over their first winter.

In most passerine species it is usually the female that builds the nest. The exception is where the male constructs several nests, called cock nests, as part of its courtship, presenting them to the female for her to choose her preferred nest. An example of this is the Wren and some warblers.

The Wren's nest is made up of moss, glued with saliva. Nuthatches stop up the entrance hole to their tree cavity nest so larger birds cannot enter and either steal the nest or try to take their young. Starling's add fresh green vegetation to their hole-nests about a month before nesting and continue to do this throughout the season until the young have hatched. It is thought that this reduces attacks by nest parasites. Some birds of prey also continue to add material to their nests whilst brooding and feeding young.

The Puffin constructs a burrow for a nest, sometimes utilising a rabbit burrow. They use their feet to excavate into a slope so the chamber is well below ground. The burrow can be 2 m long and 14 cm diameter and can take 2 weeks to build. They also build a side chamber that the chick uses as a toilet.

One piece of folklore is that the stones sometimes to be found in a Golden Eagle's eyrie have been brought down from the sun or a volcano by the bird to help hatch its eggs. These stones became collector's items.

In woodland many bird species utilise tree cavities, such as Woodpeckers, Nuthatch, Treecreeper, Starling, Blue and Great Tit, owls and Pied Flycatcher. Most nest sites require dead standing trees except where a nest hole can be drilled, such as with the woodpeckers or where use is made of crevices, such as owls. Managed woodlands, especially with young trees, provide few nesting opportunities. House Sparrows traditionally build their nests near human habitation but one pair's nest was found 600 m down a mine shaft!

Male Oystercatchers build several simple scrape nesting areas in their shingle home and the female then selects the most suitable one. Usually waders and terns nest on simple scrapes on the ground, sometimes on shingle, where the eggs are cryptically coloured against predation. An exception is the Green Sandpiper that nests in trees, using an old thrush's or pigeon's nest. Goosanders, Smew and Goldeneye also nest in tree cavities. When fledged the young jump from their nest to the ground without injury.

Breeding densities can be limited by the availability of suitable nest sites even where there is sufficient food. Some conservation measures have included installing artificial nest sites and several species have benefitted from this. Nest boxes and water rafts have been used to assist species like the Pied Flycatcher, Kestrels, Barn Owls and the Common Tern amongst several others.

The human built environment has provided some species with new nesting opportunities. Swallows have taken to nesting almost exclusively on buildings as have the House Martin and Swift. In the past they nested on cliffs. This has led to an increase in numbers of these birds. Sand Martins have also benefitted from the creation of sand banks in worked-out gravel pits where they can nest. Building wooden rafts on old gravel pits has encouraged Common Tern to nest inland sometimes in competition from Black-headed Gulls. Falcons, such as the Peregrine and Kestrel, have taken to nesting in buildings. The highest breeding population density of Peregrines in the world is New York city! Ospreys have also adapted to nesting on human made platforms. Many gulls have moved inland and found nesting sites on buildings. Kittiwake breed inland now with the furthmost inland colony in the world of this species being located in Newcastle.

Colonial nesting occurs in a number of bird species for a variety of reasons:

- o For protection against predators, where crowds can confuse predators and they find it difficult to catch prey.
- o To make the best use of the space available, such as inaccessible cliffs, where birds have to nest in colonies to utilise the area available.
- o Improve the efficiency of finding food.

However there are disadvantages including:

- o Increased competition for food.
- o Competition for nesting material.
- o Predation of eggs and nestlings. Colonial nesters coordinate their egg laying so all the eggs are laid at once.
- o Identification of food source.

Colonial nesters include the seabirds, gulls, terns, Gannet, Puffin, Guillemot, Razorbill, Kittiwake, Manx Shearwater and Fulmar plus Fieldfare, Swifts, Rooks and Herons.

In order to minimise the risk of parasitical infections most birds keep their nests clean by removing the faecal sacs, which the young produce to contain their faeces. Not all birds do this. Some young instinctively squirt their faeces clear out of the nest. Some are not so clean. The Kingfisher excavates its nest at an incline so the wet faeces of their young drain away. The Golden Eagle adds fresh material to its nest throughout the fledging period to provide a clean top layer which possibly contains anti-bacterial material. The largest recorded nest was 4.6 m deep! The Great Crested Grebe constructs two types of nest. The first is a love nest that the couple use for copulation after their elaborate display. The second nest is a raft built for their eggs. Some birds like the Fieldfare build their nests near birds of prey to provide a measure of protection against predation by other birds like Magpies and Woodpeckers. The Firecrest builds its nest near a Goshawk. Black Grouse nests are more productive when built near a Goshawk's nest. Wrens have been seen to build their nest near a Golden Eagle's eyrie.

A strategy to increase the potential number of surviving young is to lay eggs in other birds' nests. Sometimes this is called egg dumping or brood parasitism. Species that use this strategy are some ducks such as the Goldeneye, some geese, House Sparrow, Moorhen, Oystercatcher, Shelduck, Starling and Swallow. This strategy is called partial brood parasitism. Some females lay some of their eggs in another bird's nest of the same species others in the nests of other species. Often the host is able to identify the parasitic egg and either buries it or pushes it to the edge of the nest despite the high colour variation of their eggs. Out of the 150 Cuckoo species in the world, 57 are wholly (or obligate) brood parasites. The one Cuckoo species in the UK is an obligate brood parasite, meaning that it only lays its eggs in the nest of another species.

The story of the Cuckoo's breeding strategy is truly remarkable. Each female only ever lays her eggs in the nest of a specific host species, as will her female off-spring. The most common hosts are Dunnock, Meadow Pipit, Pied Wagtail, Reed Warbler, Robin and Sedge Warbler. The eggs she lays mimic the host's eggs in colour (except for some odd reason, the Dunnock). Her eggs are proportionally small for a Cuckoo- sized bird and the shells are thicker than normal so they don't break when dropped in a nest. This ability to mimic the host's egg colour is hereditary with the egg colour deriving from the W chromosome, specific to the female. The male can mate with any female and the particular species' egg mimicry will be maintained in any female off-spring. The female is able to store sperm for many days. She observes a selected nest and at the right moment starts the 24 hour egg production process. The female retains the egg inside her body longer than normal and this leads to internal incubation with the embryo being more developed when the egg is laid. The act of laying an egg takes 3-4 seconds, in which time she ejects one of the host's eggs. At this time she also emits a call mimicking a bird of prey which frightens the host bird and distracts them from the Cuckoo's activity. She lays her eggs in the afternoon when the host is more likely to be collecting food (most birds lay their eggs in the morning). The eggs have two distinct layers with an outer chalky layer that is believed to provide resistance to cracking when the egg is dropped in the host nest. On average a female lays 9 eggs per year. The young chick, on hatching immediately and instinctively starts to eject the other eggs from the nest, using a specially developed hollow in its back. The Cuckoo chick has a voracious appetite and quadruples its weight in 4 days! The chick's begging call imitates the host species' chick's call to induce the host adults to feed the bird. The natural history of the Cuckoo took a long time to unfold. Aristotle noted that the bird did not make a nest and laid its eggs in other bird's nests and ate their eggs. Edward Jenner presented a paper to the Royal Society in 1788 giving evidence of the Cuckoo's egg laying behaviour. His paper was considered so fantastic that the Royal Society suggested "it is best to give you full scope for altering it".

Eggs

All birds reproduce by laying eggs. These are the main components of this extraordinary process:

Yolk - female birds have a single ovary (except birds of prey and humans that have two) and it contains all the ova for a lifetime of breeding. The ovary increases in weight by 10 to 50 times at the start of the breeding season. The process commences with an ovum gradually filling with yolk. The % of yolk in an egg varies. In species with altricial young it is low at 20% whilst those with precocial young have a yolk 70% of egg weight, enabling these chicks to develop further in the egg before hatching. Yolk provides fat-rich food for the developing embryo. The embryo sits at the top of the yolk. Attached to the yolk at both ends is a twisted structure, called the chalaza. This suspends the yolk in the egg and allows the developing embryo to stay on the surface of the yolk sac.

Fertilisation - once the yolk is full size it leaves the ovary to be fertilised. The egg passes into the first area of the oviduct called the infundibulum, where it is fertilised. Females can store sperm in the lower part of the oviduct which is released up the oviduct to fertilise the embryo. A membrane then covers the yolk.

Albumen – the covered yolk then moves down the oviduct to an area called the magnum. Here over about 3 hours the yolk is covered in albumen, a mix of water and proteins. The albumen acts as a cushion for the developing embryo when it moves and gives it biochemical protection against microbes. The yolk can rotate in the albumen so the embryo can remain at the top of the yolk, where it needs to be to breathe and to be nearest to the parent's warm brood patch.

Membranes – the egg then travels to the next section of the oviduct, the isthmus, where two thin, clear membranes are added. This takes about one hour.

Shell – the penultimate stage of egg production is covering the egg with a shell at the lower end of the oviduct in an area called the uterus, where it remains for about 20 hours. The shell is made by spraying calcium carbonate solution which hardens in columns, keeping the shell porous, enabling waste gases to leave the egg and air to enter. Calcium comes from the female's diet and they need to add this as a supplement for example, by eating snail shells and grit. They will often eat this supplement in the evening ready for laying her egg the next morning. Female Sandpipers eat the legs of dead lemmings found on their breeding grounds as a calcium supplement. The embryo needs to inhale oxygen and exhale carbon dioxide and water and does this through the porous shell which also allows the embryo to interact with the outside world by smell and sound. Given their aquatic environment some duck eggs are water-proof. A Cuckoo's egg shell is thicker than normal to withstand the shock of being dropped into a nest. A Great Crested Grebe's eggs have a water proof shell that allows the egg to sit in water without affecting the developing embryo, whilst still allowing water vapour to escape from inside the egg.

Colour - is applied as the last stage in the uterus. Markings are made on the various layers of the egg shell. The egg is twisted and turned for the various colours and shapes to be applied to the shell. Different ideas exist about the colouration of eggs. One is that it entices male partners to share in incubation. Another is that brighter eggs attract males or the colours provide protection from UV radiation. Guillemots' eggs are held to have the most variable patterning of all birds. This enables the adults to identify their own uniquely patterned egg on a very crowded cliff ledge nest site. The ground colour ranges from white to creamy yellow, ochre, blue or deep blue-green, with the most extraordinary variety of markings interlacing lines, spots, blotches or uniform masses of colour, ranging from bright red or brown to deep black and greenish black. Cuckoos are brood parasites and their eggs mimic the host's colouration in an attempt to ensure the host does not reject the egg. Nightjars lay their light coloured eggs on the open ground but the female is cryptically coloured and offers the ultimate in camouflage and will not budge from her eggs until an intruder is almost upon her.

Shapes - the range of egg shapes include spherical, pyriform, oval and elliptical. The shape of the egg is determined as the membrane forms in the isthmus. The conical shape of waders' eggs allows the bird to arrange them in the nest (typically four) so the female can brood them all equally. Non-spherical shapes give a greater surface area / volume ratio which improves heat transfer on incubation. The pyriform egg shape of the Guillemot was thought to ensure that if the egg is knocked it will roll in an arc and not fall off the narrow shelf. Research suggests that the shape is to keep the blunt end of the egg cleaner in a very dirty, crowded nest site. The embryo's head is located at the blunt end where it needs to breathe and be kept free from harmful microbes.

Laying - the egg is laid blunt end first having travelled down the uterus pointed end first. Eggs are usually laid in the morning having taken about 24 hours to produce. An exception is the Cuckoo which lays its egg in the afternoon whilst the host is more likely to be away from the nest feeding after laying their own egg in the morning. Unusually the Swift lays her eggs every 48 hours and can delay laying if the weather is poor and little food is available. The date of laying eggs is variable, determined by the availability of food. The Kestrel lays her eggs quite early in the season, to coincide with the breeding cycle of its vole prey and when the grass is still short enough to see its prey easily. The Sparrowhawk lays her eggs later so the male can catch the fledglings of small birds. An extreme example is Eleanor's Falcon (which breeds around the Mediterranean). They delay their nesting and egg laying until late the summer when southerly migration has commenced, when they will typically catch Swallows as they fly south. Swallows, House Martins and Swifts lay their eggs at slightly different dates because they feed off specific species of aerial insects that emerge at different times. Egg production and laying is energy intensive. For example, the female Chaffinch, weighing 22 g, lays 4 – 5 eggs weighing 2.2 g i.e. a total of about half of her own weight as eggs. The Kiwi lays one egg of about 25% its own body weight, the largest egg in proportion to body weight. The female Sanderling, on its Arctic breeding grounds, lays two broods simultaneously, with the male brooding one nest and the female the other, in order to make the best of its short breeding season.

Brooding - eggs do not produce enough heat to maintain their own temperature, so require an external heat source to develop. Females, and some males, have a brood patch, an area of bare skin on the under belly, to provide this heat. Eggs are incubated at $36^0 – 38^0$ C. Eggs once laid can be left and un-brooded, which occurs with many species that have synchronous hatching i.e. all the eggs hatch at the same time. The embryo comes to no harm and growth is triggered off when the egg's temperature rises. In contrast, birds of prey and owls commence brooding as soon as the first egg is laid. This leads to asynchronous hatching where the chick from the first egg laid commences its growth before its later-laid siblings. In years of good food supply all the chicks might survive but in years of poor food supply only the first, stronger chick will survive. In some species eggs are left for several days without harm whilst the parents are away feeding. Eggs need to be turned during incubation to ensure the embryo develops evenly. Parents (often the female) are very careful at maintaining the correct temperature in the nest so they modify their habits to let the eggs cool at little or to warm them. Great Tits have been observed to increase the temperature of their eggs in warm weather. This seems counter-intuitive but not so! In warm weather the bird's caterpillar prey will emerge earlier so the parent knows to accelerate the growth of her eggs' embryos so they hatch sooner to be greeted with a healthy supply of caterpillars. Without this adjustment, there might not be sufficient food for the brood. The female Eider broods her clutch continuously, putting up with hunger, as the male is not involved in rearing his young. To deter predators she covers her eggs in oily, green, foul-smelling excrement. She also lowers her heart rate in case predators can hear it beating. Coot chicks emerge from their eggs at slightly different times. The ones emerging later have more brightly coloured plumage around the head. This is thought to help the adults preferentially feed the later born chicks and increase their survival rates. Coots also build brooding nests used by the chicks for roosting whilst being fed by a parent.

Birds have to be ever vigilant against egg predators at the brooding stage as many animals will avail themselves of this nutrient rich food. Some nests are designed to protect against predation, like domed and chamber nests. Tree nests are less accessible. Grebes make a nest on a raft and cover their eggs over with vegetation to minimise egg loss. One reason many females are cryptically coloured is that when brooding they are not easily spotted by a predator when sitting on an open nest. Other birds have a distraction display, such as the broken wing display of plovers, partridge and Skylark. Birds that nest in colonies will vigorously mob egg thieves.

Hatching - when the embryo is ready to enter the world it lies against the blunt end of the egg with the beak touching the membrane. The embryo uses the air pocket to start breathing and sucks up the remaining yolk as food for its first day out of the egg. It closes off the blood supply from the shell into its own body. The embryo emerges by cutting through the shell with its egg tooth located on the tip of its upper mandible and eventually makes a hole through which it emerges. The whole process takes about 30 hours. Many embryos communicate with its parents or siblings whilst still in the egg so the chick can be recognised by sound or to coordinate hatching with the others eggs in the nest.

Below is a simple diagram of egg production:

EGG PRODUCTION

1. Ovum released from ovary into oviduct. Ovum made up of yolk and germinal spot - which forms the embryo.

2. Sperm released to fertilise the embryo.

3. Yolk covered with albumen - takes about 3 hours.

4. Moves down oviduct to isthumus region where shell membranes are added - takes about 1 hour.

5. Moves to uterus where the outer shell is added. The egg is turned and the patterns, colours etc. are added - takes about 20 hours.

6. Egg is laid, usually in the morning.

Egg production

Chicks – once hatched some chicks are virtually ready to face the world immediately, others are born helpless and need parental care for some time after hatching. The two broad categories of chick are:

- o **Precocial** – chicks born ready to live an independent life. These chicks are born with downy feathers, eyes open, they can regulate their body temperature and are able to feed themselves at a very early stage (with some help from a parent). Precocial chicks need to coordinate their hatching so they can all move off together as family immediately after hatching. In fact the embryos assist with this whilst still in the egg by emitting a sound to which the parents respond. Duck chicks are an example of this. Precocial chicks have a slower growth rate than altricial chicks. The egg size of precocial chicks is smaller than eggs of altricial chicks. Precocial chicks are described as nidifugous, meaning nest fleeing.

o **Altricial** – chicks born unable to fend for themselves being dependent on their parents for a significant time after birth. These chicks are born blind, featherless, are unable to feed themselves and cannot regulate their body temperature. These chicks need to stay in the nest until they are able to fledge. Altricial chicks have a higher growth rate. Most passerine species' chicks are altricial. Altricial chicks are also described as nidicolous, meaning nest loving.

A chick at the stage of development between hatching and fledging is called a pullus. The table below shows the different proportions of yolk, albumen and shell in the 2 types of chick:

Table 8 - Chick type data

Chick type:	% Yolk	% Albumen	% Shell
Precocial	37	54	9
Altricial	22	70	8

Some species' chicks hatch as an intermediate between these two extremes and are labelled semi-precocial. Owl chicks are born with some down feathers (and can keep warm) but are fed by their parents in the nest for some considerable time. Gull chicks emerge with down feathers, with some sight and mobility but remain dependent on their parents for some time.

Altricial chicks are wholly reliant on their parents until they achieve some independence. Experiments have shown that a fledgling's gape colour changes. When a parent arrives with food the normal red colour deepens to attract the attention of the parent. Chicks that have not been fed recently produce an even stronger gape colour. In an experiment with Pied Flycatchers very hungry young were placed in an active nest. These hungry chicks begged intensively for food. As a result the feeding rate by the adults increased significantly confirming that adults react to the intensity of begging by their chicks. Swallows, when feeding their young, can detect the sex of their offspring and preferentially feed the males. Immediately after hatching altricial chicks need one parent to brood them to keep them warm as they cannot regulate their own temperature. When the chicks are able to regulate their temperature both parents are able to leave the nest and provision food for their chicks.

Some young are stimulated to feed when they see their parent's beak. In fact they will beg to a false beak providing it is of a similar colour. Herring Gull chicks respond to a false beak with a red band on that replicates their parents' beak. Some species that have precocial young provide protection in unusual ways. Grebe chicks are often seen tucked up on the back of a parent for protection. This also helps keep the chicks warm. A female Woodcock under attack will fly off carrying her chick. In some bird families, particularly amongst ducks, precocial chicks form large crèches that are guarded by one female. Eiders in particular do this as the females do not feed at all whilst they are brooding and are near to starvation when their eggs hatch. By forming into large groups the chicks are protected in the way flocks of birds are by creating confusion to distract a predator. The guardian female will also raise the alarm if she detects a threat. Unusually Reed Bunting chicks leave the nest before they can fly possibly to reduce predation from nest thieves like rats and stoats. The chicks are able to fly about 5 days after leaving their nest.

About 20% of bird species have precocial young and virtually all passerine chicks are altricial. Precocial chicks have larger brains than altricial chicks, to allow them to walk, find food and eat. When adult their brains are smaller than altricial chicks. Brood parasitic chicks also have larger brains to deal with the rigours of growing as a chick in someone else's nest. A longer fledging period leads to a larger brain on reaching maturity.

Sometimes a female might lose a partner, for example through predation and then attract a new partner. In what might seem a cruel act, this new male partner will then eject any young that remain in the nest in order for his eggs to be laid. The male is only interested in his line of heredity and his breeding success.

The number of eggs laid is a function of the ability of the parents to provision sufficient food for the chicks to survive. The variation in clutch size for a range of species is shown in the table below. Clutch size varies with bird weight; larger birds having smaller clutches. Seabirds tend to lay just one egg and have only one clutch. In contrast game birds have high clutch sizes of up to 15 eggs. David Lack spent much time researching in this area and concluded that the optimum clutch size evolves to maximise the number of off-spring in a future generation. The limiting factor on clutch size is the ability to supply sufficient food. Researchers investigated the phenomenon of females pushing eggs out of their nest. The eggs were ejected during periods of bad weather which suggests that the female was making adjustments to her brood size to maximise the hatching and fledging success of the remaining eggs. In some species it is known that the female can count how many eggs she has laid through sensors in her brood patch. In one experiment with Swallows, as the female laid an egg it was taken away. She carried on producing 19 eggs (when normally it would be five).

Egg sizes vary, from the 0.3 g egg of a hummingbird to the 1 600 g egg of the Ostrich. Females laying for the first time lay smaller eggs. The last egg of a clutch is also smaller than the first. The chick from the last egg will only survive when there is a plentiful food supply. Most non-passerine and larger passerine species only have one clutch, especially birds that have a long period of chick care. With some birds the number of broods is dependent on the availability of food. In wetter summers, when worms appear in good numbers, Blackbirds will have more broods. Some birds, like the Blue Tit, will only have one brood as their caterpillar food is only available for a short period of time. If a Blue Tit loses its nest it does not attempt to lay again.

Woodpigeon are an exception as they can breed in most seasons and can have up to five clutches a year. One factor enabling this is the ability of this family of birds to produce milk in its crop from its seed food. The digestive system of a chick cannot digest seed food but they can digest this milk. The inability of chicks to digest seeds is the reason why other birds, like finches and tits, have to change to an insect diet whilst breeding. One exception is the Linnet (a member of the finch family) which continues as a seed eater all year round and feeds its young with seeds, albeit small ones. Many seabirds and herons partially digest their fish food and then regurgitate an oily digestible feed to their chick.

The table below gives the data on egg weight, incubation, fledging, clutch size and hatchling type for a range of UK birds:

Table 9 – Species breeding data

Species	Egg weight (g)	Incubation period	Fledgling period	Clutch size	Altricial / Precocial
Arctic Tern	19	22	22	1-2	Semi-P
Canada Goose	163	30	44	5-7	P
Mute Swan	340	40	135	4-7	P
Mallard	54	27	55	11-14	P
Ptarmigan	20	21	12	5-8	P
Great Crested Grebe	40	28	75	3-4	P
Woodpigeon	19	17	33	2	A

Species	Egg weight (g)	Incubation period	Fledgling period	Clutch size	Altricial / Precocial
Coot	37	22	57	5-7	P
Lapwing	26	30	37	4	P
Herring Gull	92	29	37	3	Semi-P
Great Northern Diver	167	24	75	2	P
Cormorant	58	29	50	3-4	A
Grey Heron	61	28	52	3-4	Semi-A
Golden Eagle	142	44	67	2	Semi-A
Sparrowhawk	23	33	30	4-5	Semi-A
Tawny Owl	39	30	37	2-3	Semi-A
Raven	29	21	40	4-6	A
Great Tit	1.7	14	19	7-9	A
Goldcrest	0.8	17	17	6-8	A
Willow Warbler	1.2	15	15	4-5	A
Robin	2.4	15	15	4-5	A
Song Thrush	6	14	14	4	A
Chaffinch	2.2	12	14	4-5	A

Ref. (1)

The growth rate of fledglings commences slowly and then increases rapidly. Growth rates are higher in smaller birds. Altricial chicks grow at a faster rate than precocial chicks as they don't expend energy on regulating their temperature or having to walk or fly. Feeding rates are highest around dawn, after a night with no food followed by a dip around mid day and then an increase in feeding towards dusk ready for the night. During the early period of growth some organs grow quicker than others. The gizzard and liver grow quickly in the early phases to enable the chick to digest food. Chicks will ingest grit into their gizzard to help masticate food. After this the chick has to develop the ability to thermo regulate and then set about growing flight muscles and feathers ready to face the outside world. In about 20% of species the chick grows to about 10% larger than its parents. Herring Gull chicks are an example where the size difference is easily seen as the young continue to harass a parent for food. In fact Herring Gull chicks will swop to another parent if they think the new parents might be better at feeding them. In species that nest in trees the young need to have well developed flight muscles and feathers before attempting to fledge and leave the nest. Exceptions are the Goldeneye, Goosander and Green Sandpiper all of which nest in a tree hole. Here the young precocial chicks just leap to the ground and then follow their mother to safety and food. Another exception is the Guillemot chick that leaps from its precarious cliff nest site into the sea, to be followed by their father who helps them feed until fully grown and independent. Young Kestrels put on weight quickly. At birth they weigh 14 – 18 g, doubling in 2 days and reaching 100 g in a week. They are fully feathered in 25 days.

In some species of bird, close members of the same family will help raise young, such as members of the crow family and Long-tailed Tits. Swifts fly considerable distances from their nest sites to feed. Mysteriously, adults can detect a cold weather front a considerable distance away (which has a concentration of flies ahead of it) and will fly there to feed. A radar tracking experiment showed them moving from London to the North Sea off the Lincolnshire coast. Very unusually for birds the chicks are able to slip into a state of torpor and survive for up to 5 days waiting for the returning adults. The only other birds able to slip into a torpid state are the Hummingbirds, a close relative of the Swift, being in the same order of Apodiformes.

Seabirds use regurgitation to feed their young. In several species the adults fly off across the ocean to feed and convert the fish into an oil that the young chick can easily digest.

The fledging period ends when a bird can fly. However, for some species parental care does not end there. In some species such birds of prey, owls and kingfishers the young have to learn survival skills, especially predation and feeding skills. Juveniles have to watch their parents and then practice the observed skills until they are sufficiently proficient to live an independent life. In some species of song bird the junior males need to learn their singing skills by listening to their fathers sing and then go off to practice.

CHAPTER FIVE

SENSE AND SENSIBILITY

This Chapter examines the senses that birds use to sustain their lives, at how intelligent they are plus examining the evidence for birds demonstrating emotions.

Sight

Arguably, sight is the most important of all the senses a bird possesses. Birds use sight for almost all of their activities – including:

Finding food	Catching prey	Feeding
Flying	Swimming	Navigating
Defending territory	Fighting	Building a nest
Selecting a mate	Looking for predators	
Locating a destination		

Sight is so vital that many birds even sleep with one eye open! Birds have the best vision of all vertebrates. A Golden Eagle can see a rabbit at a distance of more than 2 km., as can a Peregrine.

The sight process of a bird is similar to all vertebrates with:

- o   a cornea and lens focuses light onto a retina →
- o   which contains a large number of photoreceptors; →
- o   these encode the light falling on them; →
- o   this information is collected by nerves and →
- o   sent to the brain via the optic nerve →
- o   where the brain decodes this information into visual objects, their brightness, colour, position and movement.

The shape of the avian eye varies; some eyes are flat, others tubular but they are never round (as human eyes are). Tubular eyes are typical of raptors that need to see small prey at a considerable distance. This shape acts like a telephoto lens on a camera. Some birds have muscles which can change the shape of the cornea as well as the shape of the lens. The diagram below shows the main features of the avian eye:

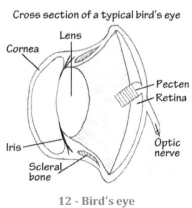

Cross section of a typical bird's eye

12 - Bird's eye

The detailed optical characteristics of the eye provide the best functionality specific to each bird's environment and life style. These include:

- o Size
- o Field of view
- o Binocular vision
- o Focussing
- o Acuity
- o Sensitivity
- o Colour vision
- o Detecting movement
- o Multiple views

Size – the size of a bird's eye determines how much light it can gather. Birds of prey have proportionally larger eyes as they need to see comparatively small prey often at a great distance. Nocturnal birds require larger eyes in order to gather the small amount of light available at night. The ability to see colours also requires a larger eye. Birds' eyes are comparatively large, with some birds possessing eyes larger than ours. The Ostrich has the largest eye of any land vertebrate - 50 mm in diameter, about twice the size of a human eye. The Kiwi has the smallest eyes in proportion to body size but this bird is entirely nocturnal and feeds by touch and smell. The White-tailed Eagle has the largest eyes (46 mm) in proportion to its body size. Often birds with larger eyes cannot rotate their eyes in its socket but rotate their heads instead. The position of a bird's eye on its head varies greatly. Many species have eyes placed on the side of their head, giving a wide field of vision whilst others are forward facing providing better binocular vision. The Barn Owl's large eyes have a 13 mm pupil (compared to 8 mm in humans) and as result the Owl cannot rotate its eyes in its socket and has to move its head round instead. It can move its head by 270^0 in each direction from the front by virtue of having 14 neck vertebrate (humans have 7) plus its arteries are placed in such a way that they are not squeezed whilst rotating its head (otherwise it would pass out with constricted blood supply to the brain).

Field of view - the width of vision afforded by the eye. The field of view in birds varies greatly by species. A key factor is the placement of the eye in the head. The Woodcock's eyes are placed on the side of its head and towards the top giving it virtually 360^0 vision. A Woodcock nests on the ground and forages on the woodland floor so its 360^0 vision helps it see any approaching predator easily. On the other hand an owl has eyes facing forward on its flat face giving it a narrow field of view at 110^0. Owls often sit in trees and need a narrower field of view in order to concentrate their vision on a small potential prey item lurking in the undergrowth. See the diagrams below which illustrate the field of view of four different species.

Binocular vision - enables a bird to locate the position of an object spatially. In order for the brain to provide this information the eyes need to be set apart and provide two slightly separated images which are merged into one image containing the spatial information required to accurately locate an object. Monocular vision occurs when there is only a single image i.e. there is no spatial information. The Woodcock, with its wide field of view, has had to trade off having binocular vision. Owls with their narrower field of view have a wider angle of binocular vision (70 °) but have a large area where they cannot see. Other birds sit somewhere between these extremes. Below are four diagrams showing both the field of view and the range of binocular and monocular vision for four different species:

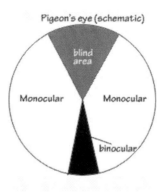

Pigeon's sight

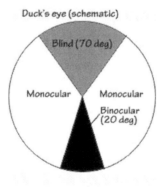

Duck's sight

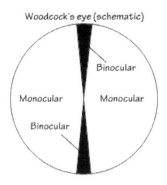

Woodcock's sight

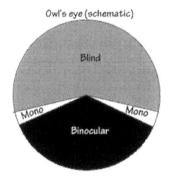

Owl's sight

Focussing - provides the ability to see an object clearly. In some birds the cornea is attached to muscles (Crampton's muscle) giving the eye a greater visual range. In all birds the lens shape can be altered by attached muscles enabling focussing on near or distant objects. Birds usually use lateral monocular vision to focus on distant objects. (See the diagrams above which show the wide area of monocular vision in many species).

Acuity - the ability to see levels of detail. The retina of the eye is covered in photoreceptors. The density of photoreceptors determines acuity. Humans have about 100 000 receptors / mm^2 whilst a Buzzard (with its very high levels of acuity) has around 1 million / mm^2. The photoreceptors are connected to panglia nerves and birds have a high density of these ensuring that more of the light detected by the photoreceptors is transmitted to the brain. Great Grey Shrikes were once used in falconry to act as a look out for incoming birds of prey. A tethered bird was set outside the falconer's hut and as the falcon was seen by the Shrike it sounded the alert long before the falconer could see anything. The Shrike also faced in the direction of the falcon. In an experiment with Golden Eagles, using a grid of lines, the distance limit for a middle aged person to distinguish the lines was 13 m whilst the

Eagle could detect the lines up to 65 m away; five times better. The Golden Eagle has the best acuity of any vertebrate.

Photoreceptors are shaped either as rods or cones. Simply put rods have a greater sensitivity to light i.e. detect low levels of light but do not gather any colour information. On the other hand cones gather colour information but cannot detect low levels of light. The proportion of rods and cones is determined by the requirements of a bird's environment and life style. Clearly nocturnal birds have a very high proportion of rods to be able to see in dark conditions. Diurnal birds have a greater proportion of cones so they able to see in colour but are not able to see in relative darkness. Owls have almost 100% rod receptors whilst diurnal birds have about 80% cone receptors. Owls have 100 x the acuity of diurnal birds (and about 2.5 x that of humans). The trade-off is that they only see in greyscale (black through to white) and do not see any colour. Some songbirds, such as the Robin, have a higher proportion of rods and are able to see soon after dawn so they awaken earlier and commence singing. This explains why in the dawn chorus some birds (like the Robin) start to sing earlier than others. Those birds that sing later have a lower proportion of rod receptors so cannot detect any light early in the morning. Species of diurnal birds that migrate at night (as many do to avoid predation) do not have night vision and sometimes collide with tall objects like lighthouses and gas platforms.

Cones are more complex than rods. Each cone detects a specific frequency of light from the light spectrum i.e. they detect different colours. Birds have four types of cone cell (known as tetrachromatic) – those that detect red, green, blue or ultra-violet frequencies. (Humans have three types which detect red, green or blue frequencies). Sensitivity to ultra-violet light is prevalent in the Charadriiformes order of waders and the Passeriformes. The Kestrel utilises this to catch its favourite prey, the Field Vole. As the rodent runs it urinates and this emits ultra-violet light, which the bird sees and uses to locate its prey. Female Blue Tits can see the ultra violet light of a prospective mate's head feathers and will select a mate on the strength of the colour. Recent research has cast doubts on this phenomenon. Female Blackbirds can see the ultra violet light content of a male's yellow beak with a stronger colouration being more attractive as a mate. It is also thought that migratory birds use their U V vision to locate the position of the sun on cloudy days as it is known that birds use the sun as a navigational aid.

Terns and gulls have special oil in their photoreceptors which helps improve contrast as they look for their underwater prey. Birds that hunt under water, like the Gannet, do not possess this.

Sensitivity - the ability of the eye to see in different light levels. Sensitivity to light determines how well a bird can see in the dark. Nocturnal birds have a large cornea compared to the length of the eye which provides maximum sensitivity. They also have a high proportion of rod photoreceptors which are more sensitive to light. Diurnal birds have longer eyes with a consequent loss of sensitivity. The large eyes of the birds of prey are optimised for spatial resolution (to see prey at a considerable distance) but not light gathering and so cannot see at night.

Colour vision - a bird's ability to see colour depends on the proportion of cone photoreceptors (see earlier paragraph). Diurnal birds with a high % of cones can see colours very well. Nocturnal birds with a low % of cones cannot perceive colour. Nor do they need to given their life style.

Detecting movement - birds are able to detect the movement of slow moving objects such as the sun and stars. This enables them to navigate using the movement of celestial objects. Also birds can resolve faster movement. Birds can resolve the rapid movement of objects at up to 100 changes a second. Humans cannot resolve movement greater than 50 changes a second (that's why we see smooth pictures on a television running at 50 frames a second). A bird watching a television can see separate frames. The ability to detect fast movement is vital to many birds in order for them to capture prey. For example, insectivorous birds need to be able to track the flight of an insect in order to catch it, which requires sight that picks up rapid movement. Research has determined that the Peregrine can register 129 changes (frames) a second helping it to be the premier avian hunter.

Multiple views - many birds are able to move each eye independently with each eye looking at something entirely different. So a bird feeding in your garden uses one eye to select its food and the other eye to look out for a predator.

The **fovea** (which is Latin for small pit) is an area of the retina that provides the clearest vision having a higher density of photoreceptors which are mainly cones, giving bright colour vision. When you see a Robin or Thrush cock its head to one side whilst foraging on your lawn, it is using the extra clarity of vision afforded by its fovea to locate a worm. Some birds have two fovea (such as birds of prey, swallows and kingfishers) with the second one used to provide clear vision in front of the bird. The blind spot occurs where the optic nerve connects to the retina, as there are no photo receptors at that point.

Some birds have the ability to sleep with one eye open, in order to be alert to any danger. To do this only one half of their brain sleeps at any one time. With the right eye open the right hand side of the brain sleeps (the visual information of the right eye is processed by the left hand side of the brain). Vigilant sleep occurs when a bird sleeps for a period and then quickly opens its eyes to scan its environment to ensure it is still safe. In flocks or communal roosts, the inner birds can sleep with both eyes shut and the outer birds sleep with one eye open, ready to alert the rest of the flock if there is a threat. The passerines are often called perching birds as their legs have an automatic mechanism that locks their legs whilst perched and so are able to sleep without falling off their perch. Whilst asleep the lower eye lid is raised to cover the eye.

In birds the retina does not have any blood vessels. Avian eyes have an alternative comb-like structure on part of the retina, called pecten to provide oxygen to the eye.

As with humans, birds have a bias towards one side and they use one eye more than the other. This behaviour is determined in the egg. As the embryo turns its head to one side to face the light this becomes the dominant eye.

In order to successfully catch underwater prey water birds have to adjust their angle of attack from above water by correcting for refraction. As light passes from air into water it bends, so that a fish swimming around is not where it appears to be; it is further forward:

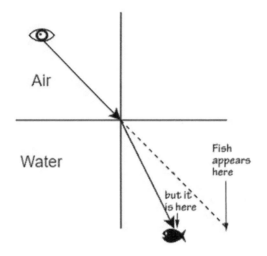

Refraction

Another distinctive feature of a bird's eyes is the presence of a third eye lid, called the nictating membrane. The word comes from the Latin nictare, meaning to blink. This clear membrane moves horizontally across the eye, giving the eye a further level of protection. A bird's eye lids are not used in blinking but the nictating membrane helps to moisturise the eye (in the way eye lids do in humans). Being translucent the membrane does not interfere with the bird's sight. Water birds use the membrane to protect their eyes whilst swimming. The eyes of raptors are kept moisturised and clear of debris by the nictating membrane when flying at speed. Woodpeckers use the membrane to protect their eyes from flying wood chips when drumming or excavating a nest hole. When observing birds, like the Dipper, the nictating membrane can often be seen moving across the eye.

The colour of a bird's iris changes with age. Hatchling Reed Warbler's iris colour is black changing to an olive colour on maturity. In the Sparrowhawk the eye colour of the hatchling is brown to black, changing quickly to pale yellow then to the adult orange colour, with adult males sometimes having red eyes. The iris colour of male and female hatchling Hen Harriers are different, enabling hatchlings to be sexed using this characteristic. In the Goldeneye and Scaup the juvenile eye colour is brown changing to yellow on maturity. Jackdaw's eyes change colour as they mature, from a blue colour as a juvenile through brown to the final white colour of maturity. It is thought that the white colouration is used as part of a threatening posture.

Birds are also able to detect polarised light i.e. light that travels in one plane. Light is polarised by clouds, especially at sunset. This assists birds locate the position of the sun used for navigation, particularly useful as many birds undertake migratory journeys at night.

Bird's eyes are also used for purposes other than sight. In Chapter 2 it was noted that Robins (and other birds) navigate using the (weak) earth's magnetic field. The bird's eyes detect photons of light with the earth's magnetic field determining the character of these electrons (by some mysterious process of quantum physics) which in turn changes the chemicals in the brain. This is then translated by the Robin's brain into a compass reading to aid navigation. A further function of the eye is to measure the duration of daylight. Recent research indicates that it might be the brain which detects light levels and not the eye. Birds can accurately measure the length of daylight and are aware of the extent of the increase or decrease in daylight. This measurement is crucial for:

- ○ **Migrating** – the trigger for migratory behaviour is the length of daylight. In late summer birds which have bred here are aware that the hours of daylight are decreasing and they must commence their preparations for migration, entering a period known as zugunruhe. See Section on Migration in Chapter 2 for more details.
- ○ **Breeding** – the trigger for commencing the breeding cycle is the increase in daylight hours in late winter. This triggers off a re-growth of the reproductive organs in both males and females, often a commencement of singing (mainly in males), setting up territory along with a partial moult into fresh breeding plumage. See Chapter 4 for more details.

Sound

The second most important sense for a bird is that of hearing. Songs and calls (along with the ability to hear and locate these accurately) are a vital aspect of avian life.

Hearing is important to birds for:

Establishing relations   Communicating
Heeding warnings   Finding food
Choosing a mate   Attracting a mate
Maintaining contact   Analysing song
Identifying: its own species, predators, young and parents

Hearing is a more important sense for nocturnal birds as they cannot rely on sight as much as diurnal birds and also for birds which live in closed environments, such as birds that breed underground or in burrows, like kingfishers, puffins, petrels and shearwaters.

The function of song and calls was dealt with in Chapter 3. This Section will look specifically at avian hearing. Most bird's ears are located behind and below the eyes and are covered by feathers, called auriculars and usually face outwards. The auriculars protect the ear and possibly help direct sound into the ear. In seabirds these feathers prevent water entering the ear canal when diving. Owl ears are a special case (see below) and their ears are located in the facial disc. Birds do not have external ears or pinna.

The hearing process is similar to that of humans:

o   Sound is funnelled by the ear; →
o   travelling down the auditory canal or outer ear where it →
o   hits the ear drum (tympanum) in the middle ear producing vibrations; →
o   these vibrations are transferred by a single bone (the columella) to the cochlea in the inner ear. →
o   Microscopic hair cells in the fluid filled cochlea convert the vibrations into nerve impulses; they are →
o   sent to the brain for translation into sound – loudness, frequency and position.

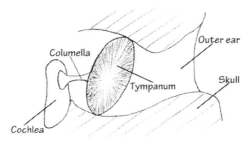

Typical bird's ear

13 - Bird's ear

Larger birds tend to have larger cochlea, helping them to hear lower frequencies. Smaller birds are more sensitive to higher frequencies. It is thought that for example thrushes emit an alarm call at about 8 KHz which other thrushes can hear but larger birds of prey cannot so the alarm call does not betray the presence of the potential prey.

Humans have three columella and our cochlea is coil shaped (the word cochlea derives from the Latin for snail), helping us to hear higher frequencies. The hair cells in a bird's cochlea are replaced if they are damaged (but human hair cells are not). Ears are also used for balance and orientation using coils inside the inner ear.

Birds such as the Corncrake and the Capercaillie call very loudly (the Corncrake at about 100 dB) and to prevent the birds being deafened by their own sound they have reflexes that cover their ears. The Bittern's low frequency voice (150 Hz) can be heard up to 3 km away. To produce this sound the vocal muscle accounts for 20% of the weight of the bird. It also has a long, modified oesophagus which helps amplify the sound. Each male has a slightly different and unique sound pattern that we can't detect but female Bitterns can. In built-up areas birds sing louder and at a higher frequency to overcome the background noise.

Overall, birds detect a narrower frequency range (low notes to high notes) than humans. Typically birds can hear in the range 100 Hz to 13 kHz whereas humans can hear in the range 20 Hz to 20 kHz. To put this in perspective A above middle C on a piano (the note from which pianos are tuned) has a frequency of 440 Hz with each octave above being double this frequency or the octave below a half. However, birds are better at sound discrimination which is very important in many situations. Humans can resolve different sounds at about 10 changes per second; at higher rates the sounds merge. Birds can differentiate more complex elements at a rate of over 10 changes per second. As noted in the Section How do they do it? in Chapter 3 birds emit multiple notes simultaneously generating more a complex sound which other birds can differentiate.

Take a Guillemot breeding colony where there are many thousands of crying, nesting birds along with many noisy fledglings. Added to this the roaring sea and wind provide a loud background sound. A parent then flies in to the colony ready to feed its chick. In amongst this cacophony the parent can pick out the call of their chick and the chick can hear the call of their parent. To us the noise appears as a continuum of sound. A parent can discriminate its chick's call amongst all this cliff top noise. Later in life the immature chick leaps from its cliff ledge nest (or nearby) into the ocean. The father needs to connect with the chick immediately it floats on the sea. They find each other by call – the father can hear the chick and vice versa amongst the loud noises surrounding them both. A further illustration of this sound discrimination is seen during the breeding season. A female may well listen to the song of several males of her species during the dawn chorus. Again, to us, in many species of bird, all songs sound alike but not to a female bird. She hears the subtle variety and nuances in each male's song and can discriminate between individual's vying for her attention. Furthermore, she can pick out her preferred songster against a background of other species' song and environmental noise. This was discussed in the Section Variations on a theme in Chapter 3. Interestingly, the area of the brain that processes sound shrinks outside the breeding season and re-grows at the start of the next breeding season. Also birds use a wide variety of calls. Whilst some of these calls sound identical to us, birds can identify the nature of each type of call and act accordingly.

Experiments on ducks and crows demonstrated that these birds can locate the source of sound. Each ear detected a slightly different frequency helping to locate the source of the sound. Birds can locate sound with respect to eye level, which is why many birds move their heads helping them to pin point sound. Eye movement is connected to a bird's hearing, so coordinating sight and sound. The acuity of bird hearing was used creatively during WW1 when parrots were kept at the top of the Eiffel Tower to warn of incoming enemy aircraft.

Owls have exceptionally good hearing, essential for night time hunters. Their hearing system is modified for this. These birds have the most sensitive hearing of any bird in the world. First their ears are about three times bigger that similar sized birds. Specially adapted feathers assist in directing the sound into the ears and protect the ears from dust and injury. Their ears are asymmetrically set either side of their eyes, enabling the bird to hear stereophonically and thus locate potential prey using sound, not sight. This asymmetry is unique amongst vertebrates. The bird moves its head from side to side, to get an aural positional fix on the location of its potential prey. Its left eye is slightly higher and tilted downwards and the right eye lower and tilted upwards. Owls have relatively large cochlea (9 mm in a Barn Owl compared to 5 mm in a Woodpigeon) with a larger number (16 300) of hair cells detecting sound, about 3 times the number for a bird of its size. The Barn Owl has 95 000 nerve cells in the auditory region of its brain compared to 27 000 in a Crow. The owl also retains its acute hearing into old age because (unlike humans) the hairs in the cochlea that transmit the hearing signal to the brain regenerate to maintain their hearing. The Barn Owl is capable of catching prey in complete darkness (providing it has a mental visual map of its territory). In an experiment a Barn Owl was placed in an enclosed room where the level of light was gradually reduced. Even in total darkness the owl was able to catch its mouse prey. The experimenter then covered the floor in foam rubber (so the artificial mouse made no sound as it moved) and attached a leaf to the tail of the mouse (which did make a sound as the mouse moved). The owl pounced on the leaf (in darkness) demonstrating that the bird hunted by sound. However, the bird would only pounce in total darkness if it had previously been able to learn the layout of the room so it was aware of any obstacles. Owls can detect the location of its prey to an accuracy of 1^0 horizontally and vertically. In Short-eared Owls the timing difference of a sound wave reaching each ear is about 30 millionths of a second but it does the job!

Touch

Birds use the sense of touch but not as extensively as humans. Bird skin has nerves which detect temperature, pressure, movement and pain. Touch receptors are found elsewhere such as on the beak, in the mouth and on the tongue. The tips of some birds' beaks, like ducks and waders, have sensitive tips which help them select their food. In the Mallard the lower jaw has about 180 pores each with 20 -30 nerve endings which act as touch receptors used in feeding. The duck is able to select suitable food using these sensitive receptors. The tip of a woodpecker's tongue is sensitive, enabling it to find insect food deep in the crevice of a tree trunk or underground and then extracting it using a sticky chemical on the end of its tongue. Altricial young have touch nerves at the tip of their beak to help them feed. A blind, young Cuckoo has sensors to locate the host's eggs and then to put an egg on its back and tip it out of the nest! Some airborne feeding birds, such as the Nightjar, have very sensitive rictal feathers near their mouth to help them detect their moth prey in the dark. Only filoplume feathers (see Section Types of feather in Chapter 1) have nerve endings; other types of feather do not transmit touch or movement to nerves in the skin. Sensors on the filoplumes on a bird's wings detect the movement of feathers as a bird flies enabling it to make adjustments to its flight pattern.

Herbst corpuscles sense movement in the form of vibrations and these are distributed over a bird's body – skin, legs and wings. Birds like snipe, ducks, swallows and sandpipers use Herbst corpuscles in their beaks to sense vibrations from the movement of food items. Corpuscles on the tip of a beak help a bird detect prey under the mud or ground. Clearly waders cannot see the food items they are searching for underneath the mud. Instead they locate their food with sensors on the tip of their beak. Formerly it was thought these were touch sensors but recent research shows that they are vibration sensors; they can detect the pressure waves produced by their prey when it wriggles away to evade being eaten. Knot use this method to detect their mollusc prey whilst probing in mud. Seed eaters also have similar sensors on their beaks to deal with their food.

Allopreening (discussed in the Section Courtship in Chapter 4) used in courtship may be related to a sense of touch as birds stroke each other's feathers and remove parasites. The brood patch (the bare skin on the underside of the belly on some females during the breeding season) is very sensitive. It is used to count the number of eggs laid so the female knows when to stop egg production. Once brooding commences nerves on the brood patch help measure and regulate the eggs' temperature by increasing or decreasing the blood flow to the brood patch.

Taste

Birds do have a sense of taste but it is not as strong as in humans. Depending on the species, birds have about 500 taste buds, while humans have 10 000. A bird's mouth is hard and sharp in comparison to ours which historically led observers to believe that birds had no sense of taste. Birds have taste buds on their beak, tongue and in their mouths with most having taste buds on the base of the tongue and near the back of the throat. The number of taste buds and their position varies greatly between species. Mallard ducks in one experiment could differentiate between foods, some of which had been adulterated, just by touching the food with its beak. It turns out that Mallard have taste sensitive tips to their beaks. They also use their palate to differentiate between palatable foods. In a test Great Tits and Blue Tits rejected foul tasting (and possibly poisonous) caterpillars based on taste. Insectivores use taste to select their food and reject items that are poisonous or harmful. Darwin investigated the role of colour in nature and wondered how birds rejected some kinds of colourful caterpillar and conjectured that they used taste to do this. Birds can taste sweet, sour, salt and bitter flavours helping them to learn which tastes are the most suitable and nutritious food. Birds relying on nectar have a greater sensitivity to sweet taste. Those eating fruit can differentiate between ripe and unripe fruit based on how sweet it tastes. Most birds are aware of salt taste and reject salty food as high levels of salt are dangerous. Seabirds have a mechanism in their nasal passage for filtering salt out of water. An experiment was conducted on Blue Jays (a member of the corvid family) where the birds were fed on monarch butterflies. The butterflies had previously been fed on cabbages and the bird suffered no ill effects. The next lot of butterflies were fed on milkweed, which is noxious. When the birds ate these butterflies they tasted the poison and vomited to avoid any ill-effects. After this the birds refused to eat any monarch butterflies.

Smell

Smell is one of the least important senses for most birds. Birds have smell receptors in their nasal cavity above the upper mandible. Their size and shape varies greatly with species. The olfactory bulb in the brain then interprets the signals from the small sense receptors. The sense of smell tends to be stronger in crepuscular and nocturnal birds as they can't rely on sight to hunt. Montagu carried out dissections of Woodcock beaks and observed it had "an exquisite sense of smelling" in its fleshy beak tip. Kiwis have an acute sense of smell. Uniquely, their nostrils are located at the tip of their beak. A few bird species have a well-developed sense of smell, such as vultures, which are known to hunt by smell. Turkey Vultures can smell carrion at least 1.6 km away and have the largest olfactory system of any bird.

Seabirds who hunt way out a sea, like the albatrosses, petrels and shearwaters all use their keen sense of smell to locate food sources. These birds can often smell food from great distances in vast, featureless, oceanic landscapes, even when the odour may not be noticeable to humans. Experiments on petrels and albatross have shown how these birds can locate food by smell at great distances. To locate their food they fly across the approximate, detected location and then gradually narrow the exact location down by flying in a zig-zag pattern, navigating by the strength of the smell. Sea-watchers use chum (small fish items) to attract sea-birds to their location for better views with birds locating this food by smell. Leach's Petrel locate their nesting sites by always flying downwind using smell to locate their destination. Homing pigeons use smell on the final part of their homeward journey by smelling their home loft. Shearwaters use their sense of smell to navigate in featureless oceans – see the Section on Migration in Chapter 2.

Magnetism

Many organisms can detect the earth's magnetic field e.g. bees, flies and frogs as well as birds. Up until the 1940's the idea of birds having a magnetic sense was dismissed. Magnetic lines run out from the earth's magnetic poles in large loops, upwards from the poles, curving over to be parallel at the equator, where the magnetic fields are weakest and then down to the opposite pole. Birds detect the inclination and intensity of the magnetic field at their location and use this to locate the direction of the magnetic pole which is then used as a compass. Experiments have demonstrated this sense in Robins and pigeons. Caged Robins that could see the night sky orientated in their migratory direction (continental Robins migrate to warmer areas of Europe). On nights when the stars were obscured the birds still orientated towards their migratory direction. The cage was then subject to an artificial magnetic field and the birds orientated to their modified migratory direction. In another experiment it was discovered that Robins detected the earth's magnetic field through its right eye. Recent research has shown that the Robin's navigation mechanism involves quantum physics and the behaviour of sub atomic particles! The earth's magnetic field is too weak for the bird to detect directly. Their right eye detects photons of light which create a pair of entangled electrons. The earth's magnetic field determines the character of these electrons which in turn affects the chemicals in the brain. (An understanding of quantum physics is required at this point.) This is then translated by the Robin into a compass reading for it to navigate by.

Having dealt with senses we will turn our attention to three key aspects of bird's lives – eating, drinking and sleeping followed by looking at bird intelligence and emotions.

Eating

A bird's highly energetic way of life means that they have a high metabolic rate requiring a highly efficient digestive system. Food needs to be converted into energy very quickly. Many birds are soon affected by low food intake, especially small birds, like the Goldcrest, which has to eat its own weight in food each day. As we saw earlier birds have to minimise their weight in order to fly. Hence, birds are not able to store much food, especially dense food, so they need to feed frequently and process that food quickly. In the breeding season the demands are even greater. The female Chaffinch, weighing 22 g, lays (on average) 4 eggs weighing 2.2 g, almost half her own weight in a period of 4 days. Egg laying is more demanding for the Blue Tit. The female weighs 11 g and she lays 9 eggs weighing 1.1 g each; laying about her own weight in eggs. Then the female has to brood her eggs for 2 weeks and rely on the male to provision her with food. After the chicks hatch these birds will then spend another 2 weeks feeding their chicks. After a brief respite the birds then undergo the energy intensive process of moulting. Summer migrants will later in the summer, after breeding, have to prepare for and undertake a demanding long distance migratory flight. To do this many birds have to feed voraciously to lay down enough fat for the journey, many increasing their weight by 40% or more in a few weeks of frenetic feeding. All this activity demonstrates how energy intensive a bird's life is.

Some small birds, such as the Goldcrest and the hummingbirds, have to feed continuously just to maintain their energy equilibrium. The Wren has to eat half its own body weight in food every day to stay alive. Many birds undertake flights of extreme endurance when migrating, which requires a large build up of energy reserves to make such long flights. A Bar-tailed Godwit was recorded as flying non-stop for 11 600 km. Swifts are estimated to fly 200 000 km each year. A number of tracked Arctic Terns flew 96 000 km in a year including a 8 000 km, 24 day, non-stop flight over the Indian

Ocean. Bar-headed Geese migrate at an altitude of over 8 km. Flying at high speeds or flying continuously to catch prey requires high levels of energy. Peregrines chase their prey food at high speeds and cormorants swim to considerable depths, all requiring a lot of energy. All birds moult and growing new feathers requires reserves of energy.

Birds maintain a body temperature of 40^0 C +/- 2^0 with some variation between day and night time temperatures. A bird's metabolic rate needs to maintain an equilibrium between heat generation and heat loss. Small birds have a large surface area to volume ratio leading to greater heat loss than larger birds and so require a higher metabolic rate to maintain their body temperature. In winter small birds lose heat more rapidly and have to increase their metabolic rate by up to 40% to survive.

The functions of the beak in feeding and the range of birds' diets was discussed in the Section Beaks and Bills in Chapter 1.

A summary of the process of digestion is:

- From the beak, where food might be crushed or torn into smaller bits, food passes into the oesophagus. →
- In the middle section of the oesophagus some birds have a crop which is used to store food. →
- The oesophagus is narrow in insectivorous birds but much wider in birds that eat their prey whole, such as herons, cormorants and owls. →
- After passing down the oesophagus food enters the first stomach chamber, the proventriculus, where very strong acids and enzymes start to break down the food. →
- The pre-digested food then moves into the gizzard where hard food is ground down using strong muscles and grit or small stones (ingested for this purpose). Softer foods are easier to digest and don't require grit or stones to assist. →
- The digested food then passes to the intestine. The length of the intestine varies with food type, with meat eaters only requiring a short intestine and vegetation eaters a longer one.

Eider have such strong gizzards that they are able to crush mussel shells. Pigeons forage for seeds and rather than eat them immediately (where they might be at risk of predation) they maximise their time collecting food for consumption later by storing large amounts in their crop. Also, in pigeons the crop is used to produce a milk they feed to their young (who otherwise could not digest the raw seeds). Jays collect as many acorns as they can in autumn, storing up to eight in their crop, before caching them away as a source of winter food. Birds can sometimes be seen to hold their fish or animal prey in their beak and throat for some time (especially chicks) with no ill effect, whilst digesting the item. The Great Crested Grebe feeds its young feathers, which form a pad preventing undigested food entering the intestine. A ball of feathers and undigested food is periodically regurgitated. The adults also eat tapeworms and feed them to their young, apparently without harm.

Research into the diet of urban Peregrines at three locations in the UK over a 9 year period revealed some fascinating facts. Predictably, the Feral Pigeon was the most common prey accounting for 42% of species identified and 63% by weight, along with other members of the pigeon family. However, 98 species were identified from the prey debris analysed, ranging from Goldcrest to Mallard. Also several species of prey would have been caught at night, making the falcon a night hunter in urban areas. The table overleaf shows the main species caught:

Table 10 - Peregrine's diet

Species	Number	% of total species	% of total biomass
Feral Pigeon	2208	41.9	62.7
Woodpigeon	91	1.73	3.9
Teal	126	2.4	3.9
Collared Dove	196	3.7	3.8
Starling	481	9.1	3.4
Woodcock	86	1.8	2.4
Black-headed Gull	70	1.3	2.0
Lapwing	58	1.1	1.3
Redwing	208	3.9	1.2
Snipe	120	2.3	1.3
Greenfinch	202	3.8	0.5
Budgerigar	12	0.2	0.03

Ref. (2)

Several birds change their diet seasonally. The Bearded Tit eats reed aphids in summer and reed seeds in winter. In winter there are up to 850 stones in its gizzard to aid the digestion of seeds whereas in summer there are only 30 stones for its insect diet. As a result the gizzard weighs 1 g in winter and only 0.6 g in summer. Great Tits eat seeds in winter and switch to caterpillars and other insects during the summer. With this switch the content of their gizzards changes and the intestine grows longer or shorter as required. Also their beaks are slightly thinner and longer in summer. The Knot's gizzard is thicker in winter to aid digestion of its mollusc prey and thinner in summer as

112

it turns to an insect diet. In summer Starlings eat soil invertebrates, like crane-fly larvae (leatherjackets) and in winter switch to a plant based diet. In doing so its intestine increases in length to cope with digesting this food. In some birds, like the owls, indigestible items, like bones, are separated out in the stomach, formed into a pellet and regurgitated. Fruit eaters only require a small gizzard and their food is digested very quickly, certainly in less than 1 hour. Several seabirds feed their young by regurgitating food caught at sea as an easily digestible oil, produced in their stomach.

Drinking

Water is essential for all life. In Chapter 1 we examined the key design features of a bird for achieving lightness. The proportion of water contained in a bird's body is comparatively low because water is dense and that runs counter to the need for the lightness required for flight. Birds do not perspire through sweat glands as that requires water. Instead birds have other means of regulating their temperature in hot weather, such as panting.

Some birds derive all their water requirements through the food that they eat or their way of life. Swifts obtain all the water they need from the atmosphere as they fly around. Most bird drink water by filling their lower beak and then tipping their heads back. However, a few birds, like the pigeons, can suck up water. A very novel way of providing drink occurs with the Sand Grouse which nests in very hot, dry desert land. To provide a source of water for its young the male flies to a water hole, dunks its breast feathers in the pool which absorb up to 25% of the bird's weight in water. The bird then flies back to the nest with the essential water supply for its chick.

Seabirds need to have an in-built desalination plant because if they ingested sea water the excess salt would poison them. To do this they have a gland inside their nostrils which extracts 90% of the salt from sea water to a potable level. The gland works like a kidney by extracting salt from the blood stream, which is excreted back through the nostrils.

Sleeping

Sleep is an essential component of nearly all forms of animal life, fulfilling a key restorative physiological function. The length and type of sleep varies with different animals. Birds need both non-rapid eye movement sleep (NREM) and rapid eye movement sleep (REM) as do humans. NREM stores and strengthens new information and skills. Deep, slow brain waves save memories in an organised fashion as they move from short to long term memory. REM sleep integrates new information and skills with previous experience to build up an accurate picture of the bird's environment. Birds have the ability to sleep one side of the brain at a time. One half of the brain can be in NREM sleep and the opposite side can process any signals from the one open eye, on the lookout for a predator. If birds are asleep in a flock or line, the birds on the outer edge or end of the line have to sleep one half of the brain at a time whilst for the rest of the flock their whole brains are asleep. At regular intervals the birds change position, not least so those on the outside can gain the warmth of being in the middle and so they can benefit from full brain sleep. In REM sleep the whole brain is asleep. Birds who are long distant migrants (especially those making non-stop oceanic crossing) can only sleep for very short periods at a time, getting a short power nap and then re-awakening. It is thought that migratory birds, only for the period of their migration, can survive sleep deprivation which would otherwise be detrimental to the bird's health.

Birds preparing for sleep undergo a number of posture changes. For example, the head falls down and the beak is tucked in the scapular feathers, they stand on one leg (to retain as much heat as possible) and their heart rate and respiration rate falls. Generally birds sleep for about 8 hours a day but this varies. Birds breeding in the polar regions have less sleep (around the lowest point of the sun's trajectory). Some birds are nocturnal and so sleep during the day. During the breeding season adults get less sleep. In a survey of Great Tits the female snuggles down in the nest with her young (to keep them warm) whilst the male sleeps nearby. He then awakens her at dawn with a soft call. In the period up to and sometimes beyond egg laying males sing at dawn (rising time varies by species, as the dawn chorus gradually builds up) and then sings again towards dusk to defend his territory during the breeding season.

When birds go to roost they carry out a range of functions, not just sleep. Birds at roost indulge in preening and often perform a range of social interactions. The reason why birds flock is given in the Section Flocking in Chapter 2. Flocking behaviour has been noted by humans for millennia and has given rise to many collective nouns. These are given at the end of Chapter 8.

Intelligence

There has long been a debate about the extent to which birds display intelligence or whether their behaviour is innate plus learned behaviour driven by survival. Historically humans were believed to have the monopoly on intelligence and that the animal kingdom merely behaved on instinct. This thinking changed in the 19th century especially with the emergence of the theory of evolution. Darwin believed some animal behaviour is learned, having observed, for example, that finches learned to use tools to extract larvae from underneath bark. Certainly birds utilise behaviours that humans use, as we'll see below in the evidence from various experiments. Even for humans the concept of intelligence is a complex one on which there is no full understanding or indeed agreement on how to define intelligence. One working definition of intelligence is the capacity for learning, retaining knowledge and applying this to future behaviour. Also there is no hard line between innate and learned behaviour but rather a continuum from the innate, instinctive behaviour required for surviving in a simple environment to the developed behaviours required for a complex environment.

Animal research has focussed on cognition which looks at the processes of acquiring knowledge and understanding through thought, experience and the senses. The perceived wisdom is that humans possess a whole raft of different intelligences, that's why intelligence tests assess a person's ability in a range of skills, such as language, verbal reasoning, number, spatial etc.. And so it is with birds. Scientists believe that birds who demonstrate higher levels of intelligence do so out of social necessity. One of the most intelligent families is the corvid family, with plenty of supporting evidence for this. Corvids are highly social birds, they form hierarchical social groups and to do that requires intelligence. Being bound to one mate also requires social intelligence, with many birds demonstrating this behaviour. See the Section Breeding relationships in Chapter 4 Mates mating and breeding for more detail on the various types of avian sexual and social relationship.

Areas which have been explored experimentally include self-awareness, problem solving, logic, tool use, social behaviour, recognition, learning from others and counting:

- o **Self awareness** – being able to recognise yourself requires intelligence. In one test six Magpies had a red dot placed on their throat. They then looked at themselves in a mirror. Two tried to remove the red dot from their own necks (not the mirror's reflection), showing they were able to recognise themselves in a mirror. A black dot placed on their throat elicited no response. Tests with pigeons gave the same result.

- o **Problem solving** – presented with a situation that requires prior learning to solve. Here are some examples:

    - o In a test in New Zealand a pair of Kea (a member of the parrot family – held to be an intelligent family of birds) were presented with a container full of food with a chain on two sides both of which had to be pulled to release the food. These birds are extremely curious and learned that they both needed to pull on the chain together to obtain the reward of food.
    - o Scientists have carried out experiments to verify the Aesop's fable of the crow gaining access to water in a vessel by dropping stones into it. Unsurprisingly, they found that the crow was able to solve the problem. The crows had to choose between using solid objects and hollow objects and they correctly choose the solid ones which sank rather than floated. They also had to choose between jars containing sand and

water and they correctly chose water. What is remarkable is that Aesop wrote his fables in the 6th century BC (before the time of Aristotle) and attributed the crow with high intelligence.

- o Another example of corvid intelligence is seen in Japan where crows place hard-shelled walnuts onto roads and retrieve the opened contents after passing cars have opened the nuts. They even observe the colour of the traffic lights to place and retrieve the nuts whilst the lights are on red! These experiments show that folklore about the crow being intelligent is true even though the authors of the tales were not able to prove it! Other evidence of the crow family's intelligence is their ability to use tools. In the wild if a tasty morsel of food is out of reach to the bird's beak it finds and uses a tool e.g. a stick to extract the food. See Tool use below.
- o Some decades ago (when bottled milk was delivered to door steps) Blue Tits acquired the skill of removing the foil top off bottles of milk left on door steps to get at the creamy milk! They learned which colour cap led to the creamiest milk – gold top Jersey milk!
- o Herons have been observed placing bread onto the surface of water to attract an unsuspecting fish to the surface for the bird to catch.
- o One novel observation of bird intelligence was how sparrows in New Zealand had learned to trigger a door opening sensor at a cafe to gain entry to a source of food.
- o Goldfinches were often kept in captivity, some just for show. In a painting by the Dutchman Carel Fabritius, a Goldfinch is sat on a perch with a fine chain on its foot at the end of which is a small bucket of water. The bird learns to pull the chain up in order to have a drink. The Dutch title for the painting is puttertje, meaning little weller. This explains the British local names for the Goldfinch of draw water and draw bird.

- o **Logic** - in one experiment, crows were given a pairing test. Picture cards were placed over three cups. One card, covering one of the outer cups containing food, matched the card covering the middle cup. A non-matching card covered the other empty outer cup. The crows learned quickly that only the matching card led to food. The experiment was made more sophisticated by using paired cards. Each card had two shapes drawn on it; on some cards the shapes were the same and on others the shapes were different. Again, if the middle card had two of the same shape, the card on the outer cup with food in had two identical shapes (but different shapes) to the middle cup. The card on the cup with no food in had two different shapes on it.

The crows were able to select the matching card without any training i.e. it did not learn by trial and error but successfully utilised its prior learning.

- o **Tool use** - extensive experiments have been carried out on New Caledonian Crows (same family as the UK Carrion Crow). These crows have developed sophisticated tools to extract their food. Several birds use simple sticks to prise out insect prey (such as the Nuthatch) but these crows manufacture a tool with a hook on the end, made to the exact size required to prise out its larva prey from a crevice. They even learned to cut a tool out of a pandanus leaf and use the hooks on the leaf cutting to stab an out-of-reach larva. In another experiment these crows were able to work out that they needed to drop a stone into a cylinder to release a trap door to release a juicy larva. Keas (a parrot from New Zealand) demonstrated a similar level of intelligence by working out how to roll a spherical object down a slope to push an item of food out of an enclosed container. Gulls have learned to drop molluscs onto hard ground to break open the hard shell.

- o **Social behaviour** - higher level social skills are clear evidence of intelligence, requiring the identification of individuals by mates, parents and chicks. Some falcons hunt in pairs having learned that socially cooperative behaviour leads to more efficient killing. Lorenz (of imprinting fame) observed a colony of Jackdaws, who live in hierarchical colonies. The highest level of bird only interacts with the next layer down. One dominant male chose a female from the lowest rank who had been attacked by other birds. After the male had formed a bond with the female she was no longer attacked.

- o **Recognition** - a team of researchers found that Ravens were able to remember for two months the identity of people who had tricked them. Each of seven birds was given a bit of bread but then given the opportunity to exchange their bread for a piece of cheese, which they prefer. Occasionally humans cheated a Raven out of its treat by taking the bread and then eating both the bread and cheese. Two days later the birds which had been tricked refused to trade with those people that had tricked them, trading only with fair traders. Two months later only one of the birds was willing to trade with a person that had deceived them earlier. The study shows that birds are capable of understanding when they have been cheated and associating that with an individual plus they have a long memory. In another experiment Ravens were able to recognise individual voices of other Ravens and they reacted to the voice as either a friend or an invader. They also had a good long term memory for these voices. Guillemots can recognise the unique pattern on their egg amongst all the other eggs on a crowded cliff ledge. Recognition of a bird's own species is dealt with later under Imprinting. Jays are well known for caching acorns in autumn with a reputation for finding them again. This alone takes some considerable mental ability. However, their behaviour is even more complex. Jays will not bury food when they know another bird is looking. If they have buried some nuts and suspect they were watched, they re-bury the food somewhere else later. They will also try to watch another bird hiding nuts and try to steal it later. A Jay can hide up to 5 000 acorns and is a key species in the regeneration of oak woodland, as the bird fails to retrieve all its buried treasure. Retrieval rates have been monitored and vary between 30% and 75%. The Jay buries its cache anywhere and helps woodland spread up-hill as acorns naturally only fall beneath or lower than the tree, not higher. In a German study each bird stored about 4 500 acorns, carried them up to 4 km away and travelled 175 km per day.

- o **Learning from others** - in an experiment to determine if birds can learn socially a number of Great Tits were taken into captivity and trained to retrieve food. The bird had to push a sliding door either to the right or the left to gain access to a feeder. Having learned which door led to a feeder, the birds were released into the wild along with the experimental feeders. The released birds continued to gain access to the food in the feeders by sliding the correct door. The local wild population of Great Tits copied this behaviour and continued to slide only the side they had learned, even if the opposite side also gave access to food. The wild birds had learned this behaviour socially from the trained birds.
  Song birds are able to learn songs from humans. Birds such as the Bullfinch can be taught to sing specific songs. Chicks learn to sing the species song from their fathers.

- o **Counting** - one tale relates to Japanese fishermen who have traditionally used Cormorants to fish. The bird has its neck tied (loosely) so that it can catch a fish but not swallow it. To keep the birds happy fishermen fed the bird every eighth fish caught. If a greedy fisherman failed to feed a bird the eighth fish, the bird refused to plunge into the sea until fed.

Emotions

Whether birds are able to feel emotions and express them is still a widely debated topic. Anthropomorphism is more evident in this area than any other where we interpret the behaviour of birds as if they were humans. In some cultures doves are used as symbols of peace and love and owls of wisdom. One view is that all animal (and bird) behaviour is driven solely by survival or more accurately driven by reproductive success. Others view the evidence that birds show a range of emotions, some are listed below:

- o **Love and affection** - courtship behaviour such as allopreening or presenting food demonstrates the bond between birds. Devoted mates may protect one another and share food resources. Doves are often portrayed as showing devotion. Seabirds, when they meet again after a winter apart at sea, undertake a mutual display to re-establish their bond. A male Bullfinch maintains a close watch on his mate, emitting a contact call and offering her a nibble of food when they meet. A flock of young Ravens were observed, with 152 instance of fighting behaviour noted. After the altercations within 2 minutes other Ravens came up to the combatants and offered gestures such as twinning beaks, sitting by their side and emitting soft sounds, as if they were calming the young down after a physical encounter. If one of a pair of Magpies is attacked the pair will retreat to a tree and the one will preen the other. Levels of the stress hormone cortisone are lower after allopreening, demonstrating the mutual calming of this social interaction.

- o **Fear** – birds live in fear of predation. Quick flight and escape is the most common reaction to fear. Other fear behaviours include freezing in place as well as physiological reactions like increased respiration rate. When birds detect a bird of prey they have a physiological response along with the release of cortisone, showing that the bird is reacting with fear. The heart rate of a flock of Greylag geese was monitored and the greatest increase in heart rate occurred with social conflict within the flock.

- o **Anger and rage** - anger is one of the emotions most commonly seen in birds where they use threatening postures like raising their crown feathers, flashing their coloured feathers, expanding their feathers, singing loudly, emitting loud calls, hissing, lunging, wing slapping, biting plus attacking with beaks and legs. Birds frequently show aggression and anger against intruders to their territory or encroachment on a nest site. In the air, angry birds may dive at intruders or competitors. Corvids can be seen making angry aerial attacks on Buzzards. Woodland birds that detect the presence of an owl show rage until the bird is seen off.

- o **Grief and sadness** - grief is a complex emotion and just as humans react differently when grieving, so do birds. Birds have been recorded looking for a lost mate or chick and adult corvids mourn the loss of a bird by sitting round the dead bird.

- o **Happiness and joy** - pleasure can be seen in birds through different types of exuberant behaviour. Males singing when it is not necessary to attract a mate or defend a territory, the playful games of corvids or pigeons making soft purring noises are possibly examples of birds expressing happiness.

Whether birds feel and express emotions is not clear cut with a debate over whether behaviours that look like emotional expressions might be instinctive behaviour. For example, a pair of birds engaged in courtship behaviour may not have any emotional connection because they could simply be seeking the most viable mate to produce strong, healthy offspring. Similarly, other behaviours can also be defined in terms of a bird's reproductive success. Fear is necessary to evade predators, anger helps defend a territory or feeding area and grief is an attempt to recover from the effect of losing a mate or chick. Even positive emotions such as joy and love could simply be humans viewing birds in their terms. Darwin thought that animals expressed emotions including fear, anger, surprise and happiness along a continuum from pleasure to displeasure.

Imprinting

When a chick hatches it naturally attaches itself to its mother. However, if it is presented with another object at a crucial stage in its development it will attach itself to that object. If this is a human, they will become the chick's adoptive parent. Imprinting occurs in a short period just after hatching. Once this bond is formed it is difficult to break. Auditory and visual cues can trigger a response. Ducks at about 15 hours old will respond to any moving object but not when about 28 hours old.

Imprinting occurs at a specific phase when young birds are learning their behaviours for life. This learning does not require reward or re-enforcement and is irreversible. Imprinting can be filial and sexual. Both are vital to a wild bird. Young birds need to attach themselves to their parents very early in life so they can develop from (a sometimes) helpless chick to a fully functioning adult. Altricial chicks especially require their parents' attention in the early days. Some youngsters are dependent on their parents for several months, such as the falcons which have to learn hunting skills from their parents before becoming independent. Sexual imprinting occurs later in life and is essential to ensure that the chick, when reaching sexual maturity, mates with its own species. It does this by imprinted identification. Whilst cross breeding between closely related species does occur it is comparatively rare. Carrion Crows and Hooded Crows are very closely related but the evidence is that cross-breeding rarely occurs. Carrion Crows recognise their own kind through imprinting as do Hooded Crows.

Pliny recorded imprinting behaviour in the 1st century AD. In the 12th century Eider chicks imprinted themselves on St. Cuthbert, the cleric who lived on Farne Island, as he looked after them. Experiments have shown that Bullfinch imprint onto humans when taken from the nest when very young.

These birds can recognise individual people and will bring a morsel of food to the imprinted adult, just as the male does to its mate in the wild. It is thought that they learn to sing to please their human adoptive parents.

The scientist who researched imprinting in detail in the mid 20th century is Conrad Lorenz. He studied imprinting in Greylag geese (amongst other animals) by scientific observation and built up a detailed understanding of the subject. He developed the idea that behaviour patterns were innate, triggered through the environmental stimuli.

CHAPTER SIX

POPULATIONS

Measuring populations

Measuring the size of bird populations is vital in determining how well birds are thriving, identifying problems that need to be addressed to rectify decreases and measuring the effectiveness of conservation measures.

Bird population data focuses on two key measures:

- o **abundance** - the total number of a species occupying an area i.e. how numerous
- o **distribution** – the areas a species occurs in regardless of numbers i.e. how widespread

Abundance data indicates the numbers of a species in a defined area. Trends in the data over several years indicate if bird species are thriving (an increase in abundance), maintaining their numbers or decreasing in number, indicating action is required.

Distribution data indicates if an area is supporting any birds of a particular species. If a species does not occupy an area that should suit its requirements this indicates a problem. If the number of areas occupied by a species is falling again this indicates an issue to investigate. Distribution data can show if a species is moving out of one area and into another or in a certain direction.

Both abundance and distribution data can be given for small areas like a 1 km square, larger areas like 10 km squares (these squares are often used in surveys) or at county, country or geographical area. At the global level the world is divided into zoogeographical regions - see the map below:

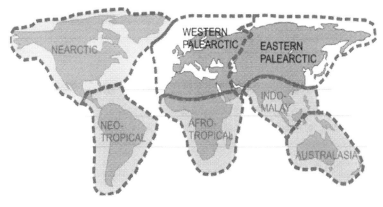

Zoogeographical areas

In stable environments bird populations remain stable, with some year- on-year fluctuations. Limits to abundance and distribution are determined by the quality and quantity of suitable habitat. Populations increase through breeding and decrease through mortality. Breeding rates are measured by counting the number of hatchlings in nests or measuring the ratio of adults to juveniles at the end of the season to arrive at the reproduction rate for that species. Ringing data is used to establish survival rates (or its converse mortality).

Reproduction rate – mortality rate = population trend

A bird's body size is also a factor: larger birds live longer → breed at a later age → have a longer annual breeding cycle → produce fewer young each year.

Survival and mortality rates are stated as a decimal fraction e.g. an adult survival rate of 0.65 means that 65 out of every 100 adults survive each year.

The table below contrasts two species:

Table 11 - Breeding data - contrasts

Factor:	Fulmar	Goldcrest
Weight (g)	340	5.4
Adult survival rate (each year)	0.97	0.15
Age first breed	9	1
Life span	44	1 ½
Number of broods	1	2
Clutch size	1	7
Incubation period (days)	52	14
Fledgling period (days)	48	19

Ref. (1)

Whilst both birds are affected by adverse conditions, like food shortages and extreme weather, the Goldcrest will suffer much higher immediate losses but its numbers recover at a much faster rate than the Fulmar suffering a similar % fall in their population. The Goldcrest breeds at an earlier age (first year), lays more eggs and has two clutches each year but has a short life (on average 1½ years) with a low adult survival rate (0.15). The Fulmar breeds later in life, at about 9 years old, lays one egg per year and has only one clutch each year but lives longer (on average 44 years) with a high adult survival rate (0.97).

Population counts are complicated by the movement of birds, especially migration. Birds will leave areas where survival and reproduction rates are low to find better breeding areas. Bird numbers in an area can recover through immigration. When birds have been culled in an area, other birds migrate into that area and numbers recover through a combination of lower first age breeding, increased reproduction rates and increased survival rates. In an experiment young Great Tits were removed from their nests. This led to an increased survival rate for the adults and more young breeding locally so the population recovered.

Population data is often published as trend data. Population numbers will inevitably rise and fall from year to year but the overall trend, over several years, will show whether the population is static, rising or falling. Statistically the annual data is smoothed out to reveal the overall trend. Also data is often presented as an index rather than as an absolute number, as this is easier to assimilate plus it enables data comparisons between species. To create an index one year is arbitrarily taken as the base year and is set at 100. The index for subsequent years is then calculated as a percentage of the current year's population against the base year's population. So, if over a 5 year period an index has risen from 100 to 110 that means the population rose 10% in the 5 years from the base year. Conversely if the index at year 5 has dropped to 85, that indicates a 15% fall in numbers over 5 years from the base year. The trend shows the underlying upward movement of the population number index, having smoothed out the rises and falls. The trend gives a much clearer indication of the overall population growth.

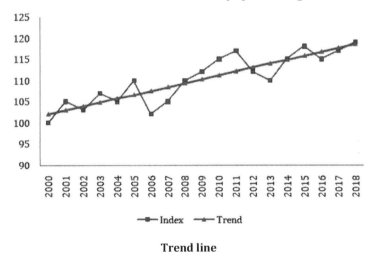

Trend line

In this illustrative graph the index is set arbitrarily = 100 in the year 2000.

Often population data is presented showing a spread of data either side of the lines on a graph (or in a table of data). The explanation for this is that bird population data is based on a sample count not a full count of all birds. This sample data provides an estimate of the actual population because a full count of the number of birds of a specific species everywhere in the UK at the same time is just impossible. Statisticians have techniques that enable them to extrapolate sample counts into population estimates. A single, stated figure (the average) is then a best estimate of the population but there is a chance (probability) that the population could be larger or smaller. Hence, graphs of data often have a coloured band either side of the average (smoothed) graph line and this shows the possible spread of the population size as a maximum number (upper limit) and minimum number (lower limit). Some data states 'within a 95% confidence limit'. This means there is a 95% chance (probability) that the stated bird population is within the stated upper and lower limits, with the most likely population as the average. Sometimes the standard deviation is quoted. This statistic measures the extent of the spread of the data either side of the average.

Overleaf is a typical graph taken from the *Wild bird populations in the UK* report of 2019:

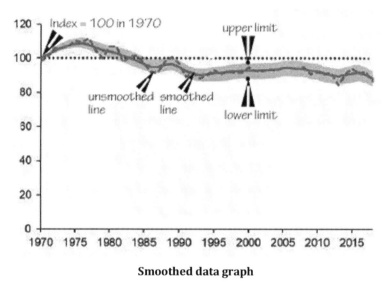

Smoothed data graph

Population levels are stable if:

births + immigration = deaths + emigration.

Inevitably there are limiting factors to the size of any bird population which can be split into extrinsic factors and intrinsic factors:

126

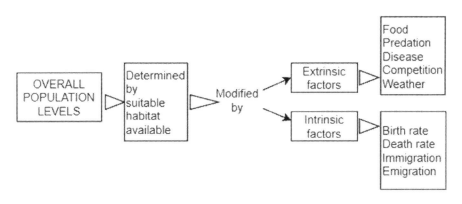

Population levels

Extrinsic factors

Food supply - this is a key determinant of the size of a population or more accurately the population density (the number of birds in a fixed area). As food becomes scarce so numbers fall and as food becomes abundant so numbers increase. The number of birds supported in a habitat depends on its size and the quality of the food supply. Some large but poor habitats will provide a low food supply and only support a limited number of birds. In a study of Dippers living on acidic rivers their breeding success rate fell as they required a larger territory of river on which to survive. The acidic water caused a fall in its food supply of nymphs and larvae so the birds needed a longer stretch of river in which to find sufficient food. Food shortages during non-breeding time affect adult mortality. Poor food supply can lead to fewer nests, fewer eggs laid, nest desertion, poor chick growth and poor fledgling survival rates. For some birds the availability of food varies from year to year and hence impacts on population levels. Bank Vole numbers vary year to year which impacts on the breeding success rates of Barn Owls. A Scottish study of Barn Owls over a 13 year period found that the number of young produced each year varied between 27 and 246. Species with a more catholic diet like the Sparrowhawk that are not affected by the availability of a specific prey item have more stable breeding rates. Migratory birds that enjoy a good food supply in their wintering areas return earlier to breed and produce more young. A study of Eider showed that in winters when there was poor food supply adult mortality increased along with later egg laying and low hatching rate. Fisheries waste levels have fallen and consequently gull numbers have decreased. If the sand eel population decreases surface feeding seabirds suffer, like Kittiwake and terns. A good food supply on the resting grounds of our summer migrants is vital as is a good food supply on the northerly breeding grounds of our winter migrants. Recently scientists have been able to track UK birds as they migrate to their resting grounds or breeding grounds and are able to discover any problems that the birds are encountering, especially food supply. See also the Section below on Habitat.

Nest sites - in some cases the population density of a species is limited by the availability of suitable nest sites rather than food. This is more likely to occur where nests sites are comparatively scarce. Birds that nest in tree cavities, like the Blue Tit, Great Tit, Little Owl, Nuthatch, Pied Flycatcher, Redstart, Starling and Treecreeper require standing dead trees to find a suitable place to nest. Where woodland is managed older trees might be felled and the younger, replacement trees do not provide the cavities these birds need for a nest site. The provision of nest boxes helps these species and the numbers nesting increases as a result. Eventually food supplies might limit a further increase in numbers (rather than providing more nests). Digging burrows for seabirds like the Puffin and Manx Shearwater helps increase the number of nest sites. Some species that defend a large territory can also limit the number of birds breeding in an area, as the resident birds repel intruders, even though there might be sufficient food for more pairs to breed. The provision of rafts, for example on worked out gravel pits, provides extra nesting sites for terns and Black-headed Gulls. Also the banks of worked out gravel pits provides nesting sites for the Sand Martin. The expansion of the built environment has seen the House Martin and Swallow nest exclusively on buildings, helping to sustain their numbers. Kittiwakes have also taken to nesting on structures such as girders on bridges. Herring Gulls have expanded their range, nesting on roofs in towns and cities, as have Kestrels and Peregrines. The first record of a Herring Gull breeding inland was in 1920. Ospreys have successfully increased in abundance and extended their range through the provision of artificial nesting platforms in areas where there is a plentiful supply of food.

Predation - the animals that predate birds include fox, mustelids, rodents, cats and hedgehogs along with avian predators like gulls, raptors, corvids and skuas. Hedgehogs are a serious predator of wader eggs. In one breeding area, protecting wader nest sites with fences increased productivity by a factor of 24. Rodents on Lundy had a catastrophic effect on the Manx Shearwater breeding population and Puffins almost became extinct there. After rodents were eradicated populations recovered. Mink escapees became problem in gull and tern colonies. Control measures to reduce the effect of predation include predator proof nest boxes, fencing, cages and diversionary feeding. Predators also affect prey species' behaviour. Birds are always on the lookout for predators and may not use the whole space available for feeding as they are wary of attacks. For example, some birds may not feed far into an open field even though food might be available nearer the centre. Other birds use bushes for cover and feed near to them so they can escape quickly to safety. Breeding densities tend to be lower in open habitats where the risk of predation is greater. Lapwing, Skylark and Yellowhammer all suffer higher predation if they nest near a field edge where Sparrowhawks lie in wait. Losses through predation are lower if nest sites are selected to provide dense cover or are located in high trees or on inaccessible cliffs.

Redshank choosing sites near bushes or trees, where the food might be better, are more likely to be predated by Sparrowhawk. Ground nesting birds are highly vulnerable to predation and their numbers can be devastated in some years. This also leads to an imbalance in male and female numbers in some species e.g. ducks as the females are often killed by predators but not the absent males who do not provide any assistance to rearing its young. In the extreme birds will abandon an area with suitable food and nest sites where the risk of predation is too high. Also, being on guard against predators takes up energy and time. Feeding in flocks reduces the time needed for an individual to scan for a predator and so feeding rates increase. Hence predators have an impact on bird populations beyond the birds they kill, as birds will not fully use the space available, with predators constraining prey behaviour. Some populations densities are not affected by predators e.g. the presence of a Sparrowhawk does not adversely affect tit and finch populations as the species compensate for this loss. Similarly, in an experiment the removal of predatory Magpies from an area had no subsequent impact on the local bird population.

Disease - all birds suffer from parasites. The effect of parasites can range from minimal to fatal. Some parasites are species specific and move from individual to individual but many parasites affect all species. Parasites can cause the spread of diseases. Birds try to remove parasites through preening, scratching, bathing, anting plus action by the immune system. Some birds make a great effort to keep their nests clean. In some species the young produce faecal sacs helping remove excrement away from the nest. Other species' nests are covered in faeces such as cliff nesting birds like the Guillemot. Birds returning to the same nest site face a resident parasite population. In an experiment Swallow's nests were cleaned of parasites and the breeding productivity of the returning birds increased. Tick numbers can increase in nesting colonies, especially species that nest very close to each other, like Guillemots. However, healthy birds are not infested by ticks, with allopreening playing an important hygiene function. Around 2005 Greenfinches across Europe suffered a parasitic infection called trichomonosis. This affected the bird's ability to eat and numbers fell. Sadly this disease is now affecting Chaffinches.

Competing species - competition between species for food can limit both abundance and distribution. Many species have a different ecological niche but still have to compete for other resources with other species of bird and other animals. Grey Herons and Egret occupy the same kind of habitat but the Egret takes smaller fish than the Grey Heron so reducing competition for food. Finches again occupy similar habitat but each species has its own niche food so reducing food competition between species. Some species are dominant. An observation session at a bird feeder will easily demonstrate a hierarchy – a Blue Tit will be pushed off by a Great Tit who will make way for a Nuthatch who will fly off quickly when a Great Spotted Woodpecker arrives. Other examples include the Gannet dominating the Herring Gull and in turn the Herring Gull dominates the Lesser Black-backed Gull at breeding sites. In woodland the Great Tit is dominant over the smaller Coal Tit and Blue Tit. This forces the subordinate species to feed elsewhere which is less productive for them. Species can compete for same habitat. For example, the Blackcap competes with the Garden Warbler, with the Blackcap being dominant. Both birds are migrants with the Blackcap arriving earlier than the Garden Warbler to establish territory first. In one experiment, Blackcap were removed from an area and Garden Warbler numbers increased. Manx Shearwater and Puffin compete for burrows on island nesting sites.

Weather - this affects the availability of food as well as impacting on habitat. Extremes of temperature, wind and rain all affect bird numbers as well as snow cover and habitat destruction. Recovery of bird populations after severe weather show early rapid recovery which then slows down as density dependent factors take effect e.g. as the expanding population increases so competition for food does then mortality rates increase to slow the rise in numbers. If severe weather events occur more frequently populations do not recover between events. In the extreme a species can be lost to an area, such as the loss of Dartford Warblers during prolonged periods of sub-zero temperatures i.e. its abundance and distribution are affected negatively. Several species will disperse to other areas in severe weather e.g. Fieldfare will move to our gardens to seek its berry food. Variations in weather affect species in different ways. For example, Blackbirds prefer some wet weather so worms are easy to catch out of the ground. Hirundines prefer drier weather so they can catch their aerial insect prey.

Populations are regulated by all these factors. Without these checks and balances numbers would either escalate or a species would become extinct.

Intrinsic factors

- o **Birth rate** – the proportion of eggs laid which mature to sexually mature adults. This comprises the number of eggs laid, the number of broods in a year, the proportion that hatch and successfully fledge and finally reach maturity.

- o **Death rate** – birds die from a range of causes – food shortages, predators, disease and accident. Ringing records are used to calculate mortality rates. The majority of birds do not live to an old age. In many species the mortality rate for each year of life is comparatively high, especially smaller birds. See table below.

- o **Immigration** – birds move into new areas that offer an improved habitat for food, shelter and nesting. They might do this temporarily during periods of adverse weather conditions. Birds on migration temporarily boost numbers locally as they move through on their way to either breeding or resting grounds. Resident populations for some species are boosted by immigrants. For example, the numbers of Blackbirds, Chaffinches and Robins in the UK increases in winter as birds migrate here.

o **Emigration** – birds move out of an area when the current habitat no longer supports the species. Birds also move out of an area as they migrate to either breeding or resting grounds. Birds like the nomadic Crossbill have to emigrate from area to area as their cone seed food ripens.

Life expectancy

Small birds are relatively short lived. Birds like the Wren are born in spring, reach maturity by the autumn, survive the winter, breed the next spring and then die the following winter. Larger birds take several years to reach maturity and then have many years of breeding. The Herring Gull takes about 4 years to gain its full adult plumage (sexual maturity can come before this) and then on average lives to the age of 12 years. Records for the oldest recorded life for a species derive from ringing data. This data is not wholly accurate with the difference between the first and last ringing recorded date being the known duration of life. Clearly the bird could have lived longer unless the bird was ringed as a nestling and subsequently found dead.

Below is a table of life expectancy and survival rates for a range of birds:

Table 12 - Lifespan and survival rates

SPECIES	LIFESPAN		SURVIVAL RATE	
	Average Years	Oldest recorded	First year[1]	Adults[2]
Canada Goose	6	31y 10m	0.76	0.72
Mute Swan	10	19y 3m	0.42 to age 3	0.85
Mallard	3	20y 5m	0.52	0.63
Ptarmigan	4	6y		0.43
Woodpigeon	3	17y 8m	0.52	0.61
Coot	5	20y 7m	0.38	0.70
Lapwing	4	21y 1m	0.6	0.7
Herring Gull	12	34y 9m	0.63 to age 4	0.88

SPECIES	LIFESPAN		SURVIVAL RATE	
	Average Years	Oldest recorded	First year[1]	Adults[2]
Arctic Tern	13	29y 1m		0.90
Cormorant	11	23y 6m	0.58	0.88
Grey Heron	5	35y 1m	0.26 to age 2	0.73
Golden Eagle	23	32y 1m	0.15 to age 4	0.95
Sparrowhawk	4	17y 1m	0.34	0.69
Tawny Owl	4	23y 5m	0.3	0.74
Raven	10	17y 11m		
Great Tit	3	15y 5m	0.38	0.54
Goldcrest	2	4y 10m		0.15
Willow Warbler	2	11y 8m	0.24	0.46
Robin	2	8y 4m	0.41	0.42
Song Thrush	3	17y 8m	0.46	.056
Chaffinch	3	14y	0.53	0.59

[1] Probability of surviving first year   [2] Probability of adult surviving each year

Ref. (1)

Habitat change

As environments and habitats change so do bird populations. These changes include habitat destruction, changes in land use, new infrastructure (e.g. roads, railways, airports, buildings), fragmentation and new structures such as wind farms and overhead cables.

The area of woodland in the UK has increased since 1998 from a very low point. In the Domesday Book woodland covered about 15% of Britain and this fell to 5% in UK by 1920 to recover to 13% in 2017 (compared to 37% in Europe). Traditional old and mixed age woodlands and the Caledonian pine forests of Scotland, which supported high levels of bio-diversity, have declined in size and become fragmented. Once large woodlands are split into smaller, isolated areas wildlife is unable to move between areas and population densities decrease as a result. Improvement projects that join up tracts of similar habitat can assist birds (and other species) in maintaining and expanding their numbers. Clear felling large areas and re-planting at high density with non-native species, like Sitka spruce, which are all the same age, leads to very low levels of bio-diversity. Conifers now account for 51% of UK woodland. A further blow to the health of UK woodland has been through diseases, like Dutch Elm disease, Ash die-back and chronic Oak die-back. An increase in the number of deer has exacerbated the problem. From 1995 – 2018 the numbers of breeding Muntjac deer increased 2.5 times. As new woodland grows certain species will move in to inhabit the new habitat until it is no longer suitable for them for example, if they cannot find suitable nest sites or their food is no longer available. Their numbers may then decline and a new species might move in if more mature woodland is suitable for them.

Changes in agricultural practices have altered farmland habitat, with many bird species no longer able to sustain populations in the changed environment, with numbers falling, some dramatically. In 1960 about 80% of cereals were sown in spring, leaving stubble and fallen seeds in the field throughout winter for birds to feed on. By 1990 80% of fields were sown in winter, depriving birds of valuable winter food. Changes in farming practices through the use of herbicides and insecticides have led to the loss of seed producing plants and a major decrease in the insect population. Changes from haymaking to silage production means that fields are cut more frequently, giving far less time for birds to raise their young. The loss of hedgerows has added to the loss of valuable habitat. Species affected include Linnet, Twite, Bullfinch, Yellowhammer and Reed, Corn and Cirl Bunting along with sparrows and Skylarks. Some species, like the finches, have been able to find other sources of food. Many farmland birds, whilst breeding, rely on insect food for their young but the use of insecticides has reduced the numbers of insects dramatically. For example, this practice has led to a collapse in the Grey Partridge population, with numbers falling by 92% in the 50 years to 2017. Similar decreases have occurred in Europe. See also the later Section on Pesticides.

Wetlands have been drained over many decades and by the 1970's over 1 million ha of wetland had been lost. About 300 000 ha of lowland wet grass land was lost between 1970 and 1985 along with 1.5 million ha of blank peat land drained in Scotland. As much as 90% of lowland ponds were lost in the 19th century. All this has led to a dramatic loss of habitat suitable for wetland birds. For data on this see the Section on Conservation below.

In the post war years the expansion of rubbish dumps led to an increase in the Herring Gull population. The increase in fishing factory ships led to an increase in the number of Fulmar, Gannets, Skuas and Great Black-backed Gulls. As ocean fish stocks reduced sand eel populations increased benefitting birds like the Puffin, terns, auks and Kittiwake. Seabirds numbered about 4.4 million pairs in 1969/70 increasing to 7.5 million pairs in 1985/6 falling to 4.5 million pairs in 1998/9. One reason for this decline was the dramatic fall in the sand eel population, leading to the breeding failure of species like the Arctic Tern. As gravel pits were worked out water fowl inhabited the area and their numbers increased.

A recent development has been the expansion of wind farms on land and sea for power generation. These large structures have become a hazard for many birds that injure themselves or worse as they fly into the large rotating blades. One innovative solution uses cameras and artificial intelligence to detect an approaching bird which then switches the generators off until the bird passes by. In one experiment Montagu's Harriers were fitted with 3 D GPS trackers to determine their height and position with respect to the blades on a wind farm. Collision risk was far lower on turbines which were taller, helping engineers design wind farms that minimised the risk of collisions and resultant injury. The simple expedient of painting wind turbine blades black reduces bird collisions.

Climate change

As a result of the build up of green house gases in the atmosphere less heat is radiated away from the earth leading to a warming of the planet. This effect is exacerbated by deforestation as less carbon dioxide is filtered out by trees. As the oceans warm they absorb carbon dioxide which acidifies the water, increasing the pH, leading to changes in the abundance and distribution of the essential plankton food. Climate change has led to oceans warming which in turn is causing oceanic creatures like plankton and sand eels to move north (to cooler waters) forcing seabirds to move north to follow their food source i.e. their distribution has changed, not necessarily their abundance. One consequence of climate change is that the timing of the seasons is changing with spring arriving earlier by 2½ days per decade. However, some wild life behaviour is not adapting to the same extent causing an imbalance. For example, migrating birds need to arrive in the UK earlier to be able to access the same food for themselves and their young, as their food supply is emerging earlier. Some species have not adapted sufficiently and are finding food more difficult to find. For example, insect food is now emerging earlier and in some cases when birds arrive the food they require is no longer available or it is less abundant e.g. caterpillar food has metamorphosed to its insect form. The Pied Flycatcher is arriving earlier but its caterpillar food is maturing even earlier with the bird's chicks hatching after the peak numbers of its food have passed. Some birds are moving further north to breed and some may cease to breed in their traditional southerly areas. Examples are Nuthatch, Blue Tit, Green Woodpecker and Barn Owl. Other species are moving north from continental Europe like the Cattle Egret, Spoonbill and Glossy Ibis, with the first two now breeding here. Some birds that breed in the far north of the UK might be lost as breeding birds to the UK like Ring Ouzel, Curlew, Golden Plover and Dotterel. Also some UK breeding birds that formerly migrated south for winters are now remaining here e.g. Blackcap and Chiffchaff. Note that some of these wintering birds are migrants from the continent. Climate change has let to extreme weather patterns and these are likely to affect populations of vulnerable birds. Whilst birds are adaptable there is a limit to this. Thereafter birds have to change genetically in order to adapt to their new conditions and this takes a longer period of time.

Hunting

A number of species became extinct in the UK as a result of the wholesale killing of birds in previous centuries. The list includes Avocet, Bittern, Black-tailed Godwit, Capercallie, Crane, Great Auk, Great Bustard, Greylag Goose and Ruff. Thankfully all but one of these species has returned to the UK after an absence. The one exception is the Great Auk which was killed to extinction by the end of the 19th century. Formerly large numbers of birds, particularly seabirds, were killed for subsistence and some communities relied on birds to eke out a living. Birds were killed for their feathers, meat, oil and whatever else could be extracted for use. Manx Shearwater and Puffin were harvested for the significant trade in salted fledglings. The eggs of many species were also taken in large numbers and sold in markets. Several examples are given later in this Section. See also the sections on Millinery and Taxidermy below.

Decoys and nets were extensively used to trap birds for killing. Decoys were introduced to England from the Netherlands. In Norfolk alone there are historical records of 30 decoy sites. With the introduction of the breach loading gun in the 19th century the use of decoys reduced. By the end of the 19th century only 5 were left in Norfolk. Decoys worked by encouraging ducks to settle on an area of water and then luring them to enter one of the many (up to ten) narrowing, curved pipes which were covered in netting. A decoy man stood behind reed screens and when there were sufficient birds in the tunnel, he jumped into the pipe and cut off the birds' retreat. The birds then flew into the narrowing pipe and found themselves trapped. Sometimes a dog was used to entice the birds further into the pipe. One record is of a single decoy trapping 1 100 Teal in one week. Another record from 1896 is a catch of 1 807 birds. These birds were then sold at market. The only use of decoys in the UK today (under licence) is to legally catch birds for ringing. The Woodcock was once eaten in large numbers. In the 13th century the market price of a Woodcock was a penny half-penny (and a Pheasant at 4 pennies). It was caught using a mesh erected in the woods where they lived, called a cock-shoot. Again, see below for examples.

Punt guns were used on wetlands. The gun had a large single bore of 50 mm, fixed flat in a punt and could fire ½ kg of shot killing up to 50 birds in one firing. The hunter lying prostrate had to manoeuvre the entire boat in order to take aim. Working in groups of 10 boats the hunters would circle a flock of waterfowl and shoot them together. In under a minute they could kill an entire flock of up to 500 birds. Since Queen Victoria's Diamond Jubilee in 1897 there has been a punt gun salute at every Coronation and Jubilee over Cowbit Wash in Lincolnshire, an area of the fens where punts were once used.

Trappers caught many birds on their southerly migration journey. Clap nets were used on water to catch the birds. Birds were lured into the net using a decoy bird set in a harness, which was pulled up as the flying birds approached and then let down to replicate a bird landing on the water. This attracted the migrating birds to land and then subsequently they were caught in the net. Another way of attracting birds into the net involved caging several birds around the net and getting them to sing. Making decoy birds sing in this later season (i.e. not the breeding season) involved the practice of stopping. This entailed keeping the birds in captivity and artificially adjusting the length of daylight so that the natural trigger for commencing singing occurred later in the year.

Legislation gave some protection to birds over the centuries, some being to protect a source of birds for aristocratic tables. Mute Swans on common land were legally protected from the 12th century as Crown property. Some bird species were pests affecting food supplies so a bounty was put on their head e.g. in the 16th century bounties were introduced for all the corvids, Buzzard, Red Kite, Harriers, Osprey, Shag, Cormorant, Green Woodpecker and Bullfinch. Church wardens were responsible for paying bounties and keeping records. In 1869 seabirds were protected but only during the breeding season. A closed season for breeding birds was introduced in the 1870's.

Game management for shoots of Red Grouse, Pheasant, Red-legged and Grey Partridge led to habitat management and wholesale predator removal (not just birds). The introduction of the breach loading gun in the 19th century was a major factor in the expansion of game shoots. This industry became economically important providing employment for a large number of people. In the 1911 census 23 000 listed their occupation as gamekeeper. The Red Grouse is famous for the shoots which start on the 'glorious twelfth' of August, established by the Game Act in 1773, and finishes on the 10th December.

Raptors have been especially targeted to protect game birds and sheep. These controls led to raptors ceasing to breed on managed estates by the end of the 19th century, including Goshawk, Marsh Harrier, Honey-buzzard and White-tailed Eagle. In other species their range was restricted e.g. Buzzard and Red Kite. This continues to be a major issue particularly with the killing of Hen Harriers on grouse moors and the killing of Golden Eagle on hill sheep farms. More recently the plight of the Hen Harrier has been much publicised, as their numbers have declined to the extent there is a clear risk that the bird might become extinct as a breeding bird in the UK. The Peregrine is still persecuted and their breeding productivity on grouse moors is about half the rate in other areas. Red Kite can be the target of persecution. Red Kite in managed areas have a first year mortality rate of 0.37 and a second year rate of 0.22 whilst in other areas the first year mortality rates are 0.54 and second year rates 0.78; a significant difference that demonstrates the major, detrimental effect of these control measures. Goshawks were killed almost to extinction for predating Pheasants kept for shooting. Gamekeepers sometimes use poisoned bate, often placed on a rabbit carcass, to kill predators and birds like the Golden Eagle, Buzzard, Red Kite and Goshawk.

Human exploitation

Below are several examples of the human exploitation of birds:

- One record of the extent of a gamekeeper's predator control is seen in the recorded killing in 3 years of 98 Peregrines, 78 Merlin, 462 Kestrels, 475 Ravens, 3 Honey-buzzards, 15 Golden Eagles, 27 White-tailed Eagles, 18 Osprey, 63 Goshawks, 275 Red Kites, 68 Harriers and 109 owls on one estate!
- An RSPB report in 2015 recorded confirmed the illegal killing of 779 protected birds of prey over a 20-year time period. Many more will have been killed but remain undetected and unrecorded. In Scotland 800 000 ha of upland is devoted to grouse shooting.
- The **Lapwing**'s eggs were taken as food and the bird was also eaten in large numbers. A record from Thetford states 3 360 eggs were taken in one year. One operator recorded taking 6-700 eggs a week and in 1820 they sold for 3/- (now 15 p) a dozen. Another record from the 1870's is of a shipment from Friesland to London of 800 000 eggs. The bird is still shot in large numbers on the continent. A record from France is of 1.6 million birds shot in the winter of 1983/4. In the Netherlands, live birds were tethered on nets luring birds to be shot. In Malta whistles were used to lure birds into shooting range. Egg collecting in Britain was eventually banned by the British Lapwing Act in 1926.
- **Guillemots** were taken on St. Kilda by lowering a man onto a rock face where he stayed all night. The birds were caught as they returned at dawn, using a white handkerchief to lure the birds and catch them when they alighted. Adults were caught early in the season when they were fat and palatable. Up to seventy birds were caught this way by one man in one night. The birds were shot for food and this led to the extinction of the bird in certain areas such as Beachy Head in Sussex. A report in 1868 reported that 168 000 birds were shot by pleasure parties over a 4 month period.
- **Puffins** were once caught in large numbers, with one estimate of 90 000 birds a year taken. The bird was caught using a fleyging,

which is a 12 foot pole with a net to catch the birds in flight. Another method involved a noose attached to a pole. The inquisitive birds were enticed towards the noose and then caught. Others used a net covering the exit from the burrow. The birds were boiled or smoked and the feathers used as down. This was often women's work with women left on remote islands for 3 weeks at a time to collect birds for their feathers. On St. Kilda more Puffins were killed than any other bird. 89 000 were killed in 1876, with 2 200 kg of feathers taken in 1894 from 90 000 birds. Puffin eggs were also taken for food. The Puffin was declared fish meat by the church and could be eaten during Lent.

o The **Black-headed Gull** was used as a substantial supply of meat and eggs. Commercial gulleries supplied up to 1 000 eggs a day and into the 1940's Leadenhall market handled 300 000 of the bird's eggs in a year. A single gullery in Scoulton, Norfolk supplied about 9 000 eggs a year for market. In levitical law Jews should not eat gulls, with gulls declared an abomination.

o On Bass Rock the colony of **Gannets** declined as the result of capture by humans and in 1885 there were no breeding birds left. Ironically the bird's scientific name is *Morus bassanus* with *bassanus* a reference to the Bass Rock colony. Numbers have recovered to about 50 000 pairs. In 1874 Gannet feathers were bought for 18 shillings (90 p) for 11 kg. Also, the breast bone was used for lamp wicks, the feet as tobacco pouches and the stomach as a fat container. Nothing went to waste! A license under a 1954 Act of Parliament is still issued for 2 000 young Gannets to be caught for meat on Sula Sgeir (meaning Gannet skerry) by men from Lewis.

o **Bitterns** were taken by taxidermists and egg collectors. At one time it was thought there were more stuffed Bitterns in Norfolk than there were live birds!

o The **Osprey** was driven to extinction in 1916 due to persecution for taking fish, by egg collectors and being killed for taxidermy and display.

o The **Red Kite** was extinct in England by 1870 and in Scotland by 1900 as a result of improved sanitation and refuse disposal, plus the destructive actions of gamekeepers and egg and skin collectors. In 1903 a Kite Committee was set up to run a nest protection scheme.

o The famous cook, Mrs. Beeton, had a recipe for **Skylark**, stuffed with bacon, beef and shallots.

o **Warblers** are still caught for consumption in some European countries, such as Cyprus, Malta and Italy. One method of catching small birds, like the Blackcap, is the use of poles covered in adhesive, known as limesticks. Nets are also used, with sound recordings used to lure the birds into the nets.

- The **Wheatear** was caught in large numbers for the table, using a noose. A record from Beachy Head (still a good place to see this bird on migration) is of a shepherd catching 1 200 birds! Catching such numbers must have been difficult as the Wheatear does not habitually form flocks. Gilbert White noted that the bird "appeared at the table of all the gentry that entertain with any degree of elegance". Daniel Defoe recorded that they tasted delicious.
- **Quail** were exported from Egypt with a recorded 3 million in 1920. The Japanese still keep Quail for their eggs, with one bird laying up to 200 eggs each year.
- In the 19th century song birds were sold for 50 shillings and bird singing competitions were held. A report from Flanders records a song contest with a row of cages containing singing birds. The number of songs each bird sang was recorded and the winner was the bird that completed the most songs in 1 hour.
- In the Middle Ages royalty and the aristocracy held enormous banquets. The list below is from the menu from the enthronement of the Archbishop of York in 1465: 204 Bittours; 204 Crane; 100 Curlew; 1 000 Egrittes; 200 Fessauntes; 2 000 Geese; 400 Heronshawes; 4 000 Mallard; 500 Partridge; 104 Peacocks; 400 Plover; 1 200 Quayles; 2 400 Reeves; 400 Swans; 4 000 Teal and 400 Woodcock totalling a staggering 17 512 birds! In 1532 when Henry VIII met the King of France in Calais 40 000 birds were consumed.
- **Ruff** (now a rare breeding bird) was shot in large numbers for the table. One fowler reported killing 600 in one 6 month period. By 1850 the bird no longer regularly bred here and it took a century to recover, albeit tenuously.
- The **Blackbird** is associated with medieval pies through the nursery rhyme *Four and twenty blackbirds baked in a pie*. Whilst this sounds gruesome in fact there was a practice of adding live birds to a pie just before serving, alarming guests when released. The tradition of placing live birds, like Blackbirds, in cooked items dates back to Roman times as a cruel means of entertaining guests at a banquet.
- **Finches** were popular as cage birds for both their colour and their song. They were kept in captivity well into the 19th century until campaigning groups changed the practice. Strangely, the normally quiet Bullfinch was kept as a caged bird because it can be taught to sing. The Bullfinch was such a good singing cage bird that they were traded. Hardy, in *Tess of the D'Urbervilles*, wrote that one of Tess' chores was to whistle to the caged Bullfinch, presumably to teach it a song. In Germany there were Bullfinch academies! The birds were kept in a darkened room and music was played to them. As they copied a few notes (which they do very well) a little light was let in

and this process continued, for about 9 months, until the birds could sing the whole song unaccompanied.

- o In the 19th century **Goldfinch** were caught in a trap that is still used today (only under licence) called a chardonneret, being the French for Goldfinch. The birds were popular as cage birds and there is a 19th century record from Worthing of 132 000 birds being caught.

Taxidermy - during the 19th century there was a widespread interest in taxidermy amongst the aristocracy. Birds were shot to order and then skilled taxidermists were employed to stuff the birds and mount them realistically for display, often in cabinets. Many examples have survived and are often exhibited in museums. The number and range of species that were used for this purpose is extraordinary but the practice was accepted as a worthy pursuit. Today museum specimens are still of value to researchers. One record from Norfolk is of Thomas Gunn (1844 - 1923) who had a taxidermist shop in Norwich. For one client alone he prepared 235 cases for exhibition. One case he prepared was of twelve male Ruff in full breeding plumage! Among the rarities shot and stuffed include Gyr Falcon, Caspian Plover, Steller's Eider and Little Shearwater. Another collection catalogued in 1897 included 434 show cases covering 336 species. In the 19th century there were bird stuffing competitions for taxidermists. Money could be made from shooting birds for collectors. One record is of £40 paid for a Pallas' Warbler shot at Cley. It was common practice for early ornithologists to have birds shot for closer inspection and dissection. Gilbert White of Selbourne fame often wrote to a friend requesting that a bird be shot and sent to him. In the early 20th century legislation was passed to protect wild birds which led to a decline in this activity. How times have changed and what was accepted then would be met with horror now.

Millinery trade - in order to satisfy the demands of the millinery trade in the 18th and 19th centuries a significant number of birds were shot for their feathers, some to the point of extinction. By the late 1880's groups of ladies joined together to campaign against the use of bird feathers. The first group, called The Plumage League, was set up in 1889 to 'discourage the wanton destruction of birds' which became the Society for the Protection of Birds in 1891. In 1904 the Society was granted its royal charter and became the RSPB. The Importation of Plumage (Prohibition) Act of 1922 which banned this trade, took 14 years to pass, although feathers could still be sold and worn. Some examples of the trade are given below:

- o The feathers of the **Great Crested Grebe** were used for the trim to collars and cuffs. The skin, complete with feathers, was used as a substitute for animal fur. By 1860 only 42 recorded breeding pairs were left in Britain.

- Terns were caught for their plumage in the 19th century. The practice was made illegal in 1922 under the Importation of Plumage (Prohibition) Act.
- In the 19th century **Grey Herons** were shot for their prized plumes, leading to protests to stop this practice. One London auction house alone in 1902 traded about 1 360 kg of Grey Heron feathers from an estimated 192 000 birds.
- The **Great White Egret** was shot in great numbers for its plumage. One kilogram of feathers required 150 birds to be shot, so 1 tonne of feathers required 150 000 birds to be shot. Between 1870 and 1920 18 400 tonnes of feathers were imported to Britain. Also, as the feathers are in prime condition during the breeding season, slaughter at this time in the season had an even greater catastrophic effect on the bird population.
- One record of feather supplies for one milliner's company in the 19th century entailed the killing of 40 000 birds.

Falconry - the use of birds of prey for hunting has a long history originating in China and Mongolia. Aristotle wrote about it in the 4th century BC. Originally birds were trained to hunt for game birds as a food supply. By the 12th century falconry had become a sport. King John (1166 – 1216) was a keen falconer and organised hunting parties where trained falcons caught ringed Grey Herons. At about the same time Frederick, Holy Roman Emperor (1194 – 1250) a keen falconer, wrote six seminal books on the subject, establishing falconry as the sport of royalty and the aristocracy. Raptors were given as valuable gifts and often exchanged when treaties were sealed, with rare birds like the gift of a Gyr Falcon. A record from the 13th century shows that Kublai Khan went hunting with 500 birds of prey. In Edward III's reign the punishment for stealing a trained raptor was the death sentence. In Burgundy the punishment for stealing a hawk was to have 170 g of flesh torn off by the stolen bird. In 1405 Henry IV granted the tenancy of the Isle of Man to Sir John Stanley for a rent of two Gyr Falcons, to be given at every subsequent coronation, which continued until 1822. In falconry there was a strict hierarchy based on the status of the person flying a bird.

The 15th century Boke of St. Albans established this hierarchy:

Table 13 - Falconry hierarchy

STATUS	BIRD
Emperor	Golden Eagle
King	Gyr Falcon
Prince	Female Peregrine
Duke	Falcon of the Loch – Osprey
Earl	Peregrine
Baron	Male Peregrine
Knight	Sacre – Saker Falcon
Esquire	Lanere – Lanner Falcon
Lady	Marylon – female Merlin
Young man	Hobby
Yeoman	Goshawk
Priest	Female Sparrowhawk
Holywater clerk	Musket – male Sparrowhawk
Knave or servant	Kestrel

Fishing - commercial fishing has had a significant effect on a number of seabirds. Seabirds are attracted to the fishing activity and then get caught in nets, lines or hooks, often with fatal consequences.

Traditional trawls catch birds in their nets as well as on the cables. Bird scaring lines help reduce the number of birds caught as well preventing the birds getting close.

Fishing using drift nets (now banned) was responsible for the deaths of a large number of birds. Long line fishing for tuna is an alternative method of catching this fish but the lines, up to 100 km long, contain 30 000 baited hooks and as the line is fed out birds dive in for the bait and are subsequently injured or killed. One estimate is that long line fishing kills 100 000 albatross each year. Worse still is the practice of unravelling a trapped bird and then cutting off its upper beak and throwing it back into the sea to die. In New Zealand 15 fishing vessels tried a new method of releasing the hooks when they are under the water and bird by-catch was reduced to zero.

Recreational fishing traditionally used lead shot on fishing lines. Inevitably some shot was lost into the water and birds picked up this shot as they were feeding. The lead shot settled in the gizzard of the birds, eventually poisoning the bird. Birds like the Mute Swan were significantly affected in the 1960's and 70's leading to the use of lead shot being banned. Lead shot for use in guns is banned in Scotland and Wales but its use is only restricted in England, with about 70% of ducks killed with lead shot. This means that the poisonous metal lead is still entering the food chain with an estimated 75 000 wild fowl dying from lead poisoning and many other birds weakened from lead entering their systems from the food they eat.

Pesticides - birds' lives are detrimentally affected by the use of pesticides along with associated pollutants, effluent and emissions. Some sprays eradicate insects and invertebrates which directly impacts on some bird species, especially insectivores, by destroying their food supply. Herbicides kill weeds which in turn affects seed production which some birds, like the finches, rely upon as food. Additionally insects would have bred on the eradicated weeds so destroying another food source for some species. Turtle Dove numbers have plummeted until the bird is now rarely seen or heard in the UK. One factor is the loss of its fumitory seed food, eradicated by herbicides. The area of crops treated with pesticides increased by 53% in the 20 years to 2016. Pesticides also kill a range of organisms not just the intended targets. They also persist in the environment for a long time and can accumulate in both predator and prey species. By doing so pesticides enter the food chain, sometimes catastrophically. They also enter waterways and again cause severe harm to animals living in an aquatic environment.

One pesticide, DDT, was sprayed on Elm trees to control Dutch Elm disease. Eventually scientists discovered DDT entered the food chain. Leaves, containing DDT, fell to the ground. As they rotted worms ate them. In turn the worms were eaten by birds like the Robin who were eventually killed by the poison. At about the same time it was observed that the Sparrowhawk's breeding success was plummeting. Scientists eventually worked out that DDT was entering the food chain and the Sparrowhawk was ingesting DDT from its bird prey. This chemical then caused the bird's egg shells to thin to the extent that the bird was no longer able to breed successfully. The Osprey's eggs were similarly affected. Eventually DDT was banned in 1984 but it took until the mid 1990's for Sparrowhawk numbers to recover. Thankfully the Sparrowhawk is now the most numerous bird of prey in the UK. As another example, Eider numbers nesting in Holland fell in the early 1960's. Scientists discovered that the mussels eaten by the bird were contaminated with organo-chlorides washing down the Rhine and the chemical had passed into the bird's digestive system. Eiders were unable to put on sufficient weight for the breeding season. This is crucial as females do not eat for the duration of incubating their eggs.

Plastics - more recently there has been an increasing awareness of the serious problem posed by non-biodegradable plastics that are having a major impact on birds, especially seabirds. Plastic rubbish does not degrade but gradually breaks up into smaller pieces which are then eventually ingested by birds with their food. These small items then sit in the gizzard and accumulate until they have a detrimental or even fatal effect on the birds as their digestive system fails. Also micro plastics discharged into the sea are entering the food chain through the plankton that ingest this plastic. In turn plankton are eaten as prey animals and further up the food chain seabirds are adversely affected, some being killed as their digestive systems fail. Observational evidence reveals that Long-tailed Tits are using synthetic fibres in building their nests, especially the outer shell. The incorporation of plastic rubbish in seabird's nests can lead to problems with entanglement and ingestion sometimes with catastrophic consequences.

Conservation

A crucial first step in any action plan for the conservation of birds (or indeed all life) is to identify those species that are most at risk. Internationally there is a system for identifying which species are at greatest risk of extinction or critically reduced abundance and / or distribution. The three categories of birds of conservation concern are based on the traffic light system of:

- o **red** for the highly vulnerable species

- o **amber** for the at risk species

- o **green** for no concern or least concern species

The criteria for each category are given below. This system applies at UK level, Europe and world levels. It is possible for a species to be categorised red for the UK and green for Europe. For example, the Nightingale is categorised as red for the UK but of least concern (green) in Europe and globally.

Such a system is crucial in order to identify which species are at risk, so action can be taken to improve the status of the bird i.e. move it from say red to amber. Beneath the categorisation lies a range of data and evidence on which conservation efforts can be focussed. Often conservation efforts are focussed on those birds that are at greatest risk. This system also enables conservation bodies to measure how successful their efforts have been in making improvements to the lives of the species at risk i.e. how many species have moved from red to amber and then to green over a period.

To be listed in a category for *Birds of Conservation Concern* the species must meet at least one of the following summarised criteria:

Red list criteria:

- o Globally threatened (using the IUCN criteria – see below)
- o Historical population decline in UK during 1800–1995
- o Severe (> 50%) decline in UK breeding population over last 25 years or longer-term period
- o Severe (> 50%) decline in UK non-breeding population over last 25 years or longer-term period
- o Severe (> 50%) contraction of UK breeding range over last 25 years or the longer-term period
- o Severe (> 50%) contraction of UK non-breeding range over last 25 years or the longer-term period

Amber list criteria:

- o Species with unfavourable conservation status in Europe
- o Historical population decline during 1800–1995 but recovering; population size has more than doubled over last 25 years
- o Moderate (25-49%) decline in UK breeding population over last 25 years or the longer-term period
- o Moderate (25-49%) contraction of UK breeding range over last 25 years or the longer-term period
- o Moderate (25-49%) decline in UK non-breeding range over last 25 years or the longer-term period
- o Moderate (25-49%) decline in UK non-breeding population over last 25 years or the longer-term period
- o Rare breeder; 1–300 breeding pairs in UK
- o Rare non-breeders; less than 900 individuals
- o Localised; at least 50% of UK breeding or non-breeding population in 10 or fewer sites but not applied to rare breeders or non-breeders
- o Internationally important; at least 20% of European breeding or non-breeding population in UK

Green list:

- o Species that occur regularly in the UK but do not qualify under any of the above criteria.

The latest report *Birds of conservation concern* – the 4th of the series (at the time of writing in 2020) was published by British Birds in 2015 as a joint report by nine UK conservation bodies. The report publishes the findings of the latest assessment of the conservation status of UK birds. Here is a summary of the key findings:

- o Of the 247 species included in the analysis:
  - o 67 were categorised red (27%)
  - o 96 were categorised amber (38.9%)
  - o 84 were categorised green (34.1%)

- Of those categorised red, 20 (30%) were new to the category, previously 18 of these were amber and 2 were green i.e. their conservation status has deteriorated.
- Three species moved from red to amber i.e. their conservation status has improved.
- Of those categorised amber, 10 (10%) were new to the category, previously 3 were red i.e. their conservation status has improved and 7 were green i.e. for 7 species their conservation status has deteriorated.
- Three species moved to the category of former breeders.
- The number of species on the green list increased by 14 as a result of 23 species moving from amber to green i.e. their conservation status has improved whilst 9 moved from green to amber or red i.e. their conservation status has deteriorated.
- The number of birds with red status has increased from 36 in 1996 to the current total of 67 – an 86% increase.

Hence, 27 species were moved from a lower category of conservation concern to a higher one and only 25 species had an improved status. The species categorised red for the first time (since the third report in 2009) included Curlew, Woodcock, Puffin, Kittiwake, Mistle Thrush, Nightingale and Pied Flycatcher. The three species moving from red to amber were Bittern, Dunlin and Nightjar. The species moving from green to amber included Mute Swan, Tawny Owl and Dipper.

The Table below provides population size and % changes plus the conservation status of a sample of UK birds:

Table 14 - Population size and conservation status

SPECIES	UK population	% change UK in last ( ) years to 2017	Conservation status
Canada Goose	55 000	137 (36)	
Mute Swan	7 000	69 (25)	Amber
Mallard	100 000	15 (25)	Amber
Grey Partridge	43 000	-67 (25)	Red
Woodpigeon	5.2 m	40 (25)	Green
Coot	26 000	3 (25) & -18 (10)	Green
Lapwing	98 000	-54 (50)	Red

SPECIES	UK population	% change UK in last ( ) years to 2017	Conservation status
Kittiwake	205 000	-44 (17)	Red
Common Tern	11 000	77 (22)	Amber
Cormorant	65 000	23 (22)	Green
Grey Heron	11 000	-17 (25)	Green
Lesser Spotted Woodpecker	800	-73 (25)	Red
Sparrowhawk	31 000	-22 (22)	Green
Tawny Owl	50 000	-31 (25)	Amber
Raven	10 000	38 (22)	Green
Great Tit	2.4 m	38 (25) & -12 (10)	Green
Starling	1.8 m	-71 (25)	Red
Willow Warbler	2.3 m	-13 (22)	Amber
Robin	7.4 m	42 (25)	Green
Song Thrush	1.3 m	30 (25)	Red
Chaffinch	5.1 m	-15 (25)	Green
Skylark	1.6 m	-18 (22)	Red

Ref. (3)

The International Union of Conservation of Nature has its own set of red list categories and criteria, which applies to all species (not just birds) and is used globally. The criteria assess the likelihood of a species becoming extinct. The categories identified are:

o   **Extinct** – where there is no reasonable doubt the last individual has died.

o   **Critically endangered** – facing an extremely high risk of extinction.

o   **Endangered** – facing a very high risk of extinction.

o   **Vulnerable** – facing a high risk of extinction.

o   **Near threatened** – is close to qualifying as one of the above in the near future.

- **Least concern**.

If a species meets any one of several criteria for a category, it is placed in that category. So if a bird species meets just one of the (many and detailed) criteria for critically endangered it is classified as that.

Below are eight UK conservation success stories:

- **Bittern**. Amber listed. This species was extinct by the late 19th century caused by wetland drainage and hunting. Small numbers bred in Norfolk in the early 20th century from where it spread slowly to reach about 80 booming males in the 1950's after which numbers fell again as wetlands were drained. A project was set up to identify the habitat requirements of the Bittern. By 2004 there were 55 booming males rising to 160 in 2016. Climate change is a potential threat to this species as rising sea levels spilling over into its wetlands home will destroy its habitat.
- **Chough**. Green listed. The Chough's breeding range steadily decreased during the 19th century as a result of being hunted as a pest and for taxidermy, leading to a few remaining pairs in Cornwall by the early 20th century. The last pair bred there in 1947. In 2001 a pair returned to the Lizard in Cornwall, this pair eventually raising 32 young. As a result of habitat restoration projects the Chough is now resident in four counties and the Isle of Man with about 400 breeding pairs. The Chough requires short grass in which to feed and arable fields in winter.
- **Cirl Bunting**. Red listed. The birds were once widespread across southern England but as a result of changes to farming practices its distribution contracted to a small area of Devon by the late 20th century. Efforts were made to create suitable habitat for the bird having identified its needs – winter stubble fields with grain seeds plus hedgerows for nesting along with the grasshoppers available as food for its young. The bird is mainly sedentary (they will only move about 2 km) so young had to be taken from their stronghold in one area of Devon to another area providing suitable habitat. The first re-location worked well and young were subsequently taken to the Roseland peninsular in Cornwall where a population has now been established. The current population is about 1 000 pairs, with some birds voluntarily moving more than the usual 2 km to establish themselves in a new area.
- **Crane**. Amber listed. Crane numbers declined from the Middle Ages and eventually ceased to breed here with the last record in 1416. In the 1980's a pair appeared in Norfolk and bred but numbers remained low with no young raised most years. Between 2000 and 2014 93 Crane chicks from Germany were hand reared in Britain. Great care was taken to avoid the chicks imprinting on their human

carers (who had to wear overalls that looked like adult Cranes!) and to train them for their eventual life in the wild, such as learning calls and reacting to predators. The young birds were gradually acclimatised to life on the Somerset Levels where there is now a thriving colony. In 2018 21 pairs attempted to breed and soon there should be a 2nd generation of re-introduced Cranes.

- **Great Bustard.** Red listed by IUCN. The bird became extinct in the UK in 1832. A re-introduction programme began in 2004, based on Salisbury Plain in Wiltshire, with wild Russian birds re-located here. In 2007 the first eggs were laid, albeit they were infertile. Nesting success followed in subsequent years with a switch to Spanish sourced eggs and chicks as the Russian birds had a strong migratory instinct and failed to stay in the UK. In 2014 33 birds were released into the wild, with half of the birds surviving their first winter.

- **Osprey**. Amber listed. The Osprey ceased to breed in Scotland in 1916 with a gap until 1954 when a pair migrating back to Scandinavia took up home in Loch Garten. The area was managed to encourage the birds to breed despite the setback of egg thieves stealing eggs on a number of occasions. Gradually numbers grew, with a UK population of about 300 pairs in 2019. Ospreys were re-introduced to Rutland Water in the 1990's leading to breeding in 2001 with a total of 117 young fledged by 2019. Now they also breed in Wales and the Lake District.

- **Red Kite**. Amber listed. The fortunes of the Red Kite have fluctuated wildly. In the Middle Ages the bird was numerous, especially in cities where it was an effective scavenger. In the 20th century the bird faced extinction with just a few birds remaining in Wales. Interestingly, the bird is now the national bird of Wales. Myxomatosis and the use of the sheep dip dieldrin adversely affected the few remaining birds. By the early 1980's the Red Kite was one of only three globally threatened species. In 1989 young birds were brought from Sweden and Spain to establish a colony in the Chilterns, leading to wild birds breeding by 1994. Birds were subsequently brought from Sweden and Germany to establish colonies elsewhere in the UK. Numbers have increased rapidly and the bird is now colonising other areas of Britain. Sadly numbers in northern Scotland remain low as the bird is still the focus of poisoning on areas managed for game shoots.

- **White-tailed Eagle**. Red listed. This bird ceased to breed in Scotland in 1916. Between 1975 and 1985 82 young birds from Norway were released on the Isle of Rhum, north Scotland. The first birds bred in 1985. A further 58 young were released between 1993 and 1998 with 85 released on the east coast of Scotland. A pair bred in Kerry, Ireland in 2013. The UK population is currently 123 pairs. After an absence of 240 years the White-tailed Eagle is being re-established on the Isle of White by introducing six birds a year from Scotland.

A major report published on behalf of 70 UK wildlife and conservation organisations entitled *State of Nature 2019* gives a detailed and thorough assessment of how the UK's wildlife has fared over the past 50 years and the current status of a large number of species, covering the abundance of about 700 species and the distribution of over 6 600 species.

The key points are:

- o Overall, average species abundance has fallen by 13% (measured on 696 species) since 1970.
- o Average distribution has fallen by 5%, measured on 6 654 species since 1970.
- o In the last 48 years the abundance of 214 priority species has fallen by 60% and the distribution of 395 priority species has fallen by 27%.
- o Using the International Union for the Conservation of Nature (IUCN) categories, 15% of UK species are at risk of extinction in the UK i.e. are critically endangered.
- o Out of 171 terrestrial and fresh water bird species 43% increased in number (1970 – 2016) due to the recovery of some species, new colonisers and an increase in wintering water bird numbers. However, the total number of birds breeding in the UK fell by 44 m in the 42 years to 2009.
- o The UK breeding seabird indicator of abundance of 22 species fell by 22% over the past 30 years.

The key pressure points on wildlife were identified as:

- o **Agricultural production** – productivity has improved 2½ times since the 1970's but the Farmland Bird Indicator (an index set at 100 in 1970) had dropped to 46 by 2017 i.e. a loss of over half the birds over the period. About 72% of UK land is agricultural with ⅓ arable and the rest pastoral. See the paragraphs below on the Defra report *Wild bird population in the UK* for data on bird numbers.

- o **Climate change** – the average UK temperature in the period 2008 – 2017 was 1^0 C warmer than the average for 1961 – 1990, with an 8% increase in rainfall and the seas 0.6^0 C warmer. Eight of the 10 warmest years for sea surface temperatures have occurred since 2002. One consequence is that terrestrial plants and invertebrates are becoming active 4 days earlier for each 1^0 rise in temperature i.e. their spring is arriving earlier but birds are becoming active 2 days earlier, creating a mis-match between food supplies and bird' breeding activity.

- o **Habitat** – in 1945 only 5% of the UK was woodland; this has risen to 13% in 2017 with about 2.4% being species rich ancient woodland. About half of woodland area is coniferous, which is species poor and often high density, giving no space for other species to thrive. See below in *Wild bird population in the UK* for data on woodland bird numbers. There are about 5 000 nature reserves in the UK covering an area 5x the size of Greater London. The restoration of worked out sand and gravel pits has provided about 8 000 ha of new wetland environment to the benefit of many species, including birds. In this period there was increased pressure from the built environment, with an expansion in road building, housing and infrastructure.

Ref: (4)

Another major report, specific to birds, *Wild bird populations in the UK 1970 – 2018* was published by Defra in 2019. The report analyses populations by habitat, analysing the changes to these environments and the effect on bird populations. The summary data is:

Table 15 – Population change by habitat

	Population change (%)	
HABITAT	**Long term (1970 – 2017)**	**Short term (2012 – 2017)**
All	-9%	No change
Farmland	-56%	-6%
Woodland	-27%	-8%
Water / wetlands	-27%	No change
Seabirds	-22%	7%
Wintering water birds	96%	No change

The key points for each habitat appear below. Data refers to 1970 – 2017 unless stated otherwise:

The native bird population (covering 130 species) fell by 11% 1970 – 2017, with little change 2012 – 2017.
- o The population of 29% of species increased
- o 39% remained static
- o 28% fell.

Farmland -19 species.
- o Overall index 45% of 1970:
  - ▪ 21% species weak increase
  - ▪ 16% static
  - ▪ 63% decline.
- o Four specialist farmland breeders, the Cirl Bunting, Grey Partridge, Turtle Dove and Tree Sparrow declined by over 90%. Rook and Reed Bunting numbers stayed the same. Two species' (Woodpigeon and Jackdaw) populations doubled.

Woodland - 37 species.
- o Overall index 71% of 1970 with populations stable from 1995:
  - ▪ 22% species increase
  - ▪ 46% static
  - ▪ 32% decline, many strong decline.
- o Five woodland species have declined by over 80% - Lesser Spotted Woodpecker, Lesser Redpoll, Spotted Flycatcher, Capercallie and Willow Tit. Blackcap and Nuthatch numbers have doubled and Great Spotted Woodpecker numbers have trebled.
- o Some species are specialist woodland breeders i.e. woodland is an essential habitat for them. The five species listed above with a decrease of over 80% have been most affected.
- o In the short term (2012 – 2017) five specialist woodland bird numbers declined – Lesser Spotted Woodpecker by 37%, Nightingale by 38% and Crossbill by 38%.
- o The fortunes of the Goldcrest, Pied Flycatcher and Chiffchaff all improved in the same period.

Water / wetlands - 26 species.
- o Overall index 83% of 1970:
  - ▪ 32% species increase
  - ▪ 36% static
  - ▪ 32% weak decline.

This environment can be usefully split into four:

- o **Slow flowing / standing water** - 6 species.
  Overall index 124% of 1970; with marked increase in Mallard and Tufted Duck numbers. However, there is a marked decrease in recent times (2012 – 2017).
- o **Fast flowing water** – 4 species.
  Overall index 83% of 1970 with a recent increase. Common Sandpiper and Grey Wagtail long term numbers have fallen

whilst Goosander numbers have doubled. Dipper numbers are static. Grey Wagtail short term numbers have increased.

- o **Reed beds** – 4 species.
  Overall index 80% of 1970 with a levelling of numbers recently. Sedge Warbler and Reed Bunting numbers have fallen 49% and 67% respectively over the long term. Cetti's Warbler numbers (a new arrival) have increase seven fold and Reed Warbler numbers have increased by 86%.
- o **Wet grassland** – 8 species.
  Overall index 47% of 1970. Snipe numbers have fallen by 79% in the long term.

Seabirds - 13 species.
- o Overall index 72% of 1970:
  - ▪ 8% species weak increase
  - ▪ 54% static
  - ▪ 38% decline.
- o Razorbill numbers have doubled in the long term. Herring Gull and Arctic Skua numbers have fallen by 59% and 82% respectively.
  In the short term 6 species have shown a recovery.

Wintering water birds - 46 species.
- o Overall index 182% of 1970:
  - ▪ 46% species increase
  - ▪ 41% static
  - ▪ 13% decline.
- o Overall numbers have declined in the short term.

  This group can usefully be split into two:

- o **Wildfowl** (ducks, geese and swans) - 27 species.
- o Overall numbers have doubled:
  - ▪ 49 % species strong or weak increase
  - ▪ 32% static
  - ▪ 19% weak decline.
- o Bewick's Swan and Eider numbers have fallen by 46% and 32% respectively. Gadwall, Greylag Goose, Brent Goose and Whooper Swan have all increased in number with some reverse in their fortunes in the short term.
- o **Waders** - 15 species.
- o Overall numbers have increase by 56%:
  - ▪ 40% species increase
  - ▪ 53% static
  - ▪ 7% decline.

153

o Avocet and Black-tailed Godwit numbers have increased 7 fold whilst Ringed Plover and Dunlin numbers have fallen 36% and 47% respectively.

The Breeding seabirds indicator of 2015, covering 13 species, shows an overall decline of 22% since 1986:

- 23% - species moderate increase
- 46% - no change
- 31% - strong to moderate decrease.

A report by the International Union for the Conservation of Nature in 2020 stated that global extinction rates had fallen by 40%, providing evidence that conservation measures are working. Critically endangered species are now twice as likely to move to the less threatened category instead of becoming extinct. A report in 2019 on bird life in North America found that the total bird population in America and Canada had fallen by 30%, a loss of 2.9 billion birds.

Natural England is 'the government's adviser for the natural environment ... helping to protect England's nature and landscapes for people to enjoy and for the services they provide' with responsibilities for promoting nature conservation which includes biodiversity, environmental land management, wildlife management and running a number of nature reserves. Natural England is the body charged with implementing the Wildlife and Countryside Act 1981 and issuing licences under this legislation. Paradoxically, in 2020 Natural England issued licences to kill three red listed species of bird – Curlew, Skylark and House Sparrow plus a number of other birds such as the Blackbird, Bullfinch, Robin, Great Tit and Lapwing. The reasons given for issuing these licences run from air safety, public health to the prevention of damage to livestock. Between 2014 and 2019 Natural England issued 2 000 licences to kill birds of 70 species including 12 000 Cormorant and 850 Curlew. Natural England is also responsible for designating and monitoring Sites of Special Scientific Interest (SSSI's) which are formal designations for the conservation of important habitats in order to protect them. If an area is designated as an SSSI the owners have a duty to manage the area to conserve its features. There are about 7 000 SSSI's in the UK. Protected areas are four times more likely to be colonised by birds than might be expected purely by chance.

The Wildlife and Countryside Act 1981 protects wild birds (except game birds) against persecution and no species can be killed or taken into captivity or their eggs taken or their nests disturbed or damaged. Traps are illegal. Licenses are issued for scientific study, including ringing. Anyone can apply for a general licenses to control birds and their nests, for birds defined in the Act as a pest species. Other species can be controlled in limited numbers by special licence e.g. for fisheries to control Cormorant, Goosander and Grey Heron numbers. Game species that can be shot outside of the close season (1st February to 31st August) include gallinules, 9 duck species, 4 goose species, plus Snipe, Woodcock and Golden Plover.

As well as land conservation areas there are now Marine Conservation Zones around the coast of the UK. The first 27 areas declared as MCZ's were introduced in 2013 in England with similar areas in Wales, Scotland and Northern Ireland and they now cover about 20% of UK waters. These designations are to protect a range of nationally important rare or threatened habitats and species. One beneficial effect of this protection will be on the food supply for seabirds.

The Joint Nature Conservation Committee is a public body set up under an Act of Parliament to advise the governments of the UK on matters relating to nature conservation. The JNCC produces a business plan and work programmes to meet its strategic objectives.

The Bern Convention, adopted in 1979, aims to ensure the conservation and protection of plants and animals and their habitats in Europe and some African countries. The UK implemented these obligations in the Wildlife and Countryside Act 1981.

UNESCO established the Convention on Wetlands of International Importance Especially as Waterfowl Habitat (RAMSAR) in 1971 for the conservation of wetlands. The convention came into force in 1975 basing the designation of areas that meet set criteria. These wetlands are of international importance for the conservation and sustainable use of wetlands. The areas are monitored to ensure that the criteria are being met. The UK has 175 RAMSAR sites.

Counting and tracking

Counts and surveys

One of the most widespread and important methods of measuring bird populations is to record observations and to undertake a count. Very many organisations undertake bird counts, from local bird watching groups, county ornithological societies to national organisations like the RSPB and BTO. The advent of information technologies has revolutionised the collection and analysis of data. It is possible to use a mobile 'phone to log the sighting of a bird in the field along with the date, time and accurate location. This data can then be sent to say the BTO remotely and the data aggregated and analysed. The BTO use a comprehensive set of codes to record the detail of an observation. It is rarely possible to count the total number of birds in a population, certainly not on a large scale e.g. a whole county. Area counts are made, for example for the Wetland Bird Survey (WeBS) organised by the BTO. On a set date trained observers count the number of birds in (say) an estuary. For other surveys sample counts are made in allocated squares (1-km, 2-km or 10-km squares). This data is then used to calculate population changes as a basis for a population estimate for that year.

Other formal surveys include the annual Breeding Birds Survey which monitors 117 breeding species throughout the breeding season. Surveyors visit allocated 1 km squares and record the birds seen and heard. The survey now includes the Waterways Breeding Bird Survey so that aquatic species are covered as well. The submitted data from over 4 000 squares is then analysed to calculate breeding success and identify trends. Alongside this the Nest Record Scheme monitors the fortunes of individual bird's nests to gather more detailed information on breeding success.

Atlases are used to present data geographically. The methodology is based on using the 10-km squares of Ordnance Survey maps and further dividing these into 25 2-km squares, each allocated a letter. Surveyors then carry out regular observations in their allocated tetrads and record sightings using a standard letter coding system, with particular emphasis on breeding status codes – possible, probable and confirmed, based on set published criteria. In addition timed tetrad visits (TTV's) are made – say two in spring and two in winter. This involves a 2 hour walk around the area to record all species seen and heard. TTV data is used to establish the relative abundance for recorded species. Data is also collected from roving records where surveyors record their observations of any and all visits to tetrads. Data collected this way is used to establish distribution data for species. The raw data then has to be validated for accuracy to identify any errors or inconsistencies as well as ensuring the accuracy of species identification which for some species can be difficult in the field. The validated data is then analysed to produce data sets that can be presented on a map using the 10-km squares of an Ordnance Survey map. The data for each square is coded using a key (usually a colour key). Maps are published for abundance and distribution, breeding and winter populations.

Ringing

The first ringing groups in the UK were formed in 1909. Early studies confirmed migration as a phenomenon giving information of where migratory birds flew to. Ringing recovery rates are very low, at about 1% and even lower for small birds. Improvements to the design of rings, particularly the use of colour rings, have increased these rates. Colour rings can be read in the field without the need to capture a bird and databases are used to identify an individual bird's history. Colour ringing data is used to calculate reproductive success rates and philopatry i.e. birds which return to their birth place. In the mid 20th century pioneering research by David Lack used ringing recovery data to predict survival and mortality rates, providing invaluable data. This analysis is still used today. Citizen science has become ever more popular where members of the public collect information and data to contribute to data collection exercises and surveys. One popular survey run by the RSPB is Garden Birdwatch with about $1/2$ million people participating. With 40 years of accumulated data it is possible to calculate trends in the population of species. One set of data gives the birds most frequently seen in gardens. The table below shows the results for 2019:

Table 16 - Garden bird survey top species

SPECIES	Mean	Rank	%
House Sparrow	4.4	1	62.8
Starling	3.1	2	40.6
Blue Tit	2.6	3	77.4
Blackbird	2.3	4	86.8
Woodpigeon	2.3	5	76.6
Goldfinch	1.8	6	33.9
Great Tit	1.5	7	57.5
Robin	1.3	8	82.2
Chaffinch	1.3	9	37.5

Mean = average number of birds seen in gardens % = proportion of gardens where species seen

The BTO published a report *Population estimates of birds in Great Britain and the United Kingdom* in 2020. The table below is an extract from this report:

Table 17 - Population estimates

SPECIES	Breeding population	Wintering population
Canada Goose	54 000 P	165 000 I
Mute Swan	7 000 P	52 500 I
Mallard	-	675 000 I
Great Crested Grebe	4 900 P	18 000 I
Woodpigeon	5.1 m P	5.1 m P
Coot	26 000 P	205 000 I

SPECIES	Breeding population	Wintering population
Lapwing	97 500 P	635 000 I
Herring Gull	130 000 P	740 000 I
Arctic Tern	53 500 P	-
Great Northern Diver	-	4 400 I
Cormorant	8 900 P	64 500 I
Grey Heron	10 500 P	45 500 I
Golden Eagle	510 P	-
Sparrowhawk	30 500 P	-
Tawny Owl	50 000 P	-
Raven	10 000 P	-
Great Tit	2.3 m T	-
Goldcrest	790 000 T	-
Willow Warbler	2.3 m T	-
Robin	7.35 m T	-
Song Thrush	1.3 m T	-
Chaffinch	5.1 m T	-

P = Pairs   T = Territories   I = individuals   - = no count

Ref. (5)

Tracking devices

o **Satellite tracking** - in 1989 remote tracking using satellites was used for the first time to track albatrosses, giving an insight into their movements at sea. Subsequently numerous studies have tracked the movement and migration of several species. Tracking has been used for migratory journeys, to identify food resources and to combat wildlife crime.

o **Geolocators** - now weigh less than $1/3$ g including a battery, light sensor, clock and a memory chip. Geolocators record light levels every few minutes. By plotting these against the recorded time, local dawn and dusk times can be estimated from which day length can be used to estimate latitude. Midpoint between dawn and dusk gives solar midday, which varies by 1 hour for every 15 degrees of longitude. Combining longitude and latitude provides an estimate of location. These tags have been used to track the migration and key dates for birds such as Swift, Nightingale, Wood Warbler and Spotted Flycatcher. Large fluctuations in light and dark during the day can indicate eggs are being incubated.

- o **Platform transmitter terminals** - tags on birds are picked up by a network of satellites devoted to environmental studies. Using the Doppler effect (the change in frequency as the satellite moves towards or away from the transmitter) PTT's can calculate the transmitter's position. These tags have low power consumption and provide instant location data.

- o **Global positioning system** - GPS gives high precision location fixes, accurate to a few metres. GPS devices weigh 1 g or more. The smallest devices only store data (but do not transmit) so birds fitted with smaller devices need to be re-caught to download data.

Devices now use technologies to download data to a base station as a bird passes by. Additional sensors are able to collect other important information. Small cameras give an indication of bird activity. Three-dimensional accelerometers detect acceleration and deceleration, as well as the device's orientation, whilst a gyroscope measures rotation. Magnetometers detect the earth's magnetic field so can act as an electronic compass. 3D visualisations of bird tracks showing the landscape are also possible. Seabirds can now be tracked whilst at sea plus sensors can detect how long they are sat on the ocean's surface as opposed to flying around. If birds sit on the water for longer periods this indicates they are moulting, providing data evidence of moulting areas, timing and duration.

As an example of how revealing these technologies are satellite data was collected from a tagged Short-eared Owl. It revealed a remarkable set of journeys. It flew from its nest in Stirlingshire → Perthshire (N Scotland) → N Scottish coast → Perthshire (to nest) → over the North Sea to Norway → nested → Galway (Ireland) → Cork → Devon → Norfolk → towards Norway when it was lost.

In 2011the British Trust for Ornithology set up a satellite tracking project to track the movement of Cuckoos from their UK breeding sites on their migratory journey. This revealed exactly where UK Cuckoos were over-wintering and the routes they took to and from these areas in Africa. The technology has advanced to the stage where anyone can look up the route and location of the birds at home on their PC. With this technology scientists can collect data on leaving and arrival dates with great accuracy as well as identifying the location of the birds' over-wintering areas. Over 80 birds have been tagged and the information gleaned has helped in the conservation of an iconic bird whose numbers have fallen dramatically in recent years.

CHAPTER 7

ORDER! ORDER!

How many?

With almost 10 000 species of birds in the world (let alone the number of species of other animals, plants etc.) and the almost bewildering variety, from the 1400 g Ostrich to the 1.6 g Bee Hummingbird, it is clear there needs to be a means by which all these birds can be sorted into some of order. The need to provide some structure was recognised many centuries ago when people like Aristotle made a first attempt to group birds into categories based on appearance or habitat. Interestingly Aristotle's methods were used well into the 17th century until more scientific methods were developed. Clearly some birds are more closely related than others and a hierarchy would make sense of this diversity and provide a clear structure. Just looking in a guide book demonstrates that birds are grouped together in some way e.g. all the ducks are listed together. Also birds do not appear in alphabetical order of their English name with guide books often commencing with the geese (as a group) and then swans (as a group) and so on. The reason for this will become apparent later.

Defining a species

A starting point for achieving some semblance of order amongst this wide variety is to start at the bottom with the individual bird species. Whilst it seems easy to identify an individual species, it actually proves to be quite difficult. For the purposes of this book we'll keep matters quite simple. At the individual, species level we need to be able state clearly what the unique defining characters are of the species to differentiate it from all other species. However, all the birds in the population of a species are not identical. It is clear that in bird species we are familiar with there is variation, sometimes to the point of confusion in the field. For example, a Buzzard's plumage varies a great deal, from light to dark. Weight and size also vary between individuals of the same sex. In other species there is a significant difference between the sexes, known as sexual dimorphism. In some species there is a significant size difference between the male and female e.g. Sparrowhawk, in other species there are differences in plumage e.g. Mallard. In times past this gave rise to confusion in the identification of species. For example, the Wren was held to be the female to the male Robin and the male and female Hen Harrier were held to be separate species.

A further critical factor in speciation is the geographical movement of birds. As members of a species spread out into new areas, the birds adapt to their new environment. Gradually, over very many generations, the birds undergo permanent genetic change and these are often manifest in changes in appearance e.g. feather colouration, beak size and shape and song. This eventually leads to the establishment of a sub-species with its own specific identity. Over a longer period of time this process of gradual change leads to the emergence of a new species, possessing unique characters that define it as a separate species. When birds spread a considerable distance, especially to an island (where interbreeding with birds from another area is less likely), they become so isolated from the parent population that a new, distinct species arises. Darwin observed this in considerable detail in his study of the so-called Galapagos finches and David Lack added to this in his study of the birds in 1938. An example nearer home is that of the geographical movement of the Herring Gull. Over a long period of time this species moved into new geographical areas and with this movement small changes took place in the bird, which became established in the population in that area. This change of character occurring with geographical movement is known as a cline. In turn these birds moved into a new area and further changes took place, spreading through Europe, Asia and North America. Eventually this led to the birds at the far end of the cline becoming a new species altogether. In this case the Herring Gull changed so much it became the separate species of the Lesser Black-backed Gull. Whilst the birds are similar, there are clear differences in appearance, like the darker back, yellow legs and being overall slightly smaller. Notably these two species do not inter-breed and are able to survive separately without serious competition, for example, for food.

There are other complications! Occasionally the male of one species mates with the female of another species to produce a hybrid. Hybridisation occurs when two similar species inter-breed, producing interspecific hybrid offspring. This more commonly occurs with ducks, geese and gulls but not exclusively so. The hybrid offspring are viable and can go onto breed themselves but they are often weaker and struggle to survive. One notable example of hybridisation caused a major problem as the offspring were both viable and able to survive. This is the case of the Ruddy Duck. This species was introduced from the USA to the UK by the Wildfowl and Wetlands Trust. Unfortunately some birds decided to escape to Spain. There they inter-breed with native White-headed Ducks and hybrids were produced. These proved stronger than the native species, which was almost driven to extinction. Eventually the Ruddy Duck had to be culled to protect the White-headed Duck. Amongst duck species there are many known hybrid crosses. The Mallard is known to hybridise with seven other species of duck. Carrion Crows and Hooded Crows can hybridise but seldom do so. The off-spring have an intermediate plumage between the two species and it is thought that the hybrids are not attractive to either species for breeding. Evidence suggests that hybridisation is a rare event.

To help arrive at some conclusion the traditional definition of a species is 'a population of birds may be considered to be of the same species if males and females can breed to produce viable offspring'. Early attempts to allocate a bird to a species were based on physical characters e.g. size, plumage, shape, beak, feet, eyes, environment, activity, song, breeding habits etc.. By observing birds and recording these characters attempts were made to define various species and identify them by name. Below is a brief history of how this developed over time.

History of taxonomy

Aristotle (384 – 322BC) was a keen observer of nature, including birds and he named the birds he saw, some of which contribute to the names we use today, especially scientific names. Aristotle identified 140 species of bird and he classified them as:

birds of prey	swimming birds
swifts, martins and swallows	all others

His methodology of classification based on a bird's attributes was used well into the 17th century. Pliny the Elder (23 – 79AD) also added to the fund of knowledge of his time, writing a book, *Naturalis Historia*, which compiled all that was known (at the time) about natural history. Again, this was a major contribution for the time and informed the naming of some birds.

The earliest extant writings in Britain date from the 6th century from records left by St. Serf and St. Columba. The first attempt to list British birds was made in the 16th century by Turner, listing 110 birds.

The Frenchman Belon (1517 – 1564) proposed six groupings of:

raptors	waterfowl	marsh birds
terrestrial birds	large arboreal birds	small arboreal birds.

His scheme included bats, as at this time bats were considered to be birds. At the same time the Swiss naturalist Gesner (1516 – 1565) identified and wrote about 217 birds. Slightly later on Aldrovandi (1522 – 1605) wrote 3 volumes on ornithology and came up with the rather odd classification based on birds that bathe in dust or dust and water! Charleton (1619 – 1672) stuck to the more traditional classification of four groups of land birds (carnivores, seed-eaters, berry eaters and insectivores) and two groups of water bird (palmipedes – web footed and fissipedes – forked feet).

The first major influential work was written by Ray in 1676, with a key contribution from his friend Willughby, who sadly died before the work was completed. The book *Ornithologiae* contained the results of the scientific examination of birds, such as dissection, with a first attempt to classify birds scientifically.

Ray's classification system is set out below:

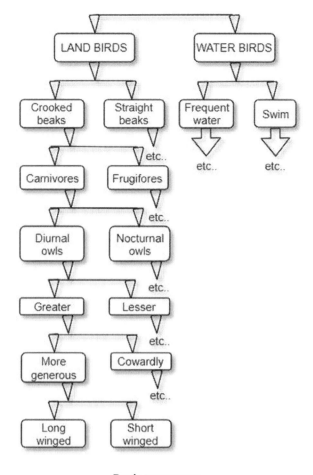

Ray's taxonomy

This classification system demonstrates which features of a bird were used to group them together i.e. physical appearance, size, feet, beaks, wings, colour, environment, food, time of activity etc.. They even used personality traits, like cowardly! Up until the publication of Darwin's game changing work this continued to be the basis for classifying birds into groups at different levels.

Gilbert White (1720 – 1793) is famous for his seminal work *The natural history and antiquities of Selborne.* Educated at Oxford University he was appointed as curate at Selborne, Hampshire where he carried out most of his studies. His work and methodology were a major influence on the study of natural history. He had a broad interest in nature, observing wild life in and around Selborne, corresponding with the leaders in the field at the time, including Pennant. As was the practice at the time, he often ordered birds for dissection and one would be shot for him. It was his curiosity and insight that made his work so notable and made him an inspiration for others.

There is good advice in the old Chinese proverb 'Wisdom begins with putting the right name on a thing'. The major breakthrough in designating a unique name for every species of living thing came with the work of Carl von Linne (1707 – 1778), a Swedish naturalist who also worked in Holland. His system for designating a species a unique scientific name is still used today and has been adopted globally. Given that he is remembered for his Latin based naming system, he is best known by the Latinate name Carolus Linnaeus. His speciality was botany but he had a wide interest in the natural world. Linnaeus published the first edition of his *Systema Naturae* in 1735 and produced the last and 10th edition in 1758, covering plants as well as animals.

He proposed a binomial nomenclature system as the basis for giving a unique name to every species. The first word would be the genus of the bird (as explained in the next paragraph) and the second word would be a specific epithet, which in combination would provide a name exclusive to that species. The words in the name are Latin but do not necessarily originate from Latin. In fact many of the scientific names of birds derive from other languages including Greek, German, Dutch and Norwegian. For example, *Rissa* (in the Kittiwake's name) is Icelandic, *Alca* in the Razorbill's name is Old Norsk and *grille* in the Black Guillemot's name is Swedish.

In addition Linnaeus helped with creating logical groupings for all living things, including birds. The first word of his binomial name structure (genus) meant this bottom level would be a group of birds sharing many common characteristics. However, he stuck with the prevailing philosophy of the time that all livings things had been created by God, which was not challenged until the 19th century. Linnaeus also stuck with the idea that there was orderliness and symmetry in nature as ordained by God and all groups of living things had six orders. For birds he proposed:

| Accipitres | Picae | Anseres |
| Grallae | Gallinae | Passeres |

split into 78 genera and 930 species.

Linnaeus' proposed taxonomic layers were:

kingdom → class → order → genus → species

The word taxonomy derives from taxis – arrangement and nomia – meaning.

Increasingly during this period importance was attached to:

- ○ Collections in museums and private houses containing specimens of birds that could be examined in detail. The British Museum opened in 1759.
- ○ Development of scientific enquiry and the emergence of biology and zoology as disciplines in universities (but rarely ornithology).

- Dissemination of scientific knowledge through publications and learned societies such as the Royal Society, founded in 1660.
- Specimens of birds were obtained (i.e. shot) for detailed examination. This enables species to be differentiated on the basis of their anatomy. Also at this time when optics were very poor and there were no guide books to assist with identification.

Further identification work was carried out by others to generate a taxonomy. Brisson (1723 - 1806) worked at a large museum in France. He carried out a detailed examination of the collection of birds, as well as their nests and eggs. He published his findings in a 6 volume catalogue. From this very detailed study he proposed a taxonomy of 26 orders (similar to the current situation) and 115 genera.

The next major, revolutionary change came with the publication of *On the origin of species by natural selection* in 1859 by Charles Darwin (1808 – 1892). Darwin's main proposition was that all life had descended over time from common ancestors. This process of evolution results from natural selection in which small inherited variations increase the ability of species to compete, survive and reproduce. He did not know how this happened and it took until the discovery of DNA in 1953 for these mechanisms to be understood. From his studies Darwin proposed that natural selection is the differential survival and reproduction of individuals due to differences in their characteristics i.e. their phenotype. Phenotype is defined as the composite of observable characteristics, which result from (as we now know) genes and an organism's environment. Over many generations these heritable traits result in a population change.

Darwin predicted that the publication of his work (along with Wallace) would cause great controversy, as it directly challenged the prevailing philosophy of the day, based on the Christian belief that God had created all things. Evolution and the Christian view of creation were seen as opposing philosophies, as evolution admitted no role for a deity or supreme being. The natural world, according to Darwin, had evolved over a very long period of time from common ancestors. Eventually Darwin went on to write that humans had evolved in the same manner as all other species. This is held to contradict the Christian belief that humans were created in the image of God and are unique. Partly as a result of this controversy Darwin's ideas took a sometime to be influential and were not adopted fully by scientists until the mid 20th century. Amongst many lay people Darwin's ideas are still controversial. Witness the divisive debate in America on the whether Darwin's theory of evolution should be taught at all. Instead only divine creation should be taught.

However, the impact of Darwin's theory of evolution meant that all the rules of taxonomy were changed. Formerly taxonomy was based on groupings of birds that possessed similar characteristics e.g. webbed feet or a long, thin beak. After Darwin taxonomy was based on descendants from common ancestors. Ascertaining these relationships however is not easy and even now there is no full agreement on which species are closely related to each other or identifying the common ancestor for a group of birds. As we will see there are several competing taxonomies. Darwin did not propose any rules for delineating species.

At around the same time Darwin was working on his theory of evolution, an Augustinian friar was conducting experiments on peas that would (eventually) start to provide an answer as to how evolution actually works. Mendel (1822 - 1884) examined in detail how the characteristics of peas e.g. seed colour, changed when two species were cross bred. He noticed that contrary to simple logic when a yellow pea was cross bred with a green pea, the off-spring were all yellow. The next generation produced one quarter green seeds and three quarters yellow seeds. Whilst Mendel called these traits we now know them to be genes. He established the laws of inheritance.

Developments in classifying birds and creating an accurate taxonomy during the 20th century included the work of:

- o   Ernst Mayer (1904 - 2005) contributed to our understanding of how separate species evolved. He defined a species as morphologically similar individuals that can breed amongst themselves. He discovered that when species become isolated by geography or food source they start to differ and eventually become a separate species.
- o   Hennig (1913 - 1976) is quoted as the founder of cladistics, which provides a framework for constructing a taxonomy (in his case of insects). The basis of cladistics is that all organisms can be categorised into groups based on their most recent common ancestor. These relationships are based on shared, derived characteristics. A clade is a group (in this case, birds) which includes the most recent common ancestor of all its members and all the descendents of that most recent common ancestor. This method of classification aims to identify only those shared characteristics which can be deduced to have originated in the common ancestor during evolution.
- o   Sibley and Ahlquist in the 1970's and '80's developed their DNA-DNA hybridisation technique. This involved measuring the similarity between the DNA of two species to determine how closely related they are. This followed the discovery of DNA in 1953 enabling new lines of experimentation. Through painstaking research Sibley and Ahlquist were able construct a taxomony of birds.

Current classification

With any classification system and taxonomy there are three caveats:

1. The information on which the taxonomy is based is subject to constant revision as new evidence is made available and new techniques are developed.
2. Taxonomies can only claim to be accurate when first published. It takes time for new lists to be compiled and approved.
3. The science behind the classification of birds is not an exact one and scientists will come to different conclusions from the available evidence and data based on their interpretation. In some cases the evidence is limited, especially when using fossil evidence. Also the science itself is not exact and conclusions are reached on the balance of probabilities rather than absolute certainty.

Divergent and convergent evolution

A further complication is that two species might, on the face of it, look very similar whereas they took an entirely different route to come to a similar place and the species are not closely related. The popular example of this is that of the Swift and Swallow. The species look similar, they are aerial insectivores, both are migratory. On that basis they might be classed together. However, they descended from entirely different ancestors. Oddly the Swift is in the same order as the hummingbirds and the same family as the Nightjar! This process is called convergent evolution where similar features giving a similar function evolved independently, not from a common ancestor. The opposite also occurs where two species, which on the face of it are quite different, are in fact close relatives. The gulls and auks appear to have different characteristics but started off as close relatives. Darwin's finches are another example, where the original finches arrived on the Galapagos and as they moved around to the various islands evolved to have quite different characteristics despite their common ancestry. This process is called divergent evolution where original common features have evolved into dissimilar features with a different function.

Geographical variations also occur in species:

- **Bergmann's rule** states that warm-blooded vertebrates tend to be larger in cooler climates as a larger body has a lower surface area to volume ratio which helps reduce heat loss. For example, Icelandic Redwings are larger than continental Redwings.

- **Gloger's rule** states that races in cool, dry climates have lighter pigments than birds from warm, humid climates.

- **Allen's rule** states that body extensions are longer in warm climates and shorter in colder regions. For example, longer legs will lose more heat than shorter legs. A study of 43 species of gulls and terns showed that legs were shorter in the coldest regions.

These rules add to the complication of grouping similar birds together, especially where a species is widespread and likely to change characteristics with its geographical location.

In addition the exact number of species is not fully known because:

- There might be species yet to be discovered.
- A species thought to be extinct might still be alive.
- A species thought to be extant could be extinct.
- The question of designating a sub-species as a separate species.
- The complication of hybrids.

This means that there is no one, single definitive list of the birds of the world or a single, agreed taxonomy. Currently there are four main lists:

1. Gill and Donsker as adopted by the International Ornithologists' Union (IOU).
2. Clements.
3. Howard and Moore.
4. BirdLife International.

The table below demonstrates the variability of the different published taxonomies:

Table 18 - Current taxonomies

Name	Date	Species	Families
Gill and Donsker	2019	10 738	245
Clements	2007	9 716	204
Morony et al	1975	8 982	158
Monroe and Sibley	1993	9 702	145
Dickinson	2003	9 721	195
Perrins	2003	9 845	172

If sub-species are included the total number increases to over 28 662! (Using the Clement's list).

To illustrate how the numbers might change, in 2019 the IOU up-dated its World Bird List. The Royal Tern (occurring in Africa and America) was previously listed as a species along with a sub-species, the West African Crested Tern. With new DNA evidence the two birds are now listed as two separate species. The birds are externally near-identical but not genetically, hence the split. A second example (admitted to the list in 2020) is where five new species and five new sub-species (based on their features, DNA and song) were discovered on a remote Indonesian island.

Whilst this might look confusing the situation is very fluid and each list has its own virtues. These lists change over time as new analyses are carried out and new lists published.

This book uses the Clement's list with the citation: (6)

Clements, J. F., T. S. Schulenberg, M. J. Iliff, D. Roberson, T. A. Fredericks, B. L. Sullivan and C. L. Wood. 2018. The eBird/Clements checklist of birds of the world: v2018

In Britain the situation is clearer; the list issued by the British Ornithologists' Union (BOU) is the one accepted list for use in the UK. The BOU has now adopted the Gill and Donsker world list issued by the IOU to determine the agreed and published classification of UK birds. So as the IOU list is amended (as it is from time to time) the BOU list will be amended accordingly. The current BOU list (9th edition 2019) covers 619 species.

To be accepted onto the list of British birds the species has to be wild (feral) and not domesticated or captive. The BOU categories of bird are:

Category A - have been recorded in an apparently natural state at least once since 1 January 1950.

Category B - have been recorded in an apparently natural state at least once between 1 January 1800 and 31 December 1949 but have not been recorded subsequently.

Category C - although introduced, now derive from the resulting self-sustaining populations:

C1 – Naturalised introduced species - species that have occurred only as a result of introduction, e.g. Egyptian Goose *Alopochen aegyptiacus*

C2 – Naturalised established species – species with established populations resulting from introduction by Man but which also occur in an apparently natural state, e.g. Greylag Goose *Anser anser*

C3 – Naturalised re-established species – species with populations successfully re-established by Man in areas of former occurrence, e.g. Red Kite *Milvus milvus*

C4 – Naturalised feral species – domesticated species with populations established in the wild, e.g. Rock Pigeon (Dove)/Feral Pigeon *Columba livia*

C5 – Vagrant naturalised species – species from established naturalized populations abroad, e.g. possibly some Ruddy Shelducks *Tadorna ferruginea* occurring in Britain. There are currently no species in category C5

C6 – Former naturalised species - species formerly placed in C1 whose naturalized populations are either no longer self-sustaining or are considered extinct, e.g. Lady Amherst's Pheasant *Chrysolophus amherstiae*

To be on the British list the species must be in Category A, B or C.

The excluded categories are:

Category D - Species that would otherwise appear in Category A except that there is reasonable doubt that they have ever occurred in a natural state. Species placed in Category D only form no part of the British List and are not included in the species totals.

Category E - Species recorded as introductions, human-assisted transportees or escapees from captivity and whose breeding populations (if any) are thought not to be self-sustaining. Category E species form no part of the British List (unless already included within Categories A, B or C).

Category F - Records of bird species recorded before 1800.

In order for a new species to be added to the list the BOU's Rarities Committee examines the evidence for admitting the species to the list. Sightings and the supporting evidence is collated by the British Birds Rarities Committee, who pass on their findings to the BOURC.

The diagram below depicts the current situation (2019) clearly showing all the taxonomic levels. It is simplified, showing the line for birds and it does not include (the complication) of super- and sub- levels.

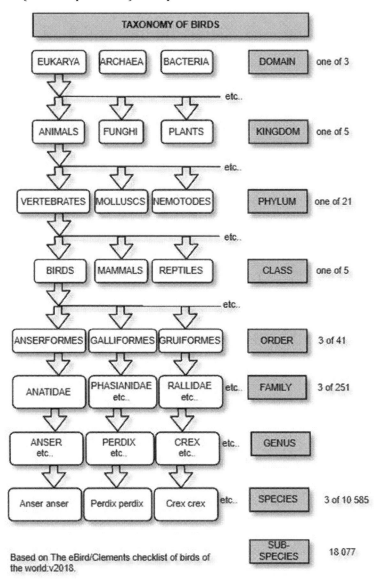

Clement's taxonomy

Below is an example of the taxonomy for a specific bird – the Blackbird:

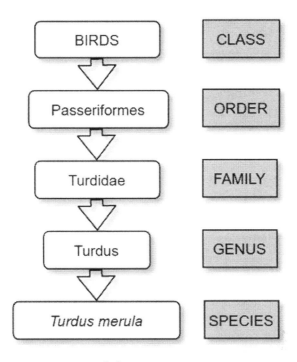

Avian taxonomy

Returning to bird guide books; the reason that geese often appear as the first entry is because, taxonomically, geese species are the oldest UK birds in evolutionary terms. Along with geese all the species in the order Anseriformes and the family Anatidae will appear first, grouped by genera. Consequently buntings often appear last because they are the most recent species to evolve in the order Passeriformes and the family Emberizidae. Guide books follow taxonomic order not alphabetical order. Some older guide books might have birds listed in a different order because the authors used an older taxonomy that placed the birds in a different sequence.

What's in a name?

When it comes to birds' names there is an enormous fund of fascinating information and meaning contained in the huge variety of names we have given to birds over the very long period of time we have been interacting with them. These names reflect birds' behaviour, habits and characteristics along with all manner of beliefs, some of which are now enshrined in myths and folklore. Birds feature in some of the oldest scripts and appear in very early art as well, such as cave drawings. An Aboriginal rock art depiction of a giant bird is possibly 40 000 years old. It is from this close attachment to birds and the relationship we have had with them for millennia that there is such a rich variety of birds' names. These names tell us a great deal about the birds themselves and our continuing close relationship with them. It also demonstrates how important birds have been in the everyday lives of people and how birds depend on us and are affected by our actions.

The derivation of some bird names are obvious and need no explanation. The Blackcap has a black cap! The Dipper dips! Others are far less obvious and some have an interesting history.

Many bird names are derived from some notable characteristic of the bird:

- **Song** - several birds' names are a phonetic representation of the bird's song i.e. onomatopoeic. For example, Chiffchaff; Chough; Curlew; Cuckoo; Quail and similarly for groups of birds such as chats; larks, a Germanic name for a songster; owls, from their howl; plovers, from the Old French plouvier related to the bird's clear call and the warblers. Sandpiper refers to the birds' shrill call. Pipit derives from the Latin pipeo, meaning a chirper. Woodpeckers have a special means of attracting attention, by drumming, usually on wood, to set up a resonance at a specific frequency.

- **Appearance** - another notable feature of birds is their colour and appearance. A number of birds' names derive from this including Blackbird; Blackcap; Bullfinch, from its bulky appearance; Coal Tit; Crossbill; Firecrest; Goldcrest; Golden Eagle; Goldeneye; Goldfinch; Great Crested Grebe; Green Sandpiper; Green Woodpecker; Greenfinch; Grey Wagtail; Long-tailed Duck; Pintail; Pink-footed Goose; Razorbill; Short-eared Owl; Tufted Duck; Waxwing; Whitethroat and Yellowhammer. Note that the word common in a bird's name, as in Common Gull and Common Scoter, means having no particular distinguishing features, rather than being numerous. Pied appears in a few bird's names, like Pied Flycatcher, with pied historically meaning coloured rather than the modern black and white.

- **Feeding habits** – e.g. Bean Goose from the bird's winter feeding habits; Carrion Crow; Chaffinch, from the historic habit of the bird eating the chaff from threshing grain; Kingfisher and Oystercatcher, with British birds preferring to eat mussels and clams and not oysters.

- **Eponyms** - one of the ultimate accolades for a naturalist or ornithologist is to have an animal or bird named after you i.e. an eponym. In the world of birds several species have been named after famous people, often experts in the subject. On the British list there are 36 birds named after individuals. These include Audouin's Gull, Bewick's Swan, Cetti's Warbler and Savi's Warbler. Some people are held in high esteem and have several birds named after them, with Pallas taking the prize with four species on the British list named after him – Pallas' Grasshopper Warbler, Reed Bunting, Sandgrouse and

174

Warbler. Pallas was born in Berlin in 1741, travelled throughout Europe, undertook expeditions to Siberia, worked in St. Petersburg and wrote many books. He also proposed a classification for birds into 7 orders and 68 families containing 425 birds. Gilbert White, famed for his innovative study of birds (recorded in the book *The natural history and antiquities of Selborne*) was commemorated with a (non-British) bird named after him - White's Thrush. Lady Amherst's Pheasant is another example with an eponym in its vernacular and scientific name - *Chrysolophus amherstiae*.

- **Human names** - some bird' names incorporate human names. For example, Jackdaw and Jack Snipe – Jack meaning small, a diminution of John. Many local names incorporate human names, such as Jenny Wren.

- **Habitat** - several formal birds' names come from the bird's habitat. These include the Corncrake; House Sparrow; Marsh Harrier; Reed Warbler; Sedge Warbler; Water Rail and Woodlark.

- **Places** – a number of birds are named after places or regions, some are accurate, others not. The Kentish Plover formerly breed in Kent but no longer and is only seen infrequently as a visitor to the UK from the continent. Three Gulls are named after regions – Mediterranean Gull, Iceland Gull and Caspian Gull as are two Terns, the Arctic Tern and Caspian Tern. Others examples include the Arctic Skua, Dartford Warbler and Scottish Crossbill.

The derivation of some names is more obscure. Several birds' names are words that are not used in any other context e.g. Teal, Fulmar and Eider. Often the name derives from an older, dead language but at the time the name given was a word which had an everyday meaning and reflected something relevant about the bird. Other names are based on what is now proved to be a myth. The Nightjar's scientific name is *Caprimulgus europaeus* linking the bird to goat's milk. For details see the Species account below. The idea that the Wren's name derives from the word hen is folklore but this is well embedded in our culture. Hence the rhyme *The Robin and Wren, are God Almighty's cock and hen*. Clearly wrong but the name stuck! In the poem *The death and burial of cock Robin* the Wren appears in "Who'll bear the pall, 'We said the Wren', Both the cock and the hen, 'And we'll bear the pall'". One poet went further and wrote: "Little Robin Redbreast sat on a tree; He made love to little Jenny Wren; Dear little Jenny, I want to marry you. Poor little Jenny she blushed quite red".

All this illustrates how closely bound we have been to birds throughout history and remain so today. Birds are so much a part of our lives that their names tell us very rich and interesting tales. Birds have also become a part of our language and Appendix 3 lists a range of idioms and phrases about birds or containing a bird's name.

Below is a description of the three categories of birds' names:

Local and common names – historical names based on common usage.

From very early times, as humans and birds interacted with each other, a wide variety of names have been ascribed to birds. This has led to a plethora of local bird names, many of which have slid into antiquity and are no longer used. The Wren alone has well over 40 recorded local names! However, the record of these names tell us a great deal about our historical relationship with birds, including our use and abuse of them, our observation of their behaviour and names related to the sometimes super-natural powers attributed to some birds. Early references to birds in British literature include *The Seafarer*, dated pre-1000 AD in which the swan (ylfete), gull (maew), eagle (earn) and tern (stearn) are all mentioned. Chaucer, in his *Parlement of Foules*, written in 1380, referred to the 35 species of bird which were used as a jury to select a bride for King Richard II. Mixed in with this are some very strange tales, myths and folklore. A few have stuck until the present day and influenced the official and accepted bird's name.

As each locality generated its own names for specific birds there are very many local variations. Attempts were made by people like Willughby and Ray in the 17th century to a create list of agreed names for birds but a variety of local names survived for a long time after this. This is not surprising as language was then predominantly an oral tradition and names would not transmit very far from the locality naming them. Few names would be written down as literacy levels were very low. Also local dialects were predominant. These dialects generated bird names that differ from other dialect names for the same bird. Sometimes the difference is the odd letter, others are more substantial. Local names persisted despite attempts to normalise them. In the 19th century scientists tried to compile a list of agreed birds' names which everyone would adopt but still common usage prevailed. This gave rise to confusion, particularly with respect to accurate bird identification, assigning birds to their correct family and identifying their near relatives. Hence some formal names are based on local names which are now known to be incorrect, for example the Wren as already mentioned. Some local names have survived and a number became the formal English name for the bird or have been incorporated into the scientific name.

The local names given to birds derived in a number of ways. Some came from the bird's colour, physical characteristics or behaviour. Others incorporated human names as a reflection of the closeness between birds and humans e.g. Jack, Madge and Gilly. Yet others came from the birds' environment. As bird observation was unrefined, the same bird name was used for several species, as a generic name e.g. willow wren (for what we now call warblers) and tit, not just for what we now call the tit family. Local names were also influenced by older names from abroad, typically from Scandinavia and continental Europe. For example, Scottish names were influenced by names from Scandinavia, the Shetlands by Iceland and S E England by Germany. Finally, various myths and folk tales were used to derive names. Local names are all written in lower case, even where the word might otherwise start with an upper case letter e.g. a human name.

Formal English name

This is the unique name that has been designated by the BOU as the correct English vernacular name for each bird on the British list. The most recent list can be found at http://www.bou.org.uk/british-list/ . This name is the official name by which each bird should be referred to in the UK for the avoidance of doubt or confusion. Historically there were several examples of confusion! The BOU also acts as the body that decides which birds are placed on the British list. The international formal English name given by the IOU can differ from the BOU name. For example, the Bittern becomes the Eurasian Bittern and the Chaffinch becomes Common Chaffinch.

Citation: (7) Amendments to the list are issued by the BOU from time to time, rather than publishing a new, complete list.

Attempts were made from the 17th century onwards to provide a definitive list of British bird names that everyone would agree to use. This endeavour was not complete until the 20th century not least because securing agreement was very difficult. In addition ornithologists still needed to achieve clarity on the identification of some species in order to provide an accurate name. A few official names are still inaccurate but we have to live with them now e.g. Stone-curlew. Some names have changed over the years. For example, the 1923 list still called a Tit, Titmouse and the Robin, Redbreast and the Dunnock incorrectly called the Hedge Sparrow.

The writing convention is that with vernacular English names each word is capitalised, unless hyphenated, when the second word is lower case e.g. Black-backed Gull. Mis-named birds, like the Honey-buzzard, have a hyphen between the two names and the second word is not capitalised.

In this book general references to a bird group e.g. owl or gull are written in lower case. Care needs to be taken with these informal labels as they can be inaccurate and scientifically mis-leading. For example, 'birds of prey' is a generic term that informally includes birds in two different orders– the hawks in the order Accipitriformes and the falcons in the order Falconiformes plus the owls. The term 'warblers' covers four different families. Ducks are sometimes split informally into dabbling ducks and diving ducks.

Scientific name

For every individual bird species (and indeed for all living organisms) there is an internationally accepted method of ascribing each species a unique name using a binomial structure i.e. a name made up of two words. Linnaeus (1707 – 1778) devised this structure and is comprised of the first word being the genus of the species and the second word a specific word or epithet. So the Teal's scientific name is *Anas crecca,* with the Teal's genus being *Anas* plus the specific adjective *crecca* (from the sound it makes). That name uniquely identifies that bird and species. The English name is confusing because Teal is the UK vernacular English name but the international English name is Eurasian Teal. The genus name is unique within the class of (all) birds i.e. there is no duplication of genera in different families or orders, otherwise there would be confusion!

The British list issued by the BOU defines and publishes the unique, correct and agreed scientific name for each species of British bird and these are identical to the internationally agreed scientific name. This list is now aligned to the international list see Refs. (7) and (8).

The writing convention for a scientific name is that the first letter of the first word is upper case, the rest is in lower case (even if the specific word is a proper noun) and in scientific works the letters are italicised. When a genus name is repeated in the same passage of text, the name is abbreviated in italics to the first letter of the genus name. In a text on thrushes, for example, the first reference to a thrush, say Fieldfare, would be *Turdus pilarus* but a subsequent reference to another member of the same genus, e.g. Blackbird, would be written as *T. merula*. Where the species is not clear, say from a difficult observation, the genus name is given followed by non-italicised sp.. This might occur with long distance views of terns and this would be written as *Sterna* sp.. If this involves multiple species, the convention is to write spp.. This naming convention is governed by an international code of rules, the International Code of Zoological Nomenclature.

In some publications a citation for the scientific name is give. For example, the Gannet's name is *Morus bassanus* Linnaeus, 1758, which attributes the creation of the name to Linnaeus or for the Little Ringed Plover, *Charadrius dubius* Scopoli, 1786 to Scopoli. There is agreement that 'the first scientific name that can confidently be identified with a species is the one that will be used' along with the name of the person giving the species the name. If the genus name changes because the species is re-assigned to another genus, the original attribution is retained but the name and date is put in brackets.

However, scientific names are not fixed forever. Scientists are using more sophisticated techniques, particularly DNA analysis and this leads to birds being re-classified as closer relatives are identified. As a consequence the Robin has been re-classified into the flycatcher family of Muscicapidae but maintains its genus Erithacus within that family. So in this case the Robin's scientific name has not changed although its family location has.

A complication arises with sub-species of birds, which are given a tri-nomial name. With a number of species of bird variations occur within the species, often geographical variations. Each sub-species retains the same binomial species name but a third word is added to provide a separate identification for the sub-species. So for example, the species scientific name for the Yellow Wagtail is *Motacilla flava* but there are many sub-species, the main differences being in the head feather pattern. One bird, referred to as the nominate species, is given the repetitive third word, so for the Yellow Wagtail the nominate species is named *Motacilla flava flava*. The other sub-species are then given a trinomial name based on the nominate species. Hence, the sub-species names for the Yellow Wagtail include *Motacilla flava thunbergi*, *Motacilla flava feldegg* and *Motacilla flava cinereocapilla*. Note that sub-species and race have an identical meaning. The writing convention for sub-species is that once a trinomial name has been written in full further references to a sub-species are abbreviated in italics. So having written *Motacilla flava flava* a subsequent reference to a sub-species is written *M. f. feldegg*.

The naming convention is that names of all orders end in –formes, meaning form or type and all family names end in –idae from the Greek eidos meaning image or appearance. The formal name for orders, families and genera are capitalised but not italicised. Informal names for orders e.g. falcons for Falconiformes or for families e.g. corvids for Covidae are not capitalised.

Citations for the source of scientific names in this book: (1) (7)

Hybrids

Hybrids are named by indicating each cross species by sex. So a cross between a male Tufted Duck and a female Pochard (a known cross) is written Tufted Duck ♂ x Pochard ♀. Identification of hybrids can difficult; especially with females, as the character changes in hybrids can be subtle. Male ducks often have more noticeable distinguishing characteristics e.g. in the beak or plumage, which are different in the hybrid from the original species.

Mis-named birds

A few birds have a name which is a mis-nomer, usually an accident of history:

- o The Bearded Tit looks like a tit but is not even closely related to the tit family, Paridae. It is in a family of its own, Timaliidae, with no close relatives. Also the bird has a moustache not a beard.
- o The mar in Fulmar is an old word for gull but the bird is a tubenose, related to the albatrosses, not a gull.

- o The Honey-buzzard does not eat honey (it eats wasp's larvae) and it is not directly related to the buzzards but is closer to the kites.
- o The Long-tailed Tit, whilst looking like a tit, is in a separate family, Aegithalidae, with no other British bird in that family.
- o The name Marsh Tit links the bird to wetlands whereas it lives in woodland.
- o The Short-eared and Long-eared Owls are mis-named, as we now know the 'ears' are merely tufts and do have not auditory function.
- o The Snow Bunting has, as a result of DNA analysis, been relocated to the Calcariidae family and is strictly speaking no longer a bunting but a long spur.
- o The Stone-curlew has a really bad time as both its formal names are incorrect. It's not a Curlew nor is it in the same family as the Curlew, but its nocturnal call sounds like a Curlew. The informal grouping it is placed in, the thick knees, is incorrectly named as the large joint which you can see on its leg is in fact an ankle!
- o The name Wheatear implies a link to a grain and the bird's ear. In fact it means white rump!

Some scientific names are incorrect:

- o The Arctic Skua's name is *Stercorarius parasiticus* which translates as belonging to dung, perpetuating the story that the bird caught the dung of other birds but what it does is steal their food. The same applies to its family name of Stercorariidae and to its close relation the Great Skua.
- o With the Little Owl *noctua* means night and incorrectly associates this owl with the night.
- o The Stone-curlew's scientific name is *Burhinus oedicnemus* with oideo for swelling and kneme for knee, whereas it is the ankle that is seen.
- o The Slavonian Grebe's scientific name is *Podiceps auritus* with *auritus* meaning ear, referring to the bird's prominent head feathers but they are not ear feathers.

Suffixes

Suffixes are letters added to the end of a word to give added meaning to a word or to change its function as a word. As in the English language generally bird names are no different with a range of suffixes being used. The table below gives some examples:

Table 19 - Suffixes

SUFFIX	MEANING	EXAMPLE
-ach		trillach – Common Sandpiper, Oystercatcher and Sanderling
-ard		Mallard; Pochard
-daw	Member of crow family; knave or person of low esteem	cornish daw – Chough; Jackdaw; land daw – Carrion Crow
-erel	Small	Dotterel; pickerel – Dunlin; chickerel – Whimbrel
-et	Small	Avocet; Cygnet; kinglet – Goldcrest; martlet – Swallow; Linnet ; owlet; martinet – House Martin and Kingfisher; puffinet – Black Guillemot
-ie		wheetie – Whitethroat
-lin	Small	Dunlin; Merlin
-ling	Small	blakeling – Yellowhammer; Brambling; duckling; gosling; otterling – Common Sandpiper; Sanderling; Starling; titling – small bird
-mar	Gull family	Fulmar
-ock	Small	Dunnock; hurrock – Brent Goose; tinnock – Blue Tit; ruddock – Robin; wrannock – Wren
-ond	Duck	stokkond – Mallard
-rel		Kestrel; Petrel; pickerel – Dunlin; Whimbrel

Myth, magic and fact

Folklore abounds in many cultures. Given the close association and interaction of humans and birds and, in some instances, the economic reliance of local people on birds, it is not surprising that there are numerous tales, stories, myths, fables, legends, superstitions and lore relating to birds. Some are factual others are mythological but they all reflect how important birds have been and are to human lives in many cultures. Some are incorporated into bird's names. Much material may well be lost, as the predominantly local tales were passed down orally and seldom written down. However, we still have a rich range of material to draw on. Several of these are enshrined in our culture and live on in music, poems, stories, nursery rhymes, paintings, flags, coats of arms and songs. In some instances a lack of knowledge and understanding led to these beliefs, such as the thinking that it was the female Nightingale that sang or that the Woodcock flew to the moon in the seasons it was not seen! It was only when ornithology was established as a scientific discipline and our knowledge and understanding of birds built up that inaccurate stories and lore were corrected.

Individual cultures and epochs have ascribed certain characteristics to individual birds. Across cultures some of these are contradictory. For example, owls in some cultures are ascribed as being wise whilst in others they are evil. Birds have been used in heraldry and many nations have used birds to represent the nature of their nation in their coat of arms.

In many cultures, such as during the Greek, Roman and Scandinavian epochs, birds were given a wholly mythological status. The authors of the myths took the perceived characteristics of certain birds and used these to make a powerful point in the stories they told. For example, doves, owls, corvids and eagles appear in many mythological stories in several cultures. For some birds their names derive from these stories. Some of these perceptions still live on today, for example a dove often represents peace, an owl wisdom, a Raven evil and an eagle strength.

There is a fine line between lore, which might have some basis in reality and myths, which are purely fictional. Some folklore started off being believed as a fact only later to be proven a myth. This is clearly demonstrated by the name of the Barnacle Goose. The prevalent story of how the Goose bred was given folklore status for centuries, being believed by many and attested in writing but it turned out to be a complete myth! The Goose did not breed under water and emerge from a shell fish! The basis for this story was an attempt to explain where migratory birds went after wintering in Britain. See the Species account for more detail. Many people had a strong belief in this lore and some still persist today as superstitions, such as turning over a coin in your pocket on hearing the first Cuckoo in spring to bring good luck.

Many mythological tales and folklore are based on anthropomorphism, (attributing human characteristics to creatures, in this case, birds). In doing so we impute attributes onto birds which mainly they do not possess. Whilst a dove is a gentle bird the attribute of peace given to the bird is a human one, not avian. But we still refer to peacemakers as doves. Wisdom is exclusively a human attribute so owls do not possess wisdom. Birds possess intelligence which is not the same as wisdom. Corvids are highly intelligent birds, ranking alongside apes in solving logical problems and memory tests. Corvids also display high levels of social behaviour and experiments have concluded that Magpies demonstrate emotions, such as loss and grieving. (See the Section on Intelligence in Chapter 5).

The species accounts in the next Chapter include many and various intriguing tales, stories, superstitions, quotes, lore and myths, which appear in boxes. All of these show how important birds have been and are to us.

CHAPTER EIGHT

SPECIES ACCOUNTS

The birds are listed in taxonomic order as described in the Section Order, Order!. The species accounts are in order of orders and then families and finally the genera within each family. For each order and family there is a detailed description of the main characteristics of that order and family, giving some context and background information for each group of birds which gives an insight into why the species are grouped together as they are. Beneath this are the species accounts, grouped by genus in alphabetical order of their formal English name. The taxonomic information used in this book is taken from the Clement's list.

The entry for each bird species provides:
  o A sample of any known local names and for some their derivation and meaning. For some well known species not all local names are included as there are so many.
  o The formal English name taken from the BOU list, with an explanation of its derivation. In some instances there is no need to add any further explanation – a Greenfinch is clearly a green coloured finch!
  o The scientific name is taken from the BOU list, again with an explanation of its derivation. For each genus any explanation is given for the first species but not for subsequent species in the genus.
  o Any interesting facts, about the species, its behaviour and life style.
  o Information on the bird's interaction with humans, references to it in literature or music along with any myths and tales –will all be recorded here.

Remember these orders, families, genera and species accounts are only for the 235 birds referred to in this book. The selected 235 species cover all the main species that reside here or migrate here in winter or summer. There are birds, particularly vagrants and rarities, on the British list that are in families not mentioned in this book. The BOU's 2019 list contains 619 species.

Below is a summary of the taxonomy of the birds in this book:

Table 20 - Orders, families, genus

Order	No. of families	No. of genus	No. of species
Anseriformes	1	15	29
Galliformes	1	6	8
Podicipediformes	1	2	5
Columbiformes	1	2	5
Cuculiformes	1	1	1
Caprimulgiformes	2	2	2
Apodiformes	1	1	1
Gruiformes	2	5	5
Charadriiformes	8	31	55
Gaviiformes	1	1	3
Procellariiformes	2	3	3
Suliformes	2	2	3
Pelecaniformes	1	4	4
Accipitriformes	2	8	11
Strigiformes	2	4	5
Coraciiformes	1	1	1
Piciformes	1	4	4
Falconiformes	1	4	4
Psittaciformes	1	1	1
Passeriformes	27	53	85
TOTAL:	**59**	**150**	**235**

The description of orders and families are broad as often there is considerable variation of characteristics within these groups. Necessarily the accounts include words like 'many', 'most' and 'some'. Descriptions become more specific when describing the characteristics of a genus and more so for the species.

Geese, swans, ducks and mergansers

Order - Anseriformes

A broad group of geese, swans, ducks and mergansers, all highly adapted for an aquatic life, with webbed feet for efficient swimming. Anser is the word for goose. On some species the beak structure allows water to be sucked in and lamellae on the beak edges traps food. The tongue is fleshy. The birds are herbivores, with some foraging for insects, molluscs, crustaceans and small fish. Most birds are seasonally monogamous, with some multiple partner copulations. Pair bond formation involves complex courtship displays with body posturing and vocalizations. Pair bonds may last for several years. The young are precocial.

Within this order there is one family:

Anatidae - ducks, geese and waterfowl.

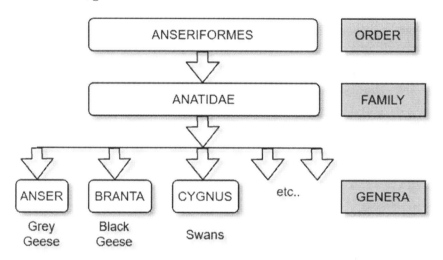

Geese and swans

Main characteristics of the Anatidae family:

Anatids are medium to large birds (30 -180 cm; 230 g - 22.5 kg) and include the geese, swans, ducks and merganser. In many species plumage is sexually dimorphic, with female ducks often being cryptically coloured to provide camouflage whilst brooding. Some species have a brightly coloured wing speculum. Often the beak is broad with lamellae which trap microscopic food particles. The beaks of some males are brightly coloured during the breeding season. The front three toes are webbed, aiding swimming. Anatidae are herbivores, although some may also forage for aquatic invertebrates. Most species are seasonally monogamous but some are polygynous. Pair formation often begins during the non-breeding season. Flock formation occurs mainly outside the breeding season. Some species retain their family grouping all year round. Courtship displays include head and wing movements, vocalisations and swimming patterns. Many males have a penis as many species mate on water. Egg hatching is synchronous within 24 hours. Chicks are precocial and can walk and swim within hours of hatching, foraging for themselves, staying close to their mother. Males in some species (especially ducks) take no role in raising their young. In some species young of the year will return to the breeding grounds with their parents for one or two years. Most ducks are sexually mature aged 1 - 2, whereas geese and swans mature aged five.

The birds in the Anatidae family are grouped in 14 genera and 29 species:

Anser - Bean Goose; Greylag Goose; Pink-footed Goose; White-fronted Goose
Branta - Barnacle Goose; Brent Goose; Canada Goose
Cygnus - Bewick's Swan; Mute Swan; Whooper Swan
Tadorna - Shelduck
Spatula - Garganey; Shoveler
Marcea - Gadwall; Wigeon
Anas - Mallard; Pintail; Teal
Aythya - Pochard; Scaup; Tufted Duck
Somateria - Eider
Melanitta - Common Scoter
Clangula - Long-tailed Duck
Bucephala - Goldeneye
Mergellus - Smew
Mergus - Goosander; Red-breasted Merganser; Ruddy Duck

Geese within the family Anatidae consist of several winter migrants who fly considerable distances to escape the severe winter in their northerly breeding grounds, areas such as Siberia, Svalbard, Iceland, Greenland and the Faroes. The two genera of geese in the UK are Anser – the grey geese, which have pink or orange legs and Branta – the black geese, which have black legs and darker bodies. Technically goose refers to the female, gander to the male and gosling to the young before fledging. The word goose derives from the Old Norse gos and the German gans. As early as the 6th century BC Aesop wrote the tale *The goose that laid the golden eggs*, the moral being not to destroy by greed anything that is of value. Geese are commonly described as silly, as in the proverb that 'it is a silly goose that comes to the fox's sermon'. From the 15th century, a silly or foolish person was referred to as a goose. Johnson stated the goose is "a large waterfowl, proverbially noted, I know not why, for foolishness". In a remarkable insight into bird migration the Bishop of Skalholt from Iceland said of these birds in the 17th century "I speak of fowl which come from abroad; t'out the winter they do not dwell amongst us... every autumn they make for neighbouring countries of England and

Scotland…". It took until the 19th century for the phenomenon of migration to be fully accepted.

Local names for the **Bean Goose** include corn goose; grey goose and wild goose.

Its scientific name is *Anser fabalis* which comes from *Anser* for goose and *fabalis* meaning of beans (from its diet).

The **Greylag Goose** has local names such as fen goose; marsh goose; stubble goose and wild goose.

The -lag in the Greylag's English name is probably from the lag-lag call made when driving geese or from the fact that they lag behind other geese when migrating.

In a famous experiment Lorenz examined imprinting by these geese. At an early age goslings will attach themselves to whoever looks after them, including humans. For more information on imprinting see the Section in Chapter 5.

The Greylag Goose (often representing geese as a group) appears in the mythology of several cultures. In mythology geese are associated with the god of fertility, Gula and were the symbol of the Egyptian sun god Ra. The goose was sacred to the Roman god Aphrodite. Geese helped the Romans to defend their last stand against their invaders in 390 BC. Geese were kept in the temples at the top of the hill and on hearing the invading Gauls they let out their loud alarm call enabling the Romans to defend the Capitol.

The bird's comic waddle and supposed lack of intelligence led to the term silly goose. In Elizabethan times goose was slang for a prostitute and goose neck for the penis. A piece of folklore was that the formation of the geese in flight could determine the number of weeks of frost to come. In Celtic culture the Goose was never eaten. In other areas the Goose was eaten as part of festivities underlined by the saying 'If you eat Goose at Michaelmas you will not want for money all year round'. The tradition of drying and pulling a wishbone came from the tradition of eating a goose at Michaelmas. One old tale was that the length and colour of the wish bone of a recently deceased goose indicated the length and severity of the oncoming winter.

The Greylag Goose has a boring and uninformative scientific name – *Anser anser*, merely meaning goose-goose!

One local name for the **Pink-footed Goose** is long-beaked goose which contradicts its scientific name of *Anser brachyrhynchus* which comes from the

Latin *Anser* for goose and the Greek brakhus for short and rhunkhos for beak. There are two populations of this species – one breeding in Iceland and Greenland and over-wintering in the UK and the other in Svalbard which over-winters in Denmark and the Netherlands. Previously this species was classified as a sub-species of the Bean Goose but is now identified separately. The UK holds 85% of the population of this species in winter.

Local names for the **White-fronted Goose** are bald goose; laughing goose and tortoise-shell goose.

Its scientific name is *Anser albifrons*, *Anser* for goose and albus white and *frons* brow, reflecting the key identification feature of this Goose – the white at the base of its beak.

Local names for the **Barnacle Goose** include bar goose; brand, from black goose; claik goose; norway barnacle; routhecock and tree goose.

The first written record of an English name for the Barnacle Goose dates from the 8th century.

An interesting question was posed relating to the physical training of the young geese who have to fly a long way very soon after they are first able to fly. The Goose breeds in Greenland and Svalbard and these populations fly to the Hebrides and Solway Firth respectively. The young have no time to train or build up their muscles. They spend about 20 minutes a day flying at their breeding grounds. Hardly a full work out! Yet they set off and complete an epic 2 500 km journey without any preparatory training. How do they do it?

> The Barnacle Goose illustrates the way in which a myth can become accepted as true and become embedded into a bird's name. In 1185 the Welsh cleric Giraldus reported "They (i.e. the birds) are produced from fir timber tossed along the sea and are at first like gum. Afterwards they hang down by their beaks as if they were a seaweed attached to the timber and are surrounded by shells in order to grow more freely. Having thus in process of time been clothed with a strong coat of feathers, they either fall into the water or fly freely away into the air. They derived their food and growth from the sap of the wood or from the sea, by a secret and most wonderful process of alimentation. I have frequently seen, with my own eyes, more than a thousand of these small bodies of birds, hanging down on the sea-shore from one piece of timber, enclosed in their shells and already formed. They do not breed and lay eggs like other birds, nor do they ever hatch any eggs, nor do they seem to build nests in any corner of the earth". This tale was repeated over the centuries, including by John Gerard in the 16th century, being affirmed as a truth. A Scottish legend from 1597 relates that fruits from a tree fell into the sea and developed into geese!   "There are ....certain trees whereon do grow

certaine shells … wherein are contained little living creatures: which ….doe open and out of them grow those little living things, which falling into the water do become fowles, which we call barnacles". Bishops in Ireland declared "do not scruple to dine off these birds at the time of fasting (i.e. Lent), because they are not flesh nor born of flesh". At the time observers in Britain did not know that the bird migrated north in summer to breed on the islands of Svalbard or Greenland. Latterly barnacle became adopted as the formal name for the bird.

The scientific name for the Barnacle Goose is *Branta leucopsis* with *branta* deriving from brandgas meaning burnt goose and *leucopsis* white faced.

The **Brent Goose** is a winter migrant with two distinct populations which are separately identified as sub-species. One arrives from its breeding grounds on the Arctic coast of Siberia and the other from Greenland. The Brent Goose is a winter visitor to fields of eel grass, its favourite food. Local names include brant, from which the formal name Brent derives via the Greek brenthos, for a water bird. The North American name for this bird is Brant. Other names include clatter goose; crocker; horra goose; hurrock, with hurr from its whining noise plus the -ock suffix; rott goose; routherock and ware goose, with ware the local Durham name for seaweed.

Brent in the vernacular name derives from brant and is onomatopoeic for the guttural call of the bird.

The bird's scientific name *Branta bernicla* derives from brandgas meaning burnt goose and *bernicla* for barnacle. There are two sub-species of Brent Goose seen in Britain. The dark-bellied form, which winters in England and breeds in Siberia, has the scientific name *Branta bernicla bernicla* making this the nominate species. The pale-bellied sub-species *Branta bernicla horta* breeds in Greenland and over winters in Ireland and Scotland. *Horta* derives from hortus meaning garden or park. The North American form, the Black Brant, is considered a separate species, *Branta nigricans* and is a rare visitor to Britain.

The scientific name of the **Canada Goose,** *Branta canadensis* comes from brandgas meaning burnt goose and *canadensis*, Canada. The Canada Goose was introduced to Britain in the 17th century as a parkland bird and it was not until the 19th century that it became established in the wild i.e. was recohgnised as feral. The species was not listed as a wild bird by the BOU in its 1923 published list. For a bird species to be entered on the British list it must be the result of self-sustaining populations. See Section Current classification in Chapter 7.

The **Swan** genus, Cygnus includes Mute Swan, Bewick's Swan and Whooper Swan. The word swan is an Old English word, from the German schwan and Dutch zwaan which in turn derived from the Indo-European root swen (to sound, to sing), whence the Latin sonus (sound). The first written record of a name for the swan in English dates from the 8th century.

In a mythological story, Zeus fell in love with the goddess Nemesis but, when she resisted his advances, he turned himself into a swan. Aphrodite pretended to pursue him in the form of an eagle. Nemesis gave refuge to the escaping swan, only to find herself tricked into embracing Zeus. To commemorate this successful trick, Zeus placed the images of a swan and an eagle in the sky, linking these birds to the constellations Cygnus and Aquila, both being the derivative of the birds' scientific names.

Several Greek mythological characters are called Cycnus or Cygnus, the latter being the genus name of some swans today. The son of Poseidon is called Cycnus with one account saying that he was rescued as a child by fisherman who saw a swan fly over at the time. Orpheus was transformed into a swan after his murder and was placed in the sky next to his lyre, as the constellation Cygnus. In Tchaikovsky's Swan Lake Odette is a beautiful woman and a swan. Odile, the sorcerer's daughter takes on the form of a Black Swan as part of a trick against Odette's love for Siegfried.

The Greeks also associated the constellation Cygnus with the tragic story of Phaethon, the son of Helios the sun god. He demanded to ride his father's sun chariot. Phaethon, however, was unable to control the reins, forcing Zeus to destroy the chariot (and Phaethon) with a thunderbolt, causing it to plummet to the earth into the river Eridanus. According to the myth, Phaethon's brother, Cycnus, grieved bitterly and spent many days diving into the river to collect Phaethon's bones to give him a proper burial. The gods were so touched by Cycnus's devotion to his brother that they turned him into a swan and placed him among the stars. In yet another tale Cycnus fought in the Trojan War and was killed by Achilles. He was transformed into a swan after death.

The swan appears in many tales and myths and variously represents beauty, grace, haughtiness and death. Aesop wrote about the swan in his tale *The Swan and the Goose*. A rich man bought a goose and a swan in the market. He fed the one for his table and kept the other for the sake of its song. When the time came for killing the goose, the cook went to take him at night but he was not able to distinguish one bird from the other and he caught the swan instead of the goose. The swan, threatened with death, burst forth into song and made himself known by his voice and preserved his life by his melody. The moral is 'Sweet words may deliver us from peril, when harsh words would fail'.

Several cultures have the belief that swans transport the souls of the dead to their final resting place. In the Buddhist tradition the swan represents the same characteristics as the dove does in Jewish and Christian cultures. In the creation myths of some indigenous American peoples, swans played a role in creation. In a Celtic mythical story four royal children were transformed into swans by their wicked mother. They flew off and spent 900 years flying round before returning as ancient people.

A local name for the **Mute Swan** (and Bewick's Swan) is tame swan to distinguish it from the Whooper Swan which is called the wild swan.

The Mute Swan is our only resident swan. The bird is not mute; although it does not have a song it can make a series of sounds, especially a loud hiss when you get too near the bird, along with grunts! Also the wings emit a loud, vibrational sound in flight, thought to be a contact call. The word swan derives from the Anglo-Saxon meaning sounder, probably referring to the swishing sound of its wings made whilst flying. The Mute Swan is generally a very quiet bird, unlike its close relative the Whooper Swan which has an accurate onomatopoeic name. The term swan song arose in ancient Greece to represent a final effort made just before death (or lately, a final performance e.g. in the theatre) based on the belief that the swan sang a beautiful song just before dying, having been silent all its life. Although not wholly true the fable has entered popular mythology. The adult male is called a cob from the Middle English cobbe, meaning leader of a group, the adult female is a pen and the young are called cygnets, from the French cygnus for swan with the diminutive suffix –et added. The Mute Swan is one of the heaviest flying birds, weighing 12 kg. The oldest living Mute Swan recorded was 19 years old. Swan Vestas adopted the Mute Swan as a logo on its match boxes, using an Eric Hosking photograph.

The Mute Swan has long been a royal bird. Edward I used the Swan as a badge. Edward III passed protective legislation as the bird was valued as a table bird for eating. Henry VII imposed fines for stealing their eggs. The Crown still has the right to Mute Swans on the Thames from London Bridge to Henley. The beaks are marked with a nick by officials from the Vintner's and Dyer's Livery Companies in a ceremony known as upping. However, in Scotland and Ireland the folklore is that the bird is thought to contain human souls and cannot be eaten. According to CAMRA there are 451 pubs named 'Swan' and is the 4th most popular pub name in Britain and 'The White Swan' is the 38th most popular. The pub name 'Swan with two necks' is an odd name but probably comes from two nicks which are the marks made on a Swan's beak during the upping ceremony. Swans remain paired for life and practice sexual monogamy, which is rare in the world of birds. The Mute Swan was voted the Danish national bird in 1984 by TV viewers.

The Mute Swan has the scientific name *Cygnus olor* from the mythical stories of Cycnus, the son of Poseidon (related above). In another account, he was said to have had womanly white skin and fair hair, which was why he received a name which meant swan. *Olor* merely means swan.

 Bewick's Swan is named after Bewick (1753 – 1828), an early ornithologist, bird illustrator and wood engraver.

The Bewick's Swan's scientific name, *Cygnus columbianus,* is named after the Columbia River in North America where the bird breeds as well as northern Eurasia.

Finally in this genus, the **Whooper Swan** has a repetitive scientific name *Cygnus cygnus*. Bewick's Swan and Whooper Swan both breed in high northern latitudes on Arctic tundra and migrate south in family groups as winter approaches. The Whooper Swan flies at 2 500 m at a speed of 88 km / hr covering over 1 000 km in 12 hours in a temperature of - 40° C - some journey! Another record is of swans flying at an altitude of 8.2 km. The Whooper Swan was nominated the national bird of Finland in 1981.

The beaks of the Bewick's and Whooper Swan have varying amounts of yellow at the base and black at the tip. Birds can be individually identified by the distinctive pattern of colour on their beak.

The next 15 species, in nine genera, are all loosely classified as ducks. Duck is the female name to the male's drake. There is a broad split between the dabbling ducks and the diving ducks.

14 - Shelduck

The **Shelduck** is a bird of mud flats and marshes and being so large and colourful is easy to pick out. Several local names use the word goose incorrectly, for example, bar gander referring to the male's red protuberance on its beak in the breeding season; links goose; skeeling goose in Orkney and sly goose. Burrow duck comes from the habit of the bird using rabbit burrows for a nest site. At one time the Shelduck was persecuted for disturbing rabbits, when rabbits were an economic source of food. Furze duck refers to the duck's use of gorse at the entrance to the nest. Oddly some females without a nest lay their eggs in another female's nest to make a brood size of up to 30, all of which might hatch! The Shelduck has an unusual moult cycle, moulting all its feathers at once (known as a catastrophic moult), rather than sequentially as most other birds do. The males, who have little active life with their off-spring, fly off to a gathering place (traditionally the Heligoland Bight in Germany) to moult.

The formal name Shelduck comes from shield meaning variegated.

The Shelduck's scientific name *Tadorna tadorna* comes from the French tadorne for Shelduck.

The **Garganey's** local names include cricket teal; garganey teal; pied wigeon and summer teal, with a clear theme of linking the bird to the wintering ducks, Teal and Wigeon.

Garganey comes from the raucous call of the female with the Latin gargala meaning tracheal artery, an echo of the females' monosyllabic note. The Garganey is Britain's only summer visiting duck.

The Garganey's scientific name is *Spatula querquedula*, with *Spatula* referring to the duck's mandibles and *querquedula* repetitively meaning duck.

The **Shoveler** is a duck with a distinctive wide, flat beak that is an effective filter of its zooplankton food. The beak contains 200 lamellae which trap its food. Not unsurprisingly many local names refer to this, such as broad bill; scooperbill; shovel bill and spoon-billed teal. Other names include blue-winged stint, with an unclear link, as stint means small; butter duck; mud duck and swaddle duck.

The Shoveler's scientific name is *Spatula clypeata*, with *Spatula* referring to the duck's flat, wide beak and also *clypeata* referring to its shield-bearing beak.

Local names for the **Gadwall** include bastard; gadwall teal; rodge and sand wigeon.

The Gadwall's vernacular name comes from gaddel, which means incessant chatter.

The Gadwall has the scientific name *Mareca strepera* with *Mareca* from the Portuguese for small and *strepera* meaning noisy.

The **Wigeon** over-winters on Britain's estuaries and lakes in large numbers, with a UK population estimate of 450 000. The local name half duck refers to its size leading in times past to a lower value at market. The local names whew and whistler refer to the duck's clear whistle which is redolent of winter bird watching on marshes and estuaries where the bird gathers in large numbers, constantly whistling. Folklore had it that Wigeon are the souls of unchristened babies, from the sad sound of their whistle. Other names include cock winder; easterling; golden head (two names for young birds sold at market); half duck (half the size of a Mallard); lady fowl; pandle whew, with pandles being winkles that the duck will eat and smee duck. Local names for other ducks refer to the Wigeon, like freshwater wigeon for both the Goldeneye and the Pochard; red-headed wigeon for the Pochard; black-headed wigeon for the Scaup and black wigeon for the Tufted Duck.

The Wigeon's name is onomatopoeic from the Latin vibionem which translated later into wigene and thence to Wigeon.

Wigeon has the scientific name *Mareca penelope* with *Mareca* from the Portuguese for a small duck and the second word being the Greek penelops, a type of duck.

15 - Mallard

Local names for **Mallard** include grey duck; mire duck; moss duck, with moss meaning marsh; muir duck and stock duck, from the Old Norsk stokkond, stokk with the suffix –ond meaning duck.

The derivation of the formal English name Mallard is from the 14th century Middle English malarde deriving from the Old French malart or mallart for wild drake. Mallard also has the same root as male. For several centuries Mallard referred only to the male, with the female being called simply Wild Duck. Several phrases come from this bird, e.g. dead duck (as it was killed in large numbers for food), the phrase 'good weather for ducks' meaning wet weather and a duck in cricket, a 0 score said to be from the shape of the duck's egg.

The scientific name for the Mallard is *Anas platyrhynchos*, with *Anas* meaning duck, platus for broad and rhunkhos beak. In Muslim countries Anas is a boy's name indicating pleasantness, companionship and friendliness.

16 - Pintail

Local names for the **Pintail** include cracker, from its alarm call; harian, meaning an attractive child; lady bird; pheasant duck; sea pheasant; sprig tail and thin neck. From population estimates the Pintail is probably the world's most numerous duck.

The pin in Pintail meant a pointed peg, from the 2 elongated middle tail feathers. The bird breeds in Iceland, Fennoscania and across to Russia.

The scientific name for the Pintail is *Anas acuta*, with *acuta* from the Latin acutus, sharp-pointed tail.

The word **Teal** is a name which is not used in any other context. The name of the colour teal comes from the bright green speculum on the wing of the Teal. The name is onomatopoeic from the Old English tel, representing the chuckling sound of a feeding bird. In Old English the male was named tela and female tele. The Teal is Britain's smallest duck.

The scientific name for the **Teal** is *Anas crecca*, with *crecca* deriving from the Swedish name for the Teal, kricka.

The **Pochard** breeds in small numbers in Britain but these are supplemented in winter by continental birds. In winter often only males are seen as the females leave the males and migrate further south. This is not uncommon as the males return to their breeding grounds earlier to secure their nest territory before the females arrive back. Local names include blue poker; poker and red-headed poker, with poker coming from its feeding habit. Other names include bull headed wigeon, from the distinctive shape of its head; dun bird, possibly from the female's duller colour; fresh water wigeon; gold head; red-headed curre; red-headed wigeon; snuff head and well plum.

The Pochard's formal name comes from the French pocher meaning to poke - whilst feeding. The bird only began to colonise the UK in the 19th century.

The Pochard's scientific name is *Aythya farina* from the Greek aithuia simply a seabird described by Aristotle and ferinus meaning wild game.

The black and white coloration of the **Tufted Duck** gives rise to a range of interesting local names, like black curre, with curre being a generic word for a diving duck; black poker; black topping duck; black wigeon; blue billed curre and blue neb, from its beak colour; crested diver, from the distinctive crest (larger on the male in breeding plumage); golden-eye duck; magpie duck and white-sided duck. As a diving duck (as opposed to a dabbling duck) it prefers deeper water; the bird can dive to a depth of 2m. The Tufted Duck is comparatively recent arrival to Britain, first recorded as breeding in 1849.

The Tufted Duck's scientific name is *Aythya fuligula* with *Aythya* being the Greek for a seabird described by Aristotle and *fuligula* from the Latin fuligo for soot and gula for throat.

The **Scaup** is a sea duck most often observed in winter bobbing up and down on the open sea. The bird's local names reflect its habitat, though some names connect it to other ducks, for example black-headed wigeon, frosty-backed wigeon; silver pochard and spoonbill duck. These are in addition to blue neb, with neb an old word for beak; covie; dun bird; golden-eyed diver; green-headed diver; holland duck and norway duck. Mussel duck refers to its food.

The Scaup's formal English name is linked to the duck's mussel food, with skalpa word for mussel bed.

The Scaup's scientific name is *Aythya marila* which comes from the Greek aithuia for a seabird described by Aristotle and the Greek marile for charcoal embers. Marila is an English girl's name meaning bitter.

The **Eider** has been famous for its down for many centuries.

In the 7th century the hermit St. Cuthbert gave protection to the birds on Farne Island, hence the local names for the bird of cuddy's duck, St. Cuthbert's duck and cudberduce. St. Cuthbert hand reared the birds and they attached themselves to him as their protector. This is a very early record of imprinting, where young birds form a bond with humans as though they were their parents. Other local names include colk; crattick; dunter; duskey duck and great black and white duck, an ample description. The bird's nest is lined with eiderdown made from feathers plucked from the female's breast. These feathers are harvested (after the young have fledged) for pillows and quilts. It takes the feathers from 60 nests to make a kilo of down. Duvet is the French for Eider. The Inuit use Eider feathers for clothing.

The female reduces her heart beat whilst brooding to reduce the chance of detection by predators, a particular risk to ground nesting birds. Eider can eat whole mussels, crushing the shells in their stomach and excreting the ground shells. Using their wings to help them swim underwater, Eider have been known to dive down to over 20 m searching for mussels. The Eider also holds a British record, being the fastest bird in constant level flight, having been timed at 75 km / hr. The Eider is the commonest sea-duck in the world and the largest in the northern hemisphere. The first written record of an English name for the Eider dates from about 650 AD.

The vernacular name Eider comes from the Icelandic aeour, meaning down duck.

The bird's scientific name is *Somateria mollissima* with *Soma* meaning body and erion wool plus *mollis* for soft i.e. very soft woolly body.

Local names for the **Common Scoter** refer to its habit of diving, like divedop and doucker, a name used for a range of birds such as the Little Grebe, Dipper, Goldeneye, Great Northern Diver and the Tufted Duck. Other local names include black diver; sea hen; surf duck and whilk.

The Common in Common Scoter means having no particular distinguishing features, rather than being numerous. Scoter comes from soot, i.e. black as soot, referring to the bird's dark colour. An alternative source is the Old English sceotan, meaning to move rapidly (leading to the modern word scoot). The bird was declared fish, rather than fowl and so could be eaten during Lent. Unlike other diving ducks the Common Scoter opens its wings whilst diving.

The Common Scoter's scientific name is *Melanitta nigra* which comes from the Greek melas for black and netta, a duck plus the Latin niger for shining black.

The **Long-tailed Duck** is seen around our shores in winter after breeding on the Arctic coasts of North America, Europe and Russia. The bird has acquired a number of descriptive local names such as calloo and col candle wick, from its call; coal and candlelight, alluding to the male's black and white colouring; hound duck; mealy bird and old squaw, from its call; sea pheasant, also a name for the Pintail; sharp tailed duck and swallow tailed sheldrake, referring to the male's long, thin tail, with sheld meaning variegated. The duck is the deepest diving sea duck, reaching depths of 60 m, staying down for more than a minute. Very unusually this duck moults three times a year.

The Long-tailed Duck is in a genus all of its own – Clangula which means to resound, from the male's yodelling call. Its full name is *Clangula hyemalis* with *hyemalis* meaning wintry.

The **Goldeneye** is a distinctive winter migrant duck. Local names include freshwater wigeon; golden eyed garrot, from its distinctive eye; gowdy duck; grey headed duck; mussel cracker, except the duck is vegetarian; popping wigeon; rattlewings, from the sound of its rapidly beating wings; whiteside and whistler. Other local names refer to its habit of diving like divedop and doucker, names used for other birds that dive.

The male Goldeneye's courtship display involves throwing its head back, kicking its legs up and emitting a loud double whistle. The duck is unusual as it nests in tree holes. The duck is also the target of partial brood parasitism, with other Goldeneyes, other ducks and even reports of Swallows laying their eggs in the Goldeneye's nest. The precocial young leave the tree nest very soon after hatching, making the leap from far up a tree trunk to a soft landing, before joining its siblings and mother as a group to start feeding. The Goldeneye has only recently colonised Britain, helped by a tree nest box programme in Scotland. Historically, in Sweden nest boxes were installed in trees so eggs could be collected for human consumption.

The Goldeneye is seen on estuaries in England during winter and has a distinctively shaped head, reflected in the scientific name *Bucephala clangula*. The first name derives from the Latin for bull and head (which seems about right!) and *clangula* from its loud double whistle.

The next three species comprise the small group of saw-tooths, well-named as the edge of their mandibles are serrated to help them retain their prey.

Local names for the **Smew** include magpie diver, white headed goosander and white nun, all from the male's black and white colouration; small herring bar; smew merganser; vare wigeon and an unusual name - weasel coot or in North Devon vare wigeon, with vare meaning weasel and weasel duck in Norfolk, with weasel referring to the female's white throat and contrasting brown head and nape.

The word Smew possibly derives from small, being the smallest saw-tooth. The bird nests in tree holes, sometimes using an old Woodpecker's nest.

The Smew's scientific name is *Mergellus albellus* with *Mergellus* meaning little water bird and *albellus* white, referring specifically to the male's high contrast black and white summer plumage.

Local names for the **Goosander** include dun diver; fish duck; green headed goosander; horner, from its call sounding like a horn; jacksaw; land cormorant, correctly inferring that the bird is commonly seen inland; saw-neb; sawyer; spear wigeon and sparkling fowl. Raising a young Goosander requires about 30 kg of fish and Goosander are culled under licence to keep numbers down. The effectiveness of this is questionable. The males (who are not involved in rearing their young) fly 2000 km to northern Norway to a communal moulting site where they undertake a catastrophic moult i.e. shed all their feathers at once. After moulting they re-join the females.

The formal name Goosander links the species to the geese, being in the same Anatidae family. Numbers of this species have increased by 49% over 25 years to 2017.

The Goosander's scientific named are two almost identical words - *Mergus merganser* with *Mergus* meaning a waterbird plus the ending anser (meaning goose).

The **Red-breasted Merganser**'s local names include earl duck; grey diver; harle and land harlan, from its harsh call; herald; lesser toothed diver; popping wigeon; sandbill; sawbill wigeon and spear wigeon.

The Red-breasted Merganser's vernacular name is from the Latin mergus meaning waterfowl diver and anser goose. After breeding males, like the Goosander, fly off to a communal roost and undertake a catastrophic moult (this time in Scotland). In winter UK birds are joined by migrants from Iceland and Scandinavia. The Red-breasted Merganser tends to remain on the coast for winter whilst its cousin the Goosander forms roosts on inland reservoirs and lakes, feeding on streams and rivers.

The Red-breasted Merganser's scientific name is *Mergus serrator* which describes the bird well with *serrator* meaning saw.

The **Ruddy Duck**'s scientific name is *Oxyura jamaicensis* with *Oxyura* coming from the Greek for sharp-tailed, being a member of the so-called stiff-tails and Jamaica, referring to Jamaica Bay in North America where it was observed breeding.

Grouse, quails, pheasants and partridge

Order - Galliformes

This order comprises turkeys, grouse, chickens, partridges, quails and pheasants. The name galli- means rooster. These are mainly terrestrial game birds with a stocky body, small head, short rounded wings, stiff, slightly bowed primaries, short, stout, down curved beaks and large, strong legs. Most Galliformes are weak-flying birds. They have large clutches of 10 or more eggs. Galliformes are polygynous or polygamous and are sexually dimorphic. Males are territorial. Young are precocial and sedentary.

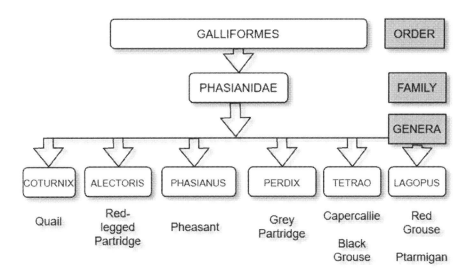

Game birds

The order contains one family – Phasianidae.

Main characteristics of the Phasianidae family:

The Phasianidae family consists of the grouse, quails, pheasants and partridge. Phasis is a river in the geographical region some of the birds came from e.g. the Pheasant. Phasianids are blunt-winged, terrestrial, ground living species. Generally they are sexually dimorphic in size, with males larger than females. They are often plump, with broad, relatively short wings and strong legs, with one or more spurs on the tarsus used for fighting. Toes are short with blunt claws and the hallux is raised. The beak is short and generally strong. Males of the larger species often have brightly coloured plumage as well as facial ornamentations such as wattles or crests. Some species are noted for their elaborate courtship displays in which males strut about, displaying their colourful plumage.

The eight species in this family are in six genera:

Coturnix - Quail
Alectoris - Red-legged Partridge
Phasianus – Pheasant
Perdix - Grey Partridge
Tetrao - Black Grouse; Capercaillie
Lagopus – Ptarmigan; Red Grouse

In Britain the **Quail** is heard more often than seen as it skulks, calling in long grass. The Quail's local names refer to its wet-me-lip call which is similar to the Corncrake (but is no relation). Other names include bobwhite; but-for-but; deadchick; fey fool; quick-me-dick and throsher. The bird was killed in large numbers, luring them using pipes replicating the bird's call. The Quail has a very short breeding cycle and young birds can breed aged only 12 weeks. This enables the bird to breed during its migratory journey, with the young continuing the journey, in a similar manner of some butterflies. In folklore the bird represents lasciviousness and resurrection.

> The Quail has been known since biblical times when the Israelites were twice given them as food whilst in the desert after fleeing from Egypt (see Exodus 16:13). The bird in fact does migrate through Israel in huge flocks. The children of Israel gathered Quail for 2 days "and the quails covered the camp". One estimate is that they ate 9 million Quail! A carved picture in an Egyptian tomb, dating from about 1350 BC, depicts trappers catching Quail in nets. Pliny wrote that migrating Quail alighted on boats (which they do) causing them to capsize (very unlikely). Chaucer wrote in *the clerkes tale* "and thou shalt make him couche as doth a quail" – make him cower like a quail, referring to the way the bird hides in its meadow environment.

The formal English name Quail is onomatopoeic. The verb to quail, meaning to feel fear or be apprehensive, is not connected with this bird which is feisty and was used as a fighting bird.

The Quail's scientific name is another repetitive name, *Coturnix coturnix* which comes from Latin *Coturnix* for quail.

The **Red-legged Partridge** was introduced from France in the 17th century. Not surprisingly local names for this bird include french partridge and frenchman. Other local names include green partridge and nut-brown bird. It is less favoured as a game bird as the bird tends to run rather than fly and its meat is less tasty. It is assumed the partridge referred to in the pear tree of the famous song *The twelve days of Christmas* is this bird. Whilst the bird does perch in trees this species is less abundant than its relation the Grey Partridge.

The name partridge derives from the Latin perdix through the French pertris to the Middle English partrich.

The Red-legged Partridge's scientific name is *Alectoris rufa* which comes from Greek alektoris for domestic hen and rufus, ruddy.

Local names for the **Pheasant** include comet, from the poacher's word for a bird with a long tail. The Long-tailed Duck is similarly called the sea pheasant and the Pintail pheasant duck. Another name was cock-up!

The name Pheasant derives from the Greek phasianos (as does the scientific name) based on the river Phasis, in modern day Western Georgia, which flows into the Black Sea, an area where the bird originated. The bird was introduced to Greece in the 4th century BC and spread to the Roman empire.

The bird was introduced into Britain by the Normans in the 11th century and possibly earlier by the Romans. The bird was killed for banquets but was rarer than the Partridge and Quail. In folklore the bird represents (not unsurprisingly) beauty and luxury as well as mother love.

The Pheasant's scientific name is *Phasianus colchicus* with *Phasi* referring to the river Phasis and Colchis a city in Georgia.

The **Grey Partridge** is a bird of open farmland whose numbers have declined by 92% over the last 50 years (to 2017) largely due to the use of herbicides that destroy the weeds the adult bird feeds on and pesticides that kill the insects the young feed on. It is also bred for sport and is easy to shoot as it flies only a short distance when disturbed and keeps to a restricted area. Local names include brown partridge; girigrick; patrig; pertriche and stumpey. Jug is a name for a group of birds roosting in a collective huddle with their heads turned out, to keeping a look-out for predators (as birds can even when sleeping). The bird also uses the broken wing display to distract predators from their nest.

> The partridge appears in Aesop's fable *The partridge and the fowler*. A fowler caught a partridge and was about to kill him. The partridge pleaded for him to spare his life, saying: "Pray, master, permit me to live and I will entice many partridges to you in recompense for your mercy to me". The fowler replied: "I shall now with the less scruple take your life, because you are willing to save it at the cost of betraying your friends and relations;" so he twisted his neck and put him in his bag with his other game. The moral of the story: 'Those who would sacrifice their friends to save themselves from harm are not entitled to mercy'.

The Grey Partridge's scientific name, *Perdix perdix,* derives from a Greek mythological tale with the Greek perdesthai meaning a maker of explosive noises. In Greek mythology Perdix was a sister of Daedalus, whose son was turned into a partridge when his uncle tried to kill him by pushing him off the top of a tower. He flew to safety but avoided heights and re-told his story in a hoarse voice. In fact the bird does not fly high or far, which makes it appealing for shooting sport.

The word grouse in **Black Grouse** means to grumble or complain. Why the Black Grouse acquired this name is unclear. The bird is associated with the 16th century word moorhen from its habitat (not the modern Moorhen species). Local names include birch hen (f); black cock (m); grigear (f); heath fowl and ruffed grouse.

The bird's tail feathers have been popular adornments in hats worn with Highland dress, most commonly associated with Glengarry and Balmoral or

Tam O'Shanter caps. They still continue to be worn by pipers of civilian and military pipe bands. Since 1904 all ranks of the Royal Scot's and King's Own Scottish Borderers have worn them in their full-dress headgear.

Black Grouse gather in leks during autumn, when no females are present, possibly to establish territory displaying their fine feathers and uttering a distinctive, grunting mating call. In Western Europe these gatherings seldom involve more than 40 birds; in Russia 150 is not uncommon and 200 have been recorded. As is common for species that compete for the right to mate the male (1 200 g) is considerably larger than the female (930 g). The bird was commonly killed for food and Gilbert White reported that the bird became extinct in Hampshire during his lifetime (1720 – 1793).

The scientific name for the Black Grouse has its roots in the records made by Aristotle who mentioned a ground bird, giving it the name tetrix. The scientific name is *Tetrao tetrix* which repeats gamebird and ground bird. Not very descriptive!

The **Capercaillie** is a large bird from the Scottish highlands that emits a loud sound to attract females. It is so loud the bird's ears have a reflex stopping action to prevent the bird going deaf from its own song! Local names include cock of the wood; giant grouse; great grouse and wood grouse. The Capercaillie was killed as game and became extinct late in the 18th century. The present population derives from birds introduced in the 19th century.

Capercaillie derives from the Gaelic words capull and coille, literally horse of the woods. Their nuptial song is likened to the sound of horses' hooves on cobbles. The Capercaillie is the world's largest grouse. The species demonstrates extreme sexual dimorphism, with the male weighing 4 300 g to the female's 2 000 g.

The Capercaillie's scientific name is *Tetrao urogallus* which comes from the Greek tetraon, being a type of gamebird and the German auerhuhn meaning mountain cock plus the Latin gallus, cock.

The **Ptarmigan**'s local names mainly refer to its snowy environment, such as snow chick; snow grouse; white grouse and white partridge as well as rock grouse and cairn bird, referring to its habitat.

The Ptarmigan's name comes from the Gaelic tarmachan meaning croaker i.e. the name is onomatopoeic. The original name was tarmigan and a silent initial P was added to the name in 1684 by Robert Sibbald to make a Greek-like word, Ptarmigan. The Ptarmigan is unique in being the only bird to have four seasonal plumages. Tennyson wrote "The Ptarmigan that whitens 'ere its hour; Woos his own end", with the poet being aware of the value of the bird's camouflage in its wintery, snowy setting. The male is 25% heavier than the 400 g female. The bird has feathered feet and toes resembling a hare. This affords its feet protection from the cold as it lives at high altitude all year round and seldom comes below 600 m. Unusually the bird has feathers on its eye lids to protect against the cold.

The Ptarmigan's scientific name is *Lagopus muta* with *Lagopus* deriving from *lago* for hare and *pus* for foot, referring to its feathered feet. *Muta* means silent but the bird croaks so it is not as silent as the name indicates. *Muta* also contradicts the formal English name as this derives from the Gaelic for croaker.

The **Red Grouse's** local names include gor cock, from its call; heath cock; moor fowl; moor poot and red ptarmigan. Young are called cheeper.

In North America the bird is called Willow Ptarmigan and the Red Grouse is a sub-species. Gamekeepers were highly vigilant at preserving stocks of the bird and shot any birds that might kill their precious game birds. A few still do, although it is illegal. Regrettably, the practice of killing wild birds of prey to protect game birds is still prevalent in some areas. The sport became popular in the 19th century as a result of the expansion of the railways and the development of the breach loading shotgun. In 1910 there were over 3 000 shoots in Scotland killing 1.5 m birds. For more detail refer to Chapter 6 and the Section on Human exploitation.

The Red Grouse also has a similar scientific name to the Ptarmigan - *Lagopus lagopus scoticus* – hare foot plus the sub-species name for this Scottish bird. The nominate species is the North American Willow Ptarmigan.

Grebes

Order - Podicipediformes

Grebes are small to medium sized aquatic birds, with large, lobed toes, making them excellent swimmers and divers. Podiceps is a combination of the Latin podex for anus and pes for foot. This refers to the fact that their legs are placed far back on the body, making walking difficult. The tail is a tuft of down feathers. Their diet ranges from fish to freshwater insects and crustaceans. Most have ornate and distinctive breeding plumages and perform elaborate display rituals. Grebes make floating nests of plant material concealed among reeds on the surface of the water. The young are precocial.

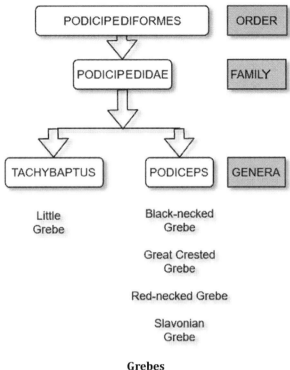

Grebes

There is only one family in this order - **Podicipedidae**.

Main characteristics of the Podicipedidae family:

The family of grebes is a widely distributed family of freshwater diving birds, some moving to the sea when migrating and in winter. Grebes are small to medium-large in size and are excellent swimmers and divers. Their toes are large, with broad lobes and small webs connecting the front three toes. The hind toe also has a small lobe, which works like a hydrofoil blade. Their feet are located to the rear of the body making them clumsy on land. Grebes have narrow wings. They respond to danger by diving rather than flying. Beaks vary from short and thick to long and pointed. Their diet ranges from fish to freshwater insects and crustaceans. Grebe plumage is dense and waterproof. Unusually the underside feathers grow at right-angles to the skin, curling at the tip. By pressing their feathers against their body, grebes can adjust their buoyancy, often swimming low in the water. In the non-breeding season, grebes are plain-coloured dark browns and white. Most have ornate, distinctive breeding plumages and perform elaborate display rituals. Grebes exhibit no sexual dimorphism in plumage. The young are often striped and retain some of their juvenile plumage even after reaching full size. When preening, grebes eat their own feathers and feed them to their young, possibly to assist with pellet formation and reduce vulnerability to gastric parasites. Grebes make floating nests of plant material. The young are precocial and able to swim from birth.

The five species in this family are in two genera:

Tachybaptus - Little Grebe
Podiceps - Black-necked Grebe; Great Crested Grebe; Red-necked Grebe; Slavonian Grebe

The **Little Grebe** is Britain's smallest grebe and is found on reed fringed pools and lakes. It readily dives to feed and to escape any perceived danger. Local names refer to its habit of diving like divedop and doucker, a name used for a diverse range of birds such as the Common Scoter, Dipper, Goldeneye, Great Northern Diver and Tufted Duck. A rather eclectic mixture, except they are all water birds. The common name dabchick is still used by bird watchers. Dabchick derives from the Middle English dobchick, with doppe being a diving bird.

The word Grebe derives from the French, griaibe and grèbe.

The only British Grebe not in the genus Podiceps is the Little Grebe, whose scientific name is *Tachybaptus ruficollis*, with *Tachybaptus* coming from the Greek takhos meaning fast or quick and bapto to sink (as in baptism) reflecting how quickly the bird dives at the least disturbance. *Ruficollis* is from the Latin rufus reddish and collus neck. Again, a simple, clear description of the nature of this bird.

17 - Black-necked Grebe

The **Black-necked Grebe** is a globally widespread bird, found on every continent except Australasia and Antarctica. Oddly it is an inefficient flier,

209

being almost flightless for 9 months of the year before contradictorily making a 6 000 km migratory journey.

Its scientific name is *Podiceps nigricollis* with *Podiceps* from the Latin podex for anus and pes for foot plus *nigricollis* coming from the Latin niger for black and *collis* for neck. The UK conservation status of this species is amber but is of least concern in Europe.

Local names for the **Great Crested Grebe** include ash coloured loon, with a reference to its similarity in the water to the divers; carr goose, with carr meaning marsh; hell diver, from its speed and agility under water; greater dabchick, correctly placing the bird in the same family as the Little Grebe; muffler, from its tuft of feathers (muffle) and rolling pin, reflects the birds habit of rolling on its side to preen its under feathers and water witch. The bird has dense feathers, with over 20 000 feathers on its body, compared to 7 000 on a Golden Eagle. It was the attraction of its feathers which nearly drove the bird to extinction in the 19th century. For more detail refer to Chapter 6 and the Section on Human exploitation.

The Great Crested Grebe has the scientific name *Podiceps cristatus* with *cristatus* meaning simply crest.

A local, Sussex name for the **Red-necked Grebe** is rolling pin, also a name for the Great Crested Grebe.

The Red-necked Grebe's scientific name is *Podiceps grisegena* with *grisegena* oddly meaning grey cheeks rather than referring to the more distinctive red neck.

The **Slavonian Grebe**'s local names include devil-diver, possibly because of its bright red eyes; hell-diver; pink-eyed diver and water-witch. Other names include dusky grebe; horned grebe and magpie diver. The bird is a rare breeder in Scotland with numbers supplemented in winter with birds from Scandinavia.

Slavonian predictably comes from the country with that name.

Its scientific name is *Podiceps auritus* with *auritus* meaning ear, referring to the prominent head feathers (except they are not ear feathers) which are highly prominent in breeding plumage.

Pigeons and doves

Order - Columbiformes

This order contains the pigeons and doves. Columba is the Latin for dove. They are plump land birds with small heads and short, scaly legs and short toes, short beaks with a down-curved culmen and a fleshy cere. All have a large crop and most have a muscular gizzard for digesting their seed food. Food consists primarily of fruits, seeds and grain. The birds have broad, rounded, powerful wings, combined with large wing muscles. The sexes are often very similar. The birds often perform an elaborate courtship display. Most species flock and many breed in colonies. The young are altricial. These species are monogamous.

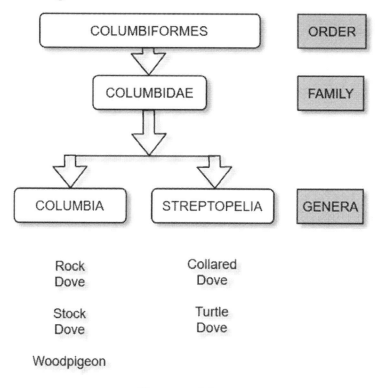

Pigeons and doves

There is only one family in this order:

Columbidae.

Main characteristics of the Columbidae family:

Pigeons and doves constitute the family Columbidae. *Columba* is associated with the Romans, who bred the birds in dovecotes called columbariums. The names dove and pigeon are interchangeable; pigeon derives from French and dove from Anglo-Saxon. Pigeons are distributed across the globe (except for the driest areas and the polar regions). Pigeons feed on seeds, fruit and plants. Both sexes have a large crop, which becomes glandular in the breeding season and secretes a milky fluid (pigeon's milk) that aids the digestion of food for the young. Some pigeons remain sexually active all year and potentially can breed at any time. Pigeons build flimsy nests from sticks and debris, placed in trees, on ledges or on the ground. They lay one or two eggs and both parents care for the young.

The five species in this family are in two genera:

Columba – Rock Dove; Stock Dove; Woodpigeon
Streptopelia - Collared Dove; Turtle Dove

The word pigeon derives from the Latin pipire, to chirp through the Old French pijon to the English pigeon. The first written record of an English name for Woodpigeon dates from c.685 AD. The earliest evidence of pigeons appears in a Sumerian temple drawing dating back to 4 000 BC. The bird was associated with their goddess of fertility. The word also means someone who is easily cheated linked to the phrase stool pigeon, coming from the use of the Woodpigeon as a decoy in falconry. The word dove possibly derives from the Old English word dufan, meaning to dive, as in its courtship display.

The famous but now extinct species, the Dodo, was a flightless member of this family, endemic to Mauritius. The bird was hunted to extinction in the 17th century not least because it was easy to catch. The Portuguese name for the bird, doido, means stupid.

The **Rock Dove** was for a long time confused with the Stock Dove, with a clear distinction made in the 19th century. Local names include blue dove; cliff pigeon; rock doo; sea pigeon; sod and white-backed dove.

The Rock Dove is named after its habitat of rocks and cliffs. The word dove was associated with death and the preferred name for this bird was culver, from the Latin columba. The menu for Richard III's Christmas dinner in 1387 included 1 200 pigeons (along with 16 oxen and 120 sheep). Its droppings were used as fertiliser, in the leather tanning process and as a source of potassium nitrate for gunpowder. The Rock Dove appears in the crest of the Tactical Communication Wing of the Royal Air Force.

The Rock Dove's scientific name is *Columba livia* with *livia* shortened from the female name Olivia which means life. Possibly the name is connected to the olive branch which signified to Noah the return of life on earth after the biblical flood.

The **Stock Dove** has many local names including blue pouter, from the way the bird can pout by inflating its crop; burrow pigeon, from its habit of nesting in old rabbit burrows; craig doo; hill pigeon; hole dove and wood culver associating the bird with woods rather than as a domestic bird.

The vernacular name Stock Dove arises from the bird's choice of a nest in the hole of a tree trunk.

Columba oenas is the scientific name for the Stock Dove and *oenas* comes from the Greek oinas for a pigeon.

The **Woodpigeon**'s local names include clatter dove, referring to the noise of their wings as they take off and dove is inter-changeable with pigeon; cow prise; cushat, deriving from cuscote, alluding to the bird's rapid flight; cushy-do; dow; queese and quisty, from its voice associated with the Latin questus meaning lament; ring dove, from the white feathers on the adult's neck; timmer doo, with doo meaning dove; wood culver, a 12th century name for a woodland bird and wood pig. The young birds are called squabs, which is a culinary term for the meat of young birds.

The Woodpigeon is seen in many locations not just woods and is a common bird unloved by farmers, as it has a voracious appetite for seeds. Licences are still issued by Natural England to shoot this bird, which is seen as a pest for eating crops. For many centuries the bird has been caught for food. The breast muscle accounts for 40% of the bird's weight, hence the common use of pigeon breasts in cooking.

The Woodpigeon is one of the few British birds that potentially can breed throughout the year. The male and female are both capable of mating at any time of the year. In almost all other birds both the male's and female's sex organs (the gonads) shrink to save weight, meaning they cannot reproduce until the next breeding season. One reason is that unlike most birds, both sexes produce crop milk to feed to their young, produced in lining of the crop, so the young can gain nutrition from seeds. Seeds fed directly to hatchlings are indigestible, which is why many other species change their diet in spring from seeds to insects e.g. the tit and finch families. Unusually pigeons are able to suck up water when drinking as opposed to most other birds who have to fill their mouths and then tip their heads up to take in water.

The Woodpigeon's scientific name is *Columba palumbus* with *palumbus* the Latin for woodpigeon.

The **Collared Dove** was virtually unknown in Britain up to the 1950's and since then it has spread across the country and increased in numbers. The first record of breeding in the UK is 1955. The bird spread at an average of 50 km a year across the continent. Numbers increased by over 300% in the 45 years to 2017 but there has been a decrease of 21% in the last 10 years. At the same time the numbers of its near relative, the Turtle Dove, have declined dramatically. The same rapid spread of the Collared Dove has occurred in America as well, with the bird being found in most states of the country now.

The Collared Dove's scientific name is *Streptopelia decaocto*. Streptos is collar and peleia is dove which accords with the bird's appearance. The second word comes from Greek mythology with *deca* meaning ten and *octo* eight which refers to a folk story. In this story Decaocto was an overworked, underpaid servant girl. The gods heard her prayers for help and changed her into a dove so she could escape her misery. The dove's call still echoes the mournful cries of her former life.

Local names of the **Turtle Dove** include blue pigeon; culver summer dove, with culver deriving from the Latin columba; little dove and turtur from its song, with the French word for this bird being tourterelle. The Black Guillemot also has a local name of turtur from the sound the pair make, similar to the Turtle Dove.

The name of the Turtle Dove is onomatopoeic from its soft turr-turr song, so redolent of bygone summer's days. The number of Turtle Doves in Britain has dropped dramatically, by 98%, over the past 50 years to 2017, with numbers dropping on the continent as well. It is red listed in the UK and classified in Europe (using the IUCN classification) as vulnerable. Possible reasons include changes in agricultural practice where there are fewer weed seeds, especially fumitory, for the birds to feed on. It is the only migratory dove (or pigeon – the same Columbidae family) in Europe and might be suffering from loss of habitat in its winter African resting grounds of Senegal and Sahel. The bird is still shot (illegally) on its migratory journey, reducing numbers still further. In Africa the bird gathers in huge roosts of up to 1 m birds. The bird is very tolerant of high temperatures, having been seen foraging in 45^0 heat.

For millennia the dove has been one of the most frequently mentioned birds in many cultures. The Turtle Dove is often mentioned specifically but references might be to other doves and pigeons. The bird has been used figuratively as a symbol of peace and life and many artists and writers have used this symbolism. In Christianity the dove is a symbol of the Holy Spirit, with the Matthew writing "And when Jesus was baptised ... He saw the Spirit of God descending like a dove...". A dove was also sent out of the ark twice by Noah "At the end of the 40 days Noah ... sent forth a dove but the dove found no resting place " then later "... the dove came back to him in the evening and lo, in her mouth a freshly picked olive leaf". The Turtle Dove was chosen by Abraham for a burnt offering and later the Jews were told "But if he cannot afford a lamb, then he shall bring ... two turtledoves, one for a sin offering and one for a burnt offering". In the Song of Solomon the writer clearly was an astute observer of birds, stating the Turtle Dove was the sound of the promise of spring "For lo, the winter is past, and the rain is over --- the time for the singing of birds is come, and the voice of the turtle is heard in our land". Jesus' commandment to his disciples in Matthew's gospel was "Behold I send you out ... so be ... innocent as doves".

In Islam, doves are respected and favoured because they are believed to have assisted the prophet of Islam, Muhammad, in distracting his enemies outside the cave of Thaw'r in the great Hijra. From the

Russian culture, Turgenev wrote in one of his short stories, *Bezhin Lea*, that a dove took the soul of a good person up to heaven. The symbolism of the dove has been used by organisations such as the World Peace Congress, to represent peace. Picasso's picture La Colombe was chosen as the emblem for the 1949 World Peace Congress.

In one Greek myth Venus ordered her carriage to be prepared. Four white doves emerged and they were yoked to her carriage. They took their mistress and flew upwards. Sparrows escorted the carriage of the goddess. The clouds parted and Caelus admitted his daughter to heaven where there is no fear of eagles or hawks. Aphrodite was the great Olympian goddess of joy, beauty and love. Her sacred animals included the dove and sparrow. Doves are associated with the birth of Venus. An egg was said to have fallen into the Euphrates River. Doves incubated the egg and it hatched out into Venus, the Syrian goddess. Because of this the Syrians do not eat doves, considering them as gods.

The Dove is a symbol of enduring love and fidelity, which fully reflects the bird's behaviour. Pliny (79 AD) wrote "their chastity is extreme, and adultery is unknown amongst them; although they live together with others, they do not break their marriage bond". Chaucer in 1380 wrote about their fidelity in *the Parliament of Fowls* "the wedded turtle-dove, with her faithful heart". Shakespeare wrote in *Henry VI* "Like a pair of loving turtle doves; that could not live asunder day or night" and in *A Winter's Tale* "Your hand, my Perdita, so turtles pair; That never mean to part". Two Turtle Doves appear in the song *Twelve days of Christmas*. Mendelssohn wrote about the Turtle Dove in his anthem *Oh for the wings of a Dove* which became famous through a recording made by Ernest Lough in 1927. The words come from Psalm 55 "O for the wings, for the wings of a dove! Far away, far away would I rove! In the wilderness build me a nest, and remain there for ever at rest". In modern times Tom Paxton wrote a song *My lady is a wild flying dove* and Buddy Holly also referred to them in *That'll be the day* – "giving him all her lovin' and all her turtle dovin'". Such strong imagery from one bird!

Streptopelia turtur is the scientific name for the Turtle Dove which comes from the Greek streptos for collar and peleia a dove, plus the Latin *turtur* for the Turtle Dove.

Cuckoos

Order - Cuculiformes

This order includes one British species, the Cuckoo.

Main characteristics of the Cuculidae family:

The cuckoos are a family of near passerine birds. Many cuckoos are arboreal. Temperate species are migratory. Many species in the family are brood parasites, laying their eggs in the nests of other species, with some being obligate brood parasites (i.e. always lay their eggs in the nests of another species). There is little sexual dimorphism in size. Their feet are zygodactyl. Cuckoos have long tails, short legs and long, narrow wings. Cuckoos are specialist eaters often consuming noxious, hairy caterpillars. Prior to swallowing such a caterpillar they rub off the sharp hairs with special bony plates in the back of the mouth. They shed their stomach lining regularly as their food is so abrasive.

Parasitic cuckoos are grouped into gentes, with each gens specialising in laying its eggs in a particular host's nest and usually imitating the colour of the host's own eggs. There is some evidence that the gentes are genetically different from one another.

18 - Cuckoo

The **Cuckoo** is an iconic and well-known bird not least because it is the only British bird that is wholly a brood parasite. Other British birds are partial brood parasites such as the Swallow and Moorhen.

Several spring plants are associated with the Cuckoo, such as Lady's smock which is called the cuckoo flower and Ragged robin flos-cuculi i.e. the cuckoo flower. Cuckoo spit is the froth that holds the froghopper bug. The plant Cuckoo pint derives its name from pint meaning penis. As it was not clear how the female Cuckoo mated the tale was that the phallic shaped flower of the Cuckoo pint served a reproductive purpose.

Local names for the Cuckoo include geck; gowk, which is used to mean a simpleton; hobby, from its flight silhouette resembling the bird of prey and welsh ambassador. The term cuckold for a man with an unfaithful wife derives from the female Cuckoo's behaviour of getting another bird to raise its young whilst the Cuckoo romped with the parasite's wife. Shakespeare referred to this in *Love's Labour's Lost* "The cuckoo then in every tree, Mocks married men; for thus sings he 'cuckoo, cuckoo' O, word of fear, unpleasing to the married ear". The first English record of the name Cuckoo is from 650 AD.

The Cuckoo's name is clearly onomatopoeic but only that of the male's song. The female emits a soft, bubbling sound. Research (in Hungary) has shown that male Cuckoos recognise the unfamiliar calls of intruders to their territory, differentiating them from familiar neighbours. The males reacted aggressively towards intruders whilst tolerating known neighbours. The full story of the Cuckoo's breeding strategy appears in the Section on Nesting in Chapter 4 - Mates, Mating and Breeding. Gilbert White (of Selborne fame) wrote that the Cuckoo's lifestyle was "a monstrous outrage on maternal affection". This calls into question the idea of anthropomorphism. The Cuckoo has developed a breeding strategy that works well for them, evidenced by their survival. Their behaviour is amoral and develops on a 'what works best' basis not because the bird has any sense of right and wrong.

> W H Auden wrote about the bird in *Short ode to the cuckoo* - "Compared to the arias by great performers such as the merle, your two-note act is kid-stuff, our most hardened crooks are sincerely shocked by your nesting habits. Science, Aesthetics, Ethics, may huff and puff but they cannot extinguish your magic: you marvel the commuter as you wondered the savage. Hence in my diary where I enter nothing but social engagements and, lately, the death of friends, I scribble year after year when I first hear you, of a holy moment". Delius also composed a piece about the Cuckoo's arrival and song in *On hearing the first Cuckoo in spring*. The bird also appears in Beethoven's 6th symphony, the Pastoral.
>
> The poem "In April he will come; in May he songs all day; in June he changes his tune; in July he prepares to fly; in August he must go" is quite accurate. In fact the males migrate earlier than August but he does change his tune during the season. Wordsworth wrote a poem *To the cuckoo*, saying "O blithe newcomer! I have heard, I hear thee and rejoice, O cuckoo! Shall I call thee bird, or but a wandering voice?". Certainly the male bird does wander round, often pestered by other birds who might be used as a host. Shakespeare notices that "So, when he had occasion to be seen, he was but as the cuckoo in June, heard, not regarded".

Given how well known the Cuckoo is, it is no surprise that there are many tales and lore about the bird. For example, counting the number of cuckoos the bird sings indicates how many years it will be before you marry or the number of children you will have. An Irish tale is that an unmarried person should, on hearing a Cuckoo, search the ground around them to find a hair that will match the colour of their future spouse's hair. In England this tale became if a young woman walked in a field and heard a Cuckoo, she would fine a hair the colour of her future spouse in her left shoe! Another tale is about the bird's arrival predicting the summer weather, as in 'If the Cuckoo comes on a bare bough; keep your hay and sell your cow; if the Cuckoo comes on the blooming May; keep your cow and sell your hay'. In Sussex April 14th is Cuckoo Day and if locals turn their money over they will not want for it. Better still, in Shropshire when workers heard their first Cuckoo they stopped work for the day and drank 'Cuckoo ale'.

In good British tradition, the Times newspaper prints early reports of the Cuckoo's arrival. A local name for the Cuckoo is gowk and associates the bird with simple-mindedness. Also the young, newly fledged Cuckoo is called gawky, a term we still use today, often for an uncoordinated, adolescent male. The Cuckoo also projected phallic prowess, for an amorous Zeus ravished Hera by assuming the shape of the cuckoo. Along these lines, it is a Danish symbol for fertility and longevity.

In 2011 an interesting experiment was set up by the BTO to plot the migration route of the bird. Six cuckoos were fitted with tracking devices and live data was sent plotting their outward and return routes (which differ). One tagged male arrived in the UK on 1st May after an 8 week flight from Congo and left on the 10th June. The data also shows that birds rest up for long periods on their outward flight and also use a different route to their return flight. Centuries ago, when migration was a mystery, one belief was that from August until April Cuckoos turned into Sparrowhawks. Another belief was they hibernated in tree stumps. Numbers of Cuckoos in the UK have dropped by 77% in the 50 years to 2017. Its conservation status in the UK is red but it is classified as least concern in Europe.

The Cuckoo's scientific name is *Cuculus canorus* with *canorus* meaning melodious, as in a song. In 1381 Chaucer wrote "Summer is icumen in, lhude sing cucu" with the bird's name then being very similar to the Latin *cuculus*.

Nightjars and swifts

Order - Caprimulgiformes

This globally distributed order contains the nightjars and the swifts. The derivation of the order's name is explained below, under Nightjar. They are excellent fliers with small, weak feet, a short beak and gaping mouth and they are entirely insectivorous. On some birds the mouth has long bristle sensors for detecting prey. Birds have excellent eye sight and their eyes are placed laterally on the head. The birds have long, narrow wings for fast flight. Most are cryptically coloured and are very well camouflaged. They have soft feathers. Many are nocturnal. Night flying birds face no competition for their flying insect prey. Two members of this order, the Oilbird and Cave Swift use echo-location to navigate in their very dark cave environment. The Poorwill, a North American member of this family, is the only bird that hibernates.

The two families in this order are:

Caprimulgidae and **Apodidae**.

Main characteristics of the Caprimulgidae family:

Nightjars, which make up this family, are medium-sized nocturnal or crepuscular birds with long pointed wings, short legs and very short beaks. Nightjars are found in all regions of the world. Some nightjars have the ability to go into a state of torpor during bad weather and poor food supply. Nightjars feed predominantly on moths and other large flying insects, probably catching their prey by sight. Most have small feet, of little use for walking. Their middle toe has a comb of serrated notches, possibly used to clean their rictal bristles. The Nightjar has a large head with large eyes providing strong night vision. The bird's small beak opens to reveal a large gape. Nightjars are noisy at night (hence the name) with males calling to attract females and other calls (churring) to defend territory. The Nightjar's churr is emitted at a rate of 30 notes per second. However, the bird is silent in flight. White patches on the outer primaries and outer tail feathers of the male are used in a territorial display. Open heathland is their preferred habitat. Most species are monogamous for one season. Nightjars usually nest on the ground and lay one or two camouflaged patterned eggs (patterning is unusual in non-passerine birds) directly onto bare ground. This bird will move its young if disturbed. The semi-precocial young are born with cryptically coloured down feathers. Hatchlings open their eyes after a few days and can walk. After a few days the parents will move to a new resting area away from the nest site.

19 - Nightjar

The only species in the Caprimulgidae family in the UK is the **Nightjar** which has been known to us for centuries. In the 16th century they were known as 'birdes that in the night sucke goats'. Local names include churn owl; fern owl and jar owl referring to its heath land habitat; night churr; night crow; night hawk and night swallow all refer to the bird's nocturnal habits but with little agreement on who its close relatives are! Other names are the amusing name flying toad; goat owl; lich fowl, which associates the bird with death and wheel bird, connecting the bird with the sound of a spinning wheel. Razor grinder and scissor's grinder both pick up on the bird's churring. The names puck and puckeridge refer to a disease in cattle which the bird was allegedly responsible for. Gilbert White noted a "notion that the fern owl ... is very injurious to calves ... by inflicting distemper". To add to the bird's bad reputation the Nightjar was blamed for pecking holes in the hide of cattle, rendering the hide less valuable. In fact the holes were made by a fly laying its eggs under cattle skin and the resulting maggots drilled the holes. One belief was that the calls of the Nightjar were the sound of witches hiding in the bushes. The local name gabble ratchet (corpse hound), may refer to the belief that the souls of unbaptised children were doomed to wander as nightjars until Judgement Day.

The jar in the Nightjar's name formerly meant a quivering or grating sound rather than today's meaning of discordant. Their nocturnal song disturbed or jarred peoples' sleep. The Victorian poet Meredith wrote "lone on the fir-branch, his rattle note unvaried, brooding over the gloom, spins the brown eve-jar". An accurate observation! The bird was known to Aristotle and is mentioned in the Bible as a night hawk, which states that the bird should not be eaten as it is unclean.

The Nightjar is a summer migrant to Britain and is found on open heath land. As is often the case with migratory birds, the male arrives 10 days before the female to secure its breeding territory. It is predominantly nocturnal but can be seen at sunset as it starts its night time moth hunting activity. Otherwise it is difficult to spot as its colouration blends so well into its surroundings including when the male is sitting on a tree branch or when the female is sitting fully camouflaged on its ground nest. Their soft plumage is cryptically coloured to resemble bark or leaves. Nightjar, unusually, perch along a branch, rather than across it, helping to conceal it during the day.

The Nightjar is adapted to detecting moths on the wing through a set of sensitive rictal bristles around its mouth. Prey is caught using the serrations on their toes and transferred to their mouth. These serrations are also used to keep the bristles clean. The male's rapid churring emits up to 1 800 notes per minute and seemingly without breathing! Gilbert White was staying in a hermitage when they observed a Nightjar singing "we were struck with wonder to find the organs of that little animal, when put in motion, gave a sensible vibration to the whole building".

In parts of the southeast U.S., it was once thought that the number of times a Whip-poor-will (the North American Nightjar) sang in succession indicated the number of years a man would remain a bachelor. In Sulawesi, the satanic or diabolical Nightjar *Eurostopodus diabolicus* (until recently known only from a single 1931 specimen) was named for the local belief that the call it made at night was the sound of it pulling out people's eyes!

The Nightjar has a fascinating mythological story behind its name. The myth which surrounds this bird is a tale that was believed for many centuries in many countries. Aristotle in the 3rd century BC related the story. Goat herdsmen reported that their goats produced far less milk after spending the night on high ground. Their excuse was that a night flying bird was secretly sucking the milk from the nannys' udders and causing their teats to dry up and also the nanny was blinded. The alleged culprit was the Nightjar. Thomas Elyot wrote in the 16th century "birds like to gulls which appear not by day but in the night they come into the goat pens and do suck the goats whereby the udders of them be mortified". The real reason for the low milk yield at night is that the goats are feeding on poorer upland pasture at night. Doubtless the birds were attracted to the area where the goats were herded as fires would be lit, attracting moths, being the Nightjar's diet. Possibly the birds flew close to the goats to pick off the nearby insects.

The bird's scientific name *Caprimulgus europaeus* is comprised of *capri* for goat and *mulgus* for milk. So the myth has been incorporated into its Latin name.

Main characteristics of the Apodidae family:

The family scientific name for the swifts, Apodidae, comes from the Ancient Greek, apous, meaning without feet. Swifts have very short legs with sharp curved claws, seldom settling on the ground but they can perch on vertical surfaces. They have a characteristic scythe-like wing shape with a short, forked tail. The flight has a distinctive flicking action. Swifts are wholly insectivorous and feed on the wing using their large gape to catch insects. They lack any rictal bristles. Swifts have feathering in front of their eyes to reduce glare and protect their eyes. Their long, narrow primary feathers and short secondary feathers allow for rapid flight and gliding; because they predominantly glide, they have small breast muscles. The birds are monomorphic. Swifts are highly aerial birds; they sleep and can copulate on the wing. The birds make a distinctive shrill scream whilst flying. They have large salivary glands that increase in size during the breeding season, using saliva to glue their nest together onto a vertical surface. They lay 2 eggs hatching after 20 days. The young are altricial. Both parents assist in raising the young.

The **Swift** is the only member of the Apodidae family in the UK.

 A bird which is sometimes incorrectly thought to be a relative of the Swift is the Swallow. Whilst they are both summer visiting, insectivorous aerial birds, they come from quite different families and orders. In fact the hummingbirds are a closer relative of the Swift! The Swift is in the order Caprimulgiformes and the Swallow in the order Passeriformes. However, a number of local names relate the Swift to the Swallow, such as brown swallow; crane swallow; hawk swallow and tile swallow. Black martin links the bird to the House Martin, which is a close relative of the Swallow. The association of the bird with the devil comes from its screech, which is often heard as small flocks fly around our towns. Hence names like black screech; devil's bitch; devil's screecher; devil's squeaker; devil swallow; horse martin, from its horse-like squealing cry; jack squealer; screech martin and shriek owl. Anchor bird is a local Sussex name alluding to its silhouette.

The Swift has very small and weak feet, rarely using them, as it spends most of its life on the wing. The front two toes point to the side (as opposed to pointing to the front). Its eyes are deep seated and a row of bristles protect the eyes from bright sunlight. The Swift is (for a small bird) relatively long-lived, with an average life span of 5.5 years. One ringed bird was 7 years old so given that the bird had been in constant flight and undertook several long migratory journeys, the total distance the bird flew must have been enormous. One estimate is nearly 2 million km! The young prepare for flight in the nest by doing press-ups and adjust their food intake to ensure that they have the correct muscle-to-fat ratio for flight. When they leave the nest the young fly continuously for the next 2 years and migrate without their parents' help. Gilbert White noted how the Swift never seemed to cease flying and wondered how they mated, recording "I have never seen the bird collect material for a nest but usurped sparrows from their nests". He noted that birds copulated on the wing "as they are sailing round at a great height … now and then one (would) drop on the back of another and both of them sink down together … this I take to be the juncture when the business of generation is carrying on". The eminent ornithologist David Lack (1910 – 1973) wrote a seminal work *Swifts in a tower* based on his study of Swifts in Oxford.

The name Swift comes from the Old English swifan, meaning moving fast. The Swift flies quickly but it is not the fastest bird in level flight. Its close relative the Spine-tailed Swift takes that honour with a top level flight speed of 160 km / hr. (The Peregrine is the fastest bird (in the world) reaching speeds of around 300 km / hr but that is in a burst of vertical, stoop flight). The Swift we see flies at around 40 km / hr and can reach above 80 km / hr in a burst of speed, for example when trying to impress a potential mate. Swedish researchers fitted geolocators to several Swifts and recovered 19 of them. The data showed that three of the birds never rested and all the birds were in the air 99% of the time (except when nesting). Swifts also make a long ascent to altitudes of 3 km, often at twilight. They can sleep on the wing and drink all the water they need as they fly.

The Swift demonstrates the phenomenon known as leapfrog migration, whereby the most northerly breeding Swifts migrate furtherest south in Africa. Swifts breeding in Europe migrate a shorter distance to more northerly regions of Africa. The young migrate independently of its parents and siblings. Various testimonies provide evidence of the height of their migratory flight. One observer in the Pyrenees saw a large flock descend from the clouds into a pass 2.1 km high. Pilots have seen Swifts at 2.3 km. A French airman in the 1914-18 war was gliding down behind enemy lines when at 3 km up he found himself amongst a flock of motionless Swifts. Historically the Swift, like the Swallow, was thought to hibernate during winter in the mud of ponds, rather than migrate. Jeremiah observed migration writing "the swift keep the time of their coming … but my people know not the ordinance of the Lord".

It was noted earlier that the Swift has small, weak feet and this is stated twice in its scientific name of *Apus apus* i.e. foot-less, foot-less.

Cranes, rails, crakes and gallinules

Order – Gruiformes

Gruiform means crane-like and the order contains cranes, rails, crakes and gallinules. The characteristics of birds in this order are highly variable. They are widely distributed and vary greatly in size and weight. Gruiformes are primarily black, grey or brown in colour and many species have streaked markings (except some rails and the cranes). Beak shape and size varies. The birds are mainly omnivorous, with several species vegetarian. Birds vary from competent fliers to flightless species. Many have a courtship display and use vocalisations for pairs to bond.

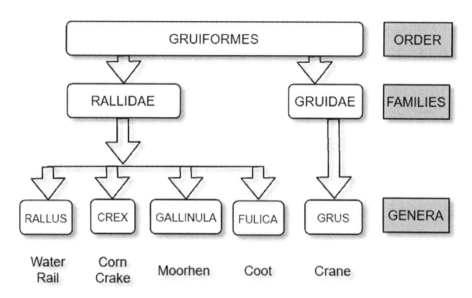

Rails, crake, gallinules and crane

The two families in this order are:

Rallidae and **Gruidae**.

Main characteristics of the Rallidae family:

The rails or Rallidae, are a large cosmopolitan family of small to medium-sized birds. The name ralus is from the Latin for the sound they make. The family includes the crakes, coots and gallinules and is one of the most widespread family of birds. They occupy dense vegetation in damp environments near lakes, swamps or rivers although some e.g. Coots prefer open water. They are shy and secretive birds and have laterally flattened bodies to aid walking through dense vegetation, hence the expression 'thin as a rail'. Rails are omnivores. Most species walk and run vigorously on strong legs and have long toes which have adapted to soft, uneven surfaces. They tend to have short, rounded wings and, although generally weak fliers, they are capable of migratory journeys. The calls of Rallidae species vary but are often a loud whistle or squeak, useful in dense vegetation or at night. Many species have long necks. Most Raillidae are solitary but some species e.g. Coots gather in large flocks. Many rails are territorial. Courtship includes displays of flank patterns or under-tail coverts or bowing. Nests are built in thick vegetation or on open water from vegetative matter. Chicks are precocial but are fed by their parents for a few weeks after fledging.

The four species in this family are in four genera:

Rallus - Water Rail
Crex - Corncrake
Gallinula - Moorhen
Fulica - Coot

The **Water Rail** is far more numerous than sightings indicate. The bird skulks in reed beds and only exits for a short time or longer when the weather is severe. It is heard more often than seen. Local names refer to the bird's habit of running from cover to cover, like bilcock; bult, meaning to move quickly; darcock, from its habit of darting from cover to cover; jack runner; rat hen; skitty cock, with skite meaning to run quickly and velver runner. Other names include brook ouzel, with a strange reference to a thrush; gutter cock and weir cock. The word rail was also used to refer to the Corncrake, when the tale was that the Corncrake (a summer migrant) turned into a Water Rail in winter. The name for the bird's call (the bird is more often heard than seen) is sharming. UK birds are sedentary but winter numbers are supplemented by migrants from Europe.

The rail in the Water Rail's name is from the French rale, a death rattle connected to this secretive bird's scraping noise. The bird is mainly insectivorous but when hungry will attack and eat other birds.

The Water Rail's scientific name is *Rallus aquaticus* with *Rallus* the Latin for rail, referring to the bird's voice and *aquaticus* to its watery environment.

The **Corncrake** is a summer migrant and where it occurs it is well known for its loud, persistent rattle, being more often heard than seen in the long grass where it lives. The call registers 100 dB i.e. it's loud! Their ears have a reflex reaction to stop them going deaf by their own call! The Corncrake was once a much more common bird than now. As a summer migrant it was thought the bird turned into a Water Rail in winter, so predictably the word rail appears in some of its local names, such as land rail. Local names include bean crake; crake gallinule, associating the bird with the Moorhen and Coot (they are in the same Rallidae family); creck, from its call; daker hen; gorse duck; grass duck, where it lives; land hen and king of the quail from its habit of taking off with migratory flocks of Quail to lead them. The male is 25% heavier than the female that weighs in at 140 g.

The Corncrake's song is recalled in two poems - first *The Landrail* by John Clare "And still they hear the craiking sound, And still they wonder why, It surely can't be underground, Nor is it in the sky. An yet 'tis heard in every vale, An undiscovered song, And makes a pleasant wonder tale, For all the summer long". An accurate observation as the bird is seldom seen. And the second *A voice of summer* by Norman MacCaig "In this one of all fields, I know best, All day and night, hoarse and melodious, sounded. A creeping Corncrake, coloured like the ground, Till the cats got him and gave the rough air

The distribution of the bird across Europe diminished greatly from the 19th century onwards. In the UK the bird is now limited mainly to the islands of western Scotland and north-west Ireland. The Corncrake has been a red listed species since 1996.

The bird's vernacular name links the bird to its habitat (corn fields) and crake is onomatopoeic.

The bird's scientific name is *Crex crex* a long-legged bird recorded by Aristotle.

Local names for the **Moorhen** include common gallinule; cuddy, from its habit of bobbing its tail, a name it strangely shares with the Dunnock, House Sparrow and Treecreeper; dabchick, a common name for the Little Grebe; dollpopper; marsh hen; mere hen; moggyhen; skitty, from its habit of seeking cover when threatened and stank hen, from still water.

The family name commonly used for the Moorhen and its relatives is gallinule. The North American name for this bird is Common Gallinule, demonstrating the variation in formal English names and the need to use the unique scientific name to accurately identify a species.

Moor is an old name for marsh, which locates the bird correctly. The Moorhen exhibits partial brood parasitic behaviour, where sometimes females lay a few of their own eggs in another couple's nest to boost their breeding success. If timed right, the host parents will incubate the egg and feed the fledgling as the host often does not recognise the addition of an extra egg. The Moorhen unusually breeds cooperatively; with older birds assisting their parents raise subsequent broods of chicks. Occasionally the bird nests in trees. The bird's eggs were taken as food and the bird was shot for meat as recently as WW 2.

The Moorhen's scientific name is an apt description of the bird, being *Gallinula chloropus* with *Gallinula* being Latin for a little hen, a diminutive of gallina (meaning hen). *Chloropus* is comprised of the Greek khloros for green (as in the green coloured gas, chlorine) and pous for foot i.e. a green footed hen; spot on!

The **Coot** is a common bird and is often found on lakes and even ponds so the bird has collected a many local names. These include bald coot and bald pate (hence the expression 'as bald as a coot'); bell poot; devil's bird, from its blackness; black diver; pout, which derives from the French poult and the Latin pulla for chicken; queet, which is a Scottish word given to the Guillemot and white faced diver. The names water crow and water hen refer to its aquatic environment. A phrase once used was 'a birde called a coute and because of its blackness is called a diuell (devil)'. Another phrase referring to the bird is 'crazy as a coot', associated with the way the birds squabble with each other. A rather odd tradition was the holding of a Coot Custard Fair in Norfolk in the 19th century. Sweet foods were made from eggs collected from Coots and Black-headed Gulls. Both birds and their eggs were a common source of food at the time. One piece of advice on keeping water fowl was to keep Coot on the same water. The bird has a reputation for being a good sentry against predators and is happy to share the same piece of water with other species, as opposed to swans which will try to exclude others.

The Coot's formal name is onomatopoeic. Coots will eat the eggs of other birds. Native birds are sedentary but in winter numbers are boosted with birds from Scandinavia. Birds gather after breeding for a communal moulting roost.

The Coot's scientific name is *Fulica atra* which comes from the Latin *Fulica* for coot and ater for black.

Main characteristics of the Gruidae family:

Gruidae is the family of cranes with the name deriving from the Latin for crane. Cranes are large, long-legged, long-necked birds. Unlike the similar-looking but unrelated herons, cranes fly with outstretched necks. Cranes' heads are bare and they have a short, wide tail and long, wide wings. The short hind toe is elevated. They are omnivores. Cranes have elaborate, noisy courtship displays or dances, raising feathers around the head and using the motions of their beaks. The ritualised fight involves leaping up with the legs folded and then using the legs to push at their mate's breast. Cranes make loud, trumpeting calls. Birds may change mates over their lifetime. The birds are gregarious and migrate in large flocks at high altitude. Cranes construct platform nests in shallow water usually laying two eggs, with brooding commencing after the first egg is laid. Both parents help to rear the young, which remain with them until the next breeding season. The young, called pipers, are precocial, grow rapidly and can fly after about 10 weeks.

20 - Crane

The **Crane** is the only member of the Gruidae family in the UK.

Standing at a height of 120 cm, the Crane is the tallest bird in Britain. The Crane is well known for its extravagant display, especially as part of courtship, with established pairs displaying each year, probably to strengthen the pair bond. The dance includes bobs, bows and pirouettes as well as calls. The Crane's trachea is elongated and coiled enabling the bird to produce a loud call that travels far. One tale is that Cranes were used as night sentries, making a loud call if they detected an intruder.

The Crane's conservation success story in the UK was related earlier in the Section Conservation in Chapter 6.

Cranes have been well known to humans for millennia. Cranes are depicted on columns in Turkey, dating back to 9 500 BC. Homer's Iliad refers to the sound of migrating Cranes writing "the Trojans marched with clamour and with shouting like unto birds, even as when there goeth up before heaven a clamour of cranes which flee from the coming of winter and sudden rain". Aristotle noted "the Grues furthermore do many things with prudence, for they seek for their convenience distant places and fly high that they might look out far and if they see clouds or a storm, betake themselves to the earth and take rest upon the ground". In ancient Greece it was noted that Cranes flew south at the time ploughing fields in autumn. Cicero wrote in the 1st century BC "Cranes in their long flights on migration assume the form of a triangle, the apex of which keeps the wind off those birds in the flanks making their course through the air easier, the lead being replaced by one of the latter birds which are said to rest by placing their heads on the backs of those in front". His

228

observation and analysis of the V formation was so prescient as was the idea that the birds migrated but the idea of bird's resting their heads is pure imagination! The Romans used the behaviour of Cranes to depict the weather. The birds are venerated in countries like Japan and India. The Grey-crowned Crane is the national bird of Uganda. The Crane appears in Irish folklore (although it is now extinct there) sometimes being kept as a pet. The Crane was used in 19181 as the basis for the design of the logo for the airline Lufthansa.

The Crane appears in an Aesop's tale. A Peacock, spreading its gorgeous tail, mocked a Crane that passed by, ridiculing the ashen hue of its plumage, and saying: 'I am robed like a king, in gold and purple, and all the colors of the rainbow; while you have not a bit of color on your wings'. 'True' replied the Crane, 'but I soar to the heights of heaven, and lift up my voice to the stars, while you walk below, like a cock, among the birds of the dunghill'. The moral being 'fine feathers don't make fine birds'.

The Crane's scientific name is *Grus grus* which is simply the Latin for Crane.

Waders, plovers, gulls, terns and guillemots

Order – Charadriiformes

This is a large and diverse order of small to medium-large birds including sandpipers, gulls, terns, plover and guillemots. Most Charadriiformes live near water and eat invertebrates or other small animals; some are pelagic. The terns dive to catch fish near the surface whilst auks, puffins and guillemot are good swimmers and catch their prey underwater. Other Charadriiformes have a diet of insects and other invertebrates. Several in this order undertake long, difficult migrations. Many species form large flocks and some are colonial nesters. The majority of species are monogamous and in some species individuals keep the same mate from one breeding season to the next. Charadriiformes build fairly simple nests, often just a lined hollow on the ground or on a rock ledge. Most shorebirds' species' young are precocial whilst most seabirds have altricial chicks. Birds in this order have a mechanism for excreting excess salt from seawater by osmoregulation.

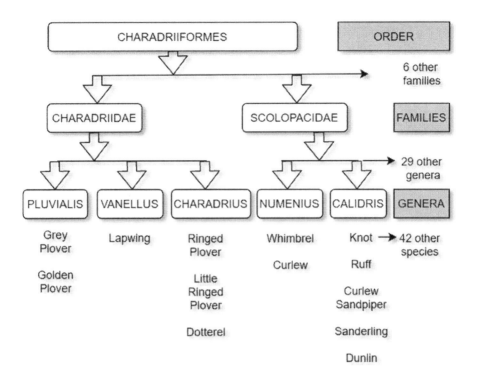

Plover and waders

The families in this order are:

Burhinidae - thick-knees
Recurvirostridae - stilts and avocets
Haematopodidae - oystercatchers
Charadriidae - plovers and lapwings
Scolopacidae - sandpipers and allies
Stercorariidae - skuas
Alcidae - auks and puffins
Laridae - gulls and terns

Main characteristics of the Burhinidae family:

The **Stone-curlew** is the only UK bird in the Burhinidae family. The family name means bull nose! Despite being classed as a wader, the bird prefers semi-arid habitats. Thick-knee refers to the prominent leg joints which are in fact ankle joints. They have round heads, slender necks and large bodies with long legs, no hind toe and long tails, with a pointed beak, large yellow or amber coloured eyes and stripes near the eyes. Males and females tend to be similar in size and are cryptically coloured. They are largely nocturnal. Their diet consists mainly of insects. Their two eggs are laid in a simple scrape. The female does most of the brooding whilst the male defends the nest.

Incubation takes about 26 days and the chicks are precocial. Young thick-knees are coloured to blend into their stony or sandy habitats.

The name curlew comes from its nocturnal call, being similar to the Curlew. The local names for this bird repeatedly associate it with the wrong family, with a range of names like goggle-eye plover; great plover; land curlew; little bustard and thick-kneed bustard, a strange association to a much larger bird; night hawk and willie reeve.

> The yellow eyes of the bird gave rise to the myth that the bird had the power to cure jaundice. According to Aelian, the Roman author, "if a man infected with jaundice gazes intently at the bird and it returns the gaze without flinching it heals the man".

The Stone-curlew's scientific name continues the unusual name theme for this bird! The name is *Burhinus oedicnemus*. *Burhinus* is comprised of the Greek bous for bull and rhinos for nose plus oideo for swelling and kneme for knee. So the bird's name becomes bull-nosed swollen knee! The bird has a comparatively short, slim beak and does not resemble a bull! As noted earlier, the knee is in fact a swollen ankle. So none of the names for this bird are wholly accurate!

Main characteristics of the Recurvirostridae family:

Members of this family, avocets and stilts, range in length from 30 - 46 cm and in weight from 140 - 435 g with males usually slightly bigger than females. The family name combines recurvi – curved and rostra – beak. All possess long, thin legs, necks and beaks. The beaks of avocets are curved upwards which they sweep from side to side when feeding in brackish or saline wetlands. They feed by touch, using thin layers of tissue (lammelae) on the beak to filter their food. The beaks of stilts are straight. The species feed on small aquatic animals. The front toes are webbed; partially in most stilts, fully in avocets, unusually (amongst waders) enabling the birds to swim whilst feeding. Their plumage has contrasting areas of black and white with the sexes similarly coloured. Stilts and avocets breed on open ground near water, often in loose colonies. They defend nesting territories vigorously. They are monogamous for the breeding season. Eggs are light-coloured with dark markings. Three to four eggs are laid in a simple nest, both parents sharing incubation duties, which last 22 - 28 days.

There is one genus and one member of this family in the UK:

Recurvirostra – Avocet

The **Avocet** has many local names including cobbler's awl and shoe awl, which refer to its beak being shaped like an awl; crooked bill; scooper, from its feeding action; and names like barker; clink; yarwhelp and yelper, from the calls made by the bird when threatened. The Avocet became extinct in Britain in 1840. It returned to breed at Minsmere in Suffolk in 1947, the unintended result of changes made during WW2 to the coastal defences which created an ideal environment for the bird to breed. The Avocet became the emblem of the Royal Society for the Protection of Birds. Numbers of breeding Avocet have increased over the last 25 years by about 500%, according to the Rare Breeding Birds Panel (reported in 2014). The bird's eggs are very pointed enabling the bird to arrange its normal clutch of 4 eggs close together so they are all evenly warmed by the adults' brood patch. The female's beak is longer than the male's, with a more prominent curve, which is ideally shaped to turn the eggs in the nest to ensure they are evenly heated.

21 - Avocet

The Avocet's vernacular name derives from its black cap, from the Italian avosetta and the French avocette, a cap once worn by European advocates or lawyers.

The Avocet's scientific name is *Recurvirostra avosetta* with recurvus meaning bent back and rostris being the beak plus *avosetta*, a Venetian name for the bird associated with lawyer's traditional dress. Also *avosetta* comes from the Latin avis for bird plus an –et diminutive ending, indicating charm and grace rather than small.

Main characteristics of the Haematopodidae family:

This is the family of Oystercatchers. The family name comes from the Greek haima for blood (red) and pous for foot. Their diet varies; inland they feed on worms and larvae, on the coast they eat bivalves, limpets and mussels. For the former diet they have a pointed beak, for the latter a chisel-shaped beak. Female's beaks are slightly longer than the male's. Oystercatchers flock to forage for food. Oystercatchers are monogamous and maintain mates and territory from year to year. Females lay 3 eggs on average and have one brood a year but will replace a lost nest. Nests are simple hollows on the ground, either unlined or lined. Both parents help incubate the eggs. Oystercatchers sometimes lay their eggs in another species nest e.g. Herring Gull. Oystercatcher chicks become fully mobile within a day of hatching and are able to run and hide from danger.

There is one genus and one member of this family in the UK:

Haematopus – Oystercatcher

A familiar sight and sound on estuaries and mud flats is the **Oystercatcher**. This distinctive bird's local names include chalder; mere pie, deriving from its variegated plumage; mussel cracker, with mussels, rather than oysters, being one of its foods of choice in Britain; sea nanpie; sea pie and trillachan, a St. Kildan name, with trill referring to its shrill call and the suffix –ach. Other names are dickie bird; gilliebride; kleeper; olive, from the woman's name; oyster plover; scolder; sea pynot; shalder and skeldro, from Orkney. The Oystercatcher can eat up to 500 cockles a day, about 40% of its own body weight, consuming 80 kg in a year! In the 1960's the bird was culled to reduce the loss of cockles on commercial beds but the cull had no effect on the number of cockles!

Southern UK birds are joined in winter by birds from Iceland and Scandinavia. Northern UK birds migrate south to France and Spain.

The Oystercatcher's scientific name is accurately descriptive: *Haematopus ostralegus* which translates as the blood-footed oyster catcher.

Main characteristics of the Charadriidae family:

The bird family Charadriidae includes the plovers, dotterels and lapwings. The family name derives from the Latin from a yellow bird and the Greek for a bird found in river valleys. They are small to medium-sized birds with compact bodies, short, thick necks with a variable length of leg and often pointed wings. Their short beaks are slightly swollen at the tip. They hunt by sight, eating insects, worms or other invertebrates caught using a run-and-pause technique. While breeding they defend their territories with highly visible aerial displays. Lapwings also have spurs on their wings used in fighting. They defend their young from predators by making loud warning calls and performing distraction displays e.g. they pretend to have a broken wing or to be incubating eggs at a fake nest. Nests are scraped indentations on the ground. Most are monogamous and most species are gregarious, migrating in large flocks.

The six species in this family are in three genera:

Pluvialis - Golden Plover; Grey Plover
Vanellus – Lapwing
Charadrius – Dotterel; Little Ringed Plover; Ringed Plover

Local names for the **Golden Plover** include black breasted plover, from its distinctive breeding plumage; bullhead; hill plover, from where it breeds; saw-beer; whistle of the waste and whistling plover.

One tale about the Golden Plover has been referred to already, with the name Plover deriving from the Old French plovier by way of the Latin pluvia, meaning to rain. It is not clear why this bird in particular is associated with rain, as many birds are traditionally associated with the weather in some way. Interestingly the word auspicious comes from the Latin avis for birds and spicere, to see, hence being able to forecast rain through the observation of birds. It could be because the Golden Plover arrives in autumn from its northern breeding grounds, (as do many other birds) which is a wet season. The bird's scientific name *Pluvialis* (meaning bringing rain) continues the connection. The cry of the bird is said to be the souls of the Jews who were doomed to wander for crucifying Jesus. Another tale is that of the seven whistlers, with six birds calling for the seventh being an augury of death or a variation is that if the six found the seventh the world would come to an end! See the entry for the Curlew for more detail.

The Golden Plover is part of the story of the creation of the Guinness Book of Records. Whilst on a shooting party the Managing Director of Guinness had an argument over which was the fastest bird. Realising there was no suitable reference book available he founded the Guinness Book of Records in 1955, which is now the best selling copyrighted book ever.

In winter the UK population is supplemented by migrants from Iceland.

The Golden Plover's scientific name is *Pluvialis apricaria*, with *apricaria* from the Latin apricus meaning sun-kissed, a reference to the bird's golden summer plumage.

The **Grey Plover** has a diverse range of local names including bull head; chuckly-head; may cock; mud plover; owl head; ox-eye; pilot; sea cock; sea plover; sheep's guide; silver plover and strand plover. Ox-eye is a local name shared with birds as diverse as the Blue and Coal Tit, Sanderling and Treecreeper.

The derivation of the word plover was given above under the Golden Plover.

The Grey Plover's scientific name is *Pluvialis squatarola* with *squatarola* an Italian name for a type of plover.

22 - Lapwing

The **Lapwing** is another bird with myriad local names (at least 50 recorded plus others that have been lost); a bird well known on the coast and inland throughout Britain. As the bird has been known for many centuries some local names derive from Old and Middle English plus many regional variations. Peewit, which is onomatopoeic, is still used today. Others include flap jack and flop wing, both from its distinctive flight, as does the name wallopie weep. Green plover, a name it shares with the Golden Plover, derived from the Old French word plouvier, related to its far reaching call; horn pie, from its colouration, with pied historically meaning coloured rather than the modern meaning of black and white. The name horry means filthy. Local names included wipe referring to the bird's crest as does the name horny wick. Lymptwigg is an Exmoor name, from the parent bird's habit of feigning a broken wing to distract predators from their young. A local Lincolnshire name for the Lapwing is pyewipe and there is a place with this name near Grimsby. Other names are old maid; teewhuppo; thieves imp and tieves nacket.

Oddly the Lapwing changes its feeding habits 2 to 3 days either side of a full moon. During this period the birds feed throughout the night and roost and sleep during the day. This behaviour is not understood! Numbers of breeding birds have fallen by 54% over the last 50 years (to 2017). The Lapwing's conservation status is red in the UK, vulnerable in Europe and near threatened by the IUCN.

> The Lapwing has the reputation of being a treacherous bird, as quoted by Chaucer "The false lapwynge, ful of trecherye" and Caxton "a foul and villanous bird". This is probably based on the bird's behaviour of feigning injury if a predator approaches. A 17th century proverb stated 'the lapwing cries the most, farthest from her nest'. This also links to the collective noun for the bird of deceit. In the 17th century prostitutes were called plovers. Lapwing chicks were held to be precocious and ran around soon after hatching with shell still on their

heads when egg thieves disturbed them, giving rise to brash people being likened to 'lapwings with shell on their heads', quoted by both Johnson and Shakespeare. A piece of folklore is that the Lapwing mocked Christ at the cross and was condemned to live homeless and call sorrowfully from its wanderings.

The vernacular name Lapwing derives from Middle English lappenwinke with lap for crest (which it has) and wince for something that moves up and down (a habit of the bird). The bird was shot in large numbers for its meat and also its eggs were collected as a source of food.

The Lapwing's scientific name is *Vanellus vanellus* with vannus the Latin for a little fan, referring to the bird's floppy flight.

The **Dotterel** is a rare summer visitor which breeds in the Highlands. Local names include dot plover, moor dotterel; spring dotterel and stone runner.

The birds are easy to approach and catch. For this they were given the name dotard and thence to the modern word dotty, meaning a fool. The diminutive suffix –erel is added to make the vernacular name of Dotterel. The birds were frequently hunted whilst on migration. The bird appears in the place name of Dotterel Hall in Cambridgeshire. It is Britain's highest altitude breeding species, seldom breeding at less than 900 m. Unusually the female is the brighter coloured bird who performs a song display to attract the male. This is known as reverse sexual dimorphism. Having mated and laid her eggs, the female leaves the incubation of the first brood to the male. She is then free to mate with another male and have a second brood in quick succession (which she incubates) to maximise productivity in the short summer breeding period.

The Dotterel's scientific name is *Charadrius morinellus* with *Charadrius* from the Latin for a yellow bird and the Greek for a bird found in river valleys and *morinellus* meaning little fool, reaffirming its dotty nature.

The **Little Ringed Plover** has the scientific name *Charadrius dubius* with the Latin *dubius* from dubare meaning to vacillate. Before the 1930's the bird was a rare vagrant. Recently disused gravel pits have provided suitable nesting sites for the bird, leading to an increase in the number of breeding birds. The species has a UK conservation status of green.

The **Ringed Plover** breeds on pebble beaches and migrants are often seen on marshes and mud flats. The bird is well known historically and has many local names. Dullwilly refers to its call; grundling, a Lancashire name, from its habit of running for cover; ring dotterel, with the Dotterel being a similar bird; ring neck, from its distinctive black neck band; sand lark and sand laverock, with laverock linking the bird to a lark and suggests betrayal from the bird's habit of feigning injury at the nest when predators appear; sandy lo, with lo being the Nordic for plover; sea lark; stone hatch, from its pebble nest; stone runner, alluding to its environment and wideawake.

The bird exhibits leap frog migration with the more northerly breeding birds from Russia migrating further south than the birds that breed in Denmark. This provides the bird with different resting grounds and so they don't compete for food.

The Ringed Plover's scientific name is *Charadrius hiaticula* which comes from the Latin hiatus, a cleft and colere, to inhabit.

Main characteristics of the Scolopacidae family:

The large Scolopacidae family includes snipe, woodcock, godwit, curlew, sandpipers and turnstones. The family name is from skolops the name for a pointed stick, perhaps a reference to their beaks. The majority of species eat small invertebrates picked out of the mud or soil. Variations in the length and shape of beaks enable different species to feed in the same habitat without competing for food. Waders have long bodies and legs and narrow wings. Most species have a narrow beak, short tails, long necks and partially webbed toes with a hind toe (except the Sanderling). Their beak tips are sensitive, allowing the birds to feel prey in the mud and sand through vibrations. They generally have a dull plumage, with cryptic brown, grey or streaked patterns. Males and females of some species display much brighter colours during the breeding season. Most species nest in open areas and some defend their territories with aerial displays. The nest is a simple scrape; typically laying three or four eggs. The Green and Wood Sandpiper nest in trees. The young of most species are precocial. Young sandpipers are coloured to blend into their habitats. Most sandpiper species are monogamous.

The 23 species in this family are in ten genera:

Nemenius – Curlew; Whimbrel
Limosa - Bar-tailed Godwit; Black-tailed Godwit
Arenaria – Turnstone
Calidris - Curlew Sandpiper; Dunlin; Knot; Little Stint; Purple Sandpiper; Ruff; Sanderling
Lymnocryptes - Jack Snipe
Gallinago – Snipe
Scolopax – Woodcock
Phalaropus - Grey Phalarope; Red Phalarope
Actitis - Common Sandpiper
Tringa - Green Sandpiper; Greenshank; Redshank; Spotted Redshank; Wood Sandpiper

Local names for the **Curlew** include calloo; cawdy mawdy; courlie; full curlew; great harvest curlew; great whaup; greater plover; jack curlew, with jack an odd reference to it being a small bird; marsh hen; musical wailer; seven whistler (explanation below) and whaup commonly used for the Curlew or birds similar to the Curlew with a long beak e.g. the Bar-tailed Godwit. Whaup is Scottish for a goblin with a long nose, used to carry off evil doers at night!

In folklore there are several stories about the seven whistlers, a local name for the Curlew. Tales were based on seven birds flying together by night with their cries forecasting disaster. This belief was fairly common among seamen and coal-miners in the 19th century. Sometimes the whistlers were said to be the spirits of the dead, especially those who had themselves been miners or fishermen, returning to warn others of imminent disaster. When they were heard, the tale was that everyone must stop work and go home or lives would be lost. Even those who knew that the cries were those of Curlews still dreaded the sound and would not work until the next day. In Leicestershire, the whistlers were said to be seven colliers who got drunk on Sunday and agreed to whistle after dark, for a bet. A whirlwind then carried them into the clouds, where they flew as Swifts forever. In Lancashire, some said the whistlers were the souls of wandering Jews, similarly doomed. The English folklorist Jabez Allies reported an 1846 account from Worcester that the country people used to talk about the Seven Whistlers. They said no more than six were ever heard to whistle at one time and they believed if the seventh whistled the world would be at an end.

The Curlew appears in a 7th century legend. St. Beuno dropped his book of sermons in the sea off the Welsh coast. The Curlew rescued the book and the Saint prayed for the protection of the bird. Hence, why it is difficult to find the bird's nest. The *Seafarer* (from AD 1000) mentions the bird: "I take my gladness in the cry of the gannet/and the sound of the curlew instead of the laughter of men".

The Curlew's formal name is onomatopoeic, based on its tumbling, gurgling flight sound. The female Curlew is 20% heavier (at 850g) than the male and has a longer beak, which can reach down to food prey the male's beak cannot reach. This enables the two sexes to share a range of hidden food deep in the mud. Numbers in the UK have fallen by 48% over the last 25 years (to 2017). The bird now has a UK conservation status of red, vulnerable in Europe and near threatened globally.

The obvious and most notable identification feature of the Curlew is its long, curved beak. Not surprisingly the scientific name is based on this, being

Numenius arquata, with *Numenius* meaning new moon i.e. crescent shaped and the second word *arquata* from the Latin arcuatus for bow-shaped.

The **Whimbrel** looks very similar to the Curlew, so many local names make this link. Being slightly smaller, predictably names include chickerel, with the diminutive suffix –erel; foolish curlew; half curlew; jack curlew, jack denoting small; little whaup and summer whaup, the meaning of whaup was given above under Curlew. Seven whistler refers to its whistling call with the folklore recounted in the entry above for Curlew. Other names are crooked-bill marlin; curlew knot; striped head, a distinguishing feature when trying to identify the bird in the field and tang whaup, from Orkney, meaning seaweed curlew.

The Whimbrel's formal name is based on the bird's whimpering call as whimmer plus the suffix – erel.

Whimbrel is named *Numenius phaeopus*, with *Numenius* as above for Curlew and *phaeopus* from the Greek phaios for dusky and pous for foot.

The **Bar-tailed Godwit** is mainly a wintering bird in the UK, living on mud-flats, breeding in northern Scandinavia. Its local names included barwit; half curlew; prine; scammel, from the bird's habit of sitting tight on its nest from the old word for limpet; sea woodcock; set hammer; shrieker; speethe; stone plover and yarwhelp. Some names are shared with other, similar birds. The Avocet and Black-tailed Godwit are called yarwhelp, from their calls. Note the links to other birds, such as the Woodcock, Curlew and Plover, based on some common characteristic.

The Bar-tailed Godwit holds the world record for the longest known non-stop flight of any bird. For details see earlier Section on Migration in Chapter 2.

The word Godwit derives from the Old English words god for good and wit for white. Good refers to how tasty they were to eat, with the bird often being on the menu at medieval banquets. There is a record that the bird 'accounted as the daintiest dish in England'.

The Bar-tailed Godwit's scientific name *Limosa lapponica* is again aptly named, with limus meaning mud and sella seat, where it is found feeding and *lapponica* from Lapland, where it breeds.

Local names for the **Black-tailed Godwit** include barker from its loud and insistent call; common godwit, being more numerous in southern England in winter (the Bar-tailed Godwit winters on northern estuaries and breeds further north); red-breasted godwit and red-breasted snipe, both referring to its striking summer plumage; shrieker; small curlew and whelp, a word used for puppies or a disparaging form of address for a boy or the name is onomatopoeic.

The Black-tailed Godwit's scientific name has the repetitive name *Limosa limosa*.

A wintering bird of the seashore that does what its name suggests is the **Turnstone**. However, the bird seems to have been mis-identified, with many local names wrongly linking the bird to other families and species, like horsefoot snipe; red-legged plover; sea dotterel; sea lark; sea quail and skirl crake. Being linked incorrectly to six other species must be a record! However, ebb picker; stanepicker; stone raw and tangle picker all correctly relate to the Turnstone's feeding habits. The name calico refers to its multi-coloured plumage. Each bird has a slight variation in plumage enabling the birds to identify those in its own group and any intruders from another group.

The Turnstone's formal name is apt with the bird being seen in winter scurrying along the shore line turning over stones to catch its food. The Turnstone has catholic tastes and will eat crustaceans, molluscs, worms and even carrion. The bird is strong enough to turn stones weighing nearly its own body weight. In the breeding season it becomes insectivorous (as do many birds) as this food is plentiful and young immature birds can digest insects.

The Turnstone's scientific name is *Arenaria interpres* with *Arenaria* from the Latin arena for sand and *interpres* meaning messenger.

The **Curlew Sandpiper**'s local names include pigmy - pigmy curlew and pigmy sandpiper.

Its formal name reflects the shape of its beak which is slightly down turned like the Curlew. The bird breeds in the Arctic and its breeding success depends on the lemming population. When there are few lemmings the bird loses its chicks to fox and skuas.

The name of the genus Calidris derives from the Greek kalidris, used by Aristotle for a grey, waterside bird.

The Curlew Sandpiper's scientific name is *Calidris ferruginea*, with ferrugo meaning rust, the breeding bird's breast colour.

The **Dunlin** is a winter migrant wader that visits Britain's estuaries in large numbers, with a small number breeding on our up-lands in summer. Local names include the diminutive jack, as in jack plover and jack snipe. Dorbie and pickerel refer to its pecking eating habit. Others names are churre and purre, from its summer call; ebb sleeper, with ebb meaning foreshore, where the bird is seen; dorbie, a Scottish word for a small wader which pecks; ox bird, possibly from the black patch on the underside of the bird in breeding plumage; plover's page and plover's slave, from its association with Golden Plover on its breeding grounds and sand mouse; sea lark; sea mouse and sea peek, from its habit of scurrying around the fore shore. A number of names include snipe (previously meaning beak) giving names like fall snipe; little snipe; sand snipe; sea snipe and tang snipe. Stint is a name for a small wader. In winter it looks similar to its rarer close relative the Little Stint.

The Dunlin's winter plumage is quite plain in contrast to its brighter summer plumage which includes a large, black belly patch. This seasonal contrast led early naturalists to believe there were two distinct species. The name dun means dull brown colour, reflecting the bird's winter plumage. The diminutive suffix –lin produces an accurate name for one of our smallest waders. The Dunlin migrates long distances, with the adults utilising a southerly route via the Baltic whilst the juveniles make their own way south from their Russian birth grounds via Norway. Prior to migrating the birds add 0.6 g of fat each day, increasing their weight from 53 g to 75 g.

The Dunlin's scientific name is *Calidris alpina*, with alpina from the Alps.

Local names for the **Knot** are ash coloured sandpiper; beach robin, referring to its red breast in breeding plumage; dun, from its dull winter colour; ebb cock, being associated with tides (see below); freckled sandpiper; gnat snap; griselled sandpiper; howster, from its call; red sandpiper and robin snipe, again referring to its bright red breeding plumage; sea snipe; silver plover, being similar to the Grey and Golden Plover and white-bellied snipe.

> The formal name Knot possibly derives from the bird's association with 11th century King Canute, Knot being an alternative name for the king. The tale goes that whilst observing Knot feeding on the seashore the King was taught a lesson about the limits of his power as King. He got his feet wet, having commanded the tide to go back. His flattering courtiers claimed he was "So great, he could command the tides of the sea to go back". The King learned that "Let all men know how empty and worthless is the power of kings. For there is none worthy of the name but God, whom heaven, earth and sea obey". Observing the Knot retreat from the incoming waves helped the King learn this lesson. The bird does indeed scurry around the edge of the waves and moves with the tide.

Birds which winter here are from Greenland or North Russia with the adults leaving the breeding grounds first to migrate here or fly further south. The Knot forms huge flocks in winter, making spectacular aerial displays. In former times the bird was shot in large numbers for food.

The Knot's scientific name *Calidris canutus* associates the bird with King Canute.

The **Little Stint**'s local names include brown sandpiper; little sandpiper; ox bird; purre, a name for the Dunlin and (oddly) the Common Tern and wagtail.

The word stint means to doing a minimum amount of work and it can mean sparingly e.g. not stinting with the wine. The bird is very similar to the Dunlin and is seen scurrying around whilst feeding.

The Little Stint's scientific name is *Calidris minuta.*

The **Purple Sandpiper** is the most northerly breeder of any UK bird and some birds over-winter in the Arctic region making them the most northerly wintering wader. The species has a wide distribution and this has led to birds from different areas having varying wing and beak lengths, with southerly birds having shorter beaks and females having slightly longer beaks.

The Purple Sandpiper's scientific name is *Calidris maritima.*

Local names for the **Ruff** include equestrian sandpiper; greenwich sandpiper; oxen-and-kine and yellow legged sandpiper.

The name Ruff technically only applies to the male bird. The female is called a Reeve. The male (who weighs 180 g) is larger than the female (weighing 110 g), being typical for a polygamous bird which has to engage in an intense sexual selection process. For details of a lek see the Section in the Chapter Mates, Mating and Breeding. Ruffs start their winter moult before migrating to winter in Kenya, with the males moulting before the females. Ruffs also have an intermediate moult between winter and summer. Siberian Ruffs undertake a return migratory flight of up to 28 000 km. The word Reeve is possibly associated with the ornate clothing of an official's robes and was used in the 15th and 16th century for both male and female birds. The word Ruff was brought into use in the 17th century and then was adopted for naming just the male bird. Some sources associate the bird with the item of clothing by the same name, others disagree stating the item of clothing comes from ruffle, meaning wrinkled or folded.

In the Middle Ages Ruff were both trapped and bred in captivity, not so much for the male's attractive plumage but for the table, having a reputation of being good to eat. The male bid was hunted for taxidermy in the 18th and 19th centuries, sometimes in large numbers. One Norfolk taxidermist prepared a display case of twelve male Ruff in full breeding plumage! One report was of one fowler killing 600 between April and September. By the end of the 18th century the bird was extinct in the UK as a breeding bird, with no records of breeding again until 1963. Sadly it still breeds in very small numbers and is red listed.

The scientific name of the Ruff is *Calidris pugnax* with *pugnax* the Latin for fight.

Local names for the **Sanderling** include beach plover; bull peep; curwillet, Cornish from its sound; ebb cock; ox bird; ox eye, a name shared with the Blue and Coal Tit, Grey Plover and the Treecreeper; ruddy plover, in breeding plumage only; sand runner, as it scoots along the shore line; sea lark; trillachan, Gaelic for trill and a –ach suffix, a name shared with the Oystercatcher and tweeky. It is the only British wader not to have a hind toe.

The Sanderling's name is simply made up of sand plus two suffix -er and -ling. The bird breeds in the high Arctic and migrates all the way to West Africa, stopping off in the UK to refuel. The bird gains weight by laying down fat for its long journey. It increases its weight from 50 g to 80 g, giving it enough fuel for almost a 3 000 km journey. On its re-fuelling stop-overs in the UK the bird can increase its weight by 4 g a day, eventually adding enough fuel for its direct flight to Greenland.

The Sanderling's scientific name is *Calidris alba,* with *alba* meaning white. Its characteristic white underside makes identifying the bird comparatively easy whilst it feeds on a muddy estuary, mixed in with other birds like Dunlin.

One local name for the **Jack Snipe** is inevitably half snipe. Others include gaverhal, meaning goat of the marsh, a name it shares with its larger relation the Snipe; jud cock and St. Martins.

The name Jack Snipe incorporates the human name Jack to denote small.

The scientific name of the Jack Snipe - *Lymnocryptes minimus* reflects its behaviour and character, with *Lymnocryptes* from the Greek limne for marsh and krupto to hide. The bird is very difficult to see as it remains hidden, until you are almost onto the bird, when it flies off quickly in a straight line (compared to the Snipe's zig-zag flight). *Minimus* means smallest.

Many of the **Snipe**'s local names refer to the distinctive sound that the male makes during it display flight. As the bird tumbles towards the ground, its two outer tail feathers beat together making a drumming sound. Hence names like heather bleat; horse gowk, with the sound being compared to a neighing horse and gowk meaning meaning awkward and mire bleater. The Old English haerferblaete means billy-goat and bleater similar to gaverhal, from the Celtic meaning goat of the marsh. The gutter in gutter snipe refers to the brooks or channels the bird feeds in and is a phrase used to describe a scruffy child.

> This distinctive display is reflected in two poems; the first by John Clare in *To the snipe* wrote "For here thy bill, suited by wisdom good, of rude unseemly length doth delve and drill The gelid mass for food". And the second by Seamus Heaney in the *The backward look* - "A snipe's bleating is fleeing its nesting ground, into dialects, into variants, transliterations whirr on the nature reserves - little goat of the air, of the evening, little goat of the frost, It is his tail feathers

The local name full snipe contrasts this bird with its cousin the smaller Jack Snipe. Others similar names are jill snipe and lady snipe. The Snipe's beak is proportionally longer than any other European bird. The bird was shot in large numbers for the table and was relatively cheap, costing 4d in the 17th century.

Snipe derives from the Middle English snite and the Old Norse myrisnipa - a mire snipe. The German snipon means a long, thin object. Snipe is used in other bird's local names to mean having a long beak. A local name for the Black-tailed Godwit is red-breasted snipe, horsefoot snipe for the Turnstone, confusingly jack snipe for the Dunlin and robin snipe for the Knot.

The Snipe is a bird that is most often seen as it makes its rapid, zig-zag escape flight when disturbed. The modern word sniper derives from this behaviour as gunmen found the Snipe so hard to shoot because of its escape flight pattern. The word was used by 18th century British soldiers in India to describe shooting from a hidden place. Snipe are so well camouflaged in their grassy wetland environment they are difficult to spot, even close-up. The Snipe breeds in Britain, in wet grassland but numbers are supplemented in winter by migrants from the colder continent, Iceland and Scandinavia. Breeding numbers have increased by 32% over the 22 years to 2017 but wintering numbers have fallen by 64% over the same period. For this reason the Snipe is amber listed.

The Snipe's scientific name is *Gallinago gallinago* which simply means hen-hen.

Local names for the **Woodcock** include the obscure ass of the partridge and the more obvious great snipe; long-bill; muckle snippeck; wood snipe and wudusnite.

The name Woodcock simply reflects this bird's environment. This bird leaves the harsh winter of Scandinavia and migrates to the UK. In the 16th century there was speculation in northern counties that the Woodcock's absence in summer was due to the fact it flew to the moon! This debate continued for 200 years! The Woodcock certainly lives in woods but the male and female are virtually identical, so there is no clear reason for the second part of the name, cock. Historically the sexes were given separate names i.e. wuduhona for the male and wuduhana for the female. The first written record of an English name for the Woodcock dates from the 8th century.

> Woodcock is used as a word for a simpleton and refers to the ease with which the bird is caught. It is so well camouflaged that the bird can be caught on the nest. Shakespeare was aware of the bird and

wrote "Among us in England this bird is infamous for its stupidity or folly so that a Woodcock is proverbially used for a simple foolish person" and "O this woodcock! What an ass it is". In *Love's Labour's Lost* when Browne discovers he and his 3 friends have fallen for the same girl, he calls them "four woodcocks in a dish". The name passed into use as a surname for someone who is simple.

One myth is that the Woodcock carried the very small Goldcrest (weighing 6 g - compare that to the 2 p coin weighing 7 g!) across the sea as the little bird would not be capable of flying so far. In fact the Goldcrest does fly solo across the North Sea! It was also thought that the Short-eared Owl piloted the Woodcock across the North Sea, as they both migrate at about the same time.

One method of killing the bird was to shine a bright light into its eyes and then to shoot the bird before it had chance to fly off. However, there is proof that if a nesting female is disturbed she can carry one of her fledglings off as she flies away. The male's twilight display flight is called a roding. The Woodcock is one of the few birds which can see through 360^0, with its eyes set either side of its head. This enables it to see a predator and remain motionless. The bird has a sensitive tip to its beak which helps locate its prey food as it forages in leaf litter. One very strange use of a bird's feather is in the production of Rolls Royce cars where they use a Woodcock's pin feather to paint the stripe down the side of the car!

The Woodcock's scientific name is *Scolopax rusticola* which comes from the Greek skolopax for the woodcock and the Latin rusticus for rural and colere to dwell.

The scientific name of the **Grey Phalarope** repeats the same meaning twice, the first word from the Greek and then the second from the Latin. The name *Phalaropus fulicarius* means coot-footed, which does not make a lot of sense as the bird is in the Sandpiper family Scolopacidae and has little in common with the Coot (except that bird does have semi-lobed feet). The female Grey Phalarope is larger (at 63 g) than the male (50 g) and the species demonstrates role reversal as the female is the brighter coloured bird, she chooses her mate and defends territory. The female arrives first at the breeding grounds and this behaviour is called protogny. Once she has laid her eggs she finds another male to mate with and leaves the first male to rear the eggs. She then sets off on her migratory journey south, leaving the males to bring up the young. The males leave the chicks before they can fly so, like many juveniles, they have to undertake their first migratory flight alone to some distant place.

A close relative of the Grey Phalarope is the **Red-necked Phalarope** whose scientific name is *Phalaropus lobatus* with *lobatus* meaning lobed. One bird tagged on Fetlar was found to have made a 16 000 km return migratory journey across the Atlantic, down to the Caribbean onwards to the Peruvian coast and back again! All this by a bird weighing a mere 36 g with a wing span of 36 cm. It is the only species known to make this trip.

Surprisingly (given how small they are) Phalaropes are truly pelagic and increase their buoyancy on water by trapping air beneath their feathers which is why they seem to sit so high in the water.

The **Common Sandpiper** breeds in some parts of upland Britain and is often seen as a migrant in autumn on its way to Africa to over-winter. Many of its local names refer to its shrill call, such as heather peeper; killy leepie; kitty needie, using a female first name; land laverock with latter word used for a lark (which this bird is not!); tatler, meaning babbler; trillachan, which derives from the Gaelic meaning trill plus an -ach suffix, a name it shares with the Oystercatcher and Sanderling; waterypleeps and willy wicket. Otterling from the French otter meaning to shake or totter, refers to the way the bird bobs up and down and shakes its tail, plus the suffix -ling; sand lark, a name for the Ringed Plover as well; shore snipe and summer snipe, again the bird is not a Snipe either and waterjuncket. Added to these are strange names such as dickie-de-dee; killie leepsie; sanny and skitter deacon.

The name Sandpiper is onomatopoeic.

The scientific name of the Common Sandpiper is *Actitis hypoleucos* which comes from aktites meaning coast dweller and hupo, below and leukos, white.

The genus Tringa is another group of waders, with Tringa deriving from the Greek trungas, which was used by Aristotle for a waterbird. There are five British birds in this genus:

Green Sandpiper; Greenshank; Redshank; Spotted Redshank; Wood Sandpiper

This group includes the **Green Sandpiper** whose local names include black sandpiper, possibly due to the dark colouration of its back and wings, contrasting with the white rump; horse gowk, a name it shares with the Snipe, Green Sandpiper and (oddly) the Sparrowhawk, with gowk meaning awkward; martin snipe, alluding to the bird's prominent white rump (like the House Martin) and whistling sandpiper. This is another wader species (like the Dunlin and Phalarope) where the male is left to rear the young whilst the female starts off first on migration to her winter resting grounds. The female is also the first and one of the earliest waders to return to their summer breeding grounds. Unusually for a wader the bird nests off the ground, often in trees, using an old thrush's or pigeon's nest. The fledged young then have to leap from their nest to the ground but being light and fluffy they come to no harm.

The scientific name is *Tringa ochropus*, with *ochropus* meaning pale yellow *ochro-* and *-pus* foot.

The **Greenshank**'s local names include barker; greater plover and green legged horseman. This bird does not have white wing bars, like many wader species, because the bird does not fly in flocks. It is thought that white wing bars assist birds which fly in flocks to stay close without colliding.

Its scientific name is *Tringa nebularia*, with the second word mysteriously meaning possessing a mist.

23 - Redshank

The **Redshank**'s piping call is redolent of walks around marshes and estuaries in winter. Local names include ebb cock, from its habit of feeding near the water's edge, also a name for the Knot; pool snipe; red-legged horseman; sandcock; warden of the marshes and watchdog, often altering other birds to a potential danger with its loud whistling call; watery peeps; whistling plover and yelper, also a name for the Avocet.

The male Redshank uses a courtship display to attract a female as well as engaging in a ritual chase with a female. The male forms up to 15 scrapes as potential nest sites and the female chooses the nest site. Again, the male continues to look after the young whilst the female sets off first on her migratory flight. Pairs remain faithful from year to year.

The Redshank's scientific name is *Tringa totanus*, with *totanus* being the Italian for the Redshank.

The **Spotted Redshank** has the local names black headed snipe; cambridge snipe; dusky godwit and spotted snipe, with the name snipe used for any bird with a long beak.

The Spotted Redshank's scientific name is *Tringa erythropus*, with *erythropus* eruthrus – red and *pus* – foot, simply red foot.

247

The association with wood in the **Wood Sandpiper**'s name is unclear. It might have been confused with the similar Green Sandpiper which is associated more with woods. However, this species sometimes nests in trees, using old nests of other species.

The Wood Sandpiper's scientific name is *Tringa glareola* from glarea the Latin for gravel, as more accurate association than wood.

Main characteristics of the Stercorariidae family:

This family consists of the skuas with the name coming from stercoreus meaning filthy or foul or stercus - excrement. They are medium to large maritime birds having medium length beaks with a hooked tip and webbed feet with sharp claws. They have a fleshy cere above the upper mandible. The sexes look alike being mainly brown with some white markings; the smaller species have projecting tail feathers and females are larger. They are strong, acrobatic fliers. Outside the breeding season, skuas take fish, offal and carrion. Many are partial kleptoparasites, chasing seabirds to steal their catches. The larger species, such as Great Skua, kill and eat adult birds as large as a Puffin. On their breeding grounds skuas eat other birds' eggs and young birds. Skuas are monogamous and pair for life and are site faithful. Skuas perform aerial displays and defend their territory with great vigour, mobbing potential predators and human intruders. They lay 2 eggs on the open ground. The birds have two brood patches, one for each egg. Brooding is asynchronous with the first chick being preferentially fed. Young are precocial and leave the nest after 1 or 2 days. Juveniles reach maturity after 2 or 3 years.

There is one genus in this family and two species:

Stercorarius - Arctic Skua; Great Skua

One local name for the **Arctic Skua** is dung bird referring to the bird's habit of chasing and harassing other birds to provoke them to disgorge their food, which the Skua then eats. This behaviour is known as kleptoparasitism. Historically observers thought that the disgorge was dung, not food! This is the derivation of the family name Stercorariidae The bird's dexterity gave inspiration for the RAF's first dive bomber, called the Blackburn Skua.

Other local names include Gaelic names like faskidar, meaning squeezer and the Shetland name shooie, from the Old Norse tju meaning thief; arctic hawk gull; chaser; dirt bird; dung hunter; gull chaser; kepshite; man of war bird; shooie, from an Old Norse word for thief and teaser, from the way bird harasses other birds, all reflecting the bird's behaviour. Added to these names are boatswain; jiddy hawk; marlinspike and trumpie.

The name skua comes from Faroese skugvur derived from German jager meaning hunter and the Norwegian skuvur from the bird's call. The Faroese

Island Skuvoy, is named after the bird. The North American name for this bird is Parasitic Jaeger.

The scientific name for the Arctic Skua is *Stercorarius parasiticus*. When translated *Stercorarius* means belonging to dung and *parasiticus* means parasitic and pirate.

The **Great Skua** is called a bonxie to this day, which in Nordic means dumpy body. Other local names include dirten alan, as the bird acts like the Arctic Skua; herdsman, from the way the bird harried White-tailed Eagles away from lambs; morrel hen, from its dark brown colouration; robber bird, referring correctly to its kleptoparastic feeding behaviour; skooie; tod bird, with tod meaning turd (the bird is traditionally associated with excrement – see above); tom harry, from its habit of chasing other birds plus the use of two human names for the bird and weasel alley.

Britain is home to 50% of the world population of the Great Skua although the UK is at the southern edge of its range. The Great Skua is the only species that breeds in both the Arctic and Antarctic. Great Skuas will pursue birds as big as a Gannet to obtain food. In attacking a Gannet the Skua will grab their wing, causing the Gannet to fall into the sea and then it is harried until it gives up its catch. Unusually, the bird has been recorded preying on Leach's Petrels at night. Adults continue to defend their breeding territory even after their young have matured and flown off. The bird is pelagic, only coming on land to breed. The bird was almost driven to extinction through being killed for food and for taxidermy.

The Great Skua's scientific name is *Stercorarius skua*. *Skua* is the Faroese name for the bird.

Main characteristics of the Alcidae family:

The Alcidae family is made up of the auks. The name comes from the Norse word alca used for the Razorbill. Alcids are good swimmers and divers but they walk clumsily, as their legs are set back. Auks have to flap their short wings rapidly in order to fly; many species need a running start to become airborne. Auks are pelagic and only come ashore for breeding. They have webbed toes. Alcids are primarily black, white and grey with little difference between the sexes. These birds have an upright posture. All species are good swimmers and divers using their wings for propulsion. Beak shape is highly variable. Auks are monogamous with some pairs divorcing. Some species nest in large colonies on cliff edges or breed in small groups on rocky coasts and the puffins nest in burrows. They exhibit strong philopatry. Both parents help incubate eggs and both feed and protect the young. Most species lay one large egg. Chicks are precocial.

The generic word for this family - auk - is from the Old Nordic alka, for neck, possibly from the habit of some birds to stretch their necks out.

The five species in this family are in five genera:

Alle - Little Auk
Uria – Guillemot
Alca – Razorbill
Cepphus - Black Guillemot
Fratercula – Puffin

The extinct flightless Great Auk was a member of this family. Its population was in the millions but the bird was killed in vast numbers. Its meat was used as a subsistence diet, along with its feathers for warmth and fat for fuel. The Great Auk gave us the word penguin, from its scientific name *Pinguinis impennis*. Mariners in the 17th century called the bird a penguin. Of course, penguins only occur in the southern hemisphere.

The **Little Auk** is one of the most numerous birds in the world, with a population estimated at 12 million pairs. The bird's scientific name is an example of a name deriving from another language, in this case Swedish. Its scientific name is *Alle alle* which simply means a seabird (local to Oland). In Greenland birds are caught for food, being placed in a seal skin with seal fat and left to ferment.

The **Guillemot** breeds in summer on precipitous rock faces and spends the winter at sea. The Scots have given the bird many names including foolish guillemot, from the ease with which it is caught for food; kiddaw, from the call of the young as is scoot; skiddaw and willock; marrot, from its guttural call and queet, a variation on coot. Sailors named the bird noddy, possibly from the French nodden, a sleepy nodding of the head. The adult birds can recognise the specific call of their young in amongst the very close packed, noisy colonies nesting on a cliff. The name shuttock refers to the very dirty mess of the colony. Murre derives from its gruff call and is the American name for the bird and the Guillemot family. Other names include eligny; longie; sea hen and spratter.

Guillemot eggs were discussed earlier in the Section Eggs in Chapter 4.

The female lays one egg each year, weighing about 100 g, the equivalent of a woman giving birth to a 12 kg baby! The eggs are very nutritional and were collected in large numbers for human consumption. One record for a single day in one place is of 6 800 eggs collected. Another 17th century record is of 16 000 eggs taken in 3 weeks.

Guillemots catch fish head first, lengthways in their beak. The head is first pre-digested in the adult's throat then the fish is turned around and presented to the hungry chick. The Guillemot is a consummate diver and can reach depths of 180 m. Guillemot chicks, called jumplings, leave their nest at about 3 weeks old, with their wings not even fully formed and leap off their nest cliff edge into the ocean. The father joins the juvenile and together they swim off to Norway, the juvenile bird maturing as it goes. Evidence shows that the father can catch more food for the juvenile whilst swimming at sea rather than making long, arduous journeys to feeding grounds and back to the cliff nest. By October the chick is fully grown and then migrates. The birds do not fly far away e.g. to the Bay of Biscay before the mature birds return to their breeding colonies.

The formal English name Guillemot comes from the French Guillaume (William).

The Guillemot's scientific name is *Uria aalge* which comes from the Greek ouriaa a water bird mentioned by Athenaeus and the Danish *aalge* meaning auk (from the Old Norwegian alka).

24 - Razorbill

Local names for the **Razorbill** include baukie; coulter neb, also a name for the puffin; hellejay; mackerel gull; parrot billed will; scout; sea blackbird; sea crow and strannie, Gaelic, based on the call.

The Razorbill's egg is proportionally very large, weighing in at 90 g, the equivalent of a woman giving birth to an 8 kg child! Each egg is also marked with an individual pattern to aid identification by the adults in a very crowded cliff face nesting site. After breeding the birds wander around the oceans as far as the Azores and Canaries, with immature birds flying further away. Razorbills are deep divers using their semi-folded wings to propel themselves. The average depth of dive is about 25 m but it can be up to 120 m. They fly more than 100 km out to sea to feed during incubation but forage closer (around 12 km away) whilst feeding their young. The fledgling leaves the nest at a young age, in the same manner as the Guillemot.

The Razorbill's scientific name shows how the Latin name can be a Latinised version of words from a different language i.e. *Alca torda* with *Alca* coming from Old Norsk and *torda* from Icelandic, both being names for the Razorbill.

Observers of the **Black Guillemot** (which is mainly seen in Scotland) have noted the devotion of the sexes to each other and compared this to the similar behaviour of doves. This led to local Scottish names such as diving pigeon; dovekie; greenland dove; sea pigeon and sex turtle. In Orkney the bird was called tyst which derived from the Old Norse word peisti, based on the sound the bird makes, as is the name turtur, a name for the Turtle Dove. Other names include black puffin; puffinet, comprised of puffin, which it resembles as a member of the auk family Alcidae and the diminutive suffix –et; spotted guillemot and tystie, which is onomatopoeic.

The Black Guillemot's scientific name is *Cepphus grylle* which comes from the Greek kepphus for a waterbird described by Aristotle and the Swedish grissla meaning guillemot.

25 - Puffin

The **Puffin** is an iconic bird, mainly because of its large and colourful breeding season beak. Names given to the Puffin often refer to its beak or large belly, such as bottlenose; bouger, from the Norwegian for belly; bulker, from the Gaelic bulgair for bird with a belly and coulter neb, coulter is Northumbrian word for plough share and neb an old name for nose. The names bass cock; ailsa cock; flamborough head pilot and lunda, are all from places where it bred; norie, used in Orkney deriving from the Icelandic nori, for something chipped off; pope and popie duck are a derogatory reference to its beak as a nose; prestur, Faroese for priest; scout; sea parrot and tammie norie, referring to a shy person. Other names include bottlenose; cockandy; helegug; marrot and tom noddy. The name of Lundy Island, in the Bristol Channel comes from the Old Norse lunde, meaning Puffin. Puffins were caught in large number for food. Details appear in the Section Human exploitation in Chapter 6.

The Puffin is often seen photographed with several sand eels in its beak. It manages to retain its catch whilst continuing to fish because its beak is hinged so that the mandibles remain parallel. Puffins are consummate swimmers using their wings for propulsion and their feet as rudders. The average depth of dive is 4 m but they have been recorded diving to 35 m. Dive times average at 28 sec with only 6 sec between dives. In one study a Puffin dived 194 times in 84 minutes. Whilst feeding their young parents were recorded diving over 1100 times in one day. Puffins do not fly far out to sea to fish; in one study 85% of flights were less than 15 km. On returning to the burrow the adult tries to land right by the nest entrance as Skuas or Great Black-backed Gulls will attack them for their beak full of food. The fledgling becomes alert to its parent's return ready to be fed but it is not clear how they know this. Using photo-luminescence the adult Puffin's beak glows in the dark to assist the chick to locate its next meal. The beak only acquires its colour in the breeding season, with the colour sheaths being shed in the autumn. The beak does not fully develop until the bird matures at the age of about four.

The young leave the nest on their own at night as the parents have flown off, previously having made sure their chick has sufficient food reserves for its first flight. Chicks leave at night to avoid predation, working out a migration route for themselves, unaided by either parent. They will remain at sea for 2 – 3 years before attaining sexual maturity. On leaving the breeding colony the adults fly off on separate migration routes and spend the winter wholly at sea. Little is known about exactly where Puffins spend winter as they disperse over a wide area. Birds moult their flight feathers all at once. Given they have a high wing loading, if they lost even a few feathers at a time they would be flightless. The high wing loading means that Puffin cannot glide, so they have to constantly flap to maintain motion. Puffins form long term relationships, remaining faithful and monogamous. In one study male fidelity was measured at 85% and over 90% returned to the same burrow. Pairs will divorce if a season's breeding success is low or a failure. In spring the adults return to the same breeding colony and re-establish their pairing with a flamboyant display, involving their colourful beak and the male flicking his head back.

The name Puffin comes from the bird's puffed out belly. The Puffin's name is the result of a muddle that existed for many years, with confusion arising between the names for the Puffin and the Manx Shearwater. The two birds are not at all similar! Juvenile Manx Shearwater were caught and killed for food and the name puffin was given to the cured carcass of that bird, which was corpulent or puffed, hence puffin. The name Mank Puffin was originally given to the Manx Shearwater and is established in the Latin name for the bird, *Puffinus puffinus*. Later the name Puffin was acquired by the bird we now know as the Puffin, which also has a puffed out belly.

The Puffin's scientific name is *Fratercula arctica* with *Frater* meaning friar or brother and *cula* small, referring to the bird's head feather pattern and *arctica* meaning northern. In Irish folklore Puffins were the re-incarnation of Celtic monks, linking it to *Frater*. An alternative meaning of *Fratercula* is a reference to the way the bird holds its feet in flight as though at prayer. A trick quiz question is 'which bird has the scientific name *Puffinus puffinus*?' Many fall for the obvious answer, Puffin, which is of course wrong.

Main characteristics of the Laridae family:

Gulls, terns and kittiwakes comprise the family Laridae. The family name laros means fat, perhaps because the birds are always eating. Most gulls are ground nesting carnivores, being predators and scavengers. Apart from the kittiwakes (which are pelagic) gulls are typically coastal. Terns are long distant migrants. Gulls are heavy-bodied, long-winged birds with an intermediate length neck and tarsi, webbed feet and heavy, slightly hooked beaks. They lack a cere on the beak. Gulls and terns are mixtures of white, black and grey. Their white belly is camouflaged against a pale sky, useful when fishing. In all species males and females have identical plumage with little difference in size. In most species the wingtips are black, the melanin pigment providing wear resistance. Terns' wings are long, slender and they have pointed, slender, sharply pointed beaks. Terns are more gregarious than gulls and often breed, forage and migrate in flocks. Gulls and terns nest colonially, sometimes in mixed colonies. Nests are rudimentary scrapes on open ground, shingle banks, rocks, cliffs or beaches. Many species engage in aerial displays and aggressively defend their nest. Eggs and chicks are cryptically coloured. Typically the birds lay 2 or 3 eggs and are single brooded. The first two chicks hatch together but the third chick may hatch a day or two later, surviving only if food is plentiful. The young are precocial.

The 16 species in this family are in nine genera:

Rissa - Kittiwake
Chroicocephalus - Black-headed Gull
Hydrocoloeus - Little Gull
Ichthyaetus - Audouin's Gull; Mediterranean Gull
Larus - Common Gull; Glaucous Gull; Great Black-backed Gull; Herring Gull; Lesser Black-backed Gull
Sternula - Little Tern
Chlidonias - Black Tern
Sterna - Arctic Tern; Common Tern; Roseate Tern
Thalasseus - Sandwich Tern

The **Kittiwake** is another coastal breeding bird that has been known to us for centuries and has many local names. Several of the names are redundant words like annet; reddag; rippack ritto; rittock and weeo. Many of these names are from north Scotland where the bird nests in large numbers and was caught for food. Tarrock is a Cornish word for the juvenile and its bold black and white colouration led observers to think the juvenile was a separate species. Some names refer to gulls, such as haddock gull; jack gull and snow gull. Some strange local names include cackreen; chitty-wecko; kishiefaik and pick-me-up. One piece of folklore is that the souls of dead children went to rest in the Kittiwake, possibly because the bird has a gentle appearance.

The Kittiwake is the only British gull that is truly pelagic, spending all its non-breeding time at sea moving as far as Greenland and Newfoundland. The Kittiwake is the most abundant breeding gull in the UK and the most numerous gull in the world. Numbers are declining, possibly as the sand eel diet required for its young is in short supply with shoals moving north into cooler waters as the seas warm up as a result of climate change. Unusually whilst young males demonstrate philopatry (i.e. on maturity return to their place of birth to breed), the females don't.

The formal name Kittiwake is onomatopoeic.

The Kittiwake's scientific name is *Rissa tridactyla* with *Rissa* deriving from the Icelandic name rita and *tridactyla* meaning three-toed.

The **Black-headed Gull** is a commonly occurring gull and has an interesting range of local names. Some names, like pick maw, include maw, which is a generic name for gulls. Black hetto; hoodie maa and pick is from pitch, referring to the black head (in breeding plumage only, of course). Swabie, an Orkney name, has its origins in the Old Norse svarbakr via swart back (black back). Pewit gull is from its association with lapwings, which it still does today, with the Gull trying to steal food from the Lapwing. Another kleptoparasitic bird! In addition there are many other local names, given the bird's association with humans, including black hatto; carr swallow, with carr meaning pool; hoodie maa, a variation on maw meaning gull; mire crow; red legged pigeon mew and redshank gull, from the bird's red legs; rittock; sea crow; sprat mew; tumbler and white crow, with 3 associations with the crow. Folklore relating to the Black-headed Gull (and this applies to other gulls as well) states that the souls of drowned sailors become seagulls and hence should not be killed.

Gull comes from the word for someone that will swallow anything thrown at them. How true! The word also means to trick or deceive. Oddly whilst gulls are synonymous with the seaside they are not particularly pelagic birds i.e. birds which live out at sea, as for example, Kittiwakes, that only come ashore to breed. More accurately gulls are coastal. In fact some gulls have recently learned to live entirely inland, in part living off our waste dumps. In winter native birds are joined by migratory birds from Iceland and Scandinavia. Young birds migrate from the UK to southern Europe.

The Black-headed Gull's has the complex scientific name of *Chroicocephalus ridibundus* which comes from Greek kroikos for coloured and kephale for head (true only in summer) and the Latin ridere to laugh plus abundare meaning abounds or abundant. The bird's UK conservation status is amber, with about 140 000 breeding pairs and a winter population of 2.2 m.

The **Little Gull**'s scientific name is *Hydrocoloeus minutus* with hudro meaning water and koloios web-footed and *minutus* meaning small. Note that all gulls have webbed feet!

Audouin's Gull has the scientific name *Ichthyaetus audouinii*, with ikhthus from fish and aetos eagle. The bird is hardly an eagle but it does eat fish (amongst other items). *Audouinii* is from Audouin, a 19th century French natural history scientist. This gull is one of the few birds to have an eponym in its scientific name.

The **Mediterranean Gull**'s scientific name is *Ichthyaetus melanocephalus* with melas meaning black and kephalos head, but only in its breeding plumage. The species only became a UK breeding bird in 1968 but its range appears to be moving north so it is seen more frequently in the UK.

The **Common Gull**'s local names include annet; barley bird, from its arrival here at the traditional time of sowing barley; cob; coddy moddy; gow; green billed bird, highlighting its distinguishing identification feature (its legs are also a yellow-green colour); mew gull; peerie maa; seed bird, from its habit of following a plough; white fool; whitie and winter bonnet as well as general names for gulls like maw and mew.

The common in Common Gull means having no particular distinguishing features, rather than being numerous. Common might also derive from the bird being seen on common land. Its current vernacular name was only adopted in 1949. Previously it was Mew Gull, the North American name for the bird.

The Common Gull's scientific name is *Larus canus* with *Larus* from the Greek laros for a seabird and *canus* meaning grey.

The **Glaucous Gull** has a number of local names including blue gull; harbour gull; ice gull; owl gull and white minister. The Glaucous Gull is in an informal grouping of gulls known as white gulls, which includes the Iceland Gull and Ivory Gull.

The vernacular name Glaucous is from glaukos, a blue / grey colour.

The Glaucous Gull's scientific name is *Larus hyperboreus*, with *hyperboreus* meaning *hyper* - over and *boreus* - the north.

The **Great Black-backed Gull** is the world's largest gull, weighing 1700 g (compared to the Herring Gull's 1200 g). One local name is goose gull, with this gull weighing more than the Brent Goose. Other names include baakie, from its cry, a name it shares with the Manx Shearwater; black back; carrion gull; cobb, a general name of a gull; hand gull; parson gull; saddle back; swaabie and swart back. Wagell is a Cornish name for the immature bird (also used for other gull species) as the young were once thought to be a separate species, based on the significantly different plumage of immature gulls. If the bird was seen inland (though it seldom is) this was a portent of bad weather or tragedy. UK birds are mainly sedentary, with migrants from the continent adding to numbers in the winter. In times past the species was hunted and its eggs were taken for food.

The scientific name for the Great Black-backed Gull is *Larus marinus*, *marinus* meaning marine.

Local names of the **Herring Gull** include black-backed maw, with maw being a generic term for gulls; scorey; silver-back; wagell, for young birds; white ack and white fool.

The Herring Gull will eat any fish, not just herring. It has learned to drop mussels on a hard surface to break the shell. Young birds feed until their weight exceeds that of their parents. They will abandon their parents and attach themselves to another pair if they think they will be better fed! Fledglings are stimulated to feed by the red band on their parents' beak. In fact they be can be fooled into begging for food from an artificial beak with a red band on it, behaviour known as super normal stimuli. The first written record of an English name for the Herring Gull dates from the 8th century.

The scientific name of the Herring Gull is *Larus argentatus,* with argent meaning silver and *tatus* ornamented.

Local names of the **Lesser Black-backed Gull** include coddy moddy, from its habit of feeding on shoals of young cod; gray gull; peedie backie; said fool; saith fowl, with saith the Icelandic for cod fry; scourie, for young birds and yellow legged gull, not to be confused with the bird's close continental relation with that name. This species is found inland (unlike its larger relative the Great Black-backed Gull) and has become a pest for polluting reservoirs. More birds are over-wintering in the UK whereas up until the 1950's birds migrated south for winter. This species is often given as an example of a cline – the way in which one species (in this case the Herring Gull) when it settles in a new geographical area changes its characteristics, eventually becoming a new species (the Lesser Black-backed Gull). For details see the Section Defining a species in Chapter 7.

The Lesser Black-backed Gull's scientific name is *Larus fuscus, fuscus* meaning dusky.

The terns in family Laridae include the Little Tern, Black Tern, Arctic Tern, Common Tern, Roseate Tern and Sandwich Tern.

Up until the 18th century terns were called sea swallows. It is easy to see why when watching them in flight, showing their prominent tail streamers. Tern derives from the Old English stearn which is onomatopoeic.

The **Little Tern**'s local names include dip-ears, from the bird diving for its food; fairy bird; lesser sea swallow; little darr, with darr being a name for the Common and Arctic Terns; little skiff; sea mice, a name for the young; shrimp-catcher and small purl, with purl a name for the Common Tern.

The Little Tern's scientific name is *Sternula albifrons* with *albifrons* meaning white brow, being a clear identifier in the field. This bird is the UK's smallest tern, weighing in at 56 g.

The genus of the **Black Tern** in its scientific name *Chlidonias niger* refers to the former English name for terns as sea swallows. The name *Chlidonias* comes from the Greek khelidon for swallow and –ios for like, along with the Latin *niger* for black.

The **Arctic Tern** predictably shares a number of local names with the Common Tern, as they look very similar and distinguishing the two species at a distance can be difficult. Arctic Terns are wholly coastal and tend to breed further north (the UK is at the southern edge of its breeding range), whereas the Common Tern will breed inland and further south. Local names include darr; pickieterno; rittack; sea swallow; sheer tail; skirr; sparling and tarrock, from the tern's harsh, shrill call and the suffix -ock.

26 - Common Tern

This Tern enjoys more daylight hours than any other bird, possibly more than any other creature, as it migrates from polar north to polar south each year. One Swedish study in 2016 tracked a bird that covered 96 000 km in one year. This is well over its 40 000 km circumnavigation journey as it includes all its rest stops and other movements and deviations. This bird holds the record for the most distant British ringing recovery, with one bird ringed on Anglesey (where is breeds) being recovered in Australia 18 000 km away. Another bird ringed in 1982 on the Farne islands (a breeding colony for the birds) was recovered in Melbourne, Australia, 22 000 km away. The average lifespan of the bird is 13 years with the oldest recorded at 29 years. A long-lived bird may well fly over $1^1/_2$ million km in a lifetime.

The Arctic Tern's scientific name is *Sterna paradisaea* with *paradisaea* meaning paradise.

The **Common Tern** is a summer breeding visitor to our shores. Local names include great sea swallow; gull teaser and kirr-mew, with mew often being a generic name for gulls. Several local names are based on its sharp, penetrating call, such as kirr mew and kipp. Its resemblance to a Swallow is reflected in the names sea swallow and shear tail. Other stranger names include darr; dip purl; great purl, with purl possibly meaning twisting, as in its flight; gull teaser; mirret; pease crow; purre, a name for the Dunlin as well; rittock, from the Icelandic; sparling; speikintares and willie fisher. The oldest living Common Tern recorded was 33 years old. Just how far this bird had flown we will never know but it's a huge distance, given its annual migratory journeys to South Africa. The Common Tern sometimes nests inland, with rafts on lakes providing a suitable nesting site. Its close cousin, the Arctic Tern, only nests on the coast.

The Common Tern has the scientific name *Sterna hirundo* with *hirundo* from hirundine, being the common family name for the swallows and martins. This links with the local names for the bird, such as sea swallow and shear tail.

The **Roseate Tern**'s scientific name of *Sterna dougallii* is unusual with the specific (second) part being an eponym. Dr. Peter McDougall first identified the bird in 1812, having shot one and sent it to Montagu (of Harrier fame) for examination. Numbers of this bird have fluctuated. Formerly it was caught for its feathers for the millinery trade and for taxidermy. In its winter quarters in Senegal and Ghana the bird is still caught as food. Roseate Terns leave their breeding colonies and gather in Dublin Bay before making their migratory journey to West Africa. In what is rare behaviour for a tern, the Roseate Tern is kleptoparasitic, stealing food from other fish-eating birds such as Puffin. It is thought they do this when the seas are rough, as plunge diving terns cannot catch fish in turbulent waters whilst diving birds like Puffin can still catch fish, which this Tern then tries to steal.

Local names for the **Sandwich Tern** are boatswain; boy's tern; crocker-kip; eric; screecher, from its raucous call; surf tern and switch tern.

The Sandwich Tern is named after the place in Kent, where specimens of the bird were sent from. It was common practice for early ornithologists to request that specimens of a species they were interested in be shot and sent to them, so they could examine the bird close up and to dissect it. Specimens were also placed in museums for display and scientific examination.

Unusually Sandwich Terns migrate as a family, with the adults assisting the young to feed as they journey to their resting grounds off the coast of West Africa as far south as the Cape of Good Hope. Breeding adults return to the same breeding grounds each year but occasionally colonies move to a new site. The young are not site faithful and don't return to their natal site.

The reference to Sandwich occurs in the bird's scientific name *Thalasseus sanvicensis* with *Thalasseus* meaning fisherman plus the reference to Sandwich. This species is an example of where a bird has been re-classified, moving in the same family from the genus *Sterna* to *Thalasseus* based on DNA evidence.

Divers

Order - Gaviiformes

 A small order of divers. In this order there is only one family:

Gaviidae.

Main characteristics of the Gaviidae family:

This is the family of divers which are the size of a large duck or a small goose. Gavia is a name given by Pliny for seabirds. Divers have palmate feet with 3 webbed toes. Their tail is comprised of 18 – 20 short, stiff feathers. Their feet are located to their rear and are the only birds whose legs are encased within the body down to the ankle joint.

The birds are consummately good swimmers and divers using their feet to swim and their wings as rudders. Divers find their prey by sight, diving to depths of 60 m. They eat mainly fish using their pointed beak to stab or grasp prey. On land they are clumsy as their feet have moved towards the rear making them unstable on land. Divers have solid rather than pneumatic bones along with modified blood making it easier to stay under water. To swim efficiently under water divers have relatively short wings. The downside is that in flight the smaller wings have to support a comparatively large body weight. Technically this leads to a high wing loading (measured as the weight supported per cm^2). The divers have a high body density. A male diver weighs 3.4 kg and has a wing span of 120 cm. By comparison a Herring Gull weighs 1.2 kg and has a wing span of 144 cm, almost a third the weight and a larger wing area to support that lower weight. Divers need large lakes in order to take-off. A diver can run for 400 m before taking-off. Also they detect the direction of the head wind and fly into it for extra lift.

Male and female divers have identical plumage; patterned black-and-white in summer, with grey on the head and neck in some species and a white belly. In winter, plumage is dark grey above, with some indistinct mottling on the wings and variable white on the chin, throat and underside. Most males are larger than females. Divers nest on freshwater lakes and build their nests close to the water. Both sexes build the nest but the male selects the site. Both incubate the 2 egg clutch for 28 days. Diver chicks are precocial. Unusually, after their first moult young divers grow a second coat of down feathers. Divers are long-lived birds.

The three species in this family are all in a single genus:

Gavia - Black-throated Diver, Great Northern Diver; Red-throated Diver

The European name diver comes from the bird's habit of catching fish by swimming calmly along the surface and then abruptly plunging into the water. The North American name loon comes from either the Old English word lumme, meaning lummox or awkward person or the Scandinavian word lum meaning lame or clumsy. Both refer to the diver's poor ability to walk on land. Alternatively it is from the Norwegian lom, which comes from Old Norse lómr, referring to the plaintive sound of the loon. Also its wailing cry is linked to lunacy, connecting loon with the modern word lunatic. Loon is also associated with a fool or simple minded person possibly from the ease with which the bird can be caught on land as it is relatively immobile.

> One myth about divers is that the birds were involved in the creation of the world. They dived into the water and brought up mud which formed land on earth. This story was prevalent in native North American cultures and also in Finland, Mongolia and Siberia. Divers are also said to wail as they accompany the souls of the dead. The divers are one of many species of bird that were used to forecast the weather. If a diver wailed incessantly it foretold rain.

27 - Black-throated Diver

The **Black-throated Diver** breeds in the far north of Scotland and Iceland. Its common name is loon, which means fool. There is also a connection to the moon, from the Latin luna alluding to the lore that the full moon made people act crazily. Local names include herring bar; lesser imber; northern ducker and speckled loon. Immer comes from the Swedish for the grey ashes of a fire, referring to the bird's dark plumage or possibly from the Latin immergo - to immerse.

The genus name Gavia refers to seabirds in general. The scientific name Gavia was once the Latin term for the Smew (*Mergellus albellus*). This small sea-duck is unrelated to divers and coincidentally is a black-and-white seabird that swims and dives for fish. The Black-throated Diver has the scientific name *Gavia arctica* i.e. northern.

The **Great Northern Diver** breeds in northern Scotland and shares the common name of loon with the Black-throated Diver (see above). Its other local names include arran hawk; bishop, from its distinctive neck pattern; bunivochi, meaning dumpy herdsman; carara; cobble; ember goose, from the Norwegian tradition that the bird appears during the ember days before Christmas (days of fasting); great doucker; gunner; holland hawk and immer diver. The Icelandic name for the bird is himbrimi. One piece of folklore is that the diver hatched its young from a hole in its wing! The bird is the state bird of Minnesota.

The Great Northern Diver's scientific name is *Gavia immer*, *immer* being the Icelandic for a surf roarer, based on the bird's ability to sit on the roughest of seas.

Local names for the **Red-throated Diver** include dun diver, a Sussex name, from the bird's dull winter plumage; red-throated loon and sprat loon, using the North American name, loon, for divers; rain goose, with the bird a portent of rain; sheep's-head-and-pluck, from Yorkshire and speckled diver.

The Red-throated Diver's scientific name is *Gavia stellata*, with *stellata* meaning starry, probably from the striking black and white pattern on the wing in summer plumage.

Shearwaters and petrels

Order - Procellariiformes

An order including the shearwaters and petrels, often called tubenoses. The word procellari is from the Latin procella meaning violent storm. They range in size from the 20 g Storm Petrel to an 11 kg Albatross. The horny beak is made of platlets. The upper beak is hooked to hold slippery prey. The birds secrete stomach oil through their beaks as a defence. They are mainly pelagic and are colonial breeders, nesting on the ground or in burrows. They exhibit strong philopatry. They are monogamous and form long-term pair bonds. They only lay a single egg per clutch with only one clutch attempt per year. Both parents participate in incubation and chick rearing. Incubation times are long compared to other birds, as are fledgling periods. Once a chick has fledged there is no further parental care.

In this order there are two UK families:

Hydrobatidae and **Procellariidae.**

Main characteristics of the Hydrobatidae family:

The storm-petrels are seabirds, ranging in size from 13 – 26 cm. Hydrobat derives from hundro for water and baino to tread. These seabirds have long legs and they patter their feet on the water as they feed on the sea's surface. They are pelagic, coming to land only to breed. They feed on planktonic crustaceans and small fish picked from the surface, typically whilst hovering. Their flight on long, narrow wings is fluttering. Their low wing loading means that as waves surge up the air easily pushes the bird up. The wings are rounded at the tips with the tenth primary shorter than the ninth. The fused tubular nostrils are prominent and span nearly half the length of the beak. They are colonial nesters, displaying strong philopatry and natal fidelity. Most species nest in crevices or burrows and all but one are nocturnal. Pairs form long term monogamous bonds and share incubation and chick feeding duties. Brooding takes up to 50 days and fledging up to 70 days. The female lays a single egg and they do not re-lay if the egg fails. Both sexes incubate in shifts of up to six days, whilst the other bird undertakes a long journey (as far as 200 km) out to sea for food. A week after hatching the chick is left alone during the day and is fed by regurgitation at night. By partly converting prey items into stomach oil, storm-petrels maximise the amount of energy the chick receives.

There is one genus in this family and one UK species:

Hydrobates – Storm Petrel

The **Storm Petrel** is a bird of the open oceans and survives atrocious weather conditions, remarkable for a small bird weighing 27 g and having a wing span of 38 cm. The Storm Petrel is Britain's smallest seabirds. The bird is a long distance migrant and British birds migrate all the way to southern Africa. Research using tracking devices revealed that the bird flies up to 300 km from its Shetland nesting site to feed. Other local names allude to the bird's habit of ejecting a foul liquid when threatened, like martin oil and oily mootie, with mootie meaning a small thing. The names gorlir and martin oil refer to the blubber and oil that was taken from the fat fledglings. The name gourder is Gaelic for whirler from the bird's flight display. Alamootie means fat, little thing. Finally, the bird has the odd names of hornfinch; mother carey's chicken and tom tailor.

Fishermen knew the bird well and gave it many names, including the link to bad weather, hence Storm in the formal name. Witch was a seaman's term for the bird 'hated by sailors, who called them witches, imagining they forbade a storm' along with storm finch. The name Petrel comes from the bird's habit of pattering their feet on waves as they fly very close to the surface of the sea, linked to St. Peter who attempted to walk on the sea. Unusually for birds this family have a good sense of smell, helping them to locate food whilst at sea. See the Section on Smell in Chapter 5. One piece of folklore involving the Storm Petrel is that the birds are the spirits of skippers who have ill-treated their crew. Another is that they are the damned souls of mariners.

The Storm Petrel's scientific name accurately describes the bird - *Hydrobates pelagicus*. This derives from the Greek hudro for water and baino to tread and pelagos for the open sea. A water-treading bird of the open sea is exactly right!

Main characteristics of the Procellariidae family:

This family comprises the fulmars and shearwaters. The procellariids are small to medium sized seabirds. Females tend to be slightly smaller. They generally have weak, set-back legs and many species move around on land by resting on their breast and pushing themselves forward. They surface feed on fish, squid, crustacean and fisheries' discard. All species are long-distance foragers and many undertake long trans-equatorial migrations. The birds have a tubular nasal passage used for smelling, helping them to find prey at sea and to locate their nesting site. They are colonial breeders, exhibiting long-term fidelity and site philopatry. Nests are in burrows or on open ground. A single egg is laid with comparatively long incubation times and fledging periods. After hatching the chick is brooded by a parent until it is large enough to independently thermo-regulate.

The two species in this family are in two genera:

Fulmarus – Fulmar
Puffinus - Manx Shearwater

Having been known to humans for a long time and being a regular breeder, the **Fulmar** acquired many local names. These include foul maa and foul gull, from its habit of ejecting foul smelling oil, incorrectly associating this bird with the gulls; john down; malle muck, from the Dutch mal for foolish and mok for gull because the birds are easy to catch on the nest; marbleheader; molly mauk; noddy; sea horse; white agdon and white puffin, possibly from their plump breasts.

The Fulmar has a particularly smelly habit of firing off the oily contents of its stomach when approached too closely by an intruder. Some predatory birds' feathers can be so fouled by this oil that it disables the bird. This did not stop the bird being trapped for its oil, which was used as a fuel. Martin Martin recorded in 1698 "and when the young fulmar is ready to take wing, he being approached, ejects a quantity of pure oyl out at his bill and will make sure to hit any that attacks him, in the face .... The inhabitants surprise him from behind by taking hold of his bill, which they tie wuth a thread and upon their return to home they untie it with a dish under to receive the oyl". In the 18th century Pennant recorded "No bird is of so much use to the islanders (of St. Kilda) as this the Fulmar supplies them with oil for their lamps, down for their beds, a delicacy for their tables, a balm for their wounds, and a medicine for their distempers".

According to the author James Fisher St. Kildan's lived off the birds with each resident consuming an average of over 100 Fulmars a year. St. Kilda has not been inhabited since 1930. Fulmars are truly pelagic birds, spending all their life at sea, except when breeding. Unusually amongst birds the so-called tubenoses have a keen sense of smell. Whilst at sea they navigate using their sense of smell and can locate food several kilometres away, living off squid, shrimps and crustaceans. They are able to fly continuously by using the up-draught from waves to soar and glide, flying with tail winds rather than into head winds, to save energy. Fulmar have comparatively long wings that are held straight and stiff, being masters of gliding, using up-draughts near cliff edges to gain height with very little wing flapping.

The Ful in their formal name comes from Old Norse into Hebridean, meaning foul plus the general word -mar for gull. The Fulmar is not closely related to the gulls (being in a different taxonomic order) but is closely related to the albatrosses.

The Fulmar is a slow breeder but a long lived bird, with an average life span of 44 years. Young birds reach breeding maturity at about 9 years old, having spent their early life at sea over a very wide area of the North Atlantic. They only lay one egg typically on a cliff ledge and if this fails they do not re-lay. Until the early 1900's the Fulmar only bred on St. Kilda but has subsequently increased in abundance and expanded its distribution, probably as a result of being able to feed off offal from fishing boats. Recently numbers have fallen and (as of 2020) is amber listed in the UK and classified as endangered in Europe.

The Fulmar's scientific name *Fulmarus glacialis* reflects the Old Norwegian for foul gull (from habits mentioned earlier) and *glacialis* from the Latin for its extreme northern range. Birds from the northern part of its range are much greyer in colour than more southerly birds.

Local names for the **Manx Shearwater** include the strange mixture such as booty; cleaver, possibly from the way the bird's wings slice through water; cockathodon, Celtic for cock of the waves; crew; hagdown; lyre, Shetland for fat; mackerel cock, from the bird's diet of mackerel fry; scraber, Hebridean for tough skin and skidden.

The Manx Shearwater once bred in large numbers on the Calf of Man, hence being named after the place. It ceased to breed there by the beginning of the 19th century when the island was over-run by rats. Efforts are being made to re-establish a colony on the Calf of Man as 90% of the world population of the Manx Shearwater breed in Britain. One third of the world population breed on the Scottish island of Rhum. This bird has a complex history of names. Willughby in the 17th century was one of the first in England to catalogue and give names to all the then known British birds. He called this bird the Mank Puffin in 1678, which has continued to cause confusion as clearly the bird is a Shearwater (order Procellariiformes) and not a Puffin (order Charadriiformes). The main connections are that both species are pelagic, they nest in burrows and both were a source of food. The word puffin means puffed, as both birds' breasts are, deriving from an older word pophyn, referring to the cured carcasses of nestling Shearwaters. The call of this bird so scared Norse sailors, they thought the Scottish island of Rhum was inhabited by trolls. It is the longest lived bird in Britain, with one living at least 55 years. The Manx Shearwater is a long-haul migrant and flies all the way to the South American coast, a journey of over 9 600 km. A 55 year old ringed bird flew about 960 000 km on its migratory flights alone and an estimated total of 8 million km! In an experiment a bird was taken to Venice and released. In 14 days it arrived back at its nest site, demonstrating that birds have a strong migratory instinct. Experiments have demonstrated that

Shearwaters navigate in the vast open oceans using their sense of smell. The birds nest in close packed colonies and the fledglings sitting in their nest hole recognise the individual calls of their parents and reply, to assist the parent in finding the nest.

The Shearwaters get their name from the way in which their wing tips just cut through the tops of waves as they fly on stiff wings at right angles to the sea.

Predictably the Manx Shearwater's scientific name is *Puffinus puffinus*.

Gannets, cormorants and shags

Order - Suliformes

A relatively new order comprising the gannets, cormorants and shags. They are coastal rather than oceanic birds. The birds have long, narrow, angled wings and a medium length, graduated tail. Their flight muscles are comparatively small and their wing loading is high. Sulids have stout legs and webbed feet, with webs connecting all four toes and some species have strongly coloured feet. The upper mandible curves down slightly at the tip which can be moved upward to accept large prey. The birds feed by plunge-diving. Their nostrils uniquely open inside the bill rather than the outside, to prevent the ingress of water whilst diving. The head and upper neck have powerful muscles for closing the beak to maintain a tight grip on slippery fish. The forward placed eyes provide binocular vision to help locate prey. Many species feed communally. Male courtship involves displaying and calling. Pairs maintain their bonds by allo-preening. Both sexes incubate.

In this order there are two UK families:

Sulidae and **Phalacrocoracidae**.

Main characteristics of the Sulidae family:

The Gannet is placed in this family. The birds are large, plunge diving seabirds. They have long narrow wings and a long tail with the central feathers shorter than the outer ones. Their bodies are streamlined for efficient diving with comparatively small wing muscles. Under water they swim using their feet. Their beak is long and deep at the base with a serrated edge. The tip of the upper mandible is flexible to help catch larger prey. Their eyes are forward facing giving them a wide field of binocular vision. Gannets have a preen gland which they use to water proof their feathers. The birds are colonial breeders. Males undertake a courtship display to attract a mate. The nest is made of mud and weed in which one egg is laid. Gannets do not have a brood patch but use their feet to brood the single egg, placing one foot either side of the egg. Young are altricial. Chicks are fed by regurgitation for 10 - 12 weeks and then the parents abandon the young bird. Young birds migrate further than adults and will stay at sea for 2 to 3 years before returning to their breeding ground.

There is one genus in this family with one UK species:

Morus - Gannet

In areas where the **Gannet** breeds there is a close association with humans, not least as the bird was an important source of food. On St. Kilda (now uninhabited) large numbers were caught and killed using a fowling rod. The birds provided vital food, feathers and skins. To give some idea of the magnitude of how many birds were caught Martin Martin recorded in 1698 "the number of Solan Geese consumed by each family the year before we came there amounted to twenty two thousand five hundred in the whole island, which they said was less then they ordinarily did, a great many being lost by the badness of the season". Its local name booby refers to the ease with which it caught. Other members of the family are called boobies, meaning fool or buffoon, from the Spanish bobo meaning stupid. Bass goose, basser and channel goose refer to the location of the bird, with the Bass Rock still a stronghold of the bird and has been from at least 1447. Albeit the bird is not a goose! Gannetries are occupied for centuries with records showing a colony on Lundy from 1274 until 1909. Solan goose derives from the crossed wing tips of the bird when sitting and sula is the Norwegian for Gannet. Mackerel gant is from its favourite food. Gannet is also slang for a greedy person e.g. 'to eat like a Gannet'. The first written record of a name in English for the Gannet dates from about 650 AD.

The name Gannet derives from the Latin ganta, merely meaning goose, then later gander. The bird is not related to geese, being in a different order. The Gannet is expert at fishing, diving from a height of 30 m, entering the water at a speed of up to 100 km / hr and diving to a depth of 20 m. To absorb the shock of hitting the water with such a great force its nostrils are blocked off (it breathes through the sides of its beak) to stop water flooding in, the base of its beak has a sponge-like damper and there are air sacs in its throat and breast. The Gannet can fly long distances to feed and often feeds in large flocks. For details on the history of hunting Gannets see the Section Human exploitation in Chapter 6.

The Gannet's scientific name is *Morus bassanus*, with *Morus* from the Greek moros meaning silly which leads to the sobriquet moron, alluding to the ease with which the bird is caught on its nest. *Bassanus* is named after the Bass Rock in Scotland where the bird breeds in large numbers.

Main characteristics of the Phalacrocoracidae family:

The cormorants and shags are dark coloured, with bare patches on their throat and face with no difference between the sexes. Phalacrocorax is the Latin for Cormorant with *Phala* meaning bald and *corax* raven, with an uncertain connection. The beak is long, thin and hooked. They are the least marine of this order and are seldom seen on the open ocean but some frequent inland water. They catch fish by diving from the surface. Birds regurgitate pellets of indigestible bones and scales. They breathe through their beak as their nostrils are blocked to prevent the ingress of water whilst diving. The birds lack air sacs and their bones are less pneumatic, increasing their density so making diving easier. They can adjust their buoyancy so they are able to sink in the water, often with little of their body showing above the water line. Their plumage is permeable aiding under water swimming but birds need to dry their feathers, hence the common sight of a Cormorant spreading its wings to dry. They have short, narrow wings with a high wing loading. At breeding time some species grow plumes. Birds in this family are colonial nesters, making nests in depressions in the ground. Both parents brood the young and use their feet to warm the eggs, rather than a brood patch. The young are altricial and are fed by regurgitation.

There is one genus and two species in this family:

Phalacrocorax - Cormorant; Shag

The **Cormorant** has long had close associations with coastal and island communities and so has many local names. These include billy diver; black diver; coal goose, but it is not a goose; cowe'en eiders; gor maw, with maw being a word for gull, which it is not; hiblin, from Old Norse referring to its white, breeding season thigh patches; lairblade; mochrum eiders; palmer; parson, from its appearance; scarf, which imitates its croaking sound and sea hen, possibly from the fact its eggs were taken as food. In Hindi the bird is called a water crow.

The vernacular name Cormorant derives from the Old French cormaran which in turn comes from the Latin name corvus marinus, meaning sea-raven. Of course, the Cormorant is not related to the Raven except they are both very black birds in winter! The Cormorant is considered a pest to fish stocks and licences are still issued to cull the bird. In times past the Cormorant was trained to fish and there was an officer of the royal household entitled Master of the Cormorants. In Japan the Cormorant is traditionally used by fishermen to catch fish. A noose is tied round the neck of the bird in such a way that it can catch a fish but not swallow it.

In South America and South Africa, huge deposits of guano have accumulated in regions with large cormorant breeding colonies. Guano is collected then sold as fertilizer and has been a large source of revenue for countries such as Peru. Between 1848 and 1875 20 million tonnes of guano was exported from Peru

> The Cormorant is associated with Liverpool. According to popular legend, the two birds on top of the Liver Building are a male and female; the female looking out to sea, watching for the seamen to return safely home whilst the male looks towards the city, making

sure the city is safe. An alternative version says that the male bird is watching over and protecting the families of the seamen. Local legend also holds that the birds face away from each other because if they were to mate and fly away, the city would cease to exist. Another legend says that if an honest man and a virgin woman were to fall in love in front of the liverbird, the couple of liverbirds would come to life, fly away and Liverpool would cease to exist.

In Paradise Lost, the Cormorant symbolises greed. Perched on top of the tree of life, Satan took the form of a Cormorant as he spied on Adam and Eve during his first intrusion into Eden. In Scandinavian they are considered good omen. A Norwegian tale is that those lost at sea come to visit their loved ones disguised as Cormorants.

The Cormorant's scientific name is *Phalacrocorax carbo* with *carbo* meaning black, as in charcoal.

28 - Shag

The name **Shag** derives from the tuft seen on the bird's head in the breeding season. This was used to differentiate the Shag from the Cormorant although the names are often inter-changeable in other countries. Local names include cole goose; crested cormorant; green cormorant, referring to the bird's iridescent green sheen; green scarf, with scarf referring to the bird's croaking sound and skart.

The Shag is a deep sea diver reaching depths of 45 m, predominantly feeding on the sea bottom. Britain holds about 40% of the world population of Shag. Like Cormorants, Shag have poor water-proofing on their wing feathers. This improves their ability to swim under water but then they have to dry their feathers by spreading out their wings. As a result of poor water-proofing they only migrate short distances. Birds are very faithful to their wintering quarters with some birds returning to the same spot on a harbour wall! During World War 2 Shag were shot as restaurant food.

The Shag was known to Aristotle and its scientific name *Phalacrocorax aristotelis* means Aristotle's cormorant, with the names Shag and Cormorant often used interchangeably.

Herons, egrets and bitterns

Order - Pelecaniformes

This order includes the herons, egrets and bitterns, as well as pelicans. Pelican derives from the Greek pelekus, the word for hatchet. They all have a bare throat (gular) patch. The nostrils are dysfunctional, breathing through their beak. Many birds have beaks with serrated edges to assist holding slimy fish. These medium to large-sized birds have long legs and necks with little size difference between the sexes. In flight the neck is retracted and their legs are held backwards. The legs are long and strong and in most species are unfeathered from the lower part of the tibia. Their feet have three forward-pointing, long, thin toes. Often they feed on fish or similar marine life. Nesting is colonial and these birds are monogamous. Pair formation and mating displays are elaborate and complex. Females defend the nest-site and construct the nest from materials collected by the male. The parents regurgitate food into their own mouths and the chicks eat from their open beaks. The young are altricial.

In this order there is one UK family:

Ardeidae - herons, egrets and bitterns.

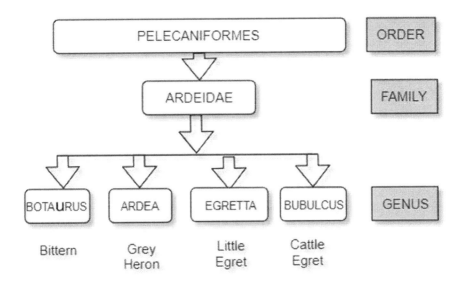

Herons, egrets and bitterns

Main characteristics of the Ardeidae family:

The herons, egrets and bitterns are wading birds which make up the Ardeidae family. The family name derives from the Latin for heron. Egrets are not a distinct group from the herons but are named because of their white, decorative plumes and they tend to be smaller. Typically herons are tall and thin, with long necks and legs, large, sharply pointed beaks, large, moveable eyes and broad wings. Their plumage is often complex, including black, white, greys or browns with distinctive plumes. The sexes are identical. The long neck of 20 – 21 cervical vertebrae (with the fifth to seventh being articulated) is S shaped in flight, giving the neck its characteristic kink. The toes are long, including the back toe and they are slightly webbed. The claw of the middle toe has a serrated edge, used in the care of plumage. Herons do not have a preen gland. Herons have well-developed eyes with a narrow field of binocular vision, aimed forward in order to sight prey. Herons capture fish, molluscs and worms by spearing them with their long beaks. They have to compensate for light refraction in the water as their underwater prey is not actually located where it appears to be. Herons also move their heads around to compensate for reflection off the water's surface. Some members of this group nest colonially in trees whilst the bitterns nest in reed beds. Although some birds are site faithful, many birds move nests or even change nesting area from one season to the next. Male herons build a nest and then indulge in a courtship display to attract their mate. Some develop delicate, lacy breeding feathers on the head, back or breast, used during courtship displays. Most species of herons are monogamous. They lay greenish or drab-coloured eggs. Chicks are altricial and are fed by regurgitation.

The feathers of species in the heron family include:

- o   filoplumes - elongated, hairy, aigrettes, with long shanks and few barbs and appear frayed.
- o   lanceolate plumes - are like long body feathers with frayed edges.
- o   powder feathers - used for grooming. Most herons have three pairs of down patches. The powder produced keeps the plumage water-repellent and probably cleans it as well.

The four species in this family are in four genera:

Botaurus - Bittern
Ardea - Grey Heron
Egretta - Little Egret
Bubulcus - Cattle Egret

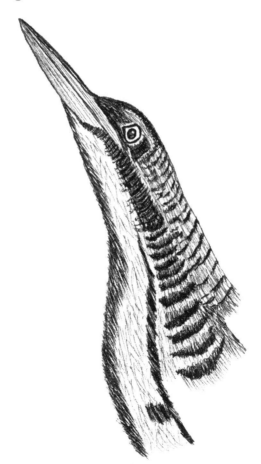

29 - Bittern

The **Bittern** is a bird which is far more often heard than seen in its reed bed and bog environment and this is reflected in some of the many local names given to the bird. This variety of names includes barrel maker; bitter bump; bog blutter; bog trotter; boomer; bull o' the bog; bumble; bumpy cors; buttle bump; clabitter; heather bluiter and mire drum. It was once thought the bird made its booming call by thrusting its beak into the mud or pushing its beak into a reed and blowing. False tales such as these became established through the local names given to the bird. In Suffolk a ship's fog-horn is called a sea bittern.

The Bittern's formal name has a long history and its roots seem to be in the Latin butio, from a bird which roars like an ox whilst mating. This moves into the Old French butor and then to bitore, bittor, bitterne and finally Bittern. Several bird names make a gradual change over time, with a few letters changing each time but eventually morphing to something quite different.

The Bittern was extinct in Britain as a breeding bird between the 1870s and 1911. For details of its recovery see the Section on Conservation in Chapter 6.

The Bittern's scientific name is *Botaurus stellaris* with *Botaurus* made up of bos meaning oxen and *taurus* bull. *Stellaris* is Latin for starry, referring to the bird's mottled plumage. In fact the formal English name also derives from the same source as *Botaurus*.

30 - Grey Heron

The **Grey Heron** has been well known for centuries and is seen throughout Britain. Some of its local names are from human names such as frank from its call; jack heron (for the male); jenny crow; joan-na-ma-crank and moll heron (for the female). Shitepoke comes from the bird's habit of defecating when flushed or when defending itself against a predator and shiterow, which was also a derogatory term for a thin, weak person. Other names include brancher and hernshaw as a name for a young heron; hegrie; herald; langleggity beastie; longie crane and long-necked longnix. Chaucer used the name heron-sewe, with sewe meaning dish, referring to the bird being eaten.

The name heron derives from the Old French hairon and eron to the English name hayroun in the 14th century.

The heron appears in Egyptian mythology and is sometimes called the Bennu. One tale is that the bird was self-created and played a role in the creation of the world. It was said to have flown over the waters of Nun that existed before creation, landing on a rock and issuing a call which led to the creation of the world. Isis' husband, Osiris, is depicted as a Heron, a bird probably well known to the ancient Egyptians. In folklore the Grey Heron symbolises fertility, forgetfulness, longevity, morning (as it stands in the water the heron is first to welcome the dawn), children and regeneration. In Angus, there was a belief that the heron waxes and wanes with the moon i.e. when the moon is full it is plump. Weather-lorists regard the heron flying up and down as a sign of bad weather and flying low as a sign of rain. In the 16th and 17th centuries the Grey Heron was hunted using a Peregrine. King John is recorded as organising hunting parties to catch ringed herons. It was a much valued bird (for hunting) and poaching the bird was punishable by having a hand chopped off.

Despite its size the Grey Heron can fly considerable distances with ringing recoveries of UK birds coming from Norway, Holland, Iceland and Morocco. In winter the UK population is supplemented by birds from Scandinavia and the Netherlands.

The Grey Heron's scientific name is *Ardea cinerea* which comes from the Latin *Ardea* for a heron and cinereus meaning ash-coloured.

The **Little Egret**'s name derives from the French aigrette for the bird's long, white head plumes that were much used in millinery. See the Section on the millinery trade in Chapter 6 Populations. Until the 1970's the bird was classified as a rarity. It slowly acclimatised to living in Britain and first bred in the UK in 1996 in Dorset. The species now has a conservation status of green in the UK.

The Little Egret's scientific name *Egretta garzetta* is based on a French and an Italian word. *Egretta* comes from the French aigrette, referring to the long, feathery neck plumes. *Garzetta* is Italian for little white heron.

The **Cattle Egret**'s scientific name is *Bubulcus ibis* with *Bubulcus* coming from the Latin for herdsman. The Cattle Egret is one of the few birds found on every continent of the world. The bird is popular with herdsmen as it rids their cattle of parasites. *Ibis* is not accurate as egrets are closely related to herons (in the Ardeidae family) not ibis, which are in a different family (with the rather complex name Threskionithidae). The bird is now established as a UK breeding bird.

Hawks, eagles, buzzards, kites and ospreys

Order - Accipitriformes

An order of birds including hawks, eagles, buzzards, kites, ospreys and vultures (but not the falcons which are more closely related to the parrots and passerines). The word accipt means to accept. Typically Accipitriformes have a sharply hooked beak with a soft cere housing the nostrils. Wings are long and broad for soaring, with the outer four to six primary feathers emarginated i.e. spread out, to reduce drag. In some species females are up to 50% heavier than males. All have strong legs and feet with raptorial claws and opposable hind claws. These birds kill their prey with their strong taloned feet. Most Accipitriformes are carnivorous, hunting by sight. They are long-lived and most have low reproductive rates. The young have a long, fast-growing fledgling stage, followed by 3–8 weeks of nest care after their first flight and then 1 to 3 years as sexually immature adults. Usually the birds are monogamous.

The terms bird of prey and raptor are generic covering a range of birds that typically hunt vertebrates or feed off carrion and possess strong feet and beaks. The word raptor derives from the Latin rapio, meaning to seize or take by force.

In this order there are two UK families:

Pandionidae and Accipitridae.

Main characteristics of the Pandionidae family:

The Osprey is a large diurnal, fish-eating raptor, about 60 cm in length with a 1.8 m wingspan. It is brown on the upperparts and predominantly greyish on the head and underparts. Both sexes are similarly coloured but the female is slightly larger. The Osprey's diet consists almost exclusively of fish. Nasal valves prevent water entering the nostrils when fishing. Its toes are of equal length, its tarsi are reticulate and its talons are rounded, rather than grooved. Males perform an aerial courtship display. Ospreys nest in trees or on an artificial nest post. Both sexes help build the nest, often using an old nest from previous years. A clutch of 2 - 4 eggs is laid which hatch asynchronously after 40 days incubation by both parents. After 3 - 4 weeks the chick's down is replaced by feathers. Hatchlings take over 50 days to fledge, after which the parents continue to feed the young bird until it has learned to catch its own fish. Ospreys reach sexually maturity at 3 - 4 years old.

There is one genus and one species in this family:

Pandion – Osprey

Local names for the **Osprey** include bald buzzard; eagle fisher; ern; fish hawk; mullet hawk; water eagle and white-headed buzzard, all quite predictable if lacking in accuracy!

The name Osprey comes from the Old French osfraie and the Latin ossifraga, which means bone breaker from the manner in which the Osprey takes fish and eats them. The first written record of a name for the Osprey in English dates from the 10th century. An Act of Parliament in 1566 declared Osprey (amongst many other birds and animals) a pest and a bounty was put on their heads. The bird was persecuted for taking salmon and trout plus it was killed for taxidermy. After becoming extinct in 1916 the bird returned naturally in 1954. For details of its recovery see the Section on Conservation in Chapter 6.

The Osprey's toes are of equal length and is the only raptor whose outer toe can turn backwards so there are two forward facing and two rear facing toes, enabling the bird to skilfully grab fish from the surface of water. It can then revert to three forward facing toes when perching. The lower surface of their toes is covered in spicules (needles) to help grasp their fish prey. A pair needs to catch about 400 fish in a breeding season, with a 1 in 4 fishing success rate. Ospreys are long distant migrants and unusually for a bird of prey they make long haul flights across the sea. Other birds of prey in this order need short sea crossings which they can soar and glide over as they cannot sustain continuous flapping flight. Adults are faithful to both their UK breeding and resting grounds in West Africa.

> One interesting piece of folklore is that the bird has such extraordinary powers they are able to make fish turn over in the water and show their white undersides, making them much easier for the Osprey to see and catch. A 16th century play recorded this: "I will provide thee of a princely osprey; That, as he flieth over fish in pools; The fish shall turn their glistering bellies up; and though shalt take they liberal choice of all". A record states another strange practice was for young Ospreys to be killed, hung outside and when adults came with a fish for its young the fish was taken for food. Shakespeare mentions the Osprey in *Coriolanus* "All places yield to him ere he sits down ... I think he'll be to Rome as is the osprey to the fish, who takes it by sovereignty of nature".

The Osprey's scientific name is *Pandion haliaetus* with *Pandion* referring to a mythical Greek king Pandion and *haliaetus* deriving from the Greek halos for sea and aetos for Eagle. Pandion appears in the myth linked to the Nightingale, as the father of Philomena who is transformed into a Nightingale. See the entry for Nightingale for the full story.

Main characteristics of the Accipitridae family:

This family comprises the kites, buzzards, vultures, eagles, harriers and hawks. *Accipiter* derives from the verb accipere meaning to grasp. The birds are generally broad winged with a strongly hooked beak and an upper mandible covered by a fleshy cere. Females are often significantly larger than males (especially hawks) enabling them to kill larger prey. Birds are usually paler below appearing less conspicuous to their prey against a bright sky. Females have duller plumage. These birds have very good visual acuity; up to 8 times better than human eyesight. They have a brow ridge above the eye to protect it from bright sunlight. Their large, tubular, fixed eyes have two fovea assisting with near and distant sharp vision. They kill their prey (up to the same weight as themselves) with their talons. Pairs generally mate for life and are highly territorial, especially when breeding. They build nests of twigs and are site faithful. Each of the 2 or 3 eggs are brooded immediately after laying leading to asynchronous hatching. In years of poor food supply the older chick survives and may kill its younger siblings. Usually the female broods and the male provides the food. Fledging is protracted.

This broad family contains ten species split into seven genera:

Pernis - Honey-buzzard
Aquila - Golden Eagle
Circus - Hen Harrier; Marsh Harrier; Montagu's Harrier
Accipter - Goshawk; Sparrowhawk
Milvus - Red Kite
Haliaeetus - White-tailed Eagle
Buteo - Buzzard

The **Honey-buzzard** is completely mis-named! The bird does not eat honey, although it eats bees and wasp grubs, having adapted not to be stung by them as it forages through a nest! One estimate is that one bird will eat 90 000 grubs a year. Also it is not a buzzard. The bird is closely related to kites rather than to buzzards.

An older name for the bird is bee hawk; at least hawk is accurate. The bird was shot by gamekeepers and its skin and eggs were taken by collectors. Gilbert White records having one shot for examination. In 1860 a clutch of eggs were sold for £5 and a pair of chicks for £40.

The Honey-buzzard's scientific name *Pernis apivorus* is still not wholly accurate. *Pernis* means a hawk and *apivorus* means to devour a bee.

31 - Golden Eagle

Local names for the **Golden Eagle** include black eagle; erne, a name it shares with the White-tailed Eagle, meaning soarer; jove's bird, alluding to its religious connections; ring-tailed eagle and rough footed eagle.

The word eagle drives from the Old French egle and the Latin aquila for black eagle. The term 'eagle-eyed', used for someone who is sharp sighted, has been in use since the 17th century. The Golden Eagle is indeed sharp sighted. It has 1 million cones in its eye compared to the 200 000 in a human eye. This would make the comparative size of a human eye the size of an orange. The bird also has two fovea on its retina. One provides long distance focussing to locate prey in the landscape and the other is for close distance focussing to home in on prey. The female weighs 5.3 kg compared to the smaller male's 3.7 kg. The golden in its name is from the colour of its head and neck feathers.

Aquiline means curved like an eagle's beak, again in use since the 17th century. In golf an eagle is better than a birdie because it soars higher. The Roman expression 'bird of jove' applied to the Golden Eagle, a highly prized bird in Rome, as the legendary messenger of the god Jove with thunderbolts in its talons as it sped across the heavens.

The Golden Eagle is an iconic bird and has had a close links with humans for millennia, with many references to it in the Bible and other literature, appearances on ancient buildings, in art work, on national flags and coats of arms. The bird is variously associated with courage, discord, empire, evil, faith, immortality, power, rapacity and strength.

Greek myths frequently incorporated birds in their stories. The aetos was a giant Golden Eagle which served as Zeus' personal messenger and animal companion. According to some the eagle was once a mortal king named Periphas, whose virtuous rule was so celebrated that he became honoured like a god. Zeus would have smote him with a thunderbolt but Apollo intervened transforming the king into an eagle, setting him beside the throne of Zeus. In other accounts, Zeus adopted the eagle as his bird when it first appeared to him, before the Titan War, as a good omen. The eagle was later sent by Zeus to carry the handsome youth Ganymede up to heaven to become the cupbearer of the gods. The bird received a place amongst the stars as the constellation Aquila. Its consort was Lyra, the heavenly Vulture. In Greek and Roman mythology, the eagle served as Jupiter's personal messenger.

The eagle appears in another story. Zeus was angry at Prometheus. Zeus had his servants, Force and Violence, seize Prometheus and take him to the Caucasus Mountains and chain him to a rock. Here he was tormented day and night by a giant eagle tearing at his liver. Zeus offered Prometheus two options. He could tell Zeus who the mother of the child was that would dethrone him or meet two conditions. The first was that an immortal must volunteer to die for Prometheus and the second was that a mortal must kill the eagle and unchain him. Eventually, Chiron the Centaur agreed to die for him and Heracles killed the eagle and unbound him.

The aquila was the eagle standard of a Roman legion, (another reference to the Golden Eagle's scientific name) carried by a legionnaire, known as an aquilifer. One eagle standard was carried by each legion. The Romans also used to look to the bird to decide whether to go to battle, by judging the bird's flight and demeanour - 'aves spicere' i.e. to look to the birds. This is the derivation of the word auspicious. When a Caesar died he was cremated and an eagle was sent into the flames to transport the Caesar's soul to heaven. The two-headed eagle probably symbolised ancient Rome and the new Rome, centred in Constantinople. Later Charlemagne adopted the eagle as his symbol. The Habsburgs later replaced this with the similar Imperial Eagle. A Norse mythological tale is of Hræsvelgr a giant who takes an eagles' form and sits at the end of the world causing the wind to blow when he beats his wings in flight.

In the Christian tradition the eagle represents salvation. It is associated with St. John, as the bearer of the word, hence the use of the eagle on lecterns from which the Bible is read, spreading the gospel round the world. An old legend is that the bird can look at the sun and not be blinded, so can contemplate divine splendour and thus is able to spread light i.e. salvation.

Needless to say the eagle appears many times in literature. The Bible records in Exodus (19:4) as Israel leaves Egypt for Sinai "and how I bore you on eagles' wings and brought you to myself". Job (39:27) knew about the eagle "Is it at your command that the eagle mounts up and makes his nest on high?". Isaiah (40:31) refers to the strength of an eagle "but they who wait upon the Lord ... shall mount up with wings like eagles ...". Proverbs (23:5) quotes "Wilt thou set thine eyes upon that which is not? For riches certainly make themselves wings; they fly away as an eagle towards heaven". Chaucer wrote "There mighte men the royal eagle find, That with his sharp look pierceth the sun". William Blake recorded "When thou seest an eagle, thou seest a portion of genius; lift up thine head". Tennyson wrote "He clasps the crag with crooked hands; Close to the sun in lonely lands, Ringed with the azure world he stands. The wrinkled sea beneath him crawls; He watches from the mountain walls, And like a thunderbolt he falls".

The bird appears in *The dalliance of the Eagles* by Walt Whitman "Skyward in air a sudden muffled sound, the dalliance of eagles, the rushing amorous contact high in space together, The clinching interlocking claws, a living, fierce, gyrating wheel, Four beating wings, two beaks , a swirling mass grappling, In tumbling, turning clustering loops, straight downward fall".

The eagle appears on the coat of arms of many countries to symbolise the characteristics the country wishes to convey. For example, the coat of arms of Egypt is a Golden Eagle looking left, taken from the Golden Eagle of Saladin founded on the Saladin citadel of Cairo, as are the coats of arms of Iraq and Palestine. The German coat of arms incorporates a black eagle and the Ghanaian coat contains two Golden Eagles and Iceland one. The coat of arms of Mexico has a Golden Eagle perched upon a cactus devouring a snake. The Moldavian coat of arms has an eagle holding a cross in its beak and a sceptre and a branch in its claws and the Montenegrin coat represents a two-headed eagle in flight. The great seal of the United States has a Bald Eagle on it. Napoleon used the Golden Eagle as a symbol of the new French Empire.

The eagle appears in Aesop's tale *The Eagle and the Jackdaw*. An eagle, flying down from his eyrie seized a lamb and carried it off. A Jackdaw who saw this was envious and was determined to emulate the eagle. He settled on a large sheep, with the intention of carrying it off, but his claws become entangled in its fleece and he was unable to release himself. A shepherd ran up and caught him. He clipped his

In times past in Orkney there was a law that entitled anyone who killed a Golden Eagle to a hen from every house in the parish where the bird was killed. The Golden Eagle is still shot as some farmers believe the bird is capable of killing a healthy lamb. The bird will eat the placenta and scavenge dead animals. There is little evidence that a Golden Eagle can kill a healthy lamb. In Texas the bird is shot from aeroplanes because it is a perceived threat to sheep.

The Golden Eagle's scientific name is *Aquila chrysaetos* with *Aquila* being Latin for Eagle and *chrysaetos* the Greek khrusos for gold and *aetos* for eagle. Aquila is the name of the constellation referred to above and *aetos* was the first name of the mythical eagle of Zeus.

The **Harriers** (of which there are three in Britain – the Hen, Marsh and Montagu's) are named from their behaviour of pursuing and destroying their prey, hence the verb to harry. The name Marsh Harrier is from its habitat and Montagu's from the person who correctly identified this species, separating it from the similar Hen Harrier. The harriers presented early ornithologists with quite an identification challenge. It was thought that the male Hen Harrier and the male (of what we now call) Montagu's Harrier were a pair, called a Hen Harrier and the respective females were a pair, called ringtails. This confusion arose because the male and female birds of both species have a very different appearance and the females are larger. The true identification was made by George Montagu in the late 18th century.

The three British harriers are placed in the same genus, Circus, based on the Greek for a hawk that flies in circles, being a distinctive feature of these birds.

Many local names for the **Hen Harrier** refer to the bird's colour, like blue gled, gled is a name used generally for hawks; blue hawk; blue sleeves; grey buzzard; white aboon gled and white hawk. The name ringtail is still used, referring to the female's distinctive white tail band. Furze hawk; gorse hawk and moor hawk all refer to the bird's habitat. Flapper is from its slow wing beat flight and faller from the male's courtship display flight. Other names include dove hawk and seagull hawk, possibly from the male's grey colour.

The Hen Harrier derives its names from its habit of chasing hens. The male has a spectacular courtship display flight involving somersaults and dives. Whilst feeding the young the male catches the prey food and passes it to the female whilst in flight, with the female turning on her back and catching the prey in her talons. This reduces the risk of predators identifying the location of the nest. The Hen Harrier has been heavily persecuted over the centuries and is still killed (illegally). For more detail see the Section on Conservation in Chapter 6. The species has a conservation status of red in the UK and near threatened in Europe.

The scientific name of the Hen Harrier is *Circus cyaneus*, with *cyaneus* meaning dark blue, the colour of the male (the female is more cryptically coloured).

The **Marsh Harrier** is true to its name and breeds in marshes. Local names include bald buzzard; bastard eagle; bog gled; brown hawk; duck hawk; dun pickle, with dun from the duller colour of the female and pickle from pittle (an old word for Buzzard); moor buzzard, with moor historically meaning marsh; red harrier, referring to the brighter coloured male bird; snipe hawk and white headed harpy, with harpy being a bird of prey with a woman's face and more recently meaning a woman who draws a man into her grasp. A photograph of the Marsh Harrier (taken by the famous bird photographer Eric Hosking) was adopted as the insignia of an RAF platoon. The name Harrier was also used by the RAF for the innovative vertical take-off aircraft in the 1960's.

Until the 17th century the bird was common in East Anglia. Numbers fell rapidly when the fens were drained. Then as a predatory bird it was heavily persecuted and almost driven to extinction in Britain in the 19th century. By the turn of the 20th century there were no records of the bird breeding. As numbers recovered from the mid 1920's, the Marsh Harrier was affected by the organochloride chemicals that affected many birds of prey. For more detail see the Section on Pesticides in Chapter 6. Currently numbers have recovered and the species has a conservation status of amber in the UK and least concern in Europe.

The male bird transfers food to its mate using an aerial pass. He calls to the female who leaves her nest and flies to meet the male who drops the food for the female to accurately catch in her talons. This eliminates the need for the more colourful male to go near the nest and thus reduces the risk of ground predators finding the nest. Often the female chooses an older male, even if the male already has several mates, as they are better hunters and provide more food than a young, inexperienced male would. The birds have very good hearing, possessing large ears measuring 12 mm long and 9 mm wide (almost the size of an owl's) but unlike the owls, they do not have stereo hearing i.e. the ears are placed symmetrically on their face. The ear coverts have well spaced barbs to assist the transmission of sound. Combined with good eye sight the birds are highly efficient hunters. The wing loading of the Marsh Harrier is low for a raptor at 0.3 g / cm^2 compared to a Buzzard at 0.45 g / cm^2

The Marsh Harrier's scientific name is *Circus aeruginosus*, from the Latin aerugo meaning copper and osus full, referring to the male's colouration.

The confusion over the identification and naming of the **Montagu's Harrier** was explained above under Hen Harrier. The female weighs 380 g, greater than the lighter male at 270 g.

The bird's scientific name is *Circus pygargus,* with *pygargus* from the Greek for a bird of prey mentioned by Aristotle.

The name **Goshawk** comes from goose hawk although even the larger female weighing 1 100 g would find it difficult to catch a goose. The male is smaller, weighing 850 g and was originally given the generic male hawk name of tiercel.

The Goshawk is low down the falconer's hierarchy and was flown by a cook or poor man. In falconry the Goshawk was given the name cook's bird from its ability to catch prey for the kitchen. A person who trains a Goshawk is called an austringer. The Goshawk appears on the flag of the Azores, with the name of islands deriving from the Portuguese for the bird - acor. In fact the Goshawk has never lived on the island, with the bird being confused with the Buzzard. Attila the Hun wore an image of this bird on his helmet.

The Goshawk's scientific name is *Accipiter gentilis*, with *Accipiter* indicating hawk from the verb accipere meaning to grasp and *gentilis* for noble hawk.

32 - Sparrowhawk

The **Sparrowhawk**'s local names include pigeon hawk but only the female would stand a chance of catching a pigeon, as she weighs around 260 g, 50% more than the male. Because of its smaller size the male is called a tiercel, from the French la tierce, meaning a third (smaller in size). Other names include blue hawk and blue merlin, for the male which is blue grey on the head and back; gold tip, from the colour of the fringes of the feathers; hedge hawk, where it sits spying on prey; horse gowk, with the sound being compared to a neighing horse and gowk meaning Cuckoo (having a similar flight silhouette) or awkward; spar hawk; stannin hawk and stone falcon. The use of gowk for this bird derives from the traditional tale that the Cuckoo turned into a Sparrowhawk in winter (before migration was understood). In fact this tale goes back to the time of Homer (thought to be around 800 BC) who reported that the Cuckoo disappeared in winter and turned into a Hierax (probably a Sparrowhawk). Aristotle later disagreed with this, noticing clear differences in plumage between the two birds. The Sparrowhawk is low down in the falconry hierarchy; the female being flown by priests and the male by clerks. Gilbert White commented that the Sparrowhawk "was a terror to all the dames in the village that had ducks or chickens under their care". The first written record of an English name for the Sparrowhawk dates from the 8th century.

The vernacular name Sparrowhawk derives from the Old English spearhafoc and the Middle English sperhauk. The much smaller male takes smaller birds, such as sparrows, to feed the fledglings. The Sparrowhawk breeds slightly later in the season so that other, smaller birds' chicks have already fledged ready for the male Sparrowhawk to catch as food for its younger chicks. It is difficult to see the bird as it sits out of sight, ready to pounce on its unsuspecting victims, like the birds on your bird table! It has been estimated that in one year each Sparrowhawk kills 30 kg of prey and eats about 20 kg of this. One study revealed that 82% of prey killed weighed less than 50 g but this only made up 47% of the total weight of prey killed; the balance being made up of heavier birds, up to 350 g weight. One estimate was that a breeding pair would eat the equivalent of 2 200 sparrow sized birds a year. Even so there is no clear evidence of what impact the presence of Sparrowhawks has on the population of its prey.

Sparrowhawks were quite common until numbers fell dramatically in the 1950's. After careful research, it was discovered that when the bird digested its prey, it also digested the pesticide poison DDT from the prey. The full story is recounted in the Section on Conservation in Chapter 6. Numbers recovered from that low point, although numbers have fallen by 23% in the 10 years to 2017. Mortality rates for this species are quite high – 69% for males in their first year and 51% for females. The birds are sedentary only moving a few kilometres from their birth place, with females moving further than males, possibly to reduce inter-breeding.

The bird appears in an Aesop's tale - *The Hawk, the Kite and the Pigeons*. Pigeons, terrified by the appearance of a kite, called upon the hawk to defend them. He at once consented. When they admitted him into the cote, they found that he made more havoc and slew a larger number of them in a single day, than the kite could possibly in a whole year. The moral being 'avoid a remedy that is worse than the disease'.

The Sparrowhawk's scientific name is *Accipter nisus* with *nisus* another name for the Sparrowhawk. *Nisus* derives from the myth of Nisus, King of Megara, who was turned into a bird of prey after the city was betrayed by his daughter Scylla, who was turned into a lark, forever flying in fear of her father.

Local names for the **Red Kite** include bald kite; crotch tail, from its distinctive forked tail; gled, meaning glider and puttock, meaning swooper, also a name for the Buzzard and the harriers, plus some rather strange names like baegez; barcud; boda wenol; scoul and whew.

The word kite derives from the Old English cyta, probably imitative of its distinctive cry. Also in the 16th century it was the name of a person who preyed on others.

> The Red Kite was a numerous bird in cities in the Middle Ages. The bird is associated with cowardice and baseness. In Roman times the bird was reported as taking hair from a man's head for its nest. Shakespeare mentioned this in *The Winter's Tale* - "My traffic is sheets; when the kite builds, look to lesser linen". He used the Kite's name as a reproach e.g. "detested kite" (*Lear*) and "you kite" (*Anthony and Cleopatra*) and "I should have fatted all the region kites with this slave's offal" (*Hamlet*) and he knew that the Kite took fowl "To guard the chicken from a hungry kite" (*Henry VI*). Clearly a well known bird in those times!

> The bird appears in an Aesop's tale *The Kites and the Swans*. Kites of old sang equally with the Swans. But having heard the neigh of the horse, they were so enchanted with the sound that they tried to imitate it. In trying to neigh, they forgot how to sing. The moral being: 'the desire for imaginary benefits might involve the loss of present blessings'.

The conservation story of the Red Kite is recalled in the Section on Conservation in Chapter 6.

The Red Kite's scientific name is *Milvus milvus* simply from the Latin *Milvus* a kite.

The **White-tailed Eagle** is the largest bird of prey in the UK, it has the largest wing span of any British bird at 2.2 m and is the fourth largest eagle in the world. The conservation story of the White-tailed Eagle is recalled in the Section on Conservation in Chapter 6. Fishermen had a tale that as soon as fish saw the bird they rose to the surface, belly up, to be caught. That led to fishermen using eagle fat on their bait to tempt fish to bite! The bird's Anglo-Saxon name is erne, meaning soarer. Other local names include fen eagle; grey eagle and sea eagle, a name for the immature birds.

The White-tailed Eagle's scientific name is accurate, being *Haliaeetus albicilla*. This is comprised of halos for sea, aetos for Eagle, albus for white and *cilla* for tail - a white-tailed sea eagle. The bird only has a white tail when the birds reach maturity at the age of 6 or 7. This led to the immature birds formerly being identified as a separate species named sea eagle.

Local names for the **Buzzard** include bald kite with a reference to the similar kite; barcutan; dancing hawk; gled, meaning to glide and glider, which it does masterfully; pittle; putian, meaning to push, thrust or swoop; puttock, from the Old English to swoop and shreak, from its aerial call.

The Buzzard's vernacular name comes from falconry where the name meant useless kind of hawk although it was flown by a baron in the falconry hierarchy (one level below the Peregrine). In America the word is now used as derogatory expression for someone who is worthless or stupid but there the name is also used for the Turkey Vulture. Dr Johnson described the bird as "a degenerate or mean species of hawk" and Bewick as "cowardly, inactive and slothful".

The Buzzard has in recent times become the most common bird of prey in Britain with numbers increasing by 96% in the 22 years to 2017 with a distribution across the UK. In the Middle Ages the bird was considered vermin for which a bounty was paid. Its numbers declined after the Second World War as a result of the spread of myxomatosis in its rabbit prey. Gamekeepers also persecuted the bird. The Buzzard's eyes are proportionally 50 times the size of a human eye and together give about 45º binocular vision and 150º monocular vision. The eyes cannot rotate in their sockets and are protected from direct sunlight by an eyebrow. The female (as with all species in this family) is heavier, at 1 000 g, than the male at 780 g.

The Buzzard's scientific name is *Buteo buteo* which simply repeats the name Buzzard twice!

Owls

Order - Strigiformes

The Strigiformes (Owls) are an order of birds of prey. The name of the order means screech, as many owls do. Most are solitary and hunt small mammals, insects and other birds. Owls have large forward-facing eyes and ear-holes, a hawk-like beak and a flat face. They often have a conspicuous circle of feathers around each eye called a facial disc which helps to funnel sound into their ears; some discs are placed asymmetrically. Owls have binocular, black and white vision with large eyes fixed in their sockets, with good distance vision. See the Section on Sight in Chapter 5 for more detail on this. Eye colour is correlated with the time of day an owl hunts: dark brown or black eyes indicate nocturnal activity; orange dawn or dusk and yellow eyes in diurnal birds. Serrations on the leading edge of the flight feathers reduce noise. Owls use filoplumes (small hair-like feathers) on their beak and feet to feel for their prey. Prey is captured using the sharp beak and powerful feet before swallowing it whole, regurgitating indigestible items as pellets. Most owls are solitary. They hunt and roost alone, except during the breeding season. Owls do not construct nests but use abandoned nests or crevices in trees or in buildings. Males mostly use sounds to gain a female's attention and some use a visual display. In most species, both sexes vocalise. Owl eggs are usually white and almost spherical. The eggs hatch asynchronously.

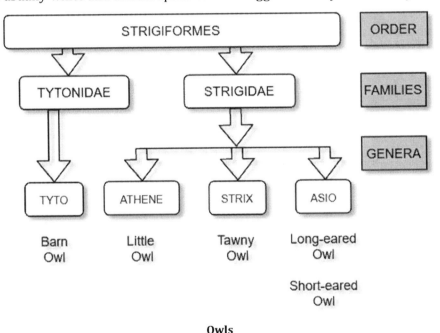

Owls

In this order in the UK there are two UK families:

Tytonidae and **Strigidae**.

Main characteristics of the Tytonidae family:

In the UK the only member of this family is the Barn Owl, one of the most widespread bird species in the world, being found on six of the seven continents. These owls have large heads and a characteristic heart-shaped faces. They have long, strong legs with powerful talons, a tufted preen gland, primary feathers that are not narrowed at the tips or emarginated. The inner toe is as long as the middle toe with comb-like serration on the inner edge of

288

the middle claw. Long ear openings are covered by a flap of skin. The heart-shaped facial disc, formed by stiff feathers, amplifies the sound, helping to locate prey. Adaptations to the wing feathers eliminate sound when flying. Barn Owls roost alone, except during courtship, emitting screeching, screaming or whistling contact calls and male Owls perform a hovering courtship flight. Barn Owls are monogamous and remain faithful for life. Eggs are laid asynchronously at two-day intervals. Their white eggs take around five weeks to hatch. Chicks hatch covered in sparse down, soon replaced by a thicker down. Incubation and brooding are undertaken by the female who is fed by the male. When the chicks are half-grown and able to keep themselves warm, the female joins in providing food for the family.

The word owl derives onomatopoeically from the bird's howl, coming from the Anglo Saxon ule and Latin ulula to howl. Ululate means to wail or lament loudly, deriving from the Roman for owl.

There is one genus and one species in this family:

Tyto – Barn Owl

The **Barn Owl** has been a familiar bird for centuries and humans have had a close relationship with it, not least because of its habit of nesting in buildings. If you get too near a Barn Owl it emits a screech that is truly frightening! The Barn Owl was given a large number of local names; up to 40. Many include human names such as billy wix, with wix from its cry; gill hooter; gillhowlet; ginny ollit; jenny owlet; madge moggy and padge (variation of Madge, from Margaret). Others include cherubim; church owl; death owl; demon owl; ghost owl, from being seen at twilight; hobgoblin; monkey-faced owl; rat owl; roarer; screech owl and white owl. All these various names reflect some observed aspect of the bird's behaviour, like its screech or hiss, or tales about the power of the bird including its link to death. The first written record of an English name for the Barn Owl dates from the 10th century.

The Barn Owl (along with other owls and birds of prey) brood their eggs asynchronously. This means that as the first egg is laid it is brooded immediately (mainly by the female). After about 48 hours she lays her next egg and broods this immediately. She can lay up to 6 eggs. The first egg laid hatches first (after 32 days of incubation) and this chick gets a head start over its yet-to-be-born siblings. When food is in good supply all the hatchlings will fledge. However, in years of poor food supply the younger siblings will often die of starvation. The strategy means that at least the oldest chicks will survive. For the Barn Owl this makes sense as they rely heavily on Short-tailed Field Voles and the numbers of this rodent vary greatly from year to year.

The Owl is an extremely skilful hunter, using its highly enhanced sense of hearing to locate prey. It is a specialised feeder, preferring Short-tailed Voles to any other rodent. The breeding success of the Barn Owl is directly correlated to the population of this Vole. The hearing of the Barn Owl is fully described in the Section on Hearing in Chapter 5 Sense and sensibility. Their flight feathers are specially adapted to be very quiet and emit sound at 1 kHz which does not interfere with the sound emitted by their prey. Gilbert White noted "the plumage of the remiges ... is remarkably soft and pliant. Perhaps it may be necessary that the wings of these birds should not make any resistance or rushing that they may be enabled to steal through the air unheard upon a nimble and watchful quarry". How right he was! This adaptation was used with inventiveness to solve an engineering problem. Developing the Japanese Railway's Bullet train to run at high speed created a complex aerodynamic problem with its pantographs. The chief development engineer for the Japanese Railways turned to the owl for inspiration. In particular he looked at the design feature of the owl's wing feathers which produce near-silent flight, in particular the serrations on their feathers. By adding tabs (a reproduction of the serrations on the owl's wing feathers) to the pantograph's structure the wind noise and turbulence was much reduced. Problem solved.

Owls have been attributed with a range of characteristics in many cultures over a long time. Owls are perceived sometimes as wise, other times as foolish; feared and venerated; despised and admired, with links to birth and death, weather and medicine. Inevitably there are many tales about owls as a group and the Barn Owl specifically. Here is a selection. An owl screeching at night could lead to a new born child having an unhappy life or it might become a witch. Only owls can live with ghosts, so if an owl nests in an empty house, it must be haunted. A tale of stupidity common to many owls, based on the fact that their large eyes cannot rotate, is if you walk round and round a tree in which an owl is perched, the owl will keep looking at you until it wrings its own neck! In Rome, a dead owl nailed to a house averted evil. Another Roman myth was that witches changed into owls and sucked the blood of babies or that owls were messengers for sorcerers and they danced together on the graves of the dead. The association with witches persisted into the Middle Ages, not least because owls are birds of the dark night and emit loud, frightening calls. Shakespeare referred to owls in his plays, often connected to evil and death. In *Henry VI* Henry says to the Duke of Gloucester "the owl shriek'd at thy birth - an evil sign" and is called the "fatal bellman" in *Macbeth*.

One folk tale was Owl broth was said to cure whooping cough and that powdered Owl's egg would improve eye sight. Owl's eggs were given as a cure for alcoholism or to children to prevent them from becoming alcoholics. The 14ᵗʰ century poet Geoffrey Chaucer characterised the Barn Owl as a prophet of woe and mischance. In Hindu mythology, the Barn Owl is considered to be the vehicle of Goddess Lakshmi (the goddess of wealth) and it is considered lucky if an owl resides near a house. In the Middle East the owl is associated with death and destruction. Seeing an owl before battle foretold many deaths. In India seizures could be treated with a broth of owl's eyes and, worse still, if you ate an owl's eye you would be able see in the dark! Rheumatism was treated with a gel of owl's meat.

In Aesop's tales the owl is portrayed as being wise. The tale recounts that once, a long time ago, when the first oak sprouted in the forest, the owl called all the other birds together and said to them, "You see this tiny tree? If you take my advice, you will destroy it now when it is small: for when it grows big, the mistletoe will appear upon it, from which birdlime will be prepared for your destruction". Again, when the first flax was sown, she said to them "Go and eat up that seed, for it is the seed of the flax, out of which men will one day make nets to catch you". Once more, when she saw the first archer, she warned the birds that he was their deadly enemy, who would wing his arrows with their own feathers and shoot them. But they took no notice of what she said: in fact, they thought she was rather mad and laughed at her. When everything turned out as she had predicted, they changed their minds and had great respect for her wisdom. Now whenever she appears the birds listen in the hope of hearing something that may be for their good.

The Barn Owl's scientific name is *Tyto alba* with *Tyto* meaning owl and *alba*-white, a very apt name!

Main characteristics of the Strigidae family:

The typical owls are in the Strigidae family. These owls vary greatly in size having large, rounded heads, forward-facing eyes, facial discs of feathers and strong, hooked beaks. They have solid, stocky bodies with dense feathering, moderately short tails, strong feet with talons and subtle colouration. These owls are mainly arboreal and their prey is mainly mammals, birds and reptiles. They regurgitate the indigestible parts of their food as pellets. Their wings are large, broad, rounded and long. Many owl species exhibit reverse sexual dimorphism in size but not plumage. Several species have so-called ear-tufts, feathers on the sides of the head, thought to have a camouflage or defensive function. The feathers of the facial disc channel sound to the ears. Hearing in owls is highly sensitive and their asymmetrical ears help locate sound to assist catching prey at night. See the Section on Sound in Chapter 5 for more detail on this. Owls have massive eyes relative to their body size. Flight feathers facilitate silent flight, with the surface of most of the feathers covered in a very fine down. The flight feathers on the trailing edge are soft. Most owls have feathers down to their talons giving protection from rodent bites. Most owls are solitary. Courtship involves vocalisations, displays and feeding. Nest sites are holes in trees, crevices or other birds' nests. The number of eggs varies depending on the availability of food. Eggs are laid asynchronously. The female incubates the eggs whilst the male hunts for food. Chicks are altricial.

The four species in this family are in three genera:

Athene - Little Owl
Strix - Tawny Owl
Asio - Long-eared Owl; Short-eared Owl

33 - Little Owl

Several attempts to introduce the **Little Owl** into Britain from the Middle East were made in the 19th century, some with limited success. Eventually the bird bred in 1879. Further introductions were made by a keen Northants' ornithologist. From there it spread across the UK. Local names include belgian owl and dutch owl plus sparrow owl, referring to the small size of the owl.

> The wisdom attributed to owls partially derives from Greek mythology. In the story of Athena, the Greek goddess of wisdom, she is often portrayed with an owl as a companion. Athena got fed up with her crow companion, who was a prankster and banished it. Impressed with the owl's wisdom, Athena chose the Little Owl to be her mascot. The Little Owl was found in places like the Acropolis. Coins were minted with Athena's face on one side and an owl on the reverse. The story continues with Lilith, the goddess of death, who is flanked by owls. When the Athenians won the battle of Marathon from the Persians in 490 BC, the warrior goddess Athena assumed the shape of an owl and led them from above.

> Roman tales include one that a dead owl nailed to the door of a house cancelled all the evil which the owl had caused earlier. To hear the hoot of an owl predicted imminent death. The deaths of Julius Caesar, Augustus, Commodus Aurelius and Agrippa apparently were all predicted by an owl. Owl feathers and internal organs were used in magical potions and pharmaceutical remedies. For example, the ashes of an owl's feet were an antidote to snakebite and an owl's heart placed on the breast of a sleeping woman forced her to tell all her secrets.

The Little Owl's scientific name is *Athene noctua* with *Athene* meaning wise, from the connection to Athene, the Greek god of wisdom. *Noctua* was an owl sacred to Minerva, a Roman goddess of wisdom. However, *noctua* means night and incorrectly associates this owl with the night as it is active during the day and twilight rather than being nocturnal.

34 - Tawny Owl

The **Tawny Owl** is well known particularly in tales and folklore. It is more often heard than seen as the owl is well adapted to a nocturnal life. It is also the master of camouflage as it sits high in a tree, looking like another branch. Many of its local names are based on versions of owl, like howlet, from the French huler, to hoot; owlet; ullet and yewlet, all echoic of its famous night time hooting. Other names include brown owl; cat owl; ferny hoolet; grey owl; hollering owl; screech owl; plus names including a person's name such as billy hooter; gilly hooter and jenny hoolet. The names beech owl and wood owl derive from where it lives and ivy owl from where it sometimes roosts.

The hu...huoooo hoot and a ke-wee of the Tawny Owl is a familiar woodland, night-time sound. Often these two sounds are put together as tu-whit, to-woo but the hoot is made by the male and harsher ke-wee is the female's contact call response. The Tawny Owl is one of the few British birds that duet. It is thought that this behaviour is a co-operative defence against intruders when the pair are establishing or defending their territory. The female (and less frequently the male) uses a kee-wik contact call. Shakespeare wrote in *Love's Labour's Lost* "When blood is nipped and ways be foul, then mightly sings the staring owl, Tu-who, Tu-whit, tu-who – a merry note".

Being a nocturnal hunter the bird has very large eyes and whilst it has reasonable night vision it uses its enhanced hearing to locate prey, as explained earlier in respect of the Barn Owl. More details are given in the Section on Sound in Chapter 5 Sense and sensibility.

In common with other owls, the Tawny Owl appears in tales from many cultures. These are often generic references to owls as a group rather than a particular species. Tawny Owls are often pictured as wise but are also associated with death and misfortune, from their nocturnal habit and screeching noises. In Greece owls were associated with wisdom but the Romans saw owls as omens of impending disaster. Hearing the hoot of an owl indicated an imminent death, including that of the Caesars. Shakespeare used this in *Julius Caesar* "And yesterday the bird of night did sit; Even at noon-day upon the market-place; Hooting and shrieking". The sight of an owl was a sign of defeat. They believed that a dream of an owl could be an omen of shipwreck for sailors and of being robbed. To ward off the evil caused by an owl, it was believed that the offending owl should be killed and nailed to the door of the affected house. This practice spread across Europe and was still observed by English farmers up to the 18th century to protect their livestock.

Roman mythology also includes birds in their stories. In one story Proserpine was transported to the underworld against her will by Pluto, god of the underworld and was allowed to return to her mother Ceres, providing she ate nothing whilst in the underworld. Ascalpus, however, saw her picking a pomegranate. He was turned into an owl.

Stories relating to Minerva, a Roman goddess, are similar to the Greek goddess Athena, both goddesses associating with owls for wisdom. Minerva, the Roman goddess of wisdom, was the offspring of Jupiter. She sprang from his head, completely armed. She was the virgin goddess of warriors and poetry and her favourite bird was the owl. Horace, a Roman poet, wrote that owl's feathers were an ingredient for a love potion.

The Tawny Owl is the topic of one of Aesop's fables - *The owl and the grasshopper*. An owl, who was sitting in a hollow tree, dozing on a summer's afternoon, was disturbed by a singing grasshopper. Far from keeping quiet or moving away at the request of the owl, the grasshopper sang all the more and called her an old blinker, that only came out at night when all honest people had gone to bed. The owl waited in silence for a time and then addressed the grasshopper:

"Well, my dear, if one cannot be allowed to sleep, it is something to be kept awake by such a pleasant voice. And now I think of it, I have a bottle of delicious nectar. If you will come up, you shall have a drop". The silly grasshopper came hopping up to the owl, who at once caught and killed him and finished her nap in comfort. The moral of the story is 'Flattery is not a proof of admiration'.

Wisdom is ascribed to the bird in the well known poem published in 1875 in Punch - "There was an owl liv'd in an oak; The more he heard, the less he spoke; The less he spoke, the more he heard; O, if men were all like that wise bird". Like other owls, there is often an association with dark magic, the owl being a witch's familiar or the old woman of the night. The Tawny Owl is often seen as an omen of bad luck. A Welsh superstition is that if an owl is heard amongst houses then an unmarried girl has lost her virginity. Henry Thoreau summarised a perception of owls writing "I rejoice that there are owls. Let them do the idiotic and maniacal hooting for men. It is a sound admirably suited to swamps and twilight woods which no day illustrates, suggesting a vast and underdeveloped nature which men have not recognized. They represent the stark twilight and unsatisfied thoughts which all [men] have".

The Tawny Owl's scientific name is *Strix aluco* with *Strix* being the Greek for an Owl and *aluco* deriving from the Italian allocco for Tawny Owl. *Strix* is linked to a legendary Roman nocturnal bird of ill omen that fed on human flesh and blood.

The tuft of feathers on the top of the heads of the Long-eared Owl and the Short-eared Owl are mis-named. Both have tufts but these are not ears. The tufts might have a function in changing the shape of the ear to enhance the owl's hearing but they are probably mainly decorative for use in looking fierce! As with other owls, the birds have an acute sense of hearing. Whilst they have good vision, their hearing is highly sensitive and is used to locate prey accurately making the birds highly proficient night hunters

Local names for the **Long-eared Owl** include cat owl, from its head tufts; horn coot; horny hoolet; laughing owl and long-horned ullat.

Reference has already been made to the high esteem that the wise Little Owl was accorded by the Greek goddess Athene. In contrast the Greeks held the Long-eared Owl in low esteem as it was seen as a stupid owl. The myth related earlier was that the bird was so stupid it could wring its own neck, a tale that persisted for many centuries.

The scientific name for the Long-eared Owl is *Asio otus*. The genus name *Asio* derives from a horned owl, described by Pliny two millennia ago. *Otus* was the son of Poseidon, the Greek god of the sea being renowned for his strength and daring but was seen as a simpleton.

Local names for the **Short-eared Owl** include brown yogle; cat-faced hawk; catyogle; ferny hoolet; foreign owl, possibly because it is a migrant; march owl; mouse-hawk; moss owl, with moss meaning marsh; norway owl, from the country it breeds in; short horned owl and tiger owl.

The Short-eared Owl is not a common bird but is best seen at twilight hunting low over fields in winter. Our own small population is supplemented during winter by migrants from Scandinavia. Our forebears noticed the arrival of this bird in early winter and gave it names like pilot owl; sea owl and woodcock owl. The names are based on the story that the bird can be seen flying in from the North Sea at about the same time as the migrating Woodcocks and other birds and the Owl was said to pilot them in to the safety of our shores.

The Short-eared Owl's name is *Asio flammeus* with *flammeus* referring to the fiery streaked plumage of the bird.

Kingfishers

Order – Coraciiformes

This order includes the families of kingfishers, bee-eaters, rollers, hoopoes and hornbills. The name Coraciiformes means raven-like, being a misnomer, with corax the Latin for Raven. Generally, all species are small- to medium-sized birds with short legs, rather small, weak feet and short toes, short necks and large beaks. Sexes are similar in most species. All members of the order have syndactylous toes, with two toes partially joined. Most beaks are long, pointed and colourful, and their long tails have bright, colourful plumage. They dig cavity nests in soft banks. Male and female pairs mate for life and generally share the duties of nest construction, chick defence and food delivery, with the female performing most of the incubation. Hatchlings are altricial.

In this order there is one UK family:

Alcedinidae.

Main characteristics of the Alcedinidae family:

The kingfishers are a family of brightly coloured birds that have large heads, short necks, compact bodies, short, rounded wings and a short tail. The family name comes from the Greek for kingfisher. See myth recounted later in this entry. The sexes are alike. Kingfishers' feet have three front toes that are fused at the base. The comparatively large beak is long and straight. Most have a fast, direct flight. The bird uses binocular vision for sighting prey and is able to turn its head through a wide angle to locate its prey. When diving, kingfishers have to compensate for refraction. Kingfishers dig their nests in earth banks, building the nest together. Tunnels are about 60 cm deep, usually sloping upwards so debris, faeces and water drains off and end in a rounded nest chamber. The eggs are pure white, being easier to see in the dark. The female usually incubates. Hatchlings are naked and blind with no down feathers. They acquire their adult feathers immediately, which emerge enclosed in a thin tube or sheath. Until the sheaths break, the hatchlings look like prickly little hedgehogs!

There is one genus and one species in this family:

Alcedo – Kingfisher

35 - Kingfisher

The **Kingfisher** has surprisingly few local names. Dipper and fisher are two names along with halcyon, deriving from the Greek myth recounted below. The bird is a prodigious fisher and one pair were recorded taking 115 fish in one day. Over a good breeding season, with a pair having three broods, they can catch 8 000 fish! The bird can hover to locate its prey but more frequently sits on a branch and waits patiently. The bird only dives at a low speed, of about 15 km / hr. As the bird dives it closes its eyes, using a third, nictitating eyelid and shuts its throat to stop water entering. The bird catches its fish prey by opening its mouth, rather than stabbing it. If the fish is for feeding to its young or the male wants to present it to a potential female mate, it knows to turn the fish's head to face out so the spines do not stick in the recipient's throat. The nest is a chamber at the end of a tunnel. Whilst the chamber is dark the young have white tips on their beak to help the adults locate their beaks for accurate feeding. The bird's third and fourth toes are fused together strengthening their feet to help dig their nest holes. A tell-tale sign of a nest site are the white droppings down the side of a sandy river bank. The Kingfisher also has a strategy of asynchronous hatching of its eggs (like birds of prey) i.e. the parents start to brood their eggs as soon as they are laid, with the first laid hatching first. This ensures that in times of food shortage the older, first laid siblings will survive and in times of plenty the whole brood will.

The Kingfisher's bright turquoise colouring of its feathers is produced by iridescence. The feathers have an intricate construction which causes interference of the light waves in such a way that the turquoise wavelength is transmitted. In very low light the feathers that appear turquoise in bright light are in fact brown. Colouration is normally achieved by white light being absorbed by the feather's pigments, except for the wavelength of the colour we see.

The Kingfisher appears in Greek mythology. The bird is a key part of the mythological story of Ceyx, who was drowned by Zeus and his wife Alcyone visited him in a dream. Grief stricken, she wandered down to the shore. At the same time, the waves carried Ceyx's body to her. She threw herself into the water but the gods, seeing her terrible grief, lifted her up and turned the couple into Kingfishers - halcyon birds, who mate each year at the start of winter. The female halcyon bird builds a nest of fish bones that floats on the sea and she tends the nest for fourteen days either side of the winter solstice. During this time, Aeolus (father of Alcyone) keeps the winds away and the waters calm, so that his grandchildren are kept safe, hence halcyon days. Halcyon means the sea-blue one. Also Ceyx is a genus of non-UK kingfishers as is Halcyon.

Another Greek myth relates to Alkyoneus, the eldest of the Thrakian giants. Herakles encountered the giant during his travels, disabling him with blows as he was sleeping. The hero then dragged the wounded giant beyond Pallene to die. Alkyoneus' seven mourning daughters were transformed into a flock of Kingfishers.

The tale of how the bird acquired its striking turquoise and orange colours is that Noah sent out a Dove and a Kingfisher from the ark and the latter bird flew so high that it was stained with the colours of the sun and sky. Another myth associated with the flood is that the survivors of the flood did not have any fire so the Kingfisher was sent to steal a burning brand from the gods. The bird removed the brand but scorched his chest orange. He dropped the brand and the creator threw the brand back at the bird and burnt his rump orange. There are several tales relating to hanging up the body of a dead Kingfisher. In Greek mythology this would ward off a lightning attack from Zeus. In Britain the hung bird would swing in the direction of the wind, with a similar tale in France, with the bird named vire-vent (turn in the wind). Shakespeare also referred to this belief in *King Lear* - "Bring oil to fire, snow to their colder moods; Renege, affirm and turn their halcyon beaks; With every gale and vary of their masters". In the 12th century a dead Kingfisher hung in clothes acted as a moth repellent. Also a 13th century lore is that "It is remarkable that these little birds if preserved in a dry place never decay, ... if they are hung by their beaks change their plumage each year, as if they were restored to life", a tale which persisted into the 18th century.

The Kingfisher was the inspiration for solving an intractable engineering problem. The chief development engineer on the Japanese Railway's Bullet train was charged with increasing the speed of the train to 300 km / hr. He struck a problem - when the train entered a tunnel the train created a very loud noise, caused by a shock wave. The sound exited the tunnel before the train (as sound travels faster than the train) and created a major, unacceptable disturbance. Also the compressed air slowed the train down. The engineer turned to the Kingfisher for a solution. The bird's long, sharp, narrow beak is designed to slide aerodynamically into water rather than push the water away (which causes shock waves). Having copied the complex beak shape of the Kingfisher to redesign the front of the train he solved the noise problem. No other design worked! An unexpected helping hand from nature.

The Kingfisher was a bird well known to the Greeks. Its scientific name, *Alcedo atthis*, references this connection, with *Alcedo* coming from the Greek alkuon for kingfisher. *Atthis* is name of one of Sappho's favourite young women from Lesbos. Sappho was a poet born in the 7th century BC who wrote about her love for Atthis.

Woodpeckers and wrynecks

Order – Piciformes

This order includes the woodpeckers and wrynecks as well as the toucans. The order name links to the Roman mythology of a woodpecker called Picus sacred to the god Mars. Piciformes are insectivorous and arboreal. All woodpeckers have similar jaw muscles and long tongues. Most have zygodactyl feet, helping them to climb tree trucks. Woodpeckers have strong, tapering often chisel-tipped beaks. They communicate by drumming rhythmically on hollow trees. Males and females look alike, with some differences in the colour of nape patches and feathers around the beak. These birds have strong, stiff tail feathers used to brace themselves against a tree trunk whilst climbing, hammering or drumming. They use their strong, sharp beaks to hammer out nest cavities in rotting trees and re-use nests for several years. Woodpeckers are territorial and lone breeders. Young are altricial. The chicks do not have down feathers, only true feathers. Most species do not migrate.

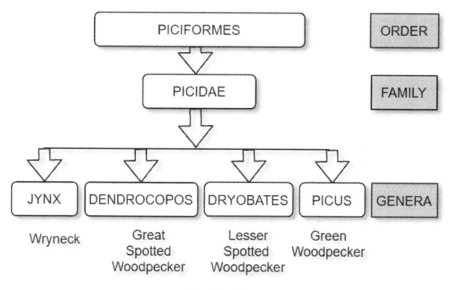

Woodpeckers

In this order there is one UK family:

Picidae.

Main characteristics of the Picidae family:

The woodpeckers and wrynecks are a family of near-passerine birds. The family name is associated with the minor god Picus who was an agricultural deity associated with the fertilisation of soil. Most species are arboreal. The sexes look alike with males having red or yellow head markings, important for signalling. Woodpeckers use their long, sticky tongues to feed; bristles aid in grabbing and extracting insects from deep in tree bark or the ground. The long tongue coils round the skull and terminates above the upper mandible. Woodpecker beaks are typically long, sharp and strong with a complex three layer structure. Many of the foraging, breeding and signalling behaviours involve drumming and hammering. Wrynecks do not drum. Woodpeckers and wrynecks have short, strong zygodactyl feet, good for grasping tree trunks, enabling the bird to walk vertically whilst foraging or excavating for a nest. Tail feathers are stiffened to support the bird when vertical; unusually these feathers are connected to the last vertebrate (except the Wryneck). Few Woodpeckers migrate (except the Wryneck). All Woodpeckers nest in excavated holes or they steal another bird's nest. Both male and female help brood and feed their altricial young with the male unusually being more involved than the female. They lay 2 - 5 white eggs which hatch in 11-14 days. Unusually fledglings do not have down feathers but grow contour feathers whilst in the nest.

The design features of the Woodpecker's beak and head, with its ability to withstand very high g forces, was used by engineers designing shock proof black box recorders for aircraft and also crash helmets.

The four species in this family are in four genera:

Jynx – Wryneck
Dendrocopos - Great Spotted Woodpecker
Dryobates - Lesser Spotted Woodpecker
Picus - Green Woodpecker

One of the UK's strangest birds is the **Wryneck**. Technically it is a member of the Woodpecker family, Picidae but that is not obvious when you see the bird. Like woodpeckers they have a long tongue used to extract insects from the ground or bark, hence the names long tongue and snake bird. In fact the Wryneck has the longest tongue of any bird, relative to its size. The name rind bird comes from the way the bird feeds on insects found in bark. Rinding means to strip bark, which is carried out at the time the migrant bird arrives. Pee bird (Surrey) and peel bird (Sussex) are from the pee pee sound it makes and snake bird is from the hissing sound the bird makes when threatened. Strangely many of the Wryneck's local names are associated with the Cuckoo. Keen observers noted that the bird arrived just before the Cuckoo, hence the names cuckoo's footman; cuckoo's leader; cuckoo's marrow, from the Midlands where marrow means mate; cuckoo's mate; cuckoo's messenger and cuckoo's waker. Emmet hunter refers to the bird's diet of ants. Twister is from the way it turns head right round. The Wryneck does not have stiffened tail feathers so is unable to cling to a vertical tree trunk in the manner of its cousins.

The vernacular name Wryneck comes from the Old English wrigian, meaning to turn.

Small numbers of Wryneck pass through Britain in spring and autumn as they migrate but the bird probably no longer breeds in Britain. In 1909 the bird was described as plentiful but the decline in abundance and distribution has been gradual. The Wryneck is more numerous in Europe where its conservation status is of least concern and its distribution stretches across Europe and Asia and into North Africa.

The Wryneck's scientific name is *Jynx torquilla* from the Greek iunx for Wryneck and *torquilla* from the Latin torquere meaning to twist. The word *Jynx* derives from a Roman myth that if you bind a Wryneck to spinning wheel (called an iynx) this would lure a potential partner or sweetheart. The phrase 'to put a jink on someone' comes from this bird.

36 - Great Spotted Woodpecker

Local names for the **Great Spotted Woodpecker** include strange names like eeckle and eequall. French pie refers to the bird's black and white plumage;

spickle pied woodpecker; woodhacker and woodpie. An earlier vernacular name for the bird was pied woodpecker.

To make the drumming sound the Woodpecker has to hit a tree trunk at just the right frequency (about 10 – 14 strikes per second) to set up a resonant frequency. The bird hits the tree with a force of about 1 kg and it has evolved a shock absorber at the base of the beak to prevent the drumming g forces causing serious brain damage. The brain is very solid and is unable to move around, plus the sponge-like cranial bone structure absorbs the shock of drumming. The lower mandible also bends slightly to absorb the impact. A nictitating membrane covers its eyes to prevent debris injuring its eyes and feathers cover the nostrils to prevent dust entering them. The inner ear has a thick, protective membrane. Both sexes drum. Recent research has shown that Woodpeckers can differentiate between the specific sounds made by individual birds.

Not unsurprisingly the Great Spotted Woodpecker's scientific name refers to its habit of drumming. The first word in *Dendrocopos major* comes from the Greek *Dendron* for tree and kopos, cutter.

The **Lesser Spotted Woodpecker** has a range of local names like barred woodpecker; crank-bird; french galley bird; hickwall; little wood pie; pump borer; speight, deriving from the Dutch specht for a woodpecker now also a surname; striated woodpecker and tapperer, as the bird taps rather than drums loudly.

Numbers of this bird have declined rapidly over the last 25 years (to 2017) by 73% and is now red listed in the UK. Its distribution has also contracted. One reason is that its larger cousin has usurped its territories in woodland, particularly by taking over the Lesser Spotted Woodpecker's nests. Also the removal of older trees from woodland deprives the bird of tree nesting sites. The bird is hard to spot although it does drum like its bigger cousin but is somewhat quieter and often remains hidden in the tree tops.

The Lesser Spotted Woodpecker has the scientific name of *Dryobates minor*. With *Dryobates* from the Greek druos meaning woodland and *bates* meaning walk. Sometimes this species is placed in the same genus as the Great Spotted Woodpecker, thus its scientific name may well be *Dendrocopos minor* in some guide and reference books.

37 - Green Woodpecker

The **Green Woodpecker** has been well known to the British for a long time and accumulated a large number of local names. The bird is associated with rain and has names like rain bird; wet bird; weathercock and whetile, from wet tail. It was believed the bird's feathers acted as a sensor of atmospheric electricity! It also has a distinctive call which is still referred to as a yaffle hence names like galley bird; laughing bird and yafflingale. It lives in trees, although it frequently feeds on the ground, leading to names like wood fucker, with fucker originating from the Dutch fokken meaning to knock (only more recently has the word become an obscenity); wood hack; wood pie; wood speck and wood sucker. The name popinjay is an early name for parrot (possibly due to the similar colouring). Other names include hew hole, the bird does make its nest in a tree hole; high hoe; jack eikle; jar peg; nicker pecker; speight, being an old word for a woodpecker from the Dutch specht and wood hack, from boring out its nest in a tree.

The number of Green Woodpeckers has almost doubled over the last 50 years (to 2017) but with a small decline of 16% in the last 10 years.

Like many of the Woodpecker family (Picidae) the Green Woodpecker has a very long tongue which it uses to find and consume its prey (typically ants). The tongue has small hooks at the end to catch its insect prey. The long tongue retracts back through the mouth and coils up round the cranium. The Green Woodpecker in fact rarely drums like its close relatives the Great and Lesser Spotted Woodpeckers. It does however excavate a hole in a tree for its nest. Also it feeds mainly on the ground. In the 16th century the bird was culled as it drilled holes in the wooden roofs of buildings making them unsafe.

> The Green Woodpecker is another bird associated with creation. The lore is that when God had finished making the earth He ordered birds to dig out hollows for seas, rivers and lakes. The Woodpecker refused to do this and as retribution God condemned the bird to peck at wood and to cry for rain, as the bird was not allowed to drink from lakes and streams. This connects to the local names for the bird like rain bird, weathercock and wet bird, from the belief that the calling bird predicted rain. A Roman myth is that a Woodpecker helped the wolf feed Romulus and Remus. A Roman coin shows two Woodpeckers perched in a sacred fig tree with the wolf feeding the foundling twins.

The Green Woodpecker is in the genus Picus. Some stories refer to Picus as an early king of Italy. In another story by Ovid the witch Circe turns Picus into a Woodpecker when he refuses to be disloyal to his wife. The bird's scientific name is *Picus viridis* with *viridis* simply meaning viridian or green.

Falcons and kestrels

Order – Falconiformes

This order contains the falcons and kestrels. Falco derives from the Latin falcis for sickle, referring to the bird's hooked talons. Falcons are small to medium-sized carnivorous birds of prey. They kill with their beaks, not their taloned feet (as often the hawks do), taking their prey in the air. Plumage is usually brown, white, black and grey, often with barring or patterning for camouflage. Male plumage can be bolder than the female's. Most birds have compact bodies, rounded heads and short necks. Falcons do not have a bony brow ridge over their eyes (as hawks do). The birds have slender wings for fast flight. Female falcons are usually larger than males. Falcons have excellent eyesight. They are solitary hunters and breeders and are monogamous. Often they do not build nests but they will usurp other birds' nests. They lay 2 – 4 eggs, mostly incubated by the female whilst the male hunts for food. The young have a long, very fast-growing fledgling stage, followed by 3 – 8 weeks of nest care after first flight, maturing in 1 to 3 years.

In this order there is one UK family:

Falconidae.

Main characteristics of the Falconidae family:

The family Falconidae comprises the falcons, kestrels and merlins. Falcons are small to medium-sized birds of prey. The wings are long and pointed giving quick, agile flight. Birds have excellent eye sight. The upper mandible is covered by a fleshy membrane called a cere, usually yellow. They have strong, hooked beaks with some species having a notch or tooth on the upper mandible. They have sharply curved talons and a strong hind toe, with bare tarsi but often feathered thighs. The birds are solitary hunters in open country. There is some sexual dimorphism in plumage. Being paler below helps birds appear more inconspicuous to prey. Falcons are carnivores, usually predatory but they will scavenge. The birds regurgitate pellets of indigestible food, producing about one pellet per day. They use ledges for nesting or use abandoned nests. The birds are monogamous and solitary breeders. Eggs are brooded asynchronously. Incubation takes about 4 weeks with a further 4 – 6 weeks to fledge. Parents look after their offspring until they can hunt on their own.

The four species in this family are in a single genus:

Falco - Hobby; Kestrel; Merlin; Peregrine

38 - Falcon's head

Local names for the **Hobby** include oddly the name jack robin, possibly as the bird's name was linked to Robert, but the Robin eventually took this name; riphook; tree falcon and ven winged hawk.

The name Hobby is from the French hobereau to stir, referring to the bird's agility when pursuing prey and how flocks of birds (like Swallows and House Martins) fly off when they see a Hobby. Also there is a link to the French verb hober to jump about hence the French name faucon hobereau.

The Hobby has the scientific name of *Falco subbuteo*, with *subbuteo* meaning smaller than a Buzzard, (which it is) *sub* meaning smaller and *buteo* being the scientific name for the Buzzard but the two birds are not close relatives. The name of the table football game came from the Hobby's scientific name! The creator of the game tried to register the name hobby for the game but was not allowed to and so creatively improvised with the bird's Latin specific name.

39 - Kestrel

The **Kestrel** is often seen hovering and several of its local names come from this habit, like fanner hawk; fuckwind, with the first syllable meaning to beat or fan (only more recently has the word become an obscenity); hover hawk; vanner hawk; wind fanner and wind hover. In Sussex the name wind bibber derived from the local word bibber meaning to shake. Stanniel and stanyel means stone yeller, with stone meaning intense (as in stone deaf) and from its habit of calling whilst perched on a stone. Other names refer to the bird as a hawk, like blood hawk; field hawk; mouse hawk and red hawk, from the male's brighter colours. The Kestrel is now established as a falcon (the family Falconidae) and not a hawk (the family Accipitridae). The name cress hawk comes from the French crescllc, to rattle, referring to the bird's courtship call, as does the name keelie. A German name for the bird is turmfalke, meaning tower falcon from its habit of nesting in buildings. The Kestrel's diet includes rodents that it looks for whilst hovering but it will also take small birds like a House Sparrow.

Being a falcon the Kestrel kills using its beak or by the blow it inflicts on its victim. In contrast hawks kill their victims by squeezing them with their large-clawed feet. The female is larger (220 g) than the male (190 g) whose wing length is about 96% the length of the female's. This leads to dietary differences between the sexes. They differ aerodynamically and have different wing loadings. The Kestrel has a proportionally longer tail, 65% of wing length compared to other falcons at 55% and a lower wing loading, typically 26 g / cm^2 compared to 37 g / cm^2 for other falcons, leading to a different diet and hunting behaviour. The prototype Harrier aircraft was named Kestrel. Numbers of the bird have fallen by 32% over the last 22 years to 2017 and has a UK conservation status of amber.

The Kestrel was the lowest bird in the falconry hierarchy and was flown by a knave. As a demonstration of how birds are still ingrained into our culture, the Kestrel was central to the famous 1969 film Kes, based on a novel entitled *A Kestrel for a knave*. In the film a down trodden boy finds redemption by establishing a relationship with a Kestrel. Ted Hughes wrote *The Hawk in the Rain* saying "Effortlessly at height hangs his still eye, His wings hold all creation in weightless quiet, Steady as hallucination in the streaming air, While banging wind kills those stubborn hedges". The war poet Julian Grenfell invoked the power of the bird writing "The Kestrel hovering by day, And the little owl that call at night, bid him be swift and keen as they, as keen of ear, as swift of sight".

The Kestrel's scientific name is *Falco tinnunculus,* with *tinnunculus* meaning shrill sounding from its call.

Local names for the **Merlin** include blue hawk, from its colouration; hawk kestrel; little blue hawk, which is accurate; peerie hawk, from Shetland meaning small; pigeon hawk; rock hawk and stone falcon, from sitting on stones to pluck its prey. References to hawk, of course, are incorrect.

The formal name Merlin may have come from the 15th century merlyon and the Anglo Norman merillon deriving from the Latin merula - Blackbird (now part that bird's scientific name), which is occasionally taken by the Merlin. The bird was popular as a falconer's bird, especially for ladies. The female at 230 g weighs more than the male at 190 g. Formerly the female was named Merlin and the male Jack (as in small). In winter some birds move down from their moorland habitat to sea level and some migrate to the continent.

The Merlin's scientific name is *Falco columbarius*, with the Latin *columba* meaning pigeon but the bird is too small to take a pigeon.

As the fastest animal on earth, (reaching up to 300 km / hr in a vertical stoop flight) the **Peregrine** was the falconers' choice of falcon and the male could only be flown by an earl and the female by a duke. Needless to say the bird has several local names, mainly linked to its status as a hunting bird. Many names use the word hawk, allocated before the difference between hawks and falcons was established. Names include blue hawk; big hawk; cliff hawk, where it often seen; duck hawk, it does catch ducks; game hawk; haggard falcon; passenger falcon; perry hawk; pigeon hawk, from its most numerous prey and spotted hawk. Tiercel gentle is the name given to the male (and to some other male birds of prey) from the French la tierce, meaning a third, which refers to the proportionally smaller size of the male. The male weighs about 670 g and the female 1100 g. Peregrine chicks are called eyases. Falconers kept moulting birds in cages called a mew, being an old word for a moulting falcon. This word is now used for a small building at the back of a house. Falconers' birds were identified by a leg ring and in Scotland anyone caught poaching a bird would be punished by having their hands cut off.

The Peregrine's feathers are not fully water proofed so the bird rarely takes its prey in water, preferring to take prey in the air. During its stoop flight the bird experiences an 18 g force. Its eyes occupy 50% of its skull (compared to 5% for humans) and the retina has two fovea, one for distance vision and one for close vision. When chasing prey the bird calculates the prey's likely flight path and intercepts the prey rather than just follow it. When it catches its prey its talons have a ratchet mechanism that locks its 2 cm talons. To ensure that its lungs do not burst whilst flying at such a high speed, the nostrils have cones to enable the bird to carry on breathing. This design was adapted by aeronautical engineers who fitted cones to the front of jet engines to reduce the effect of turbulence created at high speed, without which the engines would fail to work.

Female Peregrine's, weighing on average 1100 g, are capable of catching and killing a Great Black-backed Gull weighing 1350 g and cock Black Grouse weighing 1300 g. Records show that in the UK the total number of species caught by the Peregrine is 132 and from records in Europe the total is 210. However, the majority of its prey is Rock Doves and its close relatives the carrier and homing pigeons, much to the annoyance of pigeon breeders. Based on data from observations the estimated annual consumption of food by a family of Peregrines is 224 kg. See also Section on Eating in Chapter 5.

Some of the oldest references to birds come from the Egyptians. From texts and pictures dating to about 2 500 BC the god Horus was depicted as a man with a falcon's head, possibly a Lanner Falcon or Peregrine.

The meaning of Peregrine derives from 'the wanderer from abroad', originally an animal that has travelled per agrum, i.e. through fields. In World War 2 a law was passed allowing the bird to be culled as it was catching carrier pigeons and so hampering the war effort. Numbers recovered after the war only for them to decline in the 1950's due to the pesticide DDT causing thin egg shells. For more detail see the Section on Pesticides in Chapter 6. Happily they have recovered again and they breed (amongst other places) in city centres, nesting in tall buildings, where the pigeon population provides easy meals for the birds. The Peregrine now has a green conservation status in the UK with 1 769 breeding pairs recorded in 2014. The highest density of breeding Peregrine in the world is found in New York City, where the bird has adapted to city life.

The Peregrine is the most widespread falcon in the world. Its scientific name is *Falco peregrinus* with *peregrinus* means wanderer, hence the word peregrination for journey or voyage.

Parrots

Order – Psittaciformes

One species from a new (to the UK) order of birds has recently established itself – the **Ring-necked Parakeet** in the order Psittaciformes. These British birds are now the most northerly breeding parrot population in the world. It is Britain's only naturalised parrot having established itself in the wild in 1969, probably from escapees. The Ring-necked Parakeet has in recent times become a common bird in SE England, to the extent that, for some, it is now a pest, as it usurps the nest holes of other birds, steals eggs and its urban roosts are very noisy. The bird is in the order Psittaciformes and the family Psittaculidae. The scientific name for the bird is *Psittacula krameri* with *Psittacula* being a diminutive of psittacus for parrot and *krameri* after the 18th century scientist W H Kramer.

 The next order is Passeriformes, which is by far the largest order of birds, accounting for around 55% of all species in the world. Inevitably such a large order contains a diverse range of birds, allocated to many families. In this analysis of the more common UK birds, there are 27 families, 53 genus and 84 species. The account below describes the common features of this order.

Passeriformes

Birds of this order are sometimes known as perching birds or, less accurately, as songbirds. The name passerine is derived from *Passer domesticus*, the scientific name of the House Sparrow. Most passerines are small birds and are one of the most diverse terrestrial vertebrate orders. Passerines are characterised by anisodactyl feet, with an irreversible hallux, facing backwards. The toes have no webbing or joining. When a bird lands on a perch the toes tighten automatically, supporting the bird. They remain tight with no effort so passerines are able to sleep whilst perched. Some birds in this order, e.g. larks and pipits, don't perch and their feet are adapted for walking, with a longer hind toe and straighter claws. Hirundine feet are weak and are not used much as the birds are predominantly aerial. Most passerines have 10 primary flight feathers and 9 secondaries. This is the only order in which singing is well developed, with birds having complex muscles controlling their syrinx. Most passerines lay coloured eggs, (in contrast with non-passerines, whose eggs are usually white). Parental care is usually by both sexes. Passerine chicks are altricial. The incubation period is often around fourteen days.

Main characteristics of the Laniidae family:

The family name of shrikes derives from the Latin word for butcher; some shrikes are known as butcher birds. Shrikes are medium-sized birds, up to 50 cm in length with grey, brown or black and white plumage. Their beaks are hooked and their calls are strident. Shrikes impale their insect or small invertebrate prey on thorns to eat their prey; this also this serves as a cache. Shrikes are territorial and sit on exposed perches to watch for prey items and to defend their territory. Males have a courtship display, showing a potential mate its cache of food. Shrikes are seasonally monogamous and build a nest of twigs and grass in a tree. The female mainly broods their 6 - 7 eggs which hatch after about 16 days and fledge after about 17 days.

There is one genus in this family and one species detailed here:

Lanius – Great Grey Shrike

Shrikes appear in low numbers in the UK, with no species being numerous. The shrike family includes the Great Grey Shrike, Lesser Grey Shrike, Red Backed Shrike and Woodchat Shrike. Shrike derives from the Old English word scric, echoic of its loud, shrieking cry.

The **Great Grey Shrike** has a number of striking local names, linked to its habit of catching its insect prey and impaling them on a spike or thorn to ensure they do not escape before being eaten. Hence the names butcher bird and murdering bird. The local name nine killer comes from the myth that the Shrike kills nine birds a day. The bird is extremely strong and can kill prey larger than itself. The ornate name white whiskey john refers to the bird's white under parts, revealed as it flicks its tail from side to side. One thesaurus of bird names lists over 700 names for this bird, which is one of the most widely distributed in the northern hemisphere. The bird has exceptionally good eyesight and the sShrike was used by trappers to alert them to an approaching bird from a great distance, with the shrike also indicating the direction of the incoming bird's flight.

The Great Grey Shrike's gruesome method of trapping its prey on spikes or thorns is reflected in its scientific name *Lanius excubitor*. *Lanius* is a butcher (hence the common name butcher bird) and *excubitor* for sentinel, as it sits and waits to single out its prey.

Members of the next family are well known – the Corvidae.

Main characteristics of the Corvidae family:

The Corvidae family contains the crows, ravens, rooks, jackdaws, jays, magpies, choughs and nutcrackers. The name corvid is from corvus for crow. The common English family name is corvid or the crow family, with crow being imitative of the bird's cry. Corvids are among the most intelligent of birds (or indeed any animal), demonstrating self-awareness, social skills and tool making ability. See the Section on Intelligence in Chapter 5. Their large brains give them a brain to body ratio equal to that of dolphins and proportionally only slightly smaller than humans. Corvids occur throughout the world and up to high altitudes. They are medium to large in size, with strong feet and beaks, rictal bristles and a single moult each year (most passerines moult twice). Most species have their nostrils either partially or completely obscured by bristles or plumes. In the majority of species, the tip of the curved upper mandible overlaps the lower mandible slightly. The feet are proportionally large and powerful, with strong, grasping toes, suited to holding large prey items; the tarsi are scaled at the front and smooth behind. Corvid wings are generally rounded and have stiffened primaries. Most corvids (except the jays and magpies which are arboreal) have a predominantly glossy black plumage. Black absorbs solar energy and radiates less heat, hence in cold environments corvids are better able to regulate their body temperature. Dark melanin-pigmented feathers are also tougher than light coloured feathers. Corvids are sexually monomorphic. Corvids utter a range of sounds but oddly (as members of the order Passeriformes) do not sing; some species perform an aerial display. Rooks and Jackdaws form mixed flocks but the only bond is between mated pairs; when a flock is disturbed only paired individuals fly off together. Most corvids are omnivorous and some corvids cache food. Corvids are largely monogamous forming strong pair bonds. Males and females build a large nest made of twigs with grass lining, in a tree or on a ledge. The female broods the clutch of 2 - 4 eggs whilst the male provides food.

The corvid family is a well known group of birds whose members appear in many myths, tales and lore. Their black colour gives them a dark character, reflected in the collective nouns of murder and mob. In fact, the Carrion Crow tends not to flock, whilst its close relative the Rook does. They are also given the attributes of evil and misfortune. A contrary attribute ascribed to the Carrion Crow is wisdom. Henry David Thoreau wrote "If men had wings and bore black feathers, few of them would be wise enough to be crows". The corvid family has proven high levels of intelligence. This intelligence was recognised long ago. In one of Aesop's tales the crow found a bottle with a little water in the bottom, which it could not reach. It found some pebbles which it dropped into the bottle until the water rose high enough for it to drink.

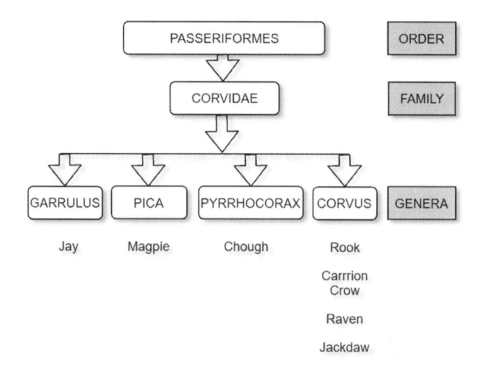

The seven species in this family are in four genera:

Garrulus – Jay
Pica – Magpie
Pyrrhocorax – Chough
Corvus - Carrion Crow; Jackdaw; Raven; Rook

The **Jay** can be seen and heard in woodlands, particularly in autumn as it gathers acorns. Some local names refer to the bright turquoise colour on its wings, such as blue jay. The bird also has a human name connection through jenny jay and references to its noisy nature in devel scritch and scold. The Gaelic name schrechag choille means screamer of the woods. Oak jackdaw associates the bird correctly with oak woodland. The bird can store up to eight acorns in its crop when gathering acorns. Jays can be seen anting in summer. They don't eat ants but use the ants to eliminate the parasites on their feathers by squeezing the ants to release formic acid which kills the parasites. The Jay is also a mimic and when it approaches carrion for a meal it makes a sound like a Buzzard to ward of intruders. As a member of the Corvidae family the Jay demonstrates high order social skills. The word jay is used to describe a foolish person. In American slang a jay is a person who chatters impertinently. Jaywalking is a term used to describe someone who carelessly crosses the street.

The Jay's vernacular name is based on the harsh, sharp sound it makes. The name comes from the Old French jai via the Modern French geai to Jay.

315

The scientific name for the Jay is *Garrulus glandarius* which reflects key elements of the bird. *Garrulus* means to chatter, linked to the English word garrulous and the bird can certainly be noisy, especially in autumn as it collects nuts for winter storage. *Glandarius* means producing acorns and the bird is highly adept at collecting and caching them. See the Section on Intelligence in Chapter 5.

Having associated with humans for centuries the **Magpie** has accumulated a large number of local names. These include chatter pie, the bird is certainly noisy; cornish pheasant, from its long tail; magget; margaret's pie, giving the bird a female name; mock-a-pie; pianet, combining pied with the name Agnes and tell pie.

The Magpie is a familiar bird seen around human habitation. In fact its name has a human connection as the Mag part of the name is a shortened version of Madge and Margaret, with its calls supposedly sounding like talkative women. Magpies are predatory and will take small birds up to the size of a Blackbird. A study into the effect of Magpie numbers on the breeding success rate and population levels of small birds found there was no correlation. Predation was not a limiting factor in population size given the large broods that most small bird have. As with most corvids they exhibit highly social behaviour.

Corvids are attracted to shiny objects and will take them. Rossini wrote an opera entitled *The thieving Magpie* in which a Magpie steals a silver spoon and hides it in its nest, only for it to be found just in time to save the heroine Ninetta's life. The Magpie has acquired the characteristics of garrulity, mischievousness and noisiness. It is quite easy to see how the Magpie got this reputation. Folklore about the bird includes tales that the chattering of a Magpie predicts the arrival of a stranger. The Magpie was thought to be a great thief and it was popularly supposed that if its tongue were split into two with silver it could talk like a man. The Magpie's hoarse cry indicated disaster and misfortune. In Ireland a Magpie tapping a window foretold death. If the bird built her nest at the top of a tree the summer would be dry; if on the lower branches, the summer would be wet. No one liked to see a Magpie when starting on a journey but in certain parts of Wales, if a Magpie flew from left to right it foretold good luck; in other parts if seen at all it was considered a sign of bad luck. Another superstition was that if you saw a Magpie you should take your hat off, spit in the direction of the bird and say 'devil, devil I defy you'! Yet another is when a Magpie was seen stationary on a tree, if it flew to the left, bad luck would follow; if to the right, good luck. Also when you see a Magpie (so the tale goes) you should say 'Morning Mr Magpie, how's your wife and kids' and turn round on the spot! In the Middle Ages Magpies were housed with poultry so they would raise the alarm if there were any intruders. A well-known poem casts the Magpie in a prophetic role - 'One for sorrow, two for joy, three for a girl, four for a boy, five for silver, six for gold, seven for a secret, never to be told'. A myth is that the Magpie refused to go into Noah's ark. It perched outside and watched the floods and, because they were enjoying the sight of bad fortune, you should turn your back on a Magpie. Boris Pasternak in *Doctor Zhivago* related the lore that when Magpies are seen they are portents of snow or there will be news via a guest or a letter.

The Magpie's scientific name is simply *Pica pica*, a general name for pied birds, with pied formerly meaning coloured.

40 - Chough

A bird which was more common in times past is the **Chough**. Currently it occurs in relatively low numbers in a few locations but thankfully its abundance and distribution is increasing. It was formerly common in Cornwall, where it was kept as a pet. It has only recently returned as a breeding bird to that county. Local names include cornish daw, daw from its call, as in Jackdaw and cliff daw, referring to its habitat; fire raven, from its red beak and feet and being in the same family as the Raven; kill grew, from the Cornish village of the same name; market jew crow where market jew is an old name for Marazion (Cornish for market of Thursday), plus red-legged crow. The first written record of an English name for the Chough dates from the 10th century. The Chough appears on the Cornish coat of arms.

> The Chough is associated with the legend of King Arthur. The Cornish version is that King Arthur did not die but his soul was transported into a Chough, with the red beak and legs being red from the blood of battle. According to the same legend, if the Chough was re-established as a breeding bird in Cornwall, King Arthur would return. The Chough has now returned to breed there after an absence of several decades. Don Quixote wrote that King Arthur was turned into a Raven and would return if a Raven was killed. Killing a Chough was held to be unlucky as the bird was held to contain the soul of King Arthur. The Chough was not a well-liked bird as it was a thief. Daniel Defoe reported that it stole not just food but items of cutlery and sometimes took lit candles and set fire to hay stacks and thatch. Thomas Becket, as Archbishop of Canterbury, had three Choughs on his coat of arms, as does the City of Canterbury. Chough is referred to in *King Lear* "how fearful and dizzy 'tis to cast one's eyes so low? The crows and choughs that wing the midway air..." as Edgar attempts to convince the blind Gloucester not to commit suicide.

The Chough has the scientific name *Pyrrhocorax pyrrhocorax*, from the Greek purrhos meaning flame-coloured, alluding to its bright red beak and korax meaning Raven. Its current UK conservation status is green.

The **Carrion Crow** has been associated with humans for centuries and has many local names. These include black beak; black neb, which distinguishes the bird from the Rook, whose beak is grey near the base of its beak; car crow; carner crow, with carn linked to the Latin for flesh and the French carne for meat; corbie crow, being repetitive; crake, is onomatopoeic; dowp; flesh crow, from its reputation for eating dead flesh, like still born lambs; gore crow; hoddy fraw; ket crow, with ket and gore being old words for carrion; land daw, with daw being a generic word for the crow family (as in Jackdaw) and midden crow, with midden being a refuse dump. The Carrion Crow is disliked by farmers for harassing ewes and lambs and by gamekeepers for taking young game birds.

The Carrion Crow's first name derives from eating carrion as part of its diet and the second word from its raucous sound. Its second name is linked to the Latin word for an iron bar used as a grappling hook and so to the English word crowbar. The first written record of the bird's name in English is dated 662 AD.

The bird's character has given rise to a number of well known phrases, for example the commonly used 18th century phrase 'as the crow flies' meaning the straight line distance between two places. The Carrion Crow does not particularly fly in a straight line but the phrase has stuck. Alfred Hitchcock used the birds as a frightening, dark influence in the film The Birds. The Carrion Crow is the fourth most widespread bird in Britain. Numbers of the bird have increased by 18% in the last 22 years (to 2017). In Scotland and Ireland the Hooded Crow takes the place of the all-black Carrion Crow which resides elsewhere in the UK. At one time the Hooded Crow was considered a sub-species but now it is listed as a separate species. In areas where the birds overlap the two species will inter-breed and produce hybrid off-spring. These birds however are not as robust the parent species and have low survival rates.

> The following story explains why crows (or in other versions, Ravens) are black. Coronis, daughter of Phlegyas, was one of Apollo's lovers. While Apollo was away, Coronis, already pregnant with Asclepius, fell in love with Ischys, son of Elatus. A white crow, who Apollo had left to guard her, informed him of the affair. Apollo, enraged that the bird had not pecked out Ischys' eyes as soon as he approached Coronis, put a curse on it which scorched its feathers, which is why all crows are black

The Carrion Crow's full name is *Corvus corone, Corvus*, meaning crow and *corone* being repetitive, as corone is Greek for crow.

Local names for the **Jackdaw** include caddaw, with cad meaning carrion; carder; cathedral parson; chank; chatter-jack; chauk; chofe; grey head and grey pate, from its distinctively grey head and jackie cawdaw.

The Jackdaw readily associates with humans, often nesting in chimney stacks. Jack means small i.e. a small crow, as in the low value of a jack in a pack of cards. Daw means knave or someone held in low esteem. The bird has a reputation as a thief, being attracted to shiny objects.

> In folklore the Jackdaw signifies conceit, vanity and imitativeness. The bird can be trained to imitate human speech. One item of folklore

is that the sight of a Jackdaw by a bride meant the marriage would be a happy one. Other pieces of folklore include a tale that a Jackdaw on the roof predicts a new arrival, that a Jackdaw settling on the roof of a house or flying down a chimney is an omen of death and coming across one is considered a bad omen. In the 16th century the bird could be caught as a pest as it eats seeds and grain. The bird sometimes nests in church towers or steeples and this confers protection for the bird. One old form of denial was 'I have no more knowledge of the fact than the devil has of a Jackdaw'.

The Jackdaw appears in Aesop's fable *The bird in borrowed feathers*. In this tale Jupiter was determined to create a chief amongst birds and said that on a certain day he would himself choose the most beautiful of them to be king. The Jackdaw, knowing his own ugliness, collected the feathers which had fallen from the wings of other birds and stuck them on his body. When the day arrived the birds stood before Jupiter, including the Jackdaw. Jupiter decided to make him king, on account of the beauty of his plumage. The other birds protested and each bird plucked its feathers off the Jackdaw. The Jackdaw was again nothing but a Jackdaw. The moral of the story: 'Hope not to succeed in borrowed plumes'.

The Jackdaw's scientific name is *Corvus monedula* with *monedula* being the Latin for Jackdaw.

41 - Raven

Whilst the **Raven** has been known to us for centuries there are few local names for the bird, like corbie, also a name for the Carrion Crow; croupy craw, from its croaking call; fiach; marburan and ralph, a nickname from Cheshire based on its harsh call.

The vernacular name Raven comes from the Old Norse mythological bird god hrafnagud, translated into the Old English hraefn and thence to Raven. One of the names given to Odin, the chief god in Norse mythology, is Hrafnagud, the Raven god. The tale is that he sent out two Ravens, called Hugin and Munin (thought and memory) to fly round the world during the day and return at night to report to Hrafnagud what was going on in the world. The first written record of an English name for the Raven dates from c. 699 AD.

The Raven is the national bird of Bhutan and represents the guardian deity, Jarog Dongchen. The Raven was persecuted in the countryside for it predatory habits, not least the gruesome habit of pecking the eyes out of prey and bounties were paid to have it killed. This habit also appears in Chapter 30 of Proverbs "The eye that mocks a father, that scorns an aged mother, will be pecked out by the Ravens of the valley". Clearly the bird's gruesome habits were well known millennia ago. In towns and cities it was protected, as it cleaned up the dirty streets. The Raven is associated with death. Shakespeare wrote in *Othello* "as doth the raven, o'er the infected house, boding to all". Hardy recorded that two Ravens smelt a hearse as it passed and swooped onto the coffin. An English folk song entitled *Twa corbies* is based on two Ravens feeding on a dead soldier's body. Shelley knew of this association with the dead "The obscene ravens, clamorous over the dead". Ravens are closely associated with the Tower of London. According to legend England will fall if the Ravens of the Tower of London are removed. It is thought that there have been at least six Ravens in residence at the Tower for centuries. References place them near the monument commemorating those beheaded at the Tower. This strongly suggests that the Ravens, which were notorious for gathering at gallows, were originally used to dramatise tales of imprisonment and execution at the Tower as told by the Yeomen Warders. During the Second World War, most of the Tower's Ravens perished through shock during bombing raids. Before the Tower reopened to the public in January 1946, care was taken to ensure that a new flock of Ravens was in place. In Sweden the Raven is known as the ghosts of murdered people.

The Raven appears in many tales and myths over many centuries from different cultures. The derivation of the name Raven from Norwegian mythology was described earlier. The bird appears in the Bible a number of times. In Genesis "At the end of the 40 days Noah ... sent forth a Raven". Job asked "Who provides food for the Raven when its young cry out to God and wander about for lack of food?" Elijah commanded the Ravens to feed Ahab and the Ravens brought him bread and meat. In the Qur'an's version of the story of Cain and Abel, the two sons of Adam, a Raven is mentioned as the creature who taught Cain how to bury his murdered brother. In Greek mythology

Ravens are associated with Apollo, the god of prophesy.

The Raven has a prominent role in the mythologies of the indigenous Tlingit peoples of the Pacific Northwest. The tale goes that when the Great Spirit created all things he separated them into cedar boxes. The Great Spirit gifted these boxes to the animals that existed before humans. When the animals opened the boxes all the things that comprised the world came into being. One box given to the seagull contained all the light of the world. The seagull refused to open it. All the people asked Raven to persuade the seagull to open the box and release the light. Finally the Raven became angry and stuck a thorn in the seagull's foot. The Raven pushed the thorn in deeper until the pain caused seagull to drop the box. Then out of the box came the sun, moon and stars that brought light to the world and allowed the first day to begin.

In another tale from the Pacific Northwest, at the beginning of the world an eagle was the guardian of the sun, moon, stars, water and fire. It jealously guarded these elements. However, a white coloured raven fell in love with the eagle's daughter. The Raven managed to steal all these elements and distributed them around to create the universe. In carrying fire his feathers were blackened so the Raven now has black feathers forever. In their mythology the Raven is the creator of the world but it is also considered a trickster god. In folklore the bird represents cruelty, death, falsehood and the soul of a wicked person. A native North American story is that the Raven became black after rescuing the moon, sun and stars from an owl's lair.

The Raven appears in one of Aesop's fables - *The Raven and the swan.* A Raven saw a swan and wanted to gain the same beautiful plumage. Assuming that his splendid white colour arose from washing in the water in which he swam, the Raven flew to some lakes and pools. But cleaning his feathers as often as he would, he could not change their colour but through lack of food he perished. The moral of the story: 'Change of habit cannot alter nature'.

The Raven is the largest corvid in the Corvidae family and the largest perching bird in the world. It is also one of the most widespread birds in the world, capable of living from low levels to high altitudes and in many different climates, from desert to frozen Arctic steppe. The Raven breeds very early in the year enabling it to feed off carrion such as still-born lambs and placentas. The Raven is one of only two British birds capable of breeding in winter, the Woodpigeon is the other.

The scientific name for the Raven is another repetitive name in *Corvus corax* with *corax* the Greek for Raven.

42 - Rook

Local names for the **Rook** include brancher, the name for the newly fledged young as they sit on branches; church parson; corbie; craw; croakers, from the sound it makes; farm labourer; squab, for immature birds, also for the Woodpigeon and white faced crow, from the grey patch at the base of the beak, being the way to identify a Rook from a Carrion Crow.

The formal English name Rook derives from the Old English hroc and other European languages such as the Dutch roek and the Old Norse hrokr, all of which are imitative of its raucous voice. Folklore has it that Rooks are the portents of rain, some from if they do a tumbling flight, another is if they fly to the hills or finally if they sit on a dead branch. It is a bad omen if Rooks desert a rookery. Rooks are much more likely to form flocks than its close relative the Carrion Crow and of course nest colonially in sometimes very large rookeries. In the 15th century Rooks had a reputation for eating seeds and there was a bounty on the bird so they could be shot.

The Rook's scientific name is *Corvus frugilegus* with *frugilegus* deriving from frugis meaning fruit and legere to lift.

The next family, **Panuridae**, has only one member - the **Bearded Tit.** The bird appears to be a unique songbird, being the only member of this family, with no known close relatives.

43 - Bearded Tit

The bird's formal name is one of the few formal names that is inaccurate. The bird superficially looks like a tit (which it isn't) and the bird has a moustache not a beard!

This species is a wetland specialist, breeding colonially in large reed beds by lakes or swamps. It is the only bird to live in reed beds all year round. Birds sometimes migrate in eruptive movements during very cold weather.

The Bearded Tit's scientific name is *Panurus biarmicus*. The genus name, *Panurus*, is from Ancient Greek *panu*, exceedingly and tail referring to the

324

bird's long tail. The specific *biarmicus* is from biarmia, a Latinised form of Bjarmaland formerly part of what is now the Arkhangelsk Oblast area of Russia.

Main characteristics of the Alaudidae family:

Larks make up the Alaudidae family. The name for the lark family comes from a Germanic name for a little songster. They are small to medium-sized birds, 12 - 24 cm in length weighing 15 - 75 g. They have more elaborate calls than most birds and often have a melodious display flight. Song flights are used to defend breeding territories and attract a mate. Like many ground birds, most lark species have a long hind claw providing stability whilst standing. Most have streaked brown plumage and are sexually monomorphic. Their dull appearance camouflages them on the ground. They feed on insects and seeds. Most species build nests on the ground, usually cups of dead grass. Larks' eggs are usually speckled. Larks incubate for 11 to 16 days. Adults feed their young insects initially then switch to seeds. Lark chicks are the only passerines to undergo a full moult as their first moult.

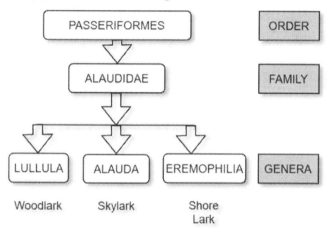

Larks

The three species in this family are in three genera:

Lullula - Woodlark
Alauda - Skylark
Eremophilia - Shore Lark

Larks are renowned songsters, giving rise to the phrase 'to sing like a lark'. Larks were formerly kept as cage birds and were subject to the extreme cruelty of being blinded to allegedly make them sing better.

The **Woodlark** is the only species (worldwide) in the genus *Lullula*. The word is onomatopoeic via the French lulu. This species is associated with woodland, seen singing in a tree on the edge of woodland.

The Woodlark's scientific name is *Lullula arborea* with *arborea* from the Latin for tree.

44 - Skylark

The **Skylark** is a well-known bird of open fields, especially for its non-stop singing from high in the sky when it is heard more often than seen. Male Skylarks recognise the local variations of their neighbours' song and can identify intruders who do not sing with the local dialect. The local name laverock derives from the Old English lawerce, meaning treason worker. This is based on the bird's habit of landing, from its song flight, a distance away from its well hidden nest to deceive possible predators. The Skylark also uses an injury feigning tactic to draw potential predators away from the nest, putting itself at potential risk, until it startles the predator by flying away! If the song attracts predators when a bird of prey approaches the bird sings louder to deter them. Other local names include lerruck, a derivation of larrock; lintwhite, a name also given to the linnet; melhuez, a Cornish name referring to the Skylark's high flight; rising lark; short-heeled lark and sky flapper.

Skylark numbers in England have fallen over the last 50 years (to 2017) by 63%, mainly due to changes in farming practice with arable crops being harvested earlier before the young have fledged. The Skylark is still caught in millions on the continent. Nets are often used measuring as much as 2 m high and 250 m long. Another method to lure birds is using a rotating mirror. As the birds are attracted to the device they are shot.

The Skylark symbolises cheerfulness, recklessness and song. In times past the word lark was used generically which might include other larks or pipits, all of which are very similar. The word has entered the language in the phrase 'to lark around', which previously had sexual connotations. The Skylark has been the subject of many poems, songs and music for centuries. Perhaps the most famous is Ralph Vaughan Williams' orchestral work, *The Lark Ascending*. This piece was voted No 1 in the Classic FM hall of fame for 9 years, a tribute to bird-inspired music. In the 16th century Edmund Spencer wrote "The merry Larke hir matins sings aloft". Shelley wrote *To a skylark* "Hail to thee, blithe spirit! Bird though never wert, That from heaven, or near it, Pourest thy full heart In profane strains of unpremeditated art. Higher still and higher from the earth thou springest Like a cloud of fire; The blue deep thou wingest, And singing still dost soar, and ever soaring singest". Tennyson wrote "And drown'd in yonder living blue, the lark becomes sightless song". Browning optimistically had this to say "The year's at the spring, and day's at the morn, ... the larks on the wing, God's in his heaven, all's right with the world". Blake wrote "His little throat labours with inspiration; every feather on throat and breast and wing vibrates with the effluence divine. All nature listens to him". Shakespeare included this in a sonnet "Haply I think on thee ... like to the lark at the break of day arising, from the sullen earth, sings hymns at heaven's gate".

The lark is the subject of one of Aesop's fables - *The lark and her Young Ones*. A lark had made her nest in the young green wheat. The brood had almost grown, when the owner of the field said "I must send to all my neighbours to help me with my harvest". One of the young larks heard him, and asked his mother where they should move for safety. "There is no occasion to move yet, my son," she replied. The owner of the field came a few days later and said "I will come myself to-morrow, and will get in the harvest". Then the lark said to her brood "It is time now to be off—he no longer trusts to his friends but will reap the field himself". The moral of the story is: 'Self-help is the best help'.

The Skylark's scientific name is *Alauda arvensis* with *Alauda* meaning lark or little songster and *arvensis* of a field, being a simple, accurate description.

The **Shore Lark** is a winter bird in Britain found on shores, hence the English name. The scientific name is *Eremophila alpestris*. The first word derives from the Greek eremos meaning desert and philos for loving. The bird is found on open land and pararies in America, where it is called the Horned Lark. *Alpestris* is Latin for the Alps or mountains where the bird breeds. A strange geographical mixture!

Main characteristics of the Hirundinidae family:

The family Hirundinidae is made up of the aerial feeding swallows and martins. Hirundo simply means swallow. They are small to medium-sized, slender, streamlined birds with pointed wings, a small beak and perching feet and excellent fliers that catch their insect prey on the wing. Their small beak has a broad gape, with a base running almost as far back as the eye. The flight muscles are strong. They fly swiftly with great manoeuvrability and endurance. Their length ranges from 10 – 24 cm and weigh from 10 – 60 g. They have 12 tail feathers, some are deeply forked. Body plumage is short and pressed close to the skin. They are usually earth-brown or a dark-and-white colour, with a green or purple iridescence. The sexes are identical. Their legs are short and they are poor walkers. Males choose and defend a nest site and then attract a female. Aggressive displays include ruffling feathers, quivering wings, beak snapping and lunging at an opponent. Birds exhibit an array of calls. Hirundines form monogamous breeding pairs but males are often promiscuous. Eggs hatch asynchronously over several days. The parents alternate in brooding.

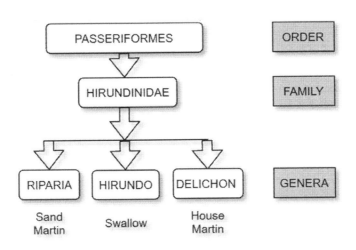

Hirundines

The three species in this family are in three genera:

Riparia - Sand Martin
Hirundo - Swallow

Delichon - House Martin

Local names for the **Sand Martin** include bank swallow, an apt name; bitter bank, meaning bite the bank, in nest making; land swallow; pit martin; sandy swallow and witchuck.

Martin in the names House Martin and Sand Martin is from the Norman name of Martin, associated with the god of war, Mars. Along with the House Martin and the Swallow all three are summer migrants to Britain. The idea of birds migrating took a long time to establish and tales to explain where the birds went in winter abounded, such as these birds hibernated under mud and revived in spring. Whilst these tales are fanciful now at the time they were taken seriously. For more detail see the Section on Migration in Chapter 2. Birds gather in huge flocks in the autumn prior to starting off on their migratory journey to Spain, across the Mediterranean at Gibraltar and then down the African coast to Senegal. The Sand Martin exhibits a loop migration pattern and returns to the UK in spring by a more easterly route over the Sahara and north through Italy.

The Sand Martin's scientific name is simply *Riparia riparia* with *ripa* meaning bank. The birds nest colonially in holes in sandy banks that can be up to 1 m in length, with a bird able to excavate at about 10 cm a day. Parents can pick out the distinctive call of their own young in a noisy colony.

45 - Swallow

A bird closely associated with human habitation is the **Swallow**. Local names are simple ones like barn swallow, which is the bird's international formal name; chimney swallow; house swallow and red-fronted swallow, from its red chin patch. Gilbert White used the name chimney swallow and noted that "it loves to haunt those stacks where there is a constant fire, no doubt for the sake of warmth".

The name Swallow derives from the Mid English swalowe and the Germanic swalwo, which means cleft stick, referring to the Swallow's forked tail. The first written record of an English name for the Swallow dates from c.685 AD. Incidentally, the forked tail is present only on adult birds. If you see Swallows flocking in autumn, ready for their perilous long migratory journey to South Africa, many birds will not have tail streamers; they are juveniles. Juveniles undertake their migratory journey without the aid of their parents. The male's tail feathers are about 20% longer than the female's, being used by the male to attract a mate. However, this is not all good news, as it takes more energy to produce longer feathers and it reduces manoeuvrability.

An early test for migration was carried out by the prior of a Cistercian monastery in the 13th century. He attached a note to a Swallow's leg which read 'Oh, swallow where do you live in winter?' The bird returned next spring with a note attached stating 'In Asia, in home of Petrus'! Olaus Magnus, Bishop of Uppsala wrote in the 16th century "in the north parts of the world, as summer weareth out, they clap their mouth to their mouth ... and so after sweet singing, fall downe into certaine great lakes ... from whence next spring they receive new resurrection; he added for proofe that the fishermen, who make holes in the ice ... do sometimes alight on these Swallowse, congealed in clods of slimy substance and that carrying them home to their stoves, the warmth restoreth them to life and flight". This explanation was given official credence by a Royal Society investigation in the 1660's. One experimenter put some Swallows in a cage under snow and found that they had died, not gone into a state of torpor. Gilbert White wrote in 1771 "..at least many of the swallow kind do not leave us in winter, but lay themselves up like insects or bats, in a torpid state ... but we must not deny migration in general (it) does subsist in some places ..... only some stragglers stay behind a long while, and do never, there is the greatest reason to believe, leave this island. Swallows seem to lay themselves up, and do come forth in a warm day, as bats do". Yet another fanciful explanation from a keen and usually accurate observer of nature.

In the 1750's a German ornithologist, Johann Frisch conducted an experiment by tying red coloured threads to the legs of Swallows. The birds returned the following year with the red thread intact. The experiment proved that Swallows did not descend into mud for the winter. Had the birds spent the winter in water the red dye would have washed out of the thread whereas they returned with a red thread on their leg. The experiment also established that Swallows returned to the same place each year. It took until the 19th century for migration to become an established and universally accepted fact.

The Swallow almost exclusively nests in buildings and will opportunistically build a nest in new buildings. Birds are faithful to their nest sites and will return to exactly the same spot as the previous year after their migratory flight from South Africa and without the use of sat-nav or GPS! In one recent study, 97% of returning males returned to their original nest site. The Swallow is the most widespread song bird on the planet.

Swallows beat their wings 4 times a second leading to 115 000 wing beats in an 8 hour flight. It is one of smallest birds that can glide which lowers the energy requirements for the bird's long migratory flight. The Swallow has a high power to weight ratio and a low wing loading. Long tail streamers help avoid stalling and aids manoeuvrability. Male streamers are 1cm longer than is optimal for flight but females are attracted by longer streamers. They grow longer during migration so they can fly well initially and then attract females later.

Swallows are breeding earlier as a result of climate warming, typically 3 days earlier each decade since the studies began in 1973. Their insect prey is emerging 4 days per decade earlier, leading to a mis-match between peak insect numbers and the hatching of Swallow chicks. Mortality rates for Swallows are low, at about 30% with an average life expectancy of 2 years, although the oldest recorded Swallow was nearly 16 years old.

Swallows work very hard to make a nest and feed young. A new nest contains up to 1400 pellets of mud and one nest examined contained 1635 rootlets, 139 pine needles and 450 pieces of dried grass. The birds can make 100 trips a day nest building, covering over 200 km, taking about a week to 10 days to complete. In an experiment a Swallow's eggs were taken away as soon as they were laid. The bird went on to lay 19 eggs instead of the 5 normally laid. The brood patch has touch sensors which count the number of eggs laid and it tells the bird when to stop laying. If there are too few eggs the bird carries on laying! Each brood will consume 150 000 insects up to fledging at about 21 days. In a paternity study of 50 nests, 30% of the young were unrelated to the male feeding them, indicating the extent of extra-pair copulations. However, if a female loses its mate and attracts a new one, he will eject all the young from the existing nest before mating with the female.

Elizabeth Barrett Browning wrote *Anacreon's ode to the swallow* writing "Thou indeed, little swallow A sweet yearly comer, Art building a hollow New nest every summer, And straight doth depart Where no gazing can follow, Past Memphis, down Nile!" Abraham Cowley wrote in *The swallow* "Foolish prater, what dost thou So early at my window do With thy tuneless serenade? Well't had been had Tereus made Thee as dumb as Philomel" which refers to the Greek myth. The phrase 'one swallow does not make a spring' was first recorded by Aristotle. In some parts April 15th is called Swallow Day.

The Swallow appears in Shakespeare's *Anthony and Cleopatra* "Swallows have built In Cleopatra's sails their nests. The augers Say they know not, look grimly And dare not speak their knowledge". This indicated that Cleopatra's ship had been left unattended for so long that Swallows had had time to nest on it and the ship was not ready for battle. Augers used the study of birds to predict the future.

The Swallow appears in many tales and lore. One Spanish story places Swallows at the crucifixion of Jesus, where they tried to remove the thorns from His brow and pricked themselves in doing so. The Russian version is that the bird pricked itself trying to remove the nails from the cross. Other stories involve the bird distracting those sent to arrest Jesus in Gethsemane or comforting Jesus on the cross. A legend is that the Swallow carried fire to earth giving it its red breast. Swallows are mentioned in the Qur'an fighting Abraha, the pagan king of Yemen who was attacking Mecca. The tiny birds hurled small stones and forced Abraha's mighty army to retreat. Moral: when God orders the smallest of His creation, miracles can happen. Other superstitions are that a broth made of crushed Swallow was said to be a remedy for epilepsy and for stammering being sympathetic magic, as the bird has a stuttering flight song. If the ashes of the bird were mixed with honey it would heal bleary eyes as would blood drawn from under the left wing. Eating a Swallow's heart would help with memory loss. Having a Swallow nesting on your house is a sign of good luck but if they abandon their nest it brings bad luck. In Wales there was a myth that 'whoever breaks a Swallow's nest shall forfeit everlasting rest'. A special stone from the bird's nest could restore sight. A northern myth was that harming the bird would lead to cows giving bloody milk or that hens would stop laying eggs.

Horatio Clare, in his book *A single Swallow*, recounts a story given to him in Niger, whilst on his epic journey following the flight path of migrating Swallows. In Niger Swallows were used in witchcraft. One potion was to boil up a Swallow with some herbs and then the resulting paste is eaten. This gives protection against car and plane accidents! Clare also recounts a story (from another book on Swallows)of an eye-witness account of a female Swallow flying with one of her nestlings in her beak to a new nest after the original nest was destroyed. A Swallow tattoo was used by sailors to demonstrate their sailing experience. One tattoo signified the sailor had travelled 8 000 km and two Swallows 16 000 km. Another piece of folklore was that as the Swallow returned to the same nest site each year, the

Swallow tattoo would ensure that the sailor would return home. If a sailor drowned at sea, the Swallow would carry his soul to heaven. Traditionally ex-Navy sailors had a Swallow tattooed on their wrists to signify a successful tour of duty and ex-prisoners had a Swallow tattooed on the back of their hand to signify 'done your bird, done your time'.

The Swallow is the national bird of Estonia and Austria. Martlet is a word used in heraldry as a swallow-like bird with no feet. The word derives from the French merlette, the name for a small, black bird i.e. merle plus the suffix –ette for small.

The Swallow's scientific name is *Hirundo rustica*, simply *Hirundo* for the swallow and *rustica* for rural. The Swallow's nesting habits mean that in Britain we closely associate it with human habitation rather than the open countryside.

Local names for the **House Martin** include black martin; easing swallow and eaves swallow, from where it nests; river swallow and window martin. The name martinet combines martin with the diminutive suffix –et, a name for the Kingfisher as well.

The bird gradually builds its nest on a vertical surface. It adds mud to the structure each morning and then feeds in the afternoon whilst the mud dries before adding another layer the next day. It takes about 1000 mud pellets to build a nest over a period of 10 days. It is thought that non-breeding birds roost on the wing at an altitude of about 900 m. House Martin numbers have fallen by 18% in the last 22 years and by 23% in the last 10 years to 2017.

The incorrect tales of where Swallows over- wintered related to the House Martin as well. Little is known about the wintering area of UK House Martins, albeit it is somewhere in Africa. The use of geo locators fitted to the birds may well help solve this puzzle but these small birds will need to be caught after their migratory journey for the collected data to be down loaded. It is possible to fix heavier transmitters on larger birds, such as Cuckoos and record the data live as the birds fly. The Hobby preys on House Martin, so the House Martin has developed a specific alarm call when it detects a Hobby.

The House Martin's scientific name is unusual in that it is an anagram; *Delichon urbicum* with *Delichon* being an anagram of the Greek khelidon (chelidon) for Swallow plus *urbicum* meaning city.

Main characteristics of the Paridae family:

The tits are a family of small passerine birds making up the Paridae family. The informal family name of tit is an abbreviation of the word titmouse, from the 14th century, when tit was used generically for any small creature and mouse referred to the tit family. The word tit derives from the Icelandic titir, a word for a small creature. Parus is the Latin for a tit. Tits are mainly small stocky woodland species with either short stout beaks (seed eaters) or thin beaks (insect eaters). They range in length from 10 - 16 cm and weigh 7 - 29 g. Tits are non-migratory, active, noisy and social birds, being highly vocal, with a large song repertoire. They are coloured with some differences between the sexes. They are territorial during the breeding season but often join mixed-species feeding flocks during the non-breeding season. Tits are highly adaptable and are amongst the most intelligent of all birds. Tits are seed eaters and generalist insectivores, often eating small caterpillars in the breeding season. Some tits cache their seed food. Tits are hole-nesting birds although some species are ground nesters. Typical clutches are 12 - 16 eggs and most tits are multi-brooded (except the Blue Tit which usually only has one). Incubation takes about 12 days and fledging a further 12 days. After this there is a period of dependency on parents for food.

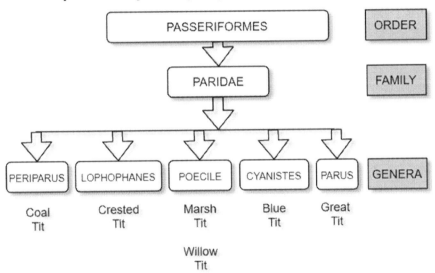

Tits

The six species in this family are in five genera:

Periparus - Coal Tit
Lophophanes - Crested Tit
Poecile - Marsh Tit; Willow Tit
Cyanistes - Blue Tit
Parus - Great Tit

Local names for the **Coal Tit** include black ox-eye, ox-eye being a name given to many of the tit family; cole titmouse; little blackcap and underground tit.

334

The Coal Tit's scientific name is *Periparus ater* which comes from *Peri* and *parus* meaning very much a tit and *ater* for black.

The **Crested Tit**'s name is *Lophophanes cristatus* which is from the Greek lophos for crest and *phanes* meaning light and the Latin *crista* for crest.

Local names for the **Marsh Tit** include predictably blackcap and black headed tit; jow ben; saw whetter and willow biter, from the way the bird bit the fingers of bird nesters, a name it shares with the Willow Tit.

The Marsh in Marsh Tit is a mis-nomer as the bird resides in broadleaf woodland not marshes. Numbers of this bird have declined dramatically, with a fall of 80% in the last 50 years to 2017 and has a UK conservation status of red.

The Marsh Tit's scientific name is *Poecile palustris* from the Greek poikolos for spotted and *palus*, a marsh. Here it is seen in bushes and trees rather than marshes.

46 - Willow Tit

The **Willow Tit** has the scientific name *Poecile montana* with *montana* from the Latin montanus for mountaineer, where it is seen in Europe as it migrates. In Britain it is sedentary and is seen, like its close relative the Marsh Tit, in bushes and trees rather than on mountain tops. Numbers of this bird have fallen even more dramatically than its close relative the Marsh Tit, with a fall of 93% in the last 50 years and also has a UK conservation status of red.

The **Blue Tit** is a very common bird that associates itself with human habitation. In the RSPB Garden Bird Survey in 2019 the Blue Tit was the third most recorded bird being seen in 77% of gardens in the survey, with an average of 2.6 birds seen. Not surprisingly the bird has many local names, including bee bird; billy biter; biting tom; blue bonnet; blue ox eye; nun; pickatee, from the bird's chirping; pickcheese; tinnock, from its song plus the suffix –ock; pridden pral, titty mouse; tom tit, a pet name and tree babbler. Again, being a bird people have known for many centuries, some names include a human name e.g. billy and tom. The word biter comes from the way the bird bites the fingers of those who interfere with its nest. Pickcheese is a Norfolk name from the habit of the bird pecking cheese. The bird's intelligence was demonstrated when it discovered that if it took the cap off milk bottles which at the time were delivered onto doorsteps, it could access the creamy milk on top. The first written record in English of the bird's name is from the 8th century.

As with many other birds, the Blue Tit can see the ultra-violet end of the light spectrum (as humans, we cannot). The male bird's blue cap emits ultra-violet light and this appears even brighter to the female and it attracts her to a suitable mate. Also the more yellow colour of the breast indicates that the male has eaten more caterpillars and so is likely to be a better provider for the female's off-spring. As a result of climate change the Blue Tit is breeding 10 days earlier than 40 years ago. This is essential as the bird has to ensure that its eggs hatch to coincide with the emergence of the hatchling's caterpillar food which is also appearing earlier in the year. The bird only lays one brood. Unusually, if the first brood is lost, there is no attempt to lay a second clutch, possibly because its codling moth caterpillar food for the young is no longer available.

The Blue Tit's scientific name emphasises the bird's colour as in *Cyanistes caeruleus* from the Latin cyaneus for dark-blue and *caeruleus* meaning blue.

The **Great Tit** has a range of interesting local names. Ox eye derives from the French for a small animal. The names black-headed bob, joe ben and tom noup, illustrate a bird acquiring a man's first name. Oddly, noup means Bullfinch. Other names are carpenter bird; saw sharpener and sawfinch, all referring to the sound made by the male in the breeding season. Others names include heckymal; lolly and sit-ye-down.

The Great Tit alters its diet in winter, eating Beech mast. To do this the bird's beak changes shape to a deeper, shorter shape. In summer the beak is thinner for eating insects. Research has shown that UK Great Tits use bird feeders more frequently than Dutch birds and as a result their beaks are slightly longer. Also UK Great Tits have a higher fledgling rate (the proportion of live chicks surviving) than its Dutch relatives. The Great Tit incubates eggs for varying lengths of time per day depending on the weather. On warmer days the female incubates for a longer period, so that her eggs hatch sooner to align with the earlier emergence of the moth caterpillars they rely on as food for their young. The caterpillars are only available for 2 weeks so the bird needs to time its egg laying accurately to maximise breeding success. The Great Tit has a loud song and, much to many a birdwatcher's irritation, it has a highly varied song. In urban areas its song is louder and higher pitched to be better heard in overcoming background noise. However, males which sing a lower note are better at attracting females and those that have a more extensive song repertoire can defend a larger territory. Also the strength of the male's breast colour varies, with a brighter colour being more attractive to females indicating a good diet and healthy feathers.

The scientific name for the Great Tit simply repeats the same as in *Parus major* i.e. the Latin *Parus* for tit and *major* for great. Easy!

Main characteristics of the Aegithalidae family:

The Long-tailed Tit is the one member in the Aegithalidae family in the UK. The family name comes from a name Aristotle gave to the birds. They are round bodied, long-tailed, small birds, 14 cm long (including the relatively long tail) and weigh 8 g. They live in mainly in woodland and are omnivorous, primarily eating insects and seeds. For a large part of the year they live in single-species flocks of related birds. They maintain contact with churring calls; their songs are quiet. The sexes are identical with black and white plumage suffused with pink. In the evening, birds roost communally, with small groups lining up together on a suitable branch. These tits build a large, domed nest (see below) in which they lay 6 – 10 white eggs. The birds are monogamous. Unusually, a breeding pair are sometimes assisted by non-breeding relatives.

The single genus in this family contains one species:

Aegithalos - Long-tailed Tit

47 - Long-tailed Tit

The **Long-tailed Tit** is often seen and heard in flocks that move quickly from tree to tree. They are dextrous birds, hanging acrobatically from branches, holding an item of food in one claw whilst eating it with its fine, stubby beak. The bird has many local names including bag; barrel tit; bellringer; bottle jug; bum towel; creak mouse; dog tail; feather poke, jack-in-a-bottle and jug pot, these names referring to its nest, with poke meaning pocket; long pod; long tailed chitterling; long tailed pie; juggy wren, with wren a name often used for small birds; long tailed chitterling; poke pudding; ragamuffin and rose muffin, from its colouration.

The bird's nest is a marvel of avian engineering. Up to 2 000 feathers are used in its construction along with moss, lichen and spiders' webs to bind it all together. The nest is dome shaped to keep predators out and the occupants warm. The nest hangs from a suitable branch and is designed to expand as the fledglings grow.

The Long-tailed Tit's scientific name is *Aegithalos caudatus* which comes from the Greek aigithalos for a tit and Latin *cauda* for tail.

Main characteristics of the Sittidae family:

Sittidae is a family of small passerine birds with one UK species, the Nuthatch. The Nuthatch has a compact body, a large head, a short squared tail, a short neck and a thin, chisel-shaped, slightly upturned beak. Both sexes are blue-grey above, white or brownish below, with a dark top of the head and a white stripe over the eye. Nuthatches forage on trees, moving with a zig-zag climbing movement and are the only UK bird that can climb head-downwards. Nuthatches use their beak to catch insects, spiders, snails and other invertebrates from the surface and crevices of tree trunks. During the spring and summer they mostly feed on invertebrates but in the winter they will eat fruit and seeds. To open an enclosed seed they wedge it into a cleft in bark and hammer the top with their beak (hence the name). They cache food in clefts. Nuthatch nest in tree holes and often narrow the entrance with mud, to keep predators out. Nuthatches are monogamous. Eggs take about 15 days to hatch and a further 24 days to fledge.

There is one genus in this family in the UK and one species:

Sitta - Nuthatch

The **Nuthatch** is a bird of woodland and its feeding habits form the basis for many of its local names, like nut jobber, where job is an old verb meaning to peck or jab; nuthack and woodcracker from its habit of tapping trees for insects. The names mud dauber and mud stopper derive from how the bird uses mud to stop up its tree nesting hole. The name jar bird was used by

Gilbert White, of Selbourne fame, from the sound the bird makes made whilst hacking.

The Nuthatch's name derives from the bird's habit of placing larger nuts it cannot eat whole in the gaps of bark and using its beak to open them i.e. hatch them. The German name is nussbrecher, meaning nut breaker.

The Nuthatch's scientific name is *Sitta europaea* with *Sitta* meaning Nuthatch and from Europe.

Main characteristics of the Certhiidae family:

This family of treecreepers are small, dull coloured, woodland birds. The family name comes from Greek kerthios for a small tree-dwelling bird described by Aristotle. The birds have strong legs and feet with long, deeply curved claws and stiffened tail feathers, enabling them to cling to side of a tree. They have a fine down-curved beak for extracting small insects from inside tree bark. The beak and claw length vary by the season depending on food availability. They climb spirally up a tree and then fly down to the base of the next tree. Birds are monogamous and defend territory. Treecreepers nest in tree cavities and lay 5 – 6 eggs, which are brooded for 14 days. Hatchlings are altricial and they fledge after 15 days.

There is one genus in this family in the UK and one species:

Certhia - Treecreeper

A woodland bird that is usually seen scurrying up the side of a tree, pecking quickly as it climbs is the **Treecreeper**. This habit is reflected in many of its local names like bark creeper; bark runner; climb tree; common creeper; creep tree; ox-eye creeper, where the term ox-eye was traditionally used for the tit family, deriving from the French term for a small bird; tree climber, noting that the Treecreeper only ever climbs up a tree (unlike the Nuthatch which can climb down a tree as well) and tree mouse, where mouse is a generic word for a small creature. Cuddy is based on the bird's habit of clinging to the side of a tree, using its tail feathers, which are stiffened, to support the bird as it seeks insect food hidden in the bark. Cuddy is also a name for a diverse range of birds including Eider, Moorhen, Dunnock and House Sparrow. Numbers of this species in the UK have fallen by 12% over the 50 years to 2017.

The Treecreeper's scientific name is *Certhia familiaris* with the Latin *familiaris* meaning familiar.

Main characteristics of the Troglodytidae family:

This is the family of wrens. Troglodyte means cave-dweller and their scientific name comes from the way some species forage in dark crevices. They are mainly small (the Wren weighs 10 g) and inconspicuous, except for their loud and often complex songs. These birds have short wings. Wrens have long and fine beaks and are largely insectivorous. The plumage of the sexes is always very similar. Wrens are often retiring and secretive. Several species often hold their tails upright and sleep on the ground. Outside the breeding season wrens form communal roosts to keep warm. An unusual breeding habit is multiple nest building. Typically the male constructs several nests (called cock nests) and the female selects the nest for breeding, to which she adds a lining. The Wren lays, on average, 6 eggs and has two broods, with brooding taking 16 days and fledging a further 16 days.

There is one genus in this family in the UK and one species:

Troglodytes - Wren

48 - Wren

One of our best known birds is the **Wren**. As a mark of this the Wren appeared on the farthing coin from 1937 until the coin was withdrawn in 1960. It readily associates with human habitation and the Wren has been given a wide variety of names over the centuries. Some of its local names include human first names such as the well-known jenny wren plus bobby wren; giller wren (from Gill); kitty wren (from Katherine) and sally. Cutty, scut and stumpit are names referring to the Wren's short tail. There are a range of regional variations based on the bird's diminutive size with puggy wren from Surrey; stumpy toddy from Cheshire; tiddy wren from Essex; titty todger from Devon and wrannock from Scotland, where –ock is a diminutive suffix. The name wren was also used for many other birds e.g. Chiffchaff, Willow Warbler and Wood Warbler were named least willow wren, ground wren and wood wren respectively. The Dartford Warbler was named furze wren and the Goldcrest gold crested wren.

The name Wren means hen as a result of the misconception that the species was all female! For a long time the Robin was thought to be the male bird and its female mate was the Wren. In Shetland the Wren was called Robin, where the Robin is rare.

A piece of folklore connected to the Wren's scientific name is well known. There was a race between an eagle and a Wren to see which bird could fly the highest. The Wren rode on the eagle's back and when it had reached its highest point the Wren leapt off and flew higher to win the race. Another race was set up to see which of the two birds could descend the lowest and the Wren won again, by diving down a mouse hole. The Wren was then given the title 'King of the birds'. Having won the title deviously the other birds condemned the Wren to seek food in crevices, hence its name, *Troglodytes*, as a cave dweller. The wren is also known as kuningilin - kinglet in Old German, a name associated with the fable recounted above on its election as the king of birds. The poet Ted Hughes wrote about this myth "The wren is a nervous wreck. Since he saw the sun from the back of an eagle. He prefers to creep. If he can't creep He'll whirr trickle-low as his shadow - Brief as a mouse's bounce from safety to safety". Dryden wrote of this saying "Fool that I was, upon my eagle's wing, I bore this wren, till he was tired of soaring, And now he mounts above me".

Wordsworth was charmed by the Wren's song, writing "So sweetly 'mid the gloom the invisible bird; Sang to herself, that there I could have made; my dwelling place, and lived for ever there; To hear such music". Shakespeare noted the bird's feisty nature writing in *Macbeth* "For the poor wren, the most diminutive of birds, will fight her young ones in her nest, against the owl".

Folklore involving the Wren includes that if a Wren's nest were destroyed this would lead to a house fire or death. A piece of Welsh lore was that 'whoever breaks a Wren's nest shall never see God's face'. Blake wrote of this "He who shall hurt the little wren, shall never be belov'd of men". The Wren, either roasted or eaten raw, was taken as a cure for kidney stones. In Devon fishermen took a Wren's feather to sea to protect them against drowning. If a bride hears a Wren it brings luck. Eating the bird's meat raw with salt was said to be a cure for kidney stones. Also the ashes of the bird taken with a little mercury effected a cure! Known as God's bird and Our lady's hen, harm would come to anyone hurting the bird. However, there is a ritual of hunting Wrens between Christmas and Epiphany. A traditional tale is that the Wren alerted guards to St. Stephen's attempted escape from gaol which led to him becoming the first Christian martyr. Wren hunts took place on St. Stephen's day, 26th December. A Wren was caught, killed and paraded from house to house where feathers from the bird were exchanged for gifts.

In winter the UK population is supplemented by birds which migrate from Russia to Britain. In another marvel of migration a bird weighing 10 g flies non-stop over the North Sea, often in poor weather! The birds roost in numbers in cold weather, with one recorded roost of 63 birds in one nest! Numbers have increased in Britain by 117% in the last 50 years to 2017.

Its scientific name *Troglodytes troglodytes* i.e. cave dweller derives from the tale above via the Greek trogle for hole and dutes, a diver. Another bird's name linked to a mythical tale.

The Wren has established separate populations on Shetland, the Outer Hebrides, Fair Isle and St. Kilda. These birds have gradually evolved physically and now differ from the mainland Wren and have become sub-species of the nominate UK species *Troglodytes troglodytes troglodytes*. The sub-species are paler, have a longer, thicker beak (perhaps arising from dietary change) and a different song. This is an example of the process of speciation, where geographically isolated populations evolve different characteristics. The scientific name for the Shetland Wren is *Troglodytes troglodytes zetlandicus* with six other sub-species of Wrens in the Hebrides, Fair Isle and St. Kilda and three other areas.

Main characteristics of the Cinclidae family:

The Dipper is a member of the Cinclidae family of which there is only one genus of 5 species worldwide. Dippers are unique among passerines for their ability to dive and swim underwater and are the smallest diving bird in the world. It is the only acquatic song bird in the world. They are stocky birds, with a short tail with broad, round-tipped feathers, sturdy legs and powerful feet and a short, compressed beak without rictal bristles. Their wings are relatively short but strongly muscled, using them as flippers underwater. They have dense plumage with a large preen gland for waterproofing their feathers. Their eyes have well-developed focus muscles which can change the curvature of the lens to enhance underwater vision. They have nasal flaps to prevent water entering their nostrils. Their blood has a high haemoglobin concentration, increasing their capacity to store oxygen, allowing them to remain underwater for up to 30 seconds. Dippers forage for invertebrates such as the nymphs or larvae of various insects as well as small fish and fish eggs with molluscs and crustaceans consumed in winter. Both sexes help build the nest, typically sited in a crevice near water, with the female completing the nest with a soft lining. The female incubates the 6 white eggs for about 16 days and the young fledge after about 22 days. After fledging the young are fed by their parents until they are able to dive and feed. The birds normally have two broods each year.

There is one genus in this family in the UK and one species:

Cinclus - Dipper

The **Dipper** is found bobbing around on the water-side of streams and rivers looking for larvae to snatch from the water. Its local names incorporate names from the thrush family (but it's not a member of the Turdidae family) like brook ousel; water blackbird and water ouzel, from its white neck band (similar to the Ring Ouzel). Others are bessy doucker, again showing a bird's name incorporating a human name; ess cock, ess being a Scottish name for waterfall; river pie; water colly, meaning dark as coal; water crake, but the bird does not resemble a crake; water crow, from its dark colour and water piet, from its contrasting white breast.

The Dipper sings throughout the year to defend its territory. Experiments have shown that if higher quality food is given to fledglings they have a better, more complex song when mature. This in turn leads to higher reproduction rates.

Darwin studied the Dipper and noted the evolution of the bird to suit its acquatic environment. This includes dense feathers as insulation and a special nictitating membrane (third eye lid) to protect its eyes under water. It has solid bones to help it submerge (whereas most other birds have a lighter, honey-combed bone structure). Its body is covered in about 4 500 feathers, compared to the 3 000 on a similar sized bird. Their preen gland is 10 times larger than an equivalent sized bird to supply it with the oil it needs to keeps its feathers fully water proofed. It spends around two thirds of its day feeding (and getting very wet!).

The Dipper's scientific name is *Cinclus cinclus* repetitively the word for a waterbird known to Aristotle, from the Greek kinklos.

Main characteristics of the Regulidae family:

The family name derives from regulus meaning little king, referring to the colourful crown feathers of many of the birds in this family. Worldwide there are only six species in this family. The family was once thought to be closely related to the warblers but recent genetic evidence suggests that they are not. The Firecrest, Goldcrest and other birds in this family are amongst the smallest in the world, being 8 - 11 cm long and weighing 6 - 8 g. Sexes are a similar size with the male possessing a distinctive, colourful crown which stands erect during their courtship display. The birds are sharp-beaked, insectivores that live mainly in conifer woods. They have a high metabolic rate and have to feed almost continuously to maintain their energy levels. They have deeply grooved pads on their feet plus a long hind toe to assist perching on branches as they extract their insect food. They build nests of moss and lichen in trees. The female incubates a usual clutch of 9 eggs, using her feet to transfer heat to the eggs. Unusually the first laid eggs weigh less than the eggs laid later. Eggs hatch after about 16 days and the chicks fledge after about 21 days.

The two species in this family in the UK are in one genus:

Regulus - Goldcrest; Firecrest

49 - Goldcrest

The **Goldcrest** is Britain's smallest bird, being 8.5 cm long and weighing 6 g, the weight of a 10 p coin; half the weight of a Wren. Our resident population is supplemented in winter by migrants from Scandinavia.

One Swedish local name is kungsfagel – king bird. Another local name is herring spink, from the bird's habit of clinging to the rigging of fishing boats, plus tot o'er the seas, a small bird flying over the sea. One belief was that this tiny bird would be incapable of flying across the Baltic and North Seas so it hitched a ride on the back of the migrating Woodcock. Hence the Yorkshire name woodcock pilot. Swing tree is from the way the bird feeds upside down on branches. Other names associate the Goldcrest with the Wren with names like gold crested wren and golden cutty. Others refer to its diminutive size with names like miller's thumb; thumb bird; tidley goldfinch, tidley meaning tiny and wood titmouse. The Goldcrest loses 20% of its weight during one cold night and has to eat constantly all day, consuming twice its body weight in food each day. The bird has three broods to maintain population levels. The male looks after the first brood whilst the female moves to a new nest and tends to the next brood.

The Goldcrest's scientific name is *Regulus regulus*.

The **Firecrest**'s scientific name is *Regulus ignicapilla* with *Regulus* meaning little king, referring to the bright orange head markings on the male bird. *Ignicapilla* is from the Latin *igni* for fire and capillus for cap, again referring to the male bird's bright head markings.

The diagram below shows the five families, the five genera and 14 species:

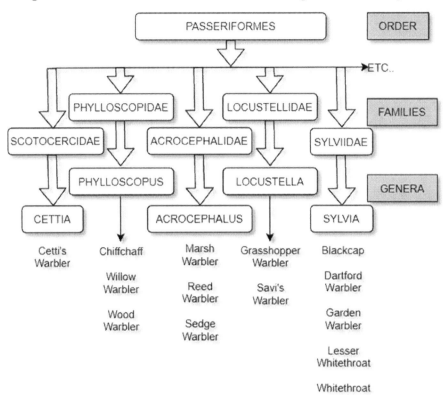

Warblers

The following five families comprise species that are often grouped informally as warblers.

Cettia - Cetti's Warbler
Phylloscopus - Chiffchaff; Willow Warbler; Wood Warbler
Acrocephallus - Marsh Warbler; Reed Warbler; Sedge Warbler
Locustella - Grasshopper Warbler; Savi's Warbler
Sylvia - Blackcap; Dartford Warbler; Garden Warbler; Lesser Whitethroat; Whitethroat

Cetti's Warbler is named after the Italian mathematician and 18th century naturalist Fransesco Cetti. The species is now placed in the family Scotocercidae, sometimes called bush warblers, that mainly occur in Asia and Africa.

Cetti's Warbler is a bird mostly heard and not often seen, with a very loud, distinctive song resembling gun-fire as it skulks in its reed bed habitat. Both sexes look alike but males are 30% heavier than females and have longer wings. Cetti's Warbler is unusual among passerine birds in having ten rectrices rather than the usual twelve. Unusually it lays bright red eggs.

David Turner in his book *Was Beethoven a birdwatcher?* suggests that the explosive opening bars of the fourth movement of Beethoven's second symphony were inspired by the bird's song. Up to the 1950's the bird was rarely seen in Britain but numbers have increased. The first record of breeding in Britain was 1973 and the population has increased rapidly in abundance and distribution since, showing a 100 fold increase for the 25 years to 2017.

The bird's scientific name is *Cettia cetti* reflecting the eponym of the vernacular name.

Main characteristics of the Phylloscopidae family:

This family is often referred to as the leaf warblers. Phylloscopus derives from the Greek phullion for leaf and skopos for watcher. UK birds of this family are summer migrants. The birds are slim, greenish with lighter underparts and some have a supercillium, others also possess noticeable wing bars. They show some plumage variation with seasons, often due to feather wear. There is little or no difference in plumage between the sexes. Each species has a distinctive song. Birds are very active, eating insects found on leaves. They nest at or near ground level. Nest building and brooding is carried out by the female alone. Their eggs are white and speckled. The birds have two broods with a first clutch of 6 - 7 eggs and the second of 4 - 5 eggs. Incubation takes 14 days and fledgling in 10 - 15 days.

The three species in this family in the UK are in one genus:

Phylloscopus - Chiffchaff; Willow Warbler; Wood Warbler

The **Chiffchaff** is a common summer migrant and, having been known for centuries, has many local names including bank bottle and feather poke, both referring to its nest; cheep; chip chop; choice; least willow wren, historically warblers were termed wrens and the Chiffchaff was seen correctly to be a close relative of the Willow Warbler; lesser pettychap; peggy, as another example of a bird acquiring a human name and wood oven, from its nest.

In spring the Chiffchaff moves quickly amongst the newly emerged leaves in the tree canopy, picking off small insects as it goes, with the male stopping frequently to emit its loud, distinctive song; the name being onomatopoeic. However, whilst we hear the song as a repetition of two notes, one sonic analysis discovered 47 variations, which presumably the females can distinguish between in order to choose a mate. Occasionally the Chiffchaff cross breeds with its close relative the Willow Warbler and the off-spring sings part of a Chiffchaff's song and part of a Willow Warbler's!

The Chiffchaff is one of the first summer migrants to arrive and one of the last to leave. The bird needs to eat 2.5 g of flies each day; a third of its own weight. The male has a contact call to attract a female. He also has a courtship display flight where he descends on spread out wings, a fanned tail and out stretched legs. The female builds the nest and the male has no active involvement in raising the young. Before migrating the bird's weight increases from 7.5 g to over 9.0 g, laying down fat for energy. Wintering birds seen in Britain are continental birds which migrate here rather than summer visitors that have remained here.

The Chiffchaff's scientific name is *Phylloscopus collybita*, with *collybita* from the Greek for money-changer, the bird's song apparently sounding like money being counted.

The **Willow Warbler** is still a common summer visitor and has been for centuries. Visually it is very similar to its close relative the Chiffchaff (there are some subtle differences, notably the leg colour), so some names confuse the two birds. However, the birds have very different and distinctive songs. Being a familiar bird some local names include human names, such as fell peggy; ground issac; sally picker; sweet billy and willie muftie. This family of warblers were given the general name wren, although they are not related to the Wren, with names such as golden wren; ground wren; muffie wren and willow wren. Other names like bank jug; feather poke, but the bird does not use feathers in its nest and ground oven refer to their distinctive nest, which, like the Long-tailed Tit's, is domed. Further names include bee bird; huck muck; nettle bird; smooth and willow sparrow.

Young birds start their migratory journey in late July, with the parents following later as they moult before migrating. The bird's scientific name is *Phylloscopus trochilus* with trokhilos being a bird mentioned by Aristotle.

The **Wood Warbler**'s scientific name, *Phylloscopus sibilatrix* is from the Latin sibilare to whistle, referring to the bird's lovely song. Based on the Breeding Bird Survey, numbers of this species have fallen by 63% in the 22 years to 2017 and it has a UK red conservation status.

Main characteristics of the Acrocephalidae family:

The name akros means highest and kephale means head; the birds in this family are flat headed. These birds have a slim beak, suited to catching insect prey. Sexes are visually similar, with uniform olive or light brown backs and lighter under sides; some have a supercillium. Each species song is different with some songs monotonous, others based on mimicry. The birds live in marshes and reed beds, often out of sight. The birds hang their nests on reed stems, mostly built by female. Clutch size is 4 - 6 eggs. Normally these birds are single brooded but in good breeding years they have two broods.

The three species in this family in the UK are in a single genus:

Acrocephalus - Marsh Warbler; Reed Warbler; Sedge Warbler

50 - Marsh Warbler

The **Marsh Warbler's** scientific name is *Acrocephalus palustris*, with *palus* meaning marsh. This bird is a master mimic of other birds' songs. For more detail see the Section Variations on a theme in Chapter 3. The bird is a rare breeder in Britain with only about 30 breeding pairs.

Local names for the **Reed Warbler** include babbler and chuckler, from its song; night warbler; reed chucker; reed tit; rush warbler; small straw and water sparrow, all referring to its habitat. Numbers of this species have remained static over the last 10 years to 2017, compared to a fall in the numbers of its close relative the Sedge Warbler.

The scientific name of the Reed Warbler is *Acrocephalus scirpaceus* with scirpus meaning reed, where the bird breeds and *aceus* - resembling.

51 - Sedge Warbler

A summer migrant that makes itself heard in reed beds is the **Sedge Warbler**. Until the 18th century there was no distinction made between this bird and the very similar Reed Warbler, so some local names refer to both birds. These names include chan chider; chitter chat; irish nightingale; night singer and thorn warbler, all referring to the bird's loud and persistent song. Other names include leg bird, possibly arising from observers being able to see the bird's legs as it straddles reeds whilst singing; fantail warbler, with another non-UK species now allocated this as its formal name; the orphean warbler, confusing this bird with the similar continental bird; reed fauvette, with the latter word being French for another warbler; sedge marine; sedge reedling; water sparrow, from the streaky, brown back and willow lark.

The Sedge Warbler's song is made up of many separate phrases, some based on mimicry. Each song is composed of a unique set of phrases. Females select the male with the widest set of song phrases. Numbers of this bird have fallen by 19% in the last 10 years to 2017.

The Sedge Warbler's scientific name is *Acrocephalus schoenobaenus* with *schoenobaenus* from the Greek skhoiniklos for reed and baino to walk.

Main characteristics of the Locustellidae family:

The name locusta means little grasshopper. This is a family of warblers with brown upper parts, lighter underneath. UK birds are migratory. The Grasshopper Warbler has a buzzing song which sounds like a grasshopper.

The birds live in brush land, mostly staying out of sight. They nest on or near the ground in thick cover. Males and females build the nest and incubate their eggs.

The two species in this family in the UK are in one genus:

Locustella - Grasshopper Warbler; Savi's Warbler

Local names for the **Grasshopper Warbler** include brake hopper and brake locustelle, from it under-growth habitat and cricket bird and reeler from its song.

The Grasshopper Warbler name is onomatopoeic and the bird's song sounds like a fisher's reel as it emits 1 400 double notes a minute (as many as 250 000 notes a night). The bird is difficult to locate as it moves its head from side to side to confuse potential predators and interested birdwatchers!

The Grasshopper Warbler's scientific name is *Locustella naevia*, with *naevia* meaning spotted plumage.

The formal name of **Savi's Warbler** recognises the 19th century Italian ornithologist Paolo Savi. Savi was given specimens of an unstreaked, dark, rufous-brown warbler which was new to science. He published a description of the bird in 1824 and it became known as Savi's Warbler. The bird is comparatively rare in the UK and is red listed here but not in Europe.

The scientific name for Savi's Warbler is *Locustella luscinoides* with luscinia meaning Nightingale and *oides* resembling. It is difficult to reconcile the sound of a grasshopper with that of the nightingale's song!

Main characteristics of the Sylviidae family:

The word sylvia means woodland sprite, associating the bird with elves, fairies and (more realistically) woodland. Birds in this family have a grey brown plumage, some being more colourful, with a number of species exhibiting sexual dimorphism. Birds have a small pointed beak with bristles at base of the beak. Their legs are stouter than other warblers. The birds are largely insectivorous but eat fruit, especially when putting on fat reserves for their long migratory journey. The birds inhabit woodland and shrubberies, hopping around and flicking their wings and tail. Songs are a fast warble, some a scratchy twitter. They build cup-shaped, open nests near the ground, sheltered in bushes. Males build cock nests (as does the Wren) i.e. the male builds several nests and the female selects one for their family. Young of this family are unspotted. Both sexes incubate the eggs.

The five species in this family in the UK are in one genus:

Sylvia – Blackcap; Dartford Warbler; Garden Warbler; Lesser Whitethroat; Whitethroat

52 - Blackcap

For a long time the **Blackcap** has been a common summer visitor to the UK and in recent times increasingly a winter migrant visitor. The bird has a very distinctive and beautiful song; some people say it equals that of the Nightingale! Our forebears also thought so and they gave the bird names like mock nightingale and northern nightingale. Its other names derive from the bird's nesting materials hence the names black-headed hay-jack; hay bird; hay chat; jack straw and nettle creeper. As a bird that lives close to humans, other names came from human first names such as black-headed peggy and jack straw. Note that it is the male which has a black cap (the female's is brown). Peggy was a word used for all warblers and jack denoted a small man, hence man of straw. Hay and straw refer to the bird's nesting material. In the 19th century the Blackcap was the most common cage bird in Europe.

The Blackcap can be seen in Britain during winter, often visiting bird tables. These birds are likely to be Blackcaps from the continent, as our UK summer visitors migrate to North Africa. Research has established that the attraction of Britain for continental birds is our love of putting up garden bird feeders. Also the birds that winter in Britain only breed with fellow travellers to Britain and do not breed with Blackcaps which have migrated to Southern Spain or Morocco. This may in time lead to separate characteristics for the two groups of Blackcaps and even the emergence of a separate species. Blackcaps wintering in Britain have narrower, longer beaks than those which winter in Spain. European Blackcap populations are probably evolving to make a winter migratory journey to Britain instead of southern Europe.

At the end the summer breeding season Blackcaps switch to a fruit diet and increase their weight in the form of fat which can be seen as fat globules on their chest. This fat then provides the fuel for their long migratory journey.

During their journey they will stop off to re-fuel ready for the next leg of their journey. Oddly these birds (along with some other migratory birds) have a leap frog pattern of migration, with the most northerly birds flying the furthest south i.e. the longest distance. The Blackcap is arriving 15 days earlier in Britain than 50 years ago as a result of climate change.

The Blackcap's scientific name is *Sylvia atricapilla,* with *Sylvia* meaning wood and *atri* for black and *capilla* for cap.

One of Britain's lightest birds (weighing 10 g) is the **Dartford Warbler** which is named after the place where a pair was shot for identification. It was commonplace for ornithologists who wanted a closer look at a bird to have one shot, inspect it close up and then perhaps give it to a museum as a specimen. Another explanation for the formal name is that the bird was discovered by a Dr. John Latham, who examined a pair given to him and he then named the species after the town where he worked.

This is the only bird of this family that is an all-year resident in Britain and is sedentary in its heathland habitat. In severe winters the population falls dramatically almost to the point of extinction. The bird holds on in small numbers and the population recovers quickly if the weather permits.

The scientific name of the Dartford Warbler is *Sylvia undata*, with *undata* meaning wavy.

The **Garden Warbler** has a wide variety of local names include billy whitethroat, with reference to a human name; cherry-chopper, it's unlikely the thin-billed warbler can crack a hard cherry stone but it does eat fruit prior to migrating in autumn; fauvette; fig-eater, another strange name as the bird is insectivorous but might eat figs as a fruit to fatten up on; greater pettychaps, from its cheerful song, with the Chiffchaff called the lesser pettychaps; lady lently n'land. Nightingale's mate refers to the bird's tuneful song, being very similar to the Blackcap's, which also has local names linking it to the Nightingale. Peggy, again a reference to the female name and small straw and strawsmear, from the straw its nest is made from.

The Garden Warbler's scientific name is *Sylvia borin* with *borin* being Italian for a type of warbler.

The **Lesser Whitethroat**'s local names include babbling warbler; haychat, from its nesting material; hazel linnet, not quite right as it's not a relative of the finch; hey-tit; mealy mouth; nettle creeper and again pettichaps.

The Lesser Whitethroat has different migration strategy from its close relatives in the Sylviidae family. This species does not fatten up very much before it leaves on its migratory journey. Unusually, it heads off towards Italy re-fuelling on the way. It then heads off for Egypt and Ethiopia before arriving at its resting grounds in Chad. It then returns in a loop migration pattern to the UK the following spring.

The Lesser Whitethroat's scientific name is *Sylvia curruca* with *curruca* being a bird named by Juvenal, a first century Roman poet.

A summer migrant that sings from our hedgerows in summer is the **Whitethroat**. Many local names refer to its nesting material with names like cut straw; hay tit; jack straw, using a man's name; nettle creeper, from its habit of nesting in nettles; small straw, from the fine pieces of hay used in its nest; straw mouse and windle straw from Shropshire, where windle means a stalk of withered grass. The bird has names linked to female first names such as great peggy and jennie cut throat and to male names in charlie mufftie and hay-jack. Mufftie refers to its distinctive white throat, seen well when it sings. Its song is reflected in the Scottish name wheetie, with wheet plus the –ie suffix. White lintie links this bird with the Linnet (lintie) but the Whitethroat is in the warbler family (Sylviidae) not in the finch family (Fringillidae). Other names include hay-chat; paddling warbler; singing skyrocket and wheety wheybeard. Hedge chicken; feather bird and meg cut-throat add to the variety of names.

In the late 1960's the numbers of Whitethroat in the UK fell dramatically due to drought in its resting grounds in the Sahel, south of the Sahara desert but numbers have recovered into the 21st century. The species now has a UK conservation status of green. The bird's migratory flight takes it non-stop over the Sahara Desert.

The scientific name of the Whitethroat is *Sylvia communis* with *communis* meaning common, as in ordinary rather than numerous.

Main characteristics of the Muscicapidae family:

The word Muscicapa derives from musca, a fly and capere, to seize. The flycatchers are mainly small to medium birds, ranging from 10 - 21 cm in length. They are arboreal insectivores. Flycatchers have large heads, broad shoulders, flattish beaks, pointed wings and small, weak legs and feet. The tails are rounded or shallowly forked. Most have a broad, flattened beak suited to catching insects in flight with the ground foraging species having finer beaks. They have stout, well-developed rictal bristles at the gape of the beak. Most have a weak song and harsh call. Many species are a dull brown in colour but the plumage of males can be much brighter. The nesting habits of flycatchers vary; the typical nest is an open cup in a tree but some nest on buildings and in concealed places.

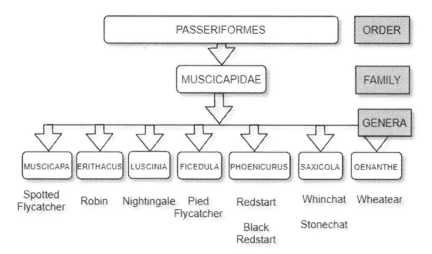

The nine species in this family in the UK are in seven genera:

Muscicapa - Spotted Flycatcher
Erithacus - Robin
Luscinia - Nightingale
Ficedula - Pied Flycatcher
Phoenicurus - Black Redstart; Redstart
Saxicola - Stonechat; Whinchat
Oenanthe - Wheatear

The **Spotted Flycatcher** was once a common bird seen sitting on the end of a branch and characteristically flying out to catch an airborne insect and returning to the same perch. Numbers have dropped by 89% over the last 50 years (to 2017) and now the species has a conservation status of red.

Its local names include beam bird; bee bird; cherry chopper and cherry sucker, the bird does not eat cherries but does feed on fruit before migrating; cobweb; lead coloured flycatcher, though it's not grey; post bird, from its habit of sitting on a post or branch; spider catcher; wall bird; wall chat and wall robin from where it nests.

The Spotted Flycatcher's scientific name of *Muscicapa striata* reflects the bird's habits. Musca is Latin for fly and capere to seize and *striata* from stria meaning line.

Possibly the most iconic bird in Britain is the **Robin**. In Britain the bird associates closely with humans and can become quite tame, especially when meal worms are involved! Ruddock was a reference to the Robin made around 1000 AD, with ruddy as the colour and a suffix of -ock. Although the breast colour is more orange, the word orange did not enter the English language until the 16th century, well after the Robin was called red! Another name referring to its colour is robin red-dock. Given its close association with humans many local names incorporate men's names, such as bobby; bob robin; thomas robin and tommy liden. For a long time the Robin was thought to be just a male bird and its female mate was the Wren. The rhyme *The robin and the wren, are God almighty's cock and hen* encapsulated this piece of folklore.

In Shetland the Wren was called Robin, where the Robin is rare. The first postmen, who had vermillion waistcoats, were called Robins, hence the appearance of Robins on Christmas cards, sometimes with a letter in their beak. Trollope noted this, writing "come in, Robin postman, and warm thee self awhile".

Tales relating to the Robin are many and varied. Several tales exist about how the Robin acquired its red breast. One is that it was singed taking water to sinners in hell. Another is that when Jesus was on his way to Calvary, the Robin picked a thorn from His crown and the blood spurted onto the Robin. This association gave the Robin a protected status and led to the legend that if a Robin was harmed it would have evil consequences. A further tale is that the Robin's red colouring came from fanning a fire to keep the baby Jesus warm in the stable. Another piece of Welsh lore is 'Whoever robs a Robin's nest shall go to hell'. If a Robin enters a house, except in November, it will lead to the death of a member of the house. If a Robin enters a church and sings, that will lead to the death of one of the congregation. Sometimes the Robin is seen as the bringer of fire - along with the Swallow and Goldfinch. The famous nursery rhyme *Who killed cock Robin?* published in about 1779 has an array of birds involved, including the Bullfinch, Linnet, Rook, Thrush, Red Kite, Skylark, House Sparrow, Tawny Owl, Turtle Dove and Wren. The rhyme commences with "Who killed Cock Robin? I, said the Sparrow, with my bow and arrow, I killed Cock Robin". It finishes with "All the birds of the air fell a-sighing and a-sobbing, when they heard the bell toll for poor Cock Robin".

The name Robin is derived from a pet diminutive of the man's name Robert. This accords with the familiarity of the Robin with humans, being a frequent visitor to gardens and bird feeders but only in Britain. Continental birds are less conspicuous, being woodland birds. Until the major revision of formal English bird names by the BOU in 1923, the formal name for the Robin was Robin Redbreast.

In the 1960's a vote, published in The Times, appointed the Robin as the national bird. In 2015 a national poll again voted the Robin as the national bird. In fact the Robin is very aggressive and will fight furiously to protect its territory. The sexes are identical. Unusually the female also sings, in autumn, probably to denote and protect her feeding territory. The average life span is just over one year. The Robin was the eighth most common bird observed in the Big Garden Birdwatch 2019.

The Robin's scientific name is *Erithacus rubecula* which comes from the Greek erithakos for robin and from the Latin ruber for red.

53 - Nightingale

The **Nightingale**'s formal name comes from the German nachtingal which means night songstress, making the historical mistake that it is the female which sings. In English the word became nyghtgale and thence to Nightingale. The Mid English word gale means to sing which the bird does exceptionally well! The first written record of an English name for the Nightingale dates from 685 AD. Oddly for a bird that has been well known for centuries there are very few recorded local names. One is barley bird, from the time of the arrival of the bird when spring sown barley is beginning to shoot.

It is the male bird that sings, despite early literature stating it was the female (but the sexes are identical in appearance). The Nightingale does sing at night and also during the day. Its song is complex and analysis has discovered 250 phrases. Its song is also very loud – up to 90 dB and the bird will sing louder to counteract any background noise. The male sings up to the time when its mate lays her eggs and then stops. If the brood is lost then the male will start to sing again. It is highly unlikely that the 'Nightingale sang in Berkeley Square' as this area would never have provided the right environment for the bird; it was probably a Robin singing, being a close relative of the Nightingale.

The Nightingale was the subject of the first ever live outdoor radio broadcast. Beatrice Harrison, a leading cellist of her generation, had the habit of playing her cello in the wooded garden of her cottage in Oxted, Surrey. One evening in 1923 a Nightingale joined in with her playing. Eventually a broadcast of the cello-Nightingale duet was made in 1924 on live radio.

Recently Nightingale numbers have fallen dramatically. A BTO survey reported a 62% drop in numbers over the 22 years and a 38% fall over 5 years, to 2017. European countries are not reporting such a severe decline. Whilst the Nightingale has a conservation status of red in the UK, it is of least concern status in Europe.

A Greek mythological story is the basis for the genus name of the Nightingale, Luscinia – a lament. Philomena was the princess of Athens and the younger of two daughters of Pandion, King of Athens. Her sister, Procne, was the wife of King Tereus of Thrace. Philomela, after being raped and mutilated by her sister's husband, Tereus, obtained her revenge and transforms into a Nightingale, a bird noted for its song. Procne was also transformed, into a Swallow. As a result of the violence associated with the myth, the song of the Nightingale is depicted as a sorrowful lament. It could be that the wrong and often repeated idea of the female Nightingale singing comes from this tale. Most listeners would not call the bird's complex, powerful and varied song a lament. Many would agree with Izak Walton who wrote "it breathes such sweet music out of her little instrumental throat that it might make mankind think miracles had not ceased". Boris Pasternak writing in *Doctor Zhivago* makes the case for the bird's song being unique "Once again I wondered at the difference between their (Nightingale's) song and that of all other birds, at the wide gulf left unabridged by nature between the others and the wealth and singularity of theirs. Such variety and power and resonance".

Several poets have written about the bird's distinctive song. For example, John Milton in *Nightingale* wrote "O nightingale, that on yon bloomy spray Warbl'st at eve, when all the woods are still, Thou with fresh hope the lover's heart doth fill, While the jolly hours lead on propitious May; Thy liquid notes that close the eye of the day, First heard before the shallow cuckoo's bill, portend success in love". Milton also wrote "Now come still evening on ... silence accompanied ... all but the wakeful nightingale; she all night her amorous descent sung". Note again how Milton thought it was the female that sang and also that it only sang at night. In 1819 John Keats wrote in *Ode to a Nightingale* "My heart aches, and a drowsy numbness pains My sense, as though of hemlock I had drunk, Or emptied some dull opiate to the drains 'Tis not through envy of thy happy lot, But being too happy in thine happiness - That thou, light-winged Dryad of the trees, In some melodious plot of beechen green, and shadows number less, Singest of summer in full-throated ease". Keats continued to wax lyrical about the bird, writing "where the nightingale doth sing, not a senseless thing, but divine melodious truth". Izak Walton wrote about the Nightingale "Lord, what music hast thou provided for the saints in heaven, when thou givest men such music on earth". Finally, Pierre Belon wrote "Could there be a man lacking in judgement who would not have admiration hearing such melody coming out of the throat of such a wild little bird ... has it ever had a master who has taught it the science of such perfect music?".

The Nightingale inevitably is the basis for many tales and myths because of its distinctive song. The bird represents sorrow or forlorn love in poems, as the song is characterised as a lament. This idea derives from the Greek mythological story recounted above. In folklore the Nightingale represents happiness and sweetness as well as forlornness and unrequited love. One tale suggests the bird presses its breast against a thorn when it sings, afraid that if it falls asleep it will be devoured by a serpent. Shakespeare used this in *The rape of Lucrece* - "and whiles against a thorn thou bear'st thy part; To keep thy sharp woes waking, wretched I; To imitate thee well, against my heart; will fix a sharp knife". He also wrote of the bird in *Romeo and Juliet* "It is not yet near day; it was the nightingale and not the lark that pierc'd the fearful hollow of thine ear. Nightly she sings on your pomegranate tree; believe me, love, it was the nightingale".

In the 12th century poem *The Owl and the Nightingale* a furious debate is heard between an owl and a Nightingale, in which they exchange insults. The Nightingale shames the owl for the screeches and shrieks she produces and equates her active time of night with vices and hatred. The owl in turn replies that the Nightingale's continuous noise is excessive and boring. The Nightingale replies that the song of the owl brings unwanted gloom, while her own is joyous and reflects the beauty of the world. The owl is quick to reply that Nightingales only sing in summer, when men's minds are filled with lechery and that singing is the Nightingale's only talent. Finally the Wren intervenes and stops them slinging insults at each other!

The Nightingale is the topic of one of Aesop's fables - *The Hawk and the Nightingale*. A Nightingale, sitting high in an oak tree, was seen by a hawk which swooped down and seized him. The Nightingale pleaded with the hawk to let him go, saying that he was not big enough to satisfy the hunger of a hawk, who ought to pursue the larger birds. The hawk said: "I should indeed have lost my senses if I should let go food ready to my hand, for the sake of pursuing birds which are not yet even within sight". The moral of the story is: 'A bird in the hand is worth two in the bush'.

The bird's scientific name is *Luscinia megarhynchos* which is a curious name. *Luscinia* comes from the Latin luctus for lament and cano to sing, i.e. singing a lamentation. *Megarhynchos* means large beak. The bird has a slim beak as expected for an insectivore.

54 - Pied Flycatcher

Local names for the **Pied Flycatcher** include cold finch, referring to its black colour and oddly epicurean warbler.

The pied in the Pied Flycatcher's name means black and white. The bird breeds in upland deciduous woods. The species' range has declined since 1994 and the bird's conservation status has moved from green to amber in 2009 and then to red in 2015. In the 5 years to 2017 there has been a slight increase in numbers, with nest box schemes assisting with this recovery.

The Pied Flycatcher's scientific name is *Ficedula hypoleuca* with *Ficedula* meaning fig eating, perhaps referring to their diet of fruit and seeds whilst migrating and *hypoleuca* the Greek hupo for below and leukos for white.

The **Black Redstart**'s name and that of its close relative the Redstart end in the word start. Historically start was the word for tail, used until the 16th century, coming from the Middle English steort. The first written record of an

English name for the Redstart dates from the 8th century. Several local names use the word start like wagstart for the Yellow Wagtail. The bird often breeds in derelict buildings in urban areas.

The Black Redstart's scientific name is *Phoenicurus ochruros* with phoinix meaning crimson and oura tail plus (confusingly) okhros pale yellow and oura tail.

55 - Redstart

Not unsurprisingly local names for the **Redstart** focus on the bird's bright red tail, found on both sexes. These names include bessy brantail; brand tail, as in fire brand; fanny redtail; fire flirt, from the movement of its tail; fire tail; nanny redtail; red stare, with stare meaning starling. The Redstart was the subject of one of the most remarkable observations of an individual species. John Buxton was captured by the Germans in Norway in 1940 and taken as a prisoner of war. From his prison he set up observations of breeding Redstart, which was eventually published as a monograph. Aristotle identified the Redstart. As he did not see them in winter he believed in transmogrification, the idea that some species magically change into others i.e. Redstarts became Robins in winter.

The name Redstart is not entirely accurate as the tail of this bird is a prominent orange colour rather than red. As with the Robin, the word orange was not part of the English language until after the name for this bird had been established.

The Redstart's scientific name is *Phoenicurus phoenicurus* with phoenix meaning orange and oura for tail.

56 - Stonechat

A bird often heard and seen on gorse covered heaths is the **Stonechat**. Its song is exactly as the names states, like two stones clinked together. The poet Norman McCaig put it eloquently as "A flint-on-flint ticking - there he is; trim and dandy - in square miles of bracken". Unsurprisingly, many local names refer to its song, such as bushchat; furze chuck; moretetter; stanechatter; stone clink and stonesmith. Jack straw refers to the Stonechat's use of straw for its nest and jack referring to a small bird and a man's name. Heath tit is correct for the place it is seen but the bird is in the chat family, Muscicapidae, not the tit family, Paridae, except tit was traditionally used for any small animal. The name blacky top is from the male's black crown.

Stonechat numbers can fall dramatically after a harsh winter but recover quickly. In a good breeding season a pair can raise four broods. Numbers

362

have increased by 87% over the 22 years to 2017. This masks a fall between 2006 – 2011, followed by a recovery, leading to a change of UK conservation status to green. The distribution of the Stonechat is moving north and to higher altitudes.

The Stonechat's scientific name is *Saxicola rubicola* which derives from the Latin saxum for rock and colere to dwell plus the Latin rubus for bramble and again colere to dwell.

Local names for the **Whinchat** include bank sparrow; blackberry eater, which it does as it fattens up for its long migratory journey in autumn; dock topper, where it might sit singing; ear tick and haytick, from its call; furze-hacker and gorse hopper, both referring to the bird's habitat; vuzzy napper and whin lintie. Lintie is a Scottish local name for the Linnet, as well as hill lintie for the Twite; sea lintie for the Rock Pipit; tree lintie for the Chaffinch and white lintie for the Whitethroat. It also means a spirited young lady.

The Whin- in the bird's name derives from the Middle English word whynne for gorse, where the bird nests.

The Whinchat's scientific name is *Saxicola rubetra* from the Latin *rubetra*, a type of small bird.

A bird often seen near the coast migrating on its way to and from its open moorland breeding area is the **Wheatear**. Many of its local names are based on some detailed observations of its behaviour, such as clot bird, from its habit of moving from clod to clod; coney chuck, from its habit of nesting in rabbit burrows; Cornish horse smatch, with the bird attracted to flies on horse dung; plus stanechacker and stone clack, as it moves from stone to stone making its clacking call. White arse comes from its prominent white rump (arse not previously being vulgar) along with white rump and white tail, plus ear bird from its ear stripe. Fallow chat; fallow finch; fallow lunch and fallow smirch, with fallow being from its habitat. Chock check bird and snorter are from its call. In folklore the Wheatear is associated with the devil from its calling in desolate places.

On the face of it the name Wheatear implies the bird eats wheat and there is something significant about its ear. Neither is true! The words wheat and ear are 16th century corruptions of white and arse, referring to the bird's white rump, which is prominent in both the male and the female. The Wheatear has the longest migratory journey of any songbird (Passeriformes) undertaking a return journey of 25 000 km, with some birds migrating from their breeding grounds in Greenland to Africa.

The Wheatear has a repetitive scientific name - *Oenanthe oenanthe* deriving from the Greek oenos for wine and anthos for flower, based on the time of the bird's return from its winter quarters, being when the vines flower in Greece.

Main characteristics of the Turdidae family:

Turdidae is the name of the family of thrushes. The family name comes from the Latin Turdus for a thrush. Thrushes are plump, soft-plumaged, small to medium-sized birds, often arboreal. Many thrushes feed on the ground. They are mainly insectivorous as well as eating worms, snails and fruit. The songs of some species are considered to be among the most beautiful in the avian world. The beak is strong and slightly decurved, sometimes with a small hook. The stout tarsi have fused horny plates and are comparatively strong and large. There are 10 primaries on their wings, the outermost often very short (except in migrants). The medium length tail has 12 feathers. In many species, adults of both sexes are alike but in others there is a marked difference. There is little seasonal variation. Most birds sing from perches. These birds are noted for their frequent sun bathing helping with feather maintenance by reducing infestation by parasites. Thrushes are monogamous but will mate with others if an opportunity arises. Thrushes build cup-shaped nests, sometimes lining them with mud. They lay 2 - 5 speckled eggs, sometimes laying two or more clutches per year. Both parents help in raising the young. Chicks are altricial and develop a coat of down before growing their first feathers.

The six species in this family in the UK are in one genus:

Turdus - Blackbird; Fieldfare; Mistle Thrush; Redwing; Ring Ouzel; Song Thrush

57 - Blackbird

The **Blackbird** is a well known British bird and has entered our culture through songs like the Beatle's *Blackbird*, the standard song *Bye Bye Blackbird* and the nursery rhyme *Four and twenty Blackbirds baked in a pie.* Local names include black ouzel; blackie, referring to its colour; colly and merle, from the French for the bird. The name woodsell was used by Shakespeare in *Midsummer Night's Dream,* writing "the Woodsell cocke, so black of hue, with orange tawny bill". In fact the male's beak colour varies from yellow to orange, with a brighter colour being more attractive to a potential mate. Ouzel is an old name for the bird and has now been adopted for the Blackbird's close relation the Ring Ouzel. The first written record in English for the Blackbird occurred in the 8th century. The Blackbird was ranked fourth in the Garden Bird Survey in 2019 and was the most frequently noted bird, seen in 87% of gardens but not in the numbers seen of the three higher ranked birds. The Blackbird was voted the Swedish national bird in 1962.

> The Blackbird appears in the tale about St. Kevin, an Irish monastic saint, which Seamus Heaney wrote about "The saint is kneeling, arms stretched out, inside his cell but the cell is so narrow, so one turned-up palm is out the window, stiff as a crossbeam, when a blackbird lands and lays in it and settles down to nest. Kevin feels the warm eggs, the small breast, the tucked neat head and claws and, finding himself linked into the network of eternal life, is moved to pity: now he must hold his hand like a branch out in the sun and rain for weeks until the young are hatched and fledged and flown".

The scientific name of the Blackbird is *Turdus merula*, with *Turdus* Latin for thrush and *merula* for black.

58 - Fieldfare

The **Fieldfare**'s local names include blue back; blue felt; blue tail; grey thrush and pigeon felt, from its colouration; storm bird and storm cock, referring to the fact the bird will sing during a storm (the Mistle Thrush is given the same name). Other names include felter; feltyfare; flirty fleer; fullfit and velverd.

The Fieldfare's name derives from the Anglo-Saxon feldefare, meaning traveller through fields. Fieldfare are winter visitors to the UK, migrating from Scandinavia and as far away as Siberia. The bird migrates at night flying continuously at about 35 km / hr covering 600 km. They commence their flight at 1 500 m and then will drop to sea level after midnight, possibly to use the wind and waves to aid navigation. The Fieldfare is a colonial nester, often nesting alongside birds of prey.

> The bird appears in 9th century literature and Chaucer mentioned them "above all the birds of winter, the frosty fieldefares". Arnold wrote about them "Hollies wuth scarlet berries gemm'd, the fellfares food", with the bird often been seen stripping berries from trees and bushes in winter. In severe weather they will come into residential gardens to eat in berries and fallen apples. Wordsworth wrote of "the fieldfares pensive flock". One piece of folklore is 'we shan't have warmer weather till the bluebacks have gone'. The Romans bred the bird in captivity for the table and there are records up to the 19th century of Fieldfare being shot for eating.

The scientific name of the Fieldfare is *Turdus pilaris*, with *pilaris* also meaning thrush. Even though the species is widespread there are no sub-species of this bird.

Thrushes have been closely linked to humans for centuries and the **Mistle Thrush** is no exception. Over 40 local names have been recorded for this bird. Many refer to its song and call such as horse thrush, where the cry is said to sound like a horse neighing; rattle thrush; screech thrush, from its alarm call; shrill cock and squawking thrush. Hollin cock refers to the habit of feeding on holly, as does holm screech. Norman gizer comes from its aggressive behaviour and gizer from the French for mistletoe. Storm cock refers to the fact that the bird continues to sing during a storm. Another name is big mavis, with mavis also a name for the similar Song Thrush. Marble thrush possibly refers its prominent breast markings. Finally, jeremy joy uses a man's first name and reflects the way the bird sings in January, as one of our early songsters.

The name Mistle is based on the fact that the bird eats mistletoe. A traditional belief was that mistletoe would not germinate unless it passed through the thrush. There is some basis in fact for this as the hard coat of the seeds are dissolved by the digestive juices of the bird and then passed out of the body. The name thrush derives from thresher. Throstle is a traditional name for a thrush from the Middle English throstel and German drostel. Mistle Thrush numbers have declined by 55% over the 50 years to 2017 with a UK conservation status of red now, moving up from amber in 2002.

The Mistle Thrush's scientific name is *Turdus viscivorus,* with *viscivorus* from the Latin viscum for mistletoe and vorare to devour. Aristotle observed this as mistletoe grows on olive trees.

The **Redwing** has been migrating to our shores from Scandinavia for centuries, hence the bird has acquired a number of local names. These include little feltyfare, with feltyfare being a name for the Fieldfare, both being winter thrushes (sometimes seen together) with the Redwing being the smaller of the two. Red thrush and redwing throlly, from the distinctive red patch on its wing; swine pipe; whin thrush and whindle, both from its whining sound and wind throstle, from the winds that aid the bird's migratory flight. Unusually, the Redwing does not return to the same location on its subsequent annual migration to its winter feeding grounds but moves to a new location.

The Redwing's scientific name is *Turdus iliacus*, with *iliacus* referring to the flanks, which are red.

The **Ring Ouzel** is a summer migrant to the UK and very much a bird of windswept upland moors. Its local names refer to this, such as fell blackbird, with the Blackbird its close cousin; heath throstle, correctly identified as a member of the thrush family; crag ouzel; fell ouzel; hill ouzel; mountain colley; rock ouzel and tor ouzel all relate to its habitat. Other names signify its song and call, such as flitterchack; hill chack and ring whistle, from its alarm call. Michaelmas blackbird refers to the time of its migration and round berry bird from the bird's preferred rowan berry food. Other names include cowboy and ditch blackie.

The ring in the Ring Ouzel's name derives from the male's clear, white, crescent shaped band across its chest. The female has a less prominent chest band and the juveniles have none. Ouzel word comes from the Old English name for the Blackbird, osel and then to ousel and finally ouzel which is used in many of its local names and for other members of this family.

The Ring Ouzel's scientific name is *Turdus torquatus*, deriving from torquis the Latin for collar; a prominent white on the male.

The **Song Thrush** is a well-known bird and is often seen in gardens and the countryside, with its loud and complex song being clearly heard in most seasons, except summer. Its traditional name is throstle, with thrush the name given its similar, close relative, the Mistle Thrush. The first written record of an English name for the Song Thrush dates from the 8th century. Other local names include grey bird; mavis, derived from the French mauvis; thrasher; throggie and whistling dick, referring to its strong song. Other names include drush; garden thrush; grey bird; thrissel, a northern variant of throstle; throg, from Cheshire as a pet name and trush drush.

> A Thrush (assuming it is a Song Thrush) appears in one of Aesop's fables *The thrush and the Swallow* which tells of migration two and a half millennia before the phenomenon was fully accepted. The tale is of a young thrush, which lived in an orchard and became friends with a Swallow. The Swallow would every now and then come and visit the thrush. The thrush would welcome him with his cheerful note. "O mother!" he said to his parent "never had creature such a friend as I have in this Swallow". "Nor ever any mother," replied the parent-bird "such a silly son as I have. Long before the approach of winter, your friend will have left you; and while you sit shivering on a leafless bough he will be sporting under sunny skies hundreds of miles away". Remarkably Aesop was able to write about migration in 600 BC.

The Song Thrush's scientific name is *Turdus philomelos*. The second part of the name, *philomelos*, is based on the Greek myth where Philomena's tongue was cut out and she was turned into a Song Thrush. *Philo* means loving and *melos* song.

Main characteristics of the Sturnidae family:

The Starling (among UK birds) is the sole UK member of the Sturnidae family.

Starlings have strong feet and direct flight. They are omnivorous, feeding on the ground. Plumage is dark with a metallic sheen. Starlings have diverse and complex vocalisations and mimic sounds from their surroundings. The birds can recognise individuals by their calls. Starlings moult only once a year, after breeding. In fresh plumage the Starling has white tips to its body feathers. These tips wear off, leaving the purple-green iridescent black plumage of the breeding season. The Starling is highly gregarious and in winter they form huge roost flocks called murmurations. They nest in cavities but do not build their own nest, lining a suitable location with soft material. They often re-use nests. The female broods on average 6 eggs for 11 days and then both sexes feed the hatchlings for about 20 days. They have 2 or 3 broods per year.

There is one genus in this family in the UK and one species:

Sturnus – Starling

59 - Starling

The **Starling** was once a very common bird in both urban and rural areas and was familiar to our ancestors. One set of local names refers to the habit of Starlings picking off the ticks on a sheep's back, hence the names sheep rack; sheep stare; shepstarling and shepster. Gyp refers to its black colour and stare is an Old English name from the German staro and Old Norse stari, linked to Starling. Pet names include jacob and jebbie. The name stinker derives from the bird's former habit of nesting in the stink pipe of toilets. Other names include black felt; jester bird; shitlegs, from the guano deposits at roosts and starnel.

The Starling's name is comprised of star, from the Old English stare, referring to the juvenile's starry plumage plus the suffix –ling. In winter numbers are supplemented by migrants from the continent forming huge flocks; some are estimated to exceed 1 million birds. At evening they gather to roost, performing magnificent displays as they fall into bushes (or buildings like Brighton pier) for the night. In 1890 Eugene Schieffelen introduced 60

Starlings into New York's Central Park (up until then it was absent in the USA) as part of a project to introduce into the USA every bird mentioned by Shakespeare! The bird readily took to its new country eventually becoming a pest and subject to control measures to limit numbers. The Starling was introduced into New Zealand (possibly to remind British migrants of their home country) and is now one on the most numerous birds there.

The Starling is a great mimic and can reproduce the songs of other birds and even alarm and 'phone sounds they hear. Birds acquire new sounds as a larger repertoire makes them more attractive to prospective mates. Shakespeare referred to this in *Henry IV*, with Hotspur saying "I'll have a starling shall be taught to speak". Mozart kept a Starling as a pet and it is believed the musical joke pieces he wrote were inspired by the bird. The Starling is one of the few British birds to practice partial brood parasitism, whereby a female will lay her eggs in the nest of another Starling if she cannot find a nest of her own.

Starling numbers in the UK, according the Breeding Bird Survey, have fallen by 52% over the 22 years and by 29% in the last 10 years to 2017. Since 2002 the species has had a UK conservation status of red, moving up from amber in that year.

The Starling's scientific name is *Sturnus vulgaris* with *Sturnus* meaning starling and *vulgaris* common or ordinary (not rude or vulgar!).

Main characteristics of the Prunellidae family:

The genus name Prunella is from the German braunelle, a diminutive form of braun, brown and the Latin prunus, also meaning brown. This is the only bird family endemic to the Palearctic. Accentors are small, drab birds with thin sharp beaks, used to catch their insect summer diet and seeds and berries diet in winter. The name accentor comes from the Latin, meaning sing with another, related to the word cantor. In winter they swallow grit and sand to help their gizzard break up seeds. Courtship involves a lot of singing. Dunnock are polygyandrous – both sexes have many mates. Dunnock females build cup nests and lay about 4 unspotted eggs which they brood for around 12 days. The young are fed by both parents and take 12 days or so to fledge. Accentors may have two to three broods a year.

There is one genus in this family in the UK and one species:

Prunella – Dunnock

The **Dunnock** has been a familiar bird to us in our gardens and countryside for generations. Not unsurprisingly it has acquired many local names over time; in excess of 45 have been recorded. Some of these include the word sparrow but this is an incorrect connection. Whilst the bird's colour resembles a sparrow's, the beak is slender. The Old English name of hegesugge and shuffle-wing derives from hege for hedge and sugge for flutterer, a correct observation of the bird's habit of fluttering its wings, especially when breeding. Many names include hedge such as hedge creeper; hedge jug, with jug a pet of Jane; hedge pick; hedge sparrow and hedge warbler, which is where it is seen. It also acquired human names such as issac, molly and philip. The bird was correctly identified as a host for the Cuckoo's egg hence the name blind dunnock, i.e. it does not see the Cuckoo laying an egg in its nest. Interestingly the Cuckoo's egg does not mimic the Dunnocks own blue egg colouration, as it does for its other host species. The blue in blue dickie; blue jig; blue sparrow and blue tom and refers to the deep blue colour of the bird's eggs and the use of two human names. Shakespeare referred to the bird in *King Lear* - "The hedge sparrow fed the cuckoo so long, that it had its head bit off by its young".

The vernacular name Dunnock is from the Old English dun- for brown, plus the suffix –ock for small. An accurate name - little brown bird. The link to sparrows led to the previous incorrect formal name of Hedge Sparrow which was changed in 1923 to Dunnock. The Dunnock is amongst Britain's most promiscuous of birds with many females mating with many males, in groups of up to 3 females and 3 males. They mate, albeit very quickly, as many times as twice an hour for 10 days. This promiscuity necessitates the male having a large cloacal protuberance associated with sperm competition. How mistaken was the Victorian clergy who advocated that his congregation follow the example of the Dunnock "Unobtrusive, quiet and retiring ... the Dunnock exhibits a pattern which many of a higher grade might imitate..."!!

The Dunnock's scientific name is *Prunella modularis* which comes from modulari, meaning to sing.

Main characteristics of the Motacillidae family:

The Motacillidae family includes the pipits and wagtails. The family name derives from the Greek mutex, a bird described by Hesychius. In Latin *Motacilla* means little mover. Pipits and wagtails are structurally very similar, having a slim, elongated body, a small rounded head and short neck, a slender pointed beak with rictal bristles, a medium to long tail (longest in the wagtails and shortest in pipits), rather long legs and toes and, especially in pipits, a long hind claw. There is no sexual dimorphism in size. The wagtails often have striking plumage, including grey, black, white and yellow, with some variation between the sexes. Wagtails prefer wetter habitats to the pipits. Wagtails often form communal roosts outside the breeding season. Pipits are cryptically coloured and patterned, usually having brown upperparts and whitish underparts. In most species the sexes are identical in plumage and there is little or no seasonal variation. The flight of wagtails and pipits is strong and often undulating. Song-flights, launched either from the ground or a perch, are characteristic of the pipits while wagtails usually sing on the ground. The Pipits song is delivered from high in the air and often continues as the bird drops back to the ground or a perch. Wagtails have a simple song. Motacillids take a wide range of invertebrate prey, especially insects plus spiders, worms and small aquatic molluscs and arthropods. Wagtails nest on the ground or in crevices, built of vegetative matter and lined with hair or feathers. The female typically lays 6 eggs and might have 2 or 3 broods per year.

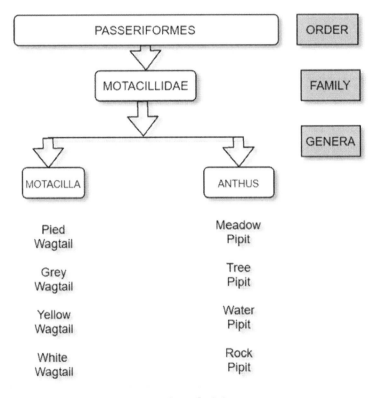

Wagtails and pipits

The eight species in this family in the UK are in two genera:

Motacilla - Grey Wagtail; Pied Wagtail; White Wagtail; Yellow Wagtail

Anthus - Meadow Pipit; Rock Pipit; Tree Pipit; Water Pipit

The **Grey Wagtail**'s local names include dishwasher and wagstart, from the way it flicks its tail up and down; barley bird and oatseed bird, except the bird is an insectivore and rocky wagtail, where it is often seen picking insects from rocks in streams. Winter wagtail identifies this bird as a species that partially winters here as opposed to its close and similar relative the summer migrant Yellow Wagtail.

The Grey Wagtail's scientific name is *Motacilla cinerea* with *cinerea* from the Latin cinereus, ash-coloured, from cinis - ashes.

60 - Pied Wagtail

The **Pied Wagtail** is a familiar bird in towns and in the countryside. Local names include dishwasher and links the bird to puddles created by washing; dishwipe; lady wagtail; polly washdish; scullery maids; waggie; wagging tale; wagstart, with start being an old word for tail; washtail and white wagtail, a name now given to the continental nominate species of this bird. The name devil's bird derives from the association of pied plumage with the devil. Pied Wagtails form noisy large roosts of up to 4 000 birds in winter and is not uncommon for roosts to form in trees in town and city centres.

The vernacular name reflects the black and white colouring of the bird and its habit of constantly wagging its tail. The bird is a partial migrant with the young dispersing after fledging, moving to Europe and North Africa. This species, along with several other wagtails, has divided into numerous geographical sub-species, many with subtle changes to the plumage, especially on the head.

> The Cornish named the bird tinner and one perching on a window sill indicated a visit from a stranger. A tale from the Borders is that the bird should wag its tale exactly nine times on alighting. Any more or less will bring bad luck to the observer. The bird was used for medicinal purposes, with one remedy for kidney stones being a concoction of its powdered bones and feathers baked together, taken with white wine.

The Pied Wagtail's scientific name *Motacilla alba yarrellii* with albus for white and *yarrellii* from the naturalist William Yarrell (1784 – 1856). He wrote the seminal, three volume work *A history of British birds* used a standard reference work for a long time. This bird's name is an example of the tri-nomial naming a sub-species. The Pied Wagtail is a sub-species, with differences in the plumage, song and calls. The nominate species is the White Wagtail, which has the scientific name *Motacilla alba alba* and is found in Europe and breeds as far north as Siberia, with some birds appearing in Britain during migration.

The **White Wagtail**'s scientific name is *Motacilla alba alba.*

The **Yellow Wagtail** is a summer visitor and was well known to our forebears. The bird is often found following cattle and sheep to pick up the flies that are attracted to the animals' dung, hence the name cow bird. Other names include barley bird and potato setter, from the time of arrival of the bird; quaketail; sunshine bird; wagstart and yellow molly. The names moll washer; peggy washer; washdish and washerwoman all refer to the characteristic flicking movement of the tail, simulating the use of the battledore, a device for beating washing. Sunshine bird and yellow molly refer to the bird's colouration.

The bird is a summer breeder in the UK. The bird migrates in flocks to their resting area in The Gambia and Senegal. The UK holds almost the whole world population of this sub-species. Numbers have fallen dramatically by 74% in the 50 years to 2017 and its distribution has contracted significantly. The species has a UK conservation status of red.

The Yellow Wagtail's scientific name is *Motacilla flava* with flavus for yellow. This species is the nominate species for eight sub-species, many showing distinctive variations to their head plumage.

A bird frequently seen on open land and moors is the **Meadow Pipit.** It is frequently used by the Cuckoo as a host species, which was accurately observed in times past, hence the names cuckoo's sandling; cuckoo's titling and gowk's fool, with gowk meaning both Cuckoo and awkward. Some of its other names include earth titling; meadow titling and tit lark, using the general name tit; moor peep and pipit lark, associating the bird with other species (larks do look very similar). Another set of names associate the bird with its habitat such as heather lintie; hill sparrow; ling bird; moor titling and moss cheeper.

Pipit derives from the Latin pipeo meaning chirper. Native birds move south in winter, some migrating to Spain and Portugal. Other birds arrive here from Greenland and Iceland for the winter.

The Meadow Pipit's scientific name is *Anthus pratensis* with *Anthus* coming from the Greek for a small grassland bird named by Aristotle and *pratensis* meaning found in meadows.

Local names for the **Rock Pipit** include the rather odd butter sparrow and gutter teetan; plus dusky lark; middin fool; rock lintie; minstrel of the sea shore; sea lark; sea titling and tang sparrow. This species is associated with the shore line and its close relative, the Water Pipit, with inland, fresh water habitats.

Logic persists in the Rock Pipit's scientific name with *Anthus petrosus* with *petrosus* meaning rock.

Local names for the **Tree Pipit** include bulking lark; chittie; cuckoo's servant; field titling; lesser crested lark, with the likely confusion with the similar larks; pipit lark, to mix the two and short heeled field lark.

The male Tree Pipit is often seen in the upper branches of a tree from where it launches itself into a characteristic song flight, returning to the same spot on the tree afterwards. The distribution of this species has moved northward with the Breeding Birds Survey showing a 72% drop in numbers in England and a corresponding increase of 72% in Scotland over 22 years to 2017. The species has a conservation status of red.

The Tree Pipit's scientific name is *Anthus trivialis* with *trivialis* meaning common as in ordinary but the bird is not numerous in Britain.

Water Pipit's scientific name is *Anthus spinoletta* with *spinoletta* the Italian for a little lark.

Main characteristics of the Bombycillidae family:

In the UK the waxwings are the one genus in the family Bombycillidae. Bombycilla is from the Greek bombukos for silk and cilla for tail, reflecting the very smooth appearance of the bird's feathers. Waxwings have soft silky plumage and unique waxy red tips to some of the wing feathers. These tips look like sealing wax, giving the group its name. The legs are short and strong and the wings are pointed. The male and female have the same plumage. Waxwing are arboreal and breed in northern Scandinavian forests. Their main food is fruit. Waxwings are well known for their irregular irruptions from their Scandinavian breeding grounds to the UK when their home winter berry food crop fails.

There is one genus in this family in the UK and one species:

Bombycilla - Waxwing

For some unknown reason the **Waxwing** is associated with plague and pestilence and has been called the plague bird. Other local names include bohemian chatterer and bohemian jay, with bohemian possibly from their supposed care-free life style or wanderings and silk tail. The Waxwing is a winter visitor to Britain and is seen in large numbers some years when the rowan berry crop in its native northern Scandinavia habitat is poor. In the winter of 2004/5 over half a million birds were recorded in Germany. The bird has a voracious appetite and one bird was observed eating 500 berries in 6 hours; about 3 times its own weight! For spiritualists the bird is a symbol of selflessness, possibly from its courtship ritual. Here the male presents a berry to a prospective female with the female returning the berry to the male who returns it to the female again, with this being repeated until copulation takes place.

The Waxwing's scientific name is *Bombycilla garrulus*. *Garrulus* means chattering, which the bird does and this might be a link to the Jay, via the same specific name of *garrulus*.

Main characteristics of the Fringillidae family:

The finches form this family. The finch family name Fringillidae derives from the Old English word fink that means a colourful, singing bird. They range in body length from 10 – 25 cm and in weight from 8 – 60 g. All have 12 tail feathers and 9 wing primaries. The true finches are small to moderately large birds and they have strong, stubby beaks, which in some species can be quite large. The shape and structure of the beak varies but all are conical-shaped, stout, short and pointed. They use their strong beaks to crush seeds and extract the edible kernel. The seed is wedged against a special groove at the side of the palate and then crushed by raising the lower jaw. The shell is removed with the tongue and the edible kernel is swallowed. Finches (except Linnet and Twite) become insectivores whilst breeding as the young cannot digest seeds. They have a bouncing flight, alternating bouts of flapping with a period of closing their wings. Most sing well. Finches have small outer primaries concealed by the wing coverts. Plumage colouration varies widely among species. Most species are dimorphic, with males more brightly coloured than females. Most species are seasonally gregarious and some are migratory. They have distinctive songs and many finches have a courtship display. The cup-shaped nest is built by the female, usually in a tree or bush. Incubation of the 3 - 4 eggs is mainly by the female, lasting about 12 days. The chicks are fed by both parents for about 14 days until the young fledge. Finches lay 2 – 3 clutches each year.

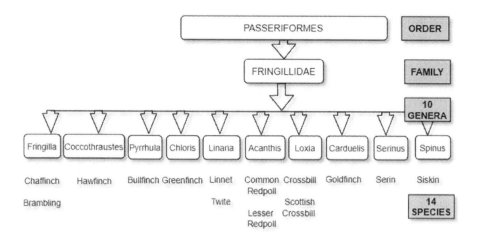

Finches

The 14 species in this family in the UK are in ten genera:

Fringilla – Brambling; Chaffinch
Coccothraustes – Hawfinch
Pyrrhula – Bullfinch
Chloris – Greenfinch
Linaria – Linnet; Twite
Acanthis - Common Redpoll; Lesser Redpoll
Loxia – Crossbill; Scottish Crossbill
Carduelis – Goldfinch
Serinus – Serin
Spinus – Siskin

The name finch entered the language as a surname, from a nickname for someone who handled or bred the birds.

Local names for the **Brambling** include brandling; cock o' the north; french linnet and french pie finch, indicating the bird is a migrant; furze chirper, from its flight call; goldie wing; mountain finch, reflected in the species' scientific name and tartan back, from its plumage;

The name Brambling refers to the striking plumage of this winter visiting Scandinavian finch, possibly from the word brandling meaning branded. Even in their winter plumage Bramblings are colourful. Its summer plumage is even more striking than the duller winter plumage we see in Britain. Numbers migrating here in winter vary depending on the availability of their favourite food, beech mast. The bird forms huge flocks in winter, with one Swiss flock in 1951 estimated at 7 million birds. In 2019 a flock in Slovenia was estimated at 5 million birds and they converged on 5 hectares of trees to roost at night.

The scientific name for the Brambling *Fringilla montifringilla* derives from a description of a bird made by Aristophanes, who lived 446 – 386 BC. The name survived in Greek as phrugilos and then into Latin as *Fringilla*. This illustrates the long history of some of our bird names. *Monti* simply means mountain plus a repeat of *fringilla*.

A bird that has been associated with human habitation for centuries is the **Chaffinch**. Over 40 local names have been recorded for this bird. A selection illustrating the wide variety of names includes apple bird; briskie; chink chawdy, from its call; copper finch; dapfinch, with dap a Devon word for hop; fleckiewing; pie finch; prink prink; sheld apple, with sheld meaning variegated; tree lintie, correctly linking the bird to the Linnet and white wing from its white wing bars. Pie is used to denote coloured. The names chink, pink and tink are all onomatopoeic. Wet bird is from the plaintive cry which was said to foretell rain. The first written record of an English name for the Chaffinch dates from 685 AD.

Like many finches the bird was prized for its song and was kept as a caged bird. In full song the bird repeats its song phrase 6 times a minute and up to 3 000 times a day! In the 19th century birds that sang well were sold in markets. Some birds were cruelly blinded, allegedly to make them sing better. Thomas Hardy wrote about this cruelty in his poem *The blinded bird* writing "So zestfully canst thou sing, And all this indignity, With God's consent, on thee, Blinded ere yet a wing, By the red-hot needle thou, I stand and wonder how, So zestfully though canst sing". Experiments on Chaffinches demonstrated that birds are born with the ability to sing but learn the specific species' song from their father. Birds reared in auditory isolation cannot sing the species' song or will learn other songs played to them. A castrated bird cannot sing but its ability to sing is restored when it's injected with testosterone.

The Chaffinch is mainly sedentary with ringed birds moving no more than 5 km. In winter numbers are supplemented by females migrating from Scandinavia.

The Chaffinch's scientific name is *Fringilla coelebs*, with *coelebs* meaning bachelor. The Chaffinch was given its scientific name by Linnaeus himself in Sweden. He correctly observed that in winter the male birds were seen in flocks with no females. The females migrate, often to Britain, where female only flocks can be seen. The males stay behind, as bachelors and are able to set up new breeding territories early in spring to await the females' later return from their winter quarters. The phenomenon of males arriving first at the breeding site is called protandry. It is not unusual amongst birds for males and females to go their separate ways after mating, some re-establishing pair bonds on their return to the breeding site. For example,

378

Puffins and Guillemots do this with the return accompanied by a flamboyant re-bonding ceremony.

61 - Hawfinch

Local names for the **Hawfinch** include berry breaker, which it does with ease; black-throated grosbeak; haw grosbeak and pie finch, placing the bird in the correct family.

The haw- in its name comes from the berries of that name or from an alternative meaning of hedge. The Hawfinch is an uncommon member of the finch family and is a difficult bird to spot as it spends much of its time in the tops of trees. The bird is capable of cracking very hard nuts with its large beak and powerful muscles. Two horny pads on each of the upper and lower jaws help hold the nut in place and distribute the massive force evenly. The Hawfinch can create a pressure of 1000 times its own weight of 50 g, the equivalent of a human creating 50 tonnes of pressure.

It has a rather long scientific name which repeats the words i.e. *Coccothraustes coccothraustes* meaning to break a kernel into pieces.

The **Bullfinch** is another British bird that has been known to us for a long time. The bird is mentioned in the rhyme *Who killed cock Robin?* as "Who'll toll the bell, I said the bull, because I can pull". Bull appears in the bird's formal name and refers to its thick neck. Local names also incorporate this such as bull spink, with spink being an old name for finch. Other local names include alp; bloor hoop; maple; mawpe and nope. Bud bird refers to the bird's love of stripping fruit trees of their buds, much to the annoyance of fruit growers. For this reason they were killed in large numbers, with a bounty of a penny a head in Elizabethan times. A record from Cheshire shows a bounty of 1d was paid with 7 000 killed in 36 years. After the 1954 Protection of Birds Act the Bullfinch could still be killed in fruit growing areas with a payment of £1 a bird. The birds are selective and prefer Morello cherry trees and Conference pears. Oddly, they don't eat buds from Hardy and Comice pears, which some fruit farmers grow to avoid predation by the bird. They will also eat buds from ornamental shrubs and ash keys. If their diet changes the birds lose their distinctive colours.

Bullfinches mate for life and are both socially and sexually monogamous, the latter being unusual in birds. Pairs remain together throughout the year, so when one is seen feeding often the other will be close by. The male bird emits a distinctive whistle which is a contact call, letting the female know where he is. When they meet again he will sometimes offer her some food. As there is no competition with rival males for the affection of a female the male has fewer sperm and no cloacal protuberance. For more detail on the Bullfinch's song see the Section Songs and calls in Chapter 3.

The scientific name of the Bullfinch is *Pyrrhula pyrrhula* which comes from the Greek purrohulas which is a worm-eating bird mentioned by Aristotle. Not quite the Bullfinch's diet!

Local names for the **Greenfinch** include barley-bird; bullyhead; green chub; green grosbeak; green lennart; green linnet and pease weep, perhaps alluding to its wheezy song. From about 2006 numbers of this species fell dramatically due to an infectious parasite, trichomonosis, also known as canker. The infection prevents the bird from swallowing its food. In 2019 Chaffinch and Hawfinch fell to the infection causing a decrease in their population.

The Greenfinch's scientific name is *Chloris chloris,* with *Chloris* referring to the bird's green colour, chlorine being a green coloured gas.

Another member of the finch family (Fringillidae) that sings well, the **Linnet**, was previously caught and kept as a cage bird. Several names refer to the male's breeding plumage of a red crown and chest like blood linnet; red headed finch and rose linnet, with brown linnet; grey linnet; thorn grey and whin grey all referring to both sexes' winter plumage plus the odd name lemon bird. Furze linnet; gorse hatcher; heather linnet and thorn linnet all refer to its habitat. The name Linnet appears in the song *My old man* recalling that "off went the van wiv me 'ome packed in it, I walked be'ind wiv me old cock Linnet.....". Lintie is a Scottish local name for the Linnet, but the name is used in hill lintie for the Twite; sea lintie for the Rock Pipit; tree lintie for the Chaffinch and white lintie for the Whitethroat. One of the collected tales in The Laird of Logan (1835) describes how Miss Jean "could sing like a linty, loup like a maukin and play on the piano to the bargain". In Scotland lintie also means a spirited young lady.

The Lin in the formal English name Linnet comes from the Latin linum for flax or linseed which the bird eats, plus the diminutive suffix –et. The Linnet, along with its close relation the Twite, are the only finches to feed seeds to its young. Other seed-eating species usually feed invertebrates to their young. Linnets, as with many other birds, can learn to sing a variety of songs or to repeat words. Birds have an innate ability to sing but have to learn the specifics of their species' song. So Linnets can be made to acquire a different song by removing young birds from its parents, before it has time to learn the Linnet's song from its parents and exposing it to the alternative songs to be learned.

The scientific name of the Linnet is *Linaria cannabina* with cannabis being hemp seed which contains a small amount of marijuana.

The **Twite**'s local names include bank linnet (not far wrong); ling linnet; lintie; little pewit, perhaps from an association with the Lapwing on its breeding grounds; moor peep, where it breeds; peepy linnart and yellow-nebbed lintie, the bird does have a yellow beak and it is a close relative of the Linnet.

Twite is a representation of the bird's tweet call. The Twite is the only British species to originate in Tibet!

The scientific name of the Twite is *Linaria flavirostris* , with *Linaria* the Latin for a linen weaver, connecting the bird to flax and flavus meaning yellow and *rostris* beak.

The scientific name of the **Common Redpoll** is *Acanthis flammea* with *Acanthis* being a bird identified by Aristotle and *flammea* being a flame, referring to the red colouration of the male's crown and breast.

Local names for the **Lesser Redpoll** include many connections to the linnet, which is very similar, like bull linnet; chevvy linnet; french linnet and smaller redpoll linnet.

The scientific name of the Lesser Redpoll is *Acanthis cabaret*, with *cabaret* meaning entertainment, with an unclear connection with the bird.

62 - Crossbill

The Scottish Gaelic name for the **Crossbill** is cam-ghob, meaning squinty beaked.

The Crossbill has the unusual ability of being able to breed at any time of the year, with its breeding cycle being linked to the abundance of its preferred food crop, the spruce pine, not to a specific time of the year. The specialised beak enables the bird to extract the seeds from the newly formed cones, whereas other birds have to wait for the cones to mature and the seeds fall out. The upper mandible is laterally in line with the body but the lower mandible is skewed to one side, helping the bird to twist and prise the seed from inside the hard exterior of the cone. The beak holds the scale open whilst the tongue extracts the seed. They can consume 3 000 seeds a day. Crossbills can store seeds in a pocket in the throat. The bird is transitory and migrates considerable distances to find food. Mysteriously, it is able to locate new sources of its cone food many kilometres away.

> The Crossbill has been known to humans for a considerable time and its odd shaped beak has made for some tales. One is that the beak acquired this shape as a result of trying to extract the nails from Jesus' cross and the red on the male bird's breast is a stain from His blood. Other tales involve superstitions that the Crossbill could effect cures for colds and rheumatism, water from which the bird had drunk was a cure for epilepsy and the body of a dead bird never decayed. A curious set of tales!

The Crossbill's scientific name is *Loxia curvirostra* deriving from loxos meaning crosswise, curvus curved and rostrum beak.

The **Scottish Crossbill,** *Loxia scotica* is now considered a separate species (i.e. it is not merely a sub-species of the Crossbill) and as such is the only bird (and indeed the only vertebrate) species that is endemic to the UK. The bird has a unique song, has a slightly different beak and does not inter-breed with Crossbill i.e. it has established a self-sustaining population. This species eats pine cone seeds and its cousin spruce cone seeds.

Another bird closely associated with humans is the **Goldfinch**. The bird has very many local names. Several relate to its bright colours, which made it attractive as a cage bird and its feathers for millinery use. This latter practice was one of the first targets in the late 19th century for the then recently formed Society for the Protection of Birds. Names include the ornate name, king harry, a reference to King Henry VIII's ornate clothing; lady with twelve flounces; proud tailor, from the white tips to its feathers; red cap, the bird has a red face rather than a red cap; seven coloured linnet and sheriff's man, from Shropshire referring to the black and yellow outfit of that county's sheriff. Brancher, grey kates and grey pate are names given to one year old young birds by bird fanciers. The Shropshire name jack nicker is from a legend that St. Nicholas gave three girls a dowry of Goldfinch. A Scottish name for the bird is gawdspinks, with spink an old name for a finch. The bird is often seen eating thistle seeds so many names are based on this like thistle finch; thistle tweaker, from the Anglo Saxon thistletuige and thistle warp, from the way the bird deftly extracts the seeds. The Goldfinch has a high degree of coordination between its beak and feet enabling it to eat thistle seeds whilst balancing precariously at the top of a stem.

> The name Goldfinch is associated with someone who is wealthy. One tale is that if the first bird a girl saw on St. Valentine's Day was a Goldfinch, she would marry someone rich. The Goldfinch represents resurrection and fertility, appearing in many old master paintings of Mary and Jesus. The association comes from the legend that its red spot was acquired at the time of Jesus' crucifixion. It flew down over the head of Christ and was taking a thorn from His crown, when it was splashed with a drop of His blood. In Raphael's painting of the Madonna he included a Goldfinch, as a symbol of Jesus' crucifixion. A similar tale exists to explain the red of the Robin's breast and the Swallow's. In the poem *Who killed cock Robin?* the Goldfinch gave the bride away at the marriage of the Robin and the Wren.
>
> Leonardo da Vinci recorded a folktale that when a Goldfinch was carried into the presence of a sick person, if the sick person was going to die, the bird turned its head away and never looked at them but if the sick person was to be saved the bird kept looking at them and was

the cause of the cure. Dante wrote that Italian children kept the bird for its health giving properties. The yellow on the bird's wings was also believed to have curative powers, similar to the yellow iris of the Stone-curlew, which was said to cure jaundice.

The scientific name of the Goldfinch is *Carduelis carduelis* with *Carduelis* being repetitive of goldfinch.

The name **Serin** comes from the French for Canary. The Serin appears to have no native English names.

The Serin's scientific name is *Serinus serinus* which comes from French serin for canary.

Local names for the **Siskin** include a mixture, like aberdevine; barley-bird, probably a confusion with the Greenfinch which does eat barley; blackheaded thistlefinch; golden wren and rather oddly tea leaves.

The name Siskin is from German and represents the bird's chirping sound.

The Siskin's scientific name is *Spinus spinus* with *Spinus* being a bird described by Aristophanes.

The **Snow Bunting** is in a separate family, **Calcariidae** and is the sole UK member of that family. The species has been re-located into Calcariidae family from the Bunting family (Emberizidae) as the result of DNA analysis. So the formal English name is now incorrect, placing it in the wrong (bunting) family.

Local names for the Snow Bunting include cherry chirper; great mountain finch, lesser mountain finch, where it breeds in small numbers; overseas bird; robin of the dreary wilds; snow fowl and white-winged lark.

The bird has feathered legs to protect it from the severe cold environment it lives in during its breeding season. The male bird returns first to the breeding area where temperatures can be as low as -30° C. It is one of only three birds to have been sighted at the North Pole. It is the most northerly breeding bird in the world along with the Raven. As there are very few natural predators the bird has a very high (75%) fledgling success rate. Unusually the Snow Bunting only moults once a year, possibly to minimise the energy drain of moulting twice. Females winter further south and are seen in small numbers on the coast in the UK. Males winter further north ready to return to their breeding grounds early and stake out their territory.

The bird's scientific name is *Plectrophenax nivalis*. *Plectrophenax* derives from the Greek plektron for cock's spur and *phenax* meaning impostor. The Greek word is accurate as the bird is now placed in the family whose common name is long-spurs. The Snow Bunting has a long hind toe nail to assist in walking. *Nivalis* is from the Latin nivus for snow.

Main characteristics of the Emberizidae family:

The Emberizidae are a large family of buntings. The name Emberiza is from Old German merely mean Bunting. Emberizids are small birds, typically around 15 cm in length, with finch-like beaks and nine primary feathers. They live in a variety of habitats, including woodland, brush, marsh and grassland. They are seed-eating birds with a distinctively shaped beak, switching to eat insects during the breeding season. Generally, males are slightly larger than females. Species tend to have brown, streaked plumage, with many species having distinctive head patterns. When singing males often sit in a conspicuous place and throw their heads back, with their crown or rump feathers ruffled. Emberizids are monogamous and often the female builds the cup-shaped nest on the ground, well hidden in vegetation. The female mainly broods the typical clutch of 4 eggs for about 12 days, with both sexes feeding the hatchlings for a further 15 days. They may have 2 or 3 clutches per year.

The four species in this family in the UK are in one genus:

Emberiza - Cirl Bunting; Corn Bunting; Reed Bunting; Yellowhammer

The word bunting derives from buntin meaning plump, hence 'baby, baby bunting' or from the German bunt for multi-coloured.

The cirl of the **Cirl Bunting**'s name derives from the Latin to chirp. The Cirl Bunting was comparatively common across England up until the 1930's and gradually its range diminished until it was confined to a few areas of west Devon. However, a recovery programme has seen the bird spread out into Cornwall and east Devon and is more numerous now. For more details see the Section on Conservation in Chapter 6.

The scientific name for the Cirl Bunting is *Emberiza cirlus* - with *cirlus* an Italian name for a bunting.

63 - Corn Bunting

The jangling song of the **Corn Bunting** was formerly common in the British countryside. With changes in farming practices numbers have fallen and the species is now extinct in Ireland (where it was once common). The Corn Bunting's local names include briar bunting; bunting lark; bush lark; common bunting; corn dumpling; ground lark; hornbill bunting; horse lark; lark bunting, a confusing connection to two separate families; skitter brottie and thistle ock. The bird is highly promiscuous, with a record of one male mating with 18 females in one season! Both the abundance and distribution of the species has fallen dramatically over the last 50 years, numbers falling by 85% (to 2017) with the decline halting after 2000; the bird's UK conservation status is red.

The scientific name for the Corn Bunting is *Emberiza calandra* which confuses the bird with the distinctly different Calandra Lark, a rarity in the UK.

The **Reed Bunting** is a resident bird found at the margins of reed beds and water. Several local names incorporate the name sparrow, like pit sparrow; reed sparrow; riverside sparrow and water sparrow, although the species is in a different family to the sparrows. Other names refer to the male's distinctive black head, like black bonnet; coaly hood; colin blackhead, again incorporating a human name and seave cap, with seave meaning reed. Unusually the Reed Bunting's song changes after mating with its song becoming more drawn out. As an indication of the bird's life style, tests show that over 50% of Reed Bunting chicks are not fathered by the male of the pair. This is one of the highest recorded extra-paternity rates.

The Reed Bunting has the cumbersome scientific name of *Emberiza schoeniclus* with *schoeniclus* meaning reed dwelling.

A popular bird of open farmland and hedgerows is the **Yellowhammer**. Popularly it is know by one of its local names - little-bit-of-bread-and-no-cheese, being a representation of its song, which can often be heard clearly as the bird perches at the top of a bush or hedge to make itself heard. Many local names refer to the bright yellow colouration of the male with names like golden amber; gouldie; yellow an-bird; yellow bunting, which was the preferred formal name until the 19th century; yellow homber and yellow yoit. Bessy blakeling combines a female name and a local name for yellow and the suffix –ling. Guler is a name from the Dutch gulden, a gold coin. The bird's eggs have exquisite fine line markings on them and local names reflecting this include scribbling lark; writing lark, except the bird is a bunting not a lark and writing master. The serpent-like marks on the eggs led to the Welsh name servant-of-the-snake, from the myth that the markings warned snakes of predators. Two other local names that seem contradictory are pretty-pretty creature and may-the-devil-take-you, the latter an alternative imitative local name!

The hammer part of the vernacular name comes from the German ammer, the name for a bunting. John Clare wrote about the bird "Close to a hill of ants where Cowslips bloom - And shed o'er meadows far their sweet perfume. - In early spring, when winds blow chilly cold, - The Yellowhammer, trailing grass will come,- To fix a place and choose an early home, With Yellow breast and head of solid gold".

The population and distribution of this species has declined markedly over the 50 years to 2017 with numbers falling by 59% and has had a UK conservation status of red since 2002.

The scientific name for the Yellowhammer is *Emberiza citrinella* with *citrinella* meaning citrus tree alluding to the bird's yellow coloration.

Main characteristics of the Passeridae family:

The Old World sparrows in the family Passeridae are small passerine birds. The genus Passer gave rise to the name of the order Passeriformes. Sparrows are small, plump brown-grey birds with short tails and stubby, powerful beaks. They are primarily seed-eaters, though they also eat small insects. Most species of sparrows are sexually dimorphic. Males are usually bigger than females and some have black on the throat, chin or throat with females and juveniles less coloured. Sparrows are usually monogamous but polygyny does occur and extra-pair copulations are common. Males defend breeding territories and attract mates by calling. Male courtship displays involves feather fluffing, wing shaking and raising the tail feathers plus calling. Their untidy lined nests are made with grass, in cavities, crevices, boxes or holes in buildings. Clutch size ranges from 4 to 5. Eggs are white with dark spots. Incubation lasts 9 to 16 days and the eggs hatch synchronously. Young are fed by both parents and fledge after 10 to 21 days.

The two species in this family in the UK are in one genus:

Passer - House Sparrow; Tree Sparrow

The **House Sparrow** was formerly very common and closely associated with human dwellings. The House Sparrow retained top spot in the Garden Birdwatch survey (2019) for the most frequently seen bird in our gardens. Its various local names include craff; cuddy, also used for the Dunnock (which was erroneously called a Hedge Sparrow for a long time); easing sparrow, from nesting in eaves; spadger, from the Old English spara; sprug; squidgie and thack sparrow from thatch. In Cockney slang 'me old cock sparra' based on this bird referred to someone small and cheeky.

The name sparrow is connected to the Old English spara and the Old German sparo. The use of the word Sparrow (or its predecessors) goes back to before the 7th century and has been used as a surname for many centuries. The name referred to a homely or chirpy person. Before 1850 there were no House Sparrows in North America. In 1851 a few birds were shipped to New York to eradicate some moths. After a further shipment the next year, the bird spread across the continent. The Sparrow became a pest, destroying fruit and vegetables and was soon being killed for bounty. The Sparrow is now one of the most widespread birds in the world.

Aphrodite was the Olympian goddess of pleasure, joy, beauty, love and procreation. Her sacred animals included the sparrow and the dove. Stories include how she travelled with four white doves attached to her chariot and sparrows escorted the carriage. Their chatter and other singing birds announced the goddess's approach. In mythology the sparrow was linked to the Roman god Venus, the god of love, beauty and fertility. One piece of folklore is that seeing a House Sparrow on Valentine's Day meant a girl would marry a farmer or marry poor and be happy.

The House Sparrow has been intimately connected with human activity for millennia. The bird is associated with lechery, because of its alleged public acts of copulation, plus lowliness and pugnacity. Chaucer wrote "lecherous as a sparrow". Shakespeare mentioned the sparrow in *Measure for Measure* when Lucio complained that "sparrows must not build in house eaves because they are lecherous". In fact the bird is no more lecherous than many other birds. He also wrote in *Hamlet* "There's a special providence in the fall of a sparrow; if it be now, 'tis not to come; if it be not to come, it will be now; if it be not now, yet it will come: the readiness is all". This links to Jesus' reference to the sparrow in Matthew 10:29 ".. are not two sparrows not sold for a farthing; and not one of them will fall to the ground without your Father's will" and later in v 31 "Fear not therefore you are of more value than many sparrows". In the rhyme *Who killed Cock Robin?* the Sparrow is the villain with "Who killed Cock Robin?, I, said the Sparrow, with my bow and arrow, I killed Cock Robin". In folklore the bird represents human attachment, lasciviousness, lowliness, melancholy and pugnacity. It is also seen as a bird which takes every opportunity to breed.

The close association of the House Sparrow to human habitation is reflected in the bird's scientific name *Passer domesticus* with domus meaning house. In the 16th century boxes were erected near houses for the House Sparrow to nest in and when the birds bred the young were caught as a source of meat. Numbers of this species have seen a large fall since 1970, especially in urban areas. Research has identified one factor in this fall is a increase in the incidence of avian malaria that particularly affects the young. However, in Scotland numbers have increased by 46% in the 22 years to 2017 and in Wales by 82% and Northern Ireland by 34%. The House Sparrow has a UK conservation status of red.

Local names for the **Tree Sparrow** include copper head; red headed sparrow, both names referring to the species' red-brown head; rock sparrow and tree finch.

It took until the 18th century for this species to be recognised separately from its close cousin the House Sparrow. In China in 1958 the bird was classified as a grain pest (along with rats, flies and mosquitoes) and was killed in large numbers. Tree Sparrow numbers have fallen as dramatically as its cousin. In the 50 years to 2017 numbers have fallen by 96% with a small recovery in recent years. In the UK the bird is red listed but is of least conservation concern status in Europe.

The Tree Sparrow's scientific name is *Passer montanus* with *montanus* meaning mountain, with no clear connection to that habitat.

Collective nouns

Humans have been aware of birds gathering together for the reasons given in the Section Flocking in Chapter 2. The names given to flocks are collective nouns. Some birds, which habitually flock, have several collective nouns. Below is a list of collective nouns, in alphabetical order of the bird's formal

English name. For ease, some species (often from the same family) which share the same collective noun appear together.

List of collective nouns:

A flock of **Avocet**s is called an orchestra.

The **Barn Owl** - parliament; stare; study and wisdom. Parliament as a collective noun is shared with the **Carrion Crow** and **Rook**. Predictably the names reflect the characteristic of wisdom that some cultures have ascribed to owls. The **Little Owl**, **Long-eared Owl**, **Short-eared Owl** and the **Tawny Owl** all share the same collective nouns.

Geese are often seen in flocks on the ground in winter as they graze in fields and also as they fly to and from feeding grounds to roost. Collective nouns for the **Barnacle Goose** include gaggle; nide; plump; skein and wedge. Gaggle refers to a group on the ground. It is also used more generally to describe a disorderly group of people. A plump refers to when they are flying closely together and skein refers to the birds in flight and wedge to the characteristic shape of their flight pattern. These collective nouns also apply to the **Bean Goose, Brent Goose, Canada Goose, Greylag Goose, Pink-footed Goose** and **White-fronted Goose**.

Wedge is also used to describe a flock of **Swans**, who also fly in a V formation. This applies to **Bewick's Swan** and the **Whooper Swan**, winter visitors to Britain. They fly considerable distances on migration in family groupings, similar to geese. The Bewick's Swan breeds on the Arctic tundra and the Whooper Swan further east.

Collective nouns for the **Bittern** include sedge and siege. These nouns also apply to flocks of **Grey Heron**. Neither bird is gregarious but will flock in extreme weather conditions.

The **Black-headed Gull** forms noisy, energetic flocks and the collective nouns reflect this, such as colony; leash; pack; screech and squabble. They form mixed flocks with other birds as they seek to chase them to pinch their food.

Flocks of **Bar-tailed Godwit** are interestingly called an omniscience; pantheon and prayer. Why this bird is referred to as all knowing is not clear. Pantheon derives from the Greek pantheion with pan meaning all and theion holy. It could be that the collective noun prayer comes from the fact that the god in Godwit means good (albeit to eat).

The **Black Grouse's** unusual lek courtship ritual has already been described in the Section on Courtship in Chapter 4. Other collective nouns include brood (shared with the **Red Grouse**); covey, a common collective noun for game birds and pack.

The **Bullfinch** is most often seen in pairs rather than in a flock. However, if they group together they are called a bellowing. Again this is strange as the Bullfinch is a quiet bird and is not given to bellowing! The birds can sing very well when trained.

A flock of **buntings** is called a mural.

A flock of **Buzzard** is called a wake.

The collective noun for a group of **Capercaillie** is tok.

Collective nouns for the **Carrion Crow** include horde; hover; mob; murder; muster; parcel; parliament and storytelling, many of which it shares with its fellow corvids.

The **Chaffinch** frequently forms flocks and names for this include charm; confusion; trembling and trimming. It shares these nouns with the **Goldfinch**. The word charm derives from the Latin carmen meaning magical song.

The **Chough** has two collective nouns, chattering and clattering. Unsurprisingly chattering is also used for some finches and also the **Magpie**.

Collective nouns for the **Collared Dove** include kit and loft.

A flock of **Common Sandpiper** is called a fling.

One collective noun for the **Common Tern** is dread.

The **Coot** is seen in loose groups on open water in winter. These have been described as a commotion, from its petulant, belligerent behaviour plus cover; fleet; pod; raft, a collective noun used for many ducks; rasp and swarm.

Cormorant are colonial nesters and collectively they are called a gulp or flight.

Curlew congregate in large flocks in winter on estuaries and has the collective nouns of head and herd.

The **Dotterel**'s collective noun is a trip as is the **Dunlin**'s.

Ducks as general group have a range of collective nouns ascribed to them including badelyne; brace, usually a dead pair; doping, when diving; flush; paddling; plump; raft, when on water; safe; skein; sord; stream; team and twack.

A flock of **Eider**s is predictably a quilt.

The **Gadwall**, being a duck shares the collective nouns of balding; paddling; raft and sord with **Pintail, Pochard, Teal, Tufted Duck** and **Wigeon**.

Collective nouns for the **Golden Eagle** include congregation, which it shares with the **Golden** and **Grey Plover** along with congress; convocation and jubilee.

The **Golden Plover** gathers in large flocks in winter, often with Lapwing. Collective nouns include band; congregation; knob, whilst on water; a rush in flight; stand and wing.

The **Goldfinch** shares the nouns charm; trembling and trimming with the **Chaffinch** plus the nouns chattering (also a noun for a flock of **Magpies**); drum; troubling and vein.

The **Goosander** shares the collective noun of doping with the **Shelduck**.

Collective nouns for the **Goshawk** are shared with the **Sparrowhawk**, a close relative (and the **Raven**) namely eyrie from the name of its nest and kettle. In addition the names cast and gross apply to the **Goshawk**. A cast is a term used in falconry to mean the number of birds a falconer releases at a time.

A collective noun for the **Great Spotted Woodpecker**, the **Green Woodpecker** and the **Lesser Spotted Woodpecker** is a descent.

The **Grey Heron**'s collective nouns are hedge; rookery, from the way the bird nests in trees colonially; scattering; sedge and siege.

The collective nouns for the **Grey Partridge** are bew; clutch; covey, jug, from the way a group huddle together with their heads turned outwards and warren.

The **Grey Plover**'s collective nouns include congregation (the same as the Golden Eagle and Golden Plover) and wing.

A breeding colony of the **Guillemot** is called a loomery. Other nouns include bazaar and raft.

A flock of **House Martin**s is called a richness.

The **House Sparrow** has a range of collective nouns, including host; knot; quarrel; tribe and ubiquity.

The **Jackdaw**'s collective nouns include clattering and train.

The close cousin of the Jackdaw, the **Jay**, has band; party and scold as collective nouns.

A flock of **Kingfisher**s is called a crown.

The **Lapwing** has a range of collective nouns including ascension, perhaps from the way flocks ascend into the sky when disturbed; bevy; deceit, from the way it deceives predators of its young by feigning injury and also a word associated with women of ill repute; desert and exaltation.

A flock of **Linnet** is called a parcel.

Like its corvid cousins, the **Magpie** enjoys a range of collective nouns, including charm; conventicle, meaning a small, unofficial religious meeting which were banned at one time; gulp; mischief; murder, from the bird's predatory behaviour; tidings; tittering and tribe.

A collective noun for a flock of **Merlin** is a leash or cast.

A flock of **Moorhen** is called a plump.

A flock of **Nuthatch**es is called a booby.

A gathering of **Pheasant**s is called a bouquet, in flight; covey; head and nide.

The **Quail**'s collective nouns include bevy; covey and drift, nouns used for several other birds.

The **Raven** has a long and varied list of collective nouns including eyrie from its lofty nest; building; clamour; congress; conspiracy; horde; murder; unkindness and storytelling. Some reflect its dark character like conspiracy, murder and unkindness.

A collective noun for **Robin**s is a worm.

The **Rock Dove**'s collective nouns include cote, from the name for a building housing the birds; dole; dule; flight; piteousness and prettying.

The **Rook** shares the collective noun parliament with the owls plus its fellow corvid the Carrion Crow. In addition the nouns building and clamour refer to the Rook.

The **Ruff**'s behaviour at a lek has already been described in the Section on Courtship in Chapter 4. In addition the nouns hill and sea apply to the bird.

A flock of **Sanderling** is called a grain.

Predictably a collective noun for the **Skylark** is ascension. Others include bevy (a common collective noun) and exaltation, which is also used for a flock of **Lapwing**.

A flock of **Snipe** is called a walk or a wisp, when flying.

A collective noun for the **Song Thrush** is hermitage and mutation plus rafter.

The **Sparrowhawk**'s collective nouns include eyrie; cast; kettle; mew, from the sound the birds make; moulting and screw.

The spectacular flocking behaviour of the **Starling** has already been mentioned and the common name for this is a murmuration. Other names include chatter, which the birds do incessantly; scintillation, which their flocking behaviour is and scourge, perhaps for the people that suffer the endless chatter of the birds or the mess they make?

Swallows are seen flocking in the autumn as they prepare for their migratory flight and these are called a flight or a gulp. Another collective noun is a kettle.

In addition to the collective nouns the **Teal** shares with other ducks, the noun spring is also used, based on the way in which a flock of Teal rise directly from the ground or water, without the usual gradual lift off.

A flock of terns is called a committee.

The now rare **Turtle Dove** has many collective nouns - bale; cote; dole; dule; flight; nest; pitying; prettying and turn, all nouns it shares with the **Woodpigeon**.

The **Wigeon** shares the collective nouns for ducks generally plus balding; bunch; coil; company; knob and trip.

The **Woodcock** has the collective nouns covey; fall, from its sudden appearance in autumn and plump, also used for flocks of ducks and geese.

The **Wren**'s collective nouns include chime and herd.

APPENDICES

Appendix 1 Zoological terms

Term	Definition
Albinism	Absence of pigment; a genetic condition or caused by malnutrition, parasites or injuries. Some birds are partially albinistic
Albumen	Clear, protein liquid surrounding the yolk of an egg
Allopatric	Geographically separated populations of a species that do not inter-breed
Allopreen	Mutual preening of the feathers; often a part of courtship or pair bond maintenance
Altricial	Sightless, immobile fledglings that require full parental care. Normally nidicolous
Alula	Bastard wing; also the first finger. Aids and disrupts air flow over the wing
Amber listed species	Unfavourable conservation status in Europe; population / range has declined moderately in recent years; population declined historically but substantial recent recovery
Anisodactyl	Arrangement of toes with three toes forward and one back. All passerines and some birds of prey
Anterior	Front half of body
Anthropogenic	Relating to or resulting from the influence that humans have on the natural world
Aptosochromatosis	A natural darkening of feathers over time; mechanism not known; possibly oxidation
Asynchronous hatching	Where the first egg laid hatches first; eggs brooded as they are laid c.f. synchronous
Apteria	Patches of bare skin with no feathers
Auriculars	Feathers under and to rear of eye
Auto cannibalism	Eating own body parts; as some long distance migrants do to lose weight

Barbs	Fine filaments that branch out from the rachis (feather shaft)
Barbules	Very fine filaments that branch out from the barbs of a feather
Biandry	A form of polygamy; female has two mates at the same time
Brachial	Upper arm supported by the humerus
Bristle	Stiff rachis with a few basal barbs
Brood parasite	Transfer of egg brooding and parental care to another bird
Brood patch	Patch on a bird's belly sensitive to touch and temperature
Brow ridge	Bony hood over the eyes; used to shade the sun – seen in hawks but not falcons
Carnivore	Feeds primarily on meat
Carpal	Pertaining to the wrist
Carpometacarpus	Fusion of the wrist and hand bones which support most of the primary flight feathers
Catastrophic moult	All feathers moult at once
Cere	Soft, fleshy swelling at base of beaks e.g. on hawks, doves, skuas
Chalazae	Two twisted strands of albumen that support the yolk in an egg
Chine	Backbone or spine
Circadian	Daily rhythmic activity cycle, based on 24-hour intervals
Circannual	Events that take place over the course of one year
Cloaca	Outlet into which the alimentary, urinary and genital ducts open in the rear of a bird
Conspecific	Of the same species c.f. heterospecific
Convergent evolution	Similar structures that evolve for specific purposes in unrelated groups

Coverts	Feathers covering part of primary and secondary wing feathers - in layers of greater, median and lesser
Crepuscular	Active at twilight or before sunrise
Crissum	Under tail covert loose feathers, covering the cloaca
Crop	Pouch at the top of the oesophagus where birds store food
Culmen	Ridge near base of upper beak
Curual feathers	Covering the upper part of the leg / tibia
Digitigrade	Walks on toes
Dimorphic	Male and female exhibit different plumages c.f. monomorphic
Dispersal	Random outward movement of young birds from the breeding locality
Diurnal	Active in daylight hours
Divergent evolution	Species once similar have developed different traits
Down	Small, soft, fluffy feathers with flexible barbs that trap air
Eclipse (plumage)	Non-breeding plumage, often dull colouration e.g. ducks
Egg tooth	Small, temporary tooth on end of a chick's upper beak used to cut the egg shell at birth
Emargination	Narrowing of outer web of primary wing feathers
Endemic	Species unique to a specific geographical area
Epideictic	Display behaviour
Eyrie	Large nest of a bird of prey
Facultative brood parasitism	Bird that sometimes lays its eggs in another bird's nest e.g. Swallow

Facultative cannism	Older fledgling eats a younger sibling, especially in years of poor food supply
Filoplume	Fine hair-like feather with long shaft and a few barbs at the tip
Fovea	Located in centre of macular region of the eye retina, giving sharp central vision
Frugivorous	Eats predominantly fruit
Gametes	Sex cells - spermatozoa and ova
Gape	Mouth opening
Gens	Host specific lineage e.g. a female Cuckoo only lays its eggs in a specific host species' nest
Gizzard	Area of alimentary tract where food is broken into a digestible form
Gliding	Method of flying where outstretched wings produce sufficient lift to maintain flight
Gonads	Primary reproductive organs
Granivores	Feeds primarily on seeds
Greater primary coverts	Feathers covering the primary flight feathers
Greater secondary coverts	Feathers covering the secondary flight feathers
Hallux	Hind toe, numbered 1 (of 4)
Hepatic	Brown colouration variant e.g. Cuckoo
Herbivore	Feeds only or mainly on plants
Heterospecific	Belonging to a different species c.f. conspecific
Humerus	Short thick bone at base of wing
Hyperphagia	Eating large quantities of food e.g. before migration
Hypoxia	Oxygen deficiency in thin air
Imprinting	Attachment behaviour of young birds – filial and sexual

Incubation	Maintaining egg temperature between 30^0 and 38^0 C to ensure growth of embryo
Insectivore	Feeds primarily on insects
Irruption	Invasion of birds from another area, often in large numbers
Keratin	Fibrous protein from which feathers are made
Kleptoparasitism	Feeding by thieving food from other birds e.g. Arctic Skua
Lammelae	Thin layers of tissue on the beak, used to filter food items e.g. Shoveler
Lek	Competitive display by a group of males e.g. Ruff
Leucistic	Pigmentation cells fail to develop properly. Can result in white patches
Lobate	Digits 2, 3 and 4 of toes have lobes of skin attached to aid swimming e.g. grebes
Lore	Area between eye and upper beak
Maculation	Variation in egg pigmentation
Mandible	Upper and lower elements of the beak
Magnatite	Magnetic mineral found in some bacteria enabling birds to sense a magnetic field
Mantle	Feathers covering fore part of back
Maximilla	Upper beak
Melanistic	Abnormal amount of dark melanin pigmentation; appearance black / dark brown
Migration	Regular movement between areas which are inhabited at different seasons
Mimic	Birds that copy other sounds in their song
Mirror	White tip on the longest primary of some birds
Monomorphic	Male and female having similar plumages c.f. dimorphic

Morph (also phase)	Variation in colouring within species that is not geographically defined
Nape	Area between neck and back
Nare	Nostrils, usually on the upper beak
Natal fidelity or natal philopatry	Young birds returning to their place of birth
Nidicolous	Fledglings that stay in nest after hatching – see altricial
Nidifugous	Fledglings that leave the nest shortly after hatching – see precocial
Nocturnal	Active at night
Obligate brood parasitism	Species that always lays all its eggs in another species' nest e.g. Cuckoo
Omnivirous	Feeds on a wide range of food
Onomatopoeic	Word representing a sound or song
Orbital ring	Thin ring of bare skin surrounding a bird's eye
Oscine	Large subgroup of passerines (Passeri) that includes most of the songbirds
Osmoregulation	System by which salt is filtered out of sea water by seabirds
Palaearctic	Zoological region of the old Arctic – Europe, N Africa, Arabia, Asia to Himalaya and C China
Palmate	Toe digits 2, 3 and 4 are webbed e.g. ducks, geese and swans
Pelagic	Open sea
Phenotype	The composite of observable characteristics
Phalanges	Toe bones
Philopatry	Remaining or returning to the same place each year
Photoperiodicity	Detecting changes to the length of daylight

Piscivore	Feeds primarily on fish
Polarised light	Light vibrating in only one plane
Polyandry	Form of polygamy; female has to two or more mates concurrently
Polygamous	Male mates with several females
Polygynandry	Both male and female have several sex partners
Polygynous	Male mates with more than one female in a single breeding season
Powder down	Down feathers that produce a powder used to provide water proofing e.g. herons
Precocial	Relatively mature hatchlings e.g. have sight, can move. Normally nidifugous
Preening	Re-arranging feathers using the beak
Primaries	Main flight feathers; most birds have 10 primaries; passerines have 9
Protandry	Male arrives at the breeding ground first to set up territory
Protogny	Female arrives at the breeding ground first to set up territory
Pterylae	Tracts of skin where contour feathers grow
Pullus	Stage of chick development between hatching and fully grown
Rachis	Feather shaft
Radius and Ulna	Supporting bones of the forearm of the wing
Rectrices	Tail feathers – number varies; often 10, ranges from 6 to 32
Red listed species	Globally threatened; population / range declined rapidly in recent years; declined historically and not shown a substantial recent recovery
Remiges	Primary, secondary and tertial flight feathers

Reticulate	Feet covered by a fine patchwork of small irregularly shaped platelets e.g. falcons and plovers
Rhynchokinesis	Flexible upper mandible enabling only the tip of the beak to open e.g. in waders
Rictal bristles	Hairs at the base of the beak. May have tactile function e.g. to catch insects
Scapulars	Feathers on back and sides, between neck and wing
Scutellate	Feet covered with a tough layer of horny keratin scales e.g. passerines
Secondary	Inner wing feathers, numbered inward from mid-point of wing
Semipalmate	Small web between digits 2, 3 and 4 e.g. some sandpipers, plovers and all grouse
Shaft	Central, thin shaft of a feather
Sibilicide	Older hatchlings who eat younger, weaker siblings when food supply is low
Soaring	Using up-draughts of warm air with out-stretched wings to maintain flight
Species	Group of birds capable of breeding producing fertile offspring, separated from other groups with which interbreeding does not (normally) happen
Speculum	Patch of colour on the secondaries e.g. ducks
Stoop	Deep, fast aerial dive of bird e.g. Peregrine
Supercilium	Stripe immediately above the eye
Sympatry	Two species that exist in the same geographical area and regularly encounter one another
Synchronous hatching	Female lays all eggs first, then commences brooding. All eggs hatch at the same time c.f. asynchronous
Syndactyl	Two or more digits of feet are fused together e.g. kingfishers

Syrinx	Sound producing organ, unique to birds
Tarsus; also tarsometatarsus	Bone between the ankle and the ball of the foot
Taxa	Taxonomic group e.g. order, family, genus
Tertials	Inner most flight feathers; usually 3 or 4
Tomia	Cutting edge on mandibles
Totipalmate	Feet with webbing that connects all four toes e.g. Gannet
Vagrant	Individual bird observed in a region outside usual range for that species
Vestigial	Organ that has become functionless
Wattle	Fleshy, colourful growth, usually on the neck or head
Tetrachromatic	Cone sensors in the eye that are sensitive to red, green, blue or ultra-violet frequencies
Zugunruhe	Rapid beating of wings denoting the onset of migration
Zygodactyl	Two toes facing forward (digits 2 and 3) and two back (digits 1 and 4) e.g. woodpeckers

Appendix 2 Record breakers

Record	Bird	Information
Biggest nest	Mallee Fowl	1 m tall; 4m wide
Deepest dive by bird	Emperor Penguin	500m; submerged for 18 min
Deepest diving duck	Long-tailed Duck	60 m
Fastest bird flight	Peregrine	At least 200 km/hr; possibly 270 km/hr
Fastest bird level flight	Spine-tailed Swift	160 km/hr
Fastest bird level flight UK	Eider	Timed speeds of 75 km/hr
Fastest recorded migratory flight	Great Snipe	6800 km non-stop; av. speed 95 km / hr.
Fastest running bird	Ostrich	Timed at 70 km/hr
Fastest swimming bird	Gentoo Penguin	40 km per hour
Fastest wingbeat	Hummingbird	90 beats / sec
Greatest diff in weight between male & female	Sparrowhawk	Female 260 g; male 150 g
Greatest number of feathers	Gentoo Penguin	~ 80 000; Mute Swan ~ 25 000
Heaviest bird ever	Moa	450 kg
Heaviest existing bird	Ostrich	160 kg
Heaviest flying bird	Kori's Bustard	18 kg; 3 m wing span
Heaviest flying bird UK	Mute Swan	12 kg; 2.2 m wing span
Highest altitude breeder UK	Dotterel	>900 m

Record	Bird	Information
Highest migratory flight	Ruppell's Griffon Vulture	Collided with an airplane at 11,278 m
	Bar-headed Geese	Flying over Himalayas above 8000 m
Largest beak	Toco Toucan	23 cm; up to 50% of body surface area
Largest egg in proportion to body size	Kiwi	450 g egg -$^1/_4$ weight of female
Largest ever flying bird	Teratornis	8.3 m wing span; weight 100 kg
Largest ever wingspan	South American Teratoron	8.3 m
Largest existing bird egg	Ostrich	15 cm long; 1.4 kg
Largest eye	Ostrich	50 mm
Largest field of vision	Woodcock	360 degrees
Largest flock	Brambling	~7 million
Largest living bird	Ostrich	115 kg; 2.5 m tall
Largest nesting colony	Passenger Pigeon	Est. 136 million in area of ~ 2000 sq / km
Largest ground nest	Dusky Scrub Fowl	11 m x 5 m; weighing 2 700 kg
Largest tree nest	Bald Eagle	6 m x 3 m; weighing 2 700 kg
Least number of feathers	Hummingbird	~940
Longest beak	Australian pelican	47 cm
Longest beak for body size UK	Snipe	7 cm beak; 25 cm body
Longest beak for body	Sword-billed	Only bird with beak longer

Record	Bird	Information
size	Hummingbird	than body
Longest comparative tongue	Wryneck	66% of body length
Longest distance ringing recovery	Arctic Tern	18 000 km - Anglesey to Australia
Longest east/west migration	Fieldfare	12 000 km round trip
Longest legs for body size	Flamingo	125 cm
Longest legs for body weight	Black-necked Stilt	23 cm ; 60% of height
Longest living species	Parrots	~100 years
Longest migratory flight by UK bird	Arctic Term	Migrates between the Arctic and Antarctica; 40 000 km with stops
Longest migratory flight by songbird	Wheatear	Greenland to sub-Sahara; 15 000 km
Longest recorded life span	Turkey buzzard	118 years
Longest recorded non-stop flight	Bar-tailed Godwit	~11 100 km; duration 8 days
Longest tail feathers	Crested Argus Pheasant	173 cm
Longest wing span	Wandering Albatross	3.8 - 4 m
Loudest bird song	White Bellbird	Average 116 dB; peak 125 dB
Most airborne bird	Sooty Tern	After leaving nest flies for 3-10 years
Most aquatic bird	Penguin	75% time at sea
Most northerly breeding bird	Snow Bunting	

Record	Bird	Information
Most numerous bird (extant)	Red-billed Quelea	Approx. 1.5 bn
Most numerous bird (extinct)	Passenger Pigeon	Extinct since 1901
Most numerous British bird	Wren	Approx. 17 m
Most numerous duck	Pintail	
Most seasonal plumages	Ptarmigan	Four
Most sensitive smell	Kiwi	Smell an earthworm through 15 cm of soil
Most widespread bird	Barn Owl	
Sharpest vision	Peregrine	Estimated can spot a pigeon at 8 km
Smallest bird	Bee Hummingbird	6.2 cm; 1.6 g
Smallest bird UK	Goldcrest	5.5 g; 9.0 cm length
Smallest egg for body size	Vervain Hummingbird	0.62 cm; 0.365 g
Smallest eye in proportion to body	Kiwi	7 mm
Smallest duck UK	Teal	36 cm; 330 g
Tallest bird	Moa	~1.8 m
Tallest breeding bird UK	Ostrich	~ 1.20 m

Appendix 3 Phrases and idioms

A bird in the hand is worth two in the bush.

A good egg.

A little bird told me.

An albatross around your neck.

As bald as a coot.

As free as a bird.

As hoarse as a crow.

As proud as a peacock.

As the crow flies.

Baby, baby bunting.

Bad egg.

Bald as a Coot.

Birds and bees.

Bird brain.

Birdie (golf).

Bird's eye view.

Birds of a feather flock together.

Bit of a lark.

Booby – (stupid person).

Booby prize

Booby trap

Charm the birds out of a tree

Chicken! (coward)

Chicken and egg (situation).

Chickens come to roost

Chicken feed.

Chicken legs.

Chicken livered.

Chicken out.

Clip (someone's) wings.

Clucking like a mother hen.

Cock and bull story

Cold turkey.

Cook one's goose.

Count one's chickens.

Crazy as a loon.

Crazy as a Coot.

Crow's feet.

Cuckoo in the nest.

Cuckolded.

Curate's egg

Dead as a Dodo.

Dead duck.

Do bird (prison)

Double eagle (golf).

Dotty (fr. Dotterel).

Duck (score zero).

Duck the question.

Eagle eyed.

Early bird catches the worm.

Eat crow.

Eat like a Gannet.

Egg on.

Egg on face.

Empty nest (syndrome).

Feather in (someone's) cap

Feather your nest.

Fine feathers make a fine bird.

Fly the nest.

For the birds.

Foul one's own nest.

Free as a bird.

Get one's ducks in a row.

Give someone the bird.

Go to work on an egg.

Goose bumps.

Goose step.

Graceful as a swan.

Grouse (grumble).

Gutter snipe.

Harpy.

Happy as a lark.

Headless chicken.

Hen party.

Hen pecked.

Hoarse as a crow.

Home bird.

Jay walking.

Jail bird.

Kill the goose that lays the golden egg.

Kill two birds with one stone.

Knock down with a feather.

Lagging behind.

Lame duck.

Lark about.

Light as a feather.

Like a chicken with its head off.

Lovely weather for ducks.

Loony – crazy (fr. divers).

Make the feathers fly.

Naked as a jay bird.

Neither fish nor fowl.

Nest egg.

Night owl.

No spring chicken.

Not a dicky bird.

Odd bird.

Old crow.

On a wing and a prayer.

One Swallow doesn't make a summer.

Out for a duck.

Parrot fashion.

Pecking order.

Pigeon chested.

Pigeon hole.

Play chicken.

Proud as a Peacock.

Put a jinks on someone.

Rare as hen's teeth.

Rare bird.

Rotten egg.

Round Robin.

Ruffle its feathers.

Rule the roost.

Say boo to a goose.

Shoot the bird.

Sick as a parrot.

Silly goose.

Sing like a canary.

Sing like a lark.

Sitting duck.

Sod this for a lark.

Soft as a feather.

Soft as down.

Some old bird.

Something to crow about.

Spread one's wings.

Spring chicken.

Stool pigeon.

Strange bird.

Strictly for the birds.

Swan around.

Swan song.

Take like a duck to water.

Take someone under your wing.

Talk turkey.

The bird has flown.

The birds and the bees.

The early bird catches the worm.

Thin as a rail.

To crow (about).

To grouse.

To harry.

To parrot.

To quail.

Try out one's wings.

To snipe.

Ugly duckling.

Up with the lark.

Watch like a hawk.

Water off a duck's back.

What's good for the goose is good for the gander.

Whirly bird.

Wild goose chase.

Wing it.

Wise old owl.

Woodcock – simpleton

Wouldn't say boo to a goose.

Yardbird.

Your goose is cooked.

REFERENCES

1. **Robinson, R.A.** *BirdFacts: profiles of birds occurring in Britain & Ireland.* Thetford. BTO. 2005.

2. **Birds, Devon.** *Devon Birds Report.* s.l. : Devon Birds. 2018. 1753-951X.

3. St. Michael's, Exeter Peregrine Falcons' project. .

4. **Woodward, I.D. et al.** *BTO/JNCC BirdTrends Report.* Thetford. BTO. 2018.

5. **Hayhow DB et. al.** *The State of Nature.* s.l. : The State of Nature Partnership. 2019.

6. **Woodward, I., et al.** *Population estimates of birds in Great Britain and the United Kingdom.* s.l. : British Birds. 2020.

7. **Clements, J. F., T. S. Schulenberg, M. J. Iliff, D. Roberson, T. A. Fredericks, B. L. Sullivan and C. L. Wood.** *The eBird/Clements checklist of birds of the world: v2018.* 2018.

8. *The British List: A Checklist of Birds of Britain (9th edition). Ibis 160: 190-240.* s.l. : British Ornithologists' Union. 2017. Vol. 160.

9. **Gill F, D Donsker & P Rasmussen (Eds).** *IOC World Bird List (v10.1).* s.l. : International Ornithologists' Union. 2020.

10. **Harris, S.J. et al.** *The Breeding Bird Survey. BTO Research Report 726.* Thetford. BTO. 2019.

Downloaded BTO graphs: Massimino, D., Woodward, I.D., Hammond, M.J., Harris, S.J., Leech, D.I., Noble, D.G., Walker, R.H., Barimore, C., Dadam, D., Eglington, S.M., Marchant, J.H., Sullivan, M.J.P., Baillie, S.R. & Robinson, R.A. (2019) BirdTrends 2019: trends in numbers, breeding success and survival for UK breeding birds. BTO Research Report 722. BTO, Thetford. www.bto.org/birdtrends

BIBLIOGRAPHY

Below are many sources from books and on the internet relevant to the subject matter of this book:

Ackerman, J., 2016. *The genius of birds.* London, Little, Brown.

A detailed examination of all aspects of bird intelligence, with plenty of research and experimental evidence discussed, albeit mainly American.

Addison, J., 1998. *Treasury of bird lore.* London, Andre Deutsch.

A book covering forty well known British birds giving a limited range of information on their names and greater detail on our relationship with the birds, relevant folklore and many quotes from literature.

Austin, O L., 1962. *Birds of the world.* London, Paul Hamlyn.

A comprehensive and well illustrated book of the orders and families of all the birds in the world.

Birkhead, T., 2008. *The wisdom of birds.* London, Bloomsbury.

An in-depth examination of all aspects of a bird's life tracing the historical development of bird science supplemented by some superb illustrations and paintings.

Birkhead, T., 2012. *Bird sense.* London, Bloomsbury.

By the same author, this book provides an in-depth examination of how birds use their senses.

Birkhead, T., 2016. *The most perfect thing: Inside (and outside) a bird's egg.* London, Bloomsbury.

A book that explores in detail all aspects of the fascinating story of a bird's egg, well written with plenty of scientific explanation.

Ed. M Brooke and T Birkhead., 1991. *The Cambridge Encyclopedia of Ornithology.* Cambridge, Cambridge University Press.

A comprehensive reference book on all aspects of ornithology. Very detailed and written by experts.

Cocker, M. ed., 2005. *Birds Britannica.* London, Chatto and Windlus.

A monumental work on all aspects of British birds, organised by bird families, with information collected from contributors around the country.

Cocker, M., 2013. *Birds and people.* London, Jonathan Cape.

A large work giving great detail on how birds have interacted with humans across the millennia in all cultures.

Davies, N., 2015. *Cuckoo - cheating by nature.* London, Bloomsbury.

A well written and detailed account of the natural history of the Cuckoo based on 30 years of research by a leading academic.

Greenoak, F., 1997. *British birds their folklore, names and literature.* London, Christopher Helm.

This book covers many popular birds on the British list in great detail, giving a list of their local names along with a wide range of information on the bird's place in history, relating many tales and myths, references in literature plus descriptions of the bird's characteristics and life.

Jackson, C., 1968. *British names of birds.* London, H F Witherby.

A very detailed dictionary style book with entries for 329 birds giving lists of local names.

Kirke Swann, K., 1913. *A dictionary of English and folk-names of British birds.* London, H F Witherby.

A well researched and detailed book listing nearly 5000 local names for British birds plus their derivation. Also folklore included. Listed in order of local names, so it is hard to compile all the names for a specific bird.

Lack, D., 1953. *The life of the Robin.* London, Pelican.

A seminal work by a famous ornithologist examining the life of the Robin in great detail.

Lederer, R., 2014. *Latin for bird lovers.* London, Timber Press.

A thorough dictionary style book of 3000 single Latin words that appear in the scientific name for birds. Covers birds worldwide and includes many illustrations and small articles giving interesting extra information about aspects of the life of birds. Does not cover all the British list and the book gives only a few full binomial scientific names for British birds.

Lockwood, W.P., 1984. *The Oxford book of British bird names.* Oxford, Oxford University Press.

This book provides a comprehensive dictionary style reference to local names for British birds. Gives detailed information on the source of the name and its derivation. Needs a lot of cross-referencing to compile all the names associated with an individual species. Does not include the vernacular or scientific names.

Newton, I., 2013. *Bird populations.* London, Harper Collins.

A comprehensive scientific examination of all aspects of UK bird populations with a detailed discussion on all the factors that affect bird numbers.

Proctor, N S and Lynch, P., 1993. *Manual of Ornithology. Avian structure and function.* London, Yale University.

A detailed undergraduate text book on avian biology, with splendid drawings and understandable text.

Rhodes, C., 2014. *An unkindness of Ravens.* London, Michael O'Mara Books.

This book covers the collective nouns for people and animals as well as birds. It provides a detailed description of the derivation of the collective nouns for many of our British birds.

Rothenberg, D., 2005. *Why birds sing?* London, Penguin.

An alternative view of what makes birds sing, suggesting it is not just a survival strategy.

Tudge, C., 2008. *Consider the birds.* London, Penguin.

A book covering many aspects of ornithology and is not limited to British birds. Contains a comprehensive section on names and taxonomy for those wanting to understand how birds are classified and a detailed description of the features of the orders and families of birds. Also interesting chapters on various aspects of the lives of birds.

Walters, M., 2003. *A concise history of ornithology.* London, Christopher Helm.

A very detailed chronological history of the main players in the world of ornithology. Shows how the science developed over the centuries.

White, G., 1789. *The Natural History and Antiquities of Selborne.*

Gilbert White's 18th century record of the natural history of a Hampshire village, of which he was curate, based mainly on letters to a friend, is one of the first works on ecology. Covers bird as well as many other animals. A fantastic read of a very perceptive man.

Below are some of the series of titles available on individual birds:

The New Naturalist series published by Collins. Monographs on birds including British Thrushes, Finches, birds of prey and Tits. These books examine the life of the individual species in great detail. Longer length books.

Hamlyn species guides - monographs on birds including Common Tern, Great Tit, Fieldfare, Barn Owl, Kestrel, Swallow and Blackcap. These books examine the life of the individual species in detail. Mid-length books.

Shire Natural History published by Shire Publishing. Monographs on a wide range of British birds. Short length books.

Below are some web useful addresses:

The **Royal Society for the Protection of Birds** - http://www.rspb.org.uk/. Information on bird identification plus survey work and projects.

The **British Ornithologists' Union** - http://www.bou.org.uk/. The BOU publishes the official list of British birds (free download) including the correct English vernacular name and the agreed scientific name. Also carries out detailed research, holds conferences and publishes scientific papers.

British Trust for Ornithology - https://www.bto.org/ The British Trust for Ornithology carries out a wide range of scientific work, data collection from surveys and issues publications. The web site has a very useful section on bird facts and survey results. The BTO also has a series of useful identification videos available on YouTube.

The **International Ornithologists' Union** - https://www.internationalornithology.org/ maintains the world lists of bird species and issues a down loadable world list of birds, including the latest taxonomic information, international English vernacular name and the agreed scientific name.

Birdguides - http://www.birdguides.com/home/default.asp. The birdwatchers' web-site with news of bird sightings, articles on all aspects of bird watching and ornithology. Some are paid-for services. Offers a free weekly e-mail news service. Some superb photographs of most British birds.

A useful site for bird song sonograms is http://fssbirding.org.uk/sonagrams.htm

A good site for bird song recordings is https://www.xeno-canto.org/ which has a huge library of downloadable files.

Most counties have a bird society, whose web-sites contain useful information. They publish annual reports giving detail of the birds seen in that county during the last year, often including papers written by local authors.

Also county or area wildlife societies have web sites with useful information on what can be seen where.

Some of the books mentioned are not easy to obtain. A useful web site is Abebooks - http://www.abebooks.co.uk/

INDEX

Abnormalities 8
Accipitridae.................................... 278
Accipitriformes.............................. 276
Acrocephalidae 348
Acuity 99
Aegithalidae.................................. 337
Aesop's tale
    Crane 229
    crow 115
    eagle................................ 281
    geese 188
    hawk...........................285, 286
    Jackdaw 320
    lark 327
    Nightingale 359
    owl 291
    partridge........................... 205
    Raven 322
    Song Thrush 368
    swan 192
    Tawny Owl 295
Age, average 131
Agricultural practices...................... 133
Agriculture 150
Air sacs 31
Alaudidae...................................... 325
Albinism... 8
Alcedinidae 297
Alcidae... 249
Allen's rule 168
Allopreening 23, 79, 108
Altricial 90
Amber list criteria.......................... 145
Anatidae 187
Anseriformes 187
Anthropomorphism......73, 118, 183, 217
Apodidae 221
Apteria... 7
Arctic Skua 248
Arctic Tern 258
Ardeidae 271
Aristotle....................................... 163
Asynchronous hatching 87
Atlases 156
Audouin's Gull............................... 256
Auriculars..................................... 104
Auto cannibalism 46
Avian eye 96
Avocet 231

Barbs...2
Barbules..2
Barn Owl 289
    hearing................................ 107
    sight....................................97
Barnacle Goose............................. 190
Bar-tailed Godwit 239
Bathing..3
Beaks 17
Bean Goose 189
Bearded Tit................................... 324
    diet 112
Belon.. 163
Bergmann's rule 168
Bewick's Swan 194
Binomial name 165
    scientific names...................... 178
Birds of conservation concern
    report 2015 145
Birds' names................................. 173
Birth rate..................................... 130
Bittern... 273
    conservation.......................... 148
Black Grouse 205
    lek 76
Black Guillemot 252
Black Redstart 360
Black Tern 258
Blackbird 364
    call sonogram 67
Blackcap 352
    migration 47
Black-headed Gull...........................255
Black-necked Grebe 209
Black-tailed Godwit........................ 239
Black-throated Diver.......................262
Blue Tit....................................... 335
Body temperature 111
Bombycillidae................................ 375
Bones..23
BOU 177
    bird categories........................ 170
Brambling.......................................377
Breeding
    relationships...........................72
Brent Goose 191
Bristles 6
Brood parasite.................................84
    obligate................................84

partial	84, 370
Brood patch	11, 87
Brooding	87
Bullfinch	380
Buzzard	287
Caged birds	60, 139, 352, 378
Calcariidae	384
Calls	66
purposes	66
Camouflage	4, 27
Canada Goose	191
Capercaillie	206
Caprimulgidae	219, 220
Caprimulgiformes	219
Carnivores	18
Carrion Crow	318
Catastrophic moult	10, 195, 201
Cattle Egret	275
Cere	21, 307
Certhiidae	340
Cetti's Warbler	346
Chaffinch	378
calls	66
Chalaza	85
Charadriidae	233
Charadriiformes	229
Chicks	89
altricial	90
precocial	89
Chiffchaff	347
Chough	318
conservation	148
Cinclidae	343
Cirl Bunting	385
conservation	148
Claws	16
Clement's list	170
Climate change	134, 150
Cline	162
Cloaca	4, 77, 80
Coal Tit	335
Cochlea	104
Cock nests	78, 82, 341, 351
Collared Dove	213
Collective nouns	390
Colour vision	101
Columbidae	211
Columbiformes	210
Columella	104
Common Gull	256
Common Redpoll	381
Common Sandpiper	246
Common Scoter	200
Common Tern	259
Compass orientation	46
Competing species	129
Conservation	144
Conservation concern categories	144
Conservation success stories	148
Coot	226
Copulation	80
Coraciiformes	297
Cormorant	269
Corn Bunting	386
Corn Crake	225
Cornea	96
Corvid intelligence	115
Corvidae	313
Counting and tracking	155
Counts and surveys	155
Courtship	75
dances	77
display	76
feeding	78
Crane	222, 228
conservation	148
Crèche	56
Crested Tit	335
Crossbill	382
Cuckoo	216
breeding	84
migration	49
tracking	159
Cuculidae	216
Cuculiformes	216
Curlew	237
Curlew Sandpiper	240
Current classification	167
Cygnus	192
Darwin	166
Dawn chorus	62, 100
DDT	143
Death rate	130
Decoys	135
Detecting movement	101
Dialects	68
Digestion	111
Dilution principle	54, 56
Dimorphism	27
Dipper	344

Disease 129
DNA.. 166
Dotterel 236
Dove 59, 214
Down 6
Drinking 113
Duetting... 69
Dunlin 49, 240
Dunnock 370
Eating 110
Egg dumping 84
Eggs 17, 85
   albumen 85
   colour... 86
   fertilisation 85
   laying.. 87
   membranes.................................. 86
   number laid 91
   shape.. 86
   shell.. 86
   size 92
   weight 92
   yolk.. 85
Eider.. 199
Emargination 5
Emberizidae 385
Emotions
   anger and rage............................ 119
   fear... 119
   grief and sadness 119
   happiness and joy........................ 119
   love and affection 119
English name, formal...................... 177
Eponyms.. 174
Evolution 166
   convergent.................................. 168
   divergent 168
Eye
   acuity... 99
   binocular vision............................ 98
   field of view 97
   focusing 99
   sensitivity................................... 100
   size 97
Falconidae 307
Falconiformes 306
Farmland, population change 152
Feathers.. 2
Fieldfare 365
Filoplumes 7, 107
   herons 273

Finch 376
   song... 60
Firecrest.. 346
Fishing... 142
Fledglings
   growth rate 93
Flight... 12
Flight feathers
   primary 5
   secondaries 5
Flight pattern
   gliding.. 38
Flight patterns 38
Flight, design 31
Flocking... 53
Flying
   lift 34
   thrust.. 34
Food supply....................................... 127
Fovea 101
Fright moult 3
Fringillidae.. 376
Frugivores 18
Fulmar... 265
Gadwall... 196
Galliformes.. 202
Game management 136
Gannet 268
Gape 21
Garden birdwatch survey................. 157
Garden Warbler................................. 353
Garganey... 196
Gavia... 260
Gaviidae 260
Gaviiformes....................................... 260
Geese... 188
Geographical movement
   species 161
Geolocators....................................... 158
Gilbert White..................................... 164
Gill and Donsker 170
Giraldus... 190
Gizzard 24, 111, 112, 210
Glaucous Gull 257
Gloger's rule...................................... 168
Goal orientation 46
Goldcrest... 345
Golden Eagle 279
Golden Plover.................................... 234
Goldeneye... 200
Goldfinch... 383

418

Goosander 201
Goshawk 284
GPS 159
Granivores 18
Grasshopper Warbler 351
Great Black-backed Gull 257
Great Bustard 149
Great Crested Grebe 210
    courtship display 77
Great Grey Shrike 313
Great Northern Diver 262
Great Skua 249
Great Spotted Woodpecker 303
Great Tit 336
    intelligence 118
    song 66
Green list 145
Green Sandpiper 246
Green Woodpecker 305
Greenfinch 380
Greenshank 247
Grey Heron 274
Grey Partridge 205
Grey Phalarope 245
Grey Plover 234
Grey Wagtail 372
Greylag Goose 189
Gruidae 227
Gruiformes 223
Guillemot 250
    call 62
    hearing 106
Habitat 151
Habitat change 132
Haematopodidae 232
Halcyon 299
Hallux 13
Harriers 282
Hatching 88
Hawfinch 379
Hearing
    process 104
    uses 104
Hen Harrier 282
Hennig 167
Herbst corpuscles 107
Herring Gull 257
Hirundinidae 328
Hobby 308
Homing pigeon 51
Honey-buzzard 278

House Martin 333
House Sparrow 388
Hovering 39
Human exploitation 137
Hunting 135
Hybrid 162
Hybridisation 162
Hybrids 179
Hydrobatidae 263
Hyperphagia 45
Hypoxia 44, 396
Imprinting 120
Infidelity 80
Insectivores 18
Intelligence 114
    crow 115
    Great Tit 118
    logic 116
    problem solving 115
    Raven 117
    recognition 117
    self awareness 115
    social behaviour 117
    tool use 117
International Ornithologists' Union ... 178
International Union
of Conservation of Nature
    categories 147
IOC 169
Iridescence 8
Jack Snipe 243
Jackdaw 319
Jay 315
    anting 3
    caching 118
Kestrel 309
King Arthur 318
King Canute 241
Kingfisher 298
Kittiwake 255
Kleptoparasite 248, 255, 260
Kleptoparastite 19
Knot 241
Lamellae 187
Lanceolate plumes
    herons 273
Laniidae 313
Lapwing 235
Laridae 254
Legs 13
Leks 55, 76, 206

Lesser Black-backed Gull.................. 257
Lesser Redpoll................................... 381
Lesser Spotted Woodpecker 304
Lesser Whitethroat........................... 353
Leucism.. 8
Life expectancy 131
Linnaeus 165, 178
Linnet 380
Little Auk 250
Little Egret 275
Little Grebe 209
Little Gull 256
Little Owl 292
Little Ringed Plover 236
Little Stint 242
Little Tern 258
Local bird names 176
Locustellidae.................................. 350
Long-eared Owl............................... 296
Long-tailed Duck 200
Long-tailed Tit................................ 338
    nest 82
Lorenz, Conrad............................... 121
Magnetic field
    detecting 103, 109
Magpie 316
    intelligence 115
Mallard 197
Mandibles... 17
Manx Shearwater............................ 266
    migration 48
Marine Conservation Zones 155
Marsh Harrier 283
Marsh Tit 335
Marsh Warbler................................ 349
    mimicry... 69
Mayer 167
Mediterranean Gull......................... 256
Melanism... 8
Mendel 167
Merlin.. 310
Messiaen 60
Migration 41
    compass systems........................... 46
    differential.................................... 43
    intermittent 43
    leap frog 43, 237, 353
    loop.....................................43, 354
    orientation.................................... 46
    partial 43
    preparing for................................ 44

Millinery trade................................ 140
Mimicry... 69
Mis-named birds.............................. 179
Mistle Thrush 366
Monogamous
    sexually 73
Montagu's Harrier 284
Moorhen.. 226
Motacillidae 371
Moulting 9
Movements
    dispersal....................................... 52
    irruptions 52
    spreading 53
Muscicapidae 354
Mute Swan 193
Myth 182
Nares 21
Natal fidelity..................................... 43
Natural England.............................. 154
Neognathes...................................... 12
Nest
    burrow 81
    domed 81
    hole... 81
    open 81
    platform.. 81
    tree 81
Nest sites 128
Nesting... 81
    colonial 83
Nictating membrane........................ 102
Nidicolous 90
Nidifugous.. 90
Nightingale..................................... 357
    song 59
    sonogram...................................... 65
Nightjar... 220
    song 62
Nuthatch 339
Oesophagus..................................... 111
Omnivores.. 18
Orientation....................................... 46
Osmoregulation.............................. 229
Osprey 277
    conservation............................... 149
    migration 49
Owl
    flight feathers................................. 7
    hearing.. 106
    sight.. 100

420

Oystercatcher 233
Paleognathes 12
Pandionidae 276
Panuridae..324
Paridae..333
Passeridae 387
Passeriformes 312
Pelagic...40, 229, 246, 249, 255, 263, 265
Pelecaniformes................................271
Peregrine...310
    diet 112
Pesticides 143
Phalacrocoracidae 268
Phasianidae 203
Pheasant 204
Phenotype.......................................166
Philopatry..43
Photoperiodicity 44
Photoreceptors
    cones..100
    rods..100
Phylloscopidae................................347
Picidae...301
Piciformes 300
Pied Flycatcher 360
Pied Wagtail 373
Pigeon...212
Pigmentation 7
Pink-footed Goose 189
Pintail..198
Piscivores 18
Plastics 144
Pochard...198
Podicipedidae..................................208
Podicipediformes............................207
Polarised light....................46, 103, 396
Polyandry 75
Polygynandry...................................75
Polygyny..74
Population estimates of birds
in the UK 2020 157
Populations
    abundance.................................123
    distribution...............................123
    estimates UK 157
    in UK 146
    measurement 123
Powder feathers
    herons.......................................273
Precocial..89
Predation...128

Preening 3
Procellariidae 264
Procellariiformes.............................263
Protandry...378
Protogny..245
Prunellidae......................................370
Psittaciformes 312
Ptarmigan 206
Pterylae 7
PTT's 159
Puffin...253
    beak...17
Pullus...90
Punt guns...135
Purple Sandpiper.............................242
Quail..204
Rachis 2
Rallidae..224
Raven 320
Ray, taxonomy 163
Razorbill..251
Rectrices 6
Recurvirostridae..............................231
Red Grouse 207
Red Kite 286
    conservation 149
Red list criteria 144
Red-breasted Merganser.................202
Red-legged Partridge.......................204
Red-necked Grebe...........................210
Red-necked Phalarope.....................246
Redshank...247
Redstart...361
Red-throated Diver..........................263
Redwing...367
Reed Bunting 386
Reed Warbler...................................349
Refraction 102
Regulidae...344
Regurgitation 94
Relationships
    monogamous.............................73
Remiges..5
Respiratory system..........................24
Reticulate 17
Reverse mounting 80
Rhynchokinesis 21
Rictal bristles...................................22
Ring Ouzel..367
Ringed Plover 236
Ringing...156

421

Ring-necked Parakeet........................ 312
Robin 355
    migration 47
Rock Dove... 212
Rock Pipit... 374
Roding 245
Rook 323
Roosts... 54
Roseate Tern.................................... 259
Ruddy Duck...................................... 202
Ruff... 242
    lek 76
Sand Martin 329
Sanderling.. 243
Sandwich Tern 260
Satellite tracking 158
Savi's Warbler.................................. 351
Saw-tooths....................................... 201
Scaup 199
Scientific names 177
Scolopacidae.................................... 237
Scottish Crossbill 383
Scutullate... 17
Seabirds, population change............. 153
Sedge Warbler 350
Semi-plume - feather......................... 6
Serin 384
Sex.. 79
Sex chromosomes 79
Sexual dimorphism.........27, 29, 161, 206
    Colouration.................................. 27
    reverse 75, 236, 291
    Size... 28
Sexual dimporphism.......................... 64
Sexual selection 76
Shag.. 271
Shelduck 195
Shore Lark.. 328
Short-eared Owl............................... 297
Shoveler.. 196
Sight 96
    process 96
    ultra-violet light 100
Siskin 384
Sittidae 339
Size, variation.................................. 25
Skeleton... 31
Skylark 326
    song 59
Slavonian Grebe 210
Sleeping.. 113

Smell 109
    navigation 51
Smew 201
Snipe... 243
Snipe, drumming 4
Snow Bunting 384
Soaring... 39
    active 39
    passive 39
Song.. 61
    dialects.. 68
    mimicry 69
    variations 68
Song Thrush 367
    song... 59
Songs and calls 58
Sonograms 67
Sound.. 104
Sparrowhawk 284
Species 161
Species, definition 162
Speculum 12, 77, 198
Sperm competition 80
Spotted Flycatcher............................ 355
Spotted Redshank............................. 247
Starling... 368
    migration 47
Stercorariidae................................... 248
Stock Dove 212
Stonechat.. 362
Stone-curlew 230
Storm Petrel 264
Strigidae... 291
Strigiformes...................................... 287
Structural colours 8
Sturnidae.. 368
Sub-species 179
Suffixes 181
Sulidae 267
Suliformes... 267
Swallow... 329
Swan 192
Swift.. 222
Swimming 40
Sylviidae... 351
Synchronous hatching....................... 87
Syrinx 62
Taste 108
Tawny Owl 294
Taxidermy 140
Taxonomy

history 163
Teal 198
Territory
    song 65
Toe arrangements............................14
Tomia 21
Touch 107
    receptors................................107
Tracking devices 158
Tree Pipit....................................375
Tree Sparrow.................................389
Treecreeper..................................340
Trend data...................................125
Troglodytidae 340
Tufted Duck..................................199
Turdidae.....................................364
Turner 163
Turnstone....................................240
Turtle Dove..................................214
Twite 381
Tympanum 104
Type of feather
    bristles 6
    contour 5
    down...6
    filoplume.......................................7
    semi-plume 6
    tail 6
    wing 5
Tytonidae 288
Ultraviolet 8
Vanes 5
Vernacular name 177
Vision
    tetrachromatic............................100
Visual displays 11
von Linne, Carl................................165
Water / wetlands
    population change 152
Water Pipit...................................375
Water Rail 225
Waxwing 375
Weather......................................130

Wetlands 133
Wheatear.....................................363
    migration 48
Whimbrel.....................................239
Whinchat 363
White gulls....................................257
White Wagtail 374
White-fronted Goose 190
White-tailed Eagle...........................286
    conservation 149
Whitethroat 354
Whooper Swan 194
Wigeon 196
Wild populations in the UK
1970 – 2018 151
Wildlife and Countryside Act 1981 154
Willow Tit 335
Willow Warbler...............................348
Wind farms 134
Wind hovering 39
Wing design 35
    aspect ratio.................................35
    wing loading.................................35
Wintering water birds
    population change 153
Wood Sandpiper 248
Wood Warbler 348
Woodcock.....................................244
Woodland
    population change 152
Woodlark......................................325
Woodpigeon 212
Wren 341
    song..63
Writing convention...........................177
    scientific names 178
Wryneck 302
Yellow Wagtail 374
Yellowhammer................................387
Young birds
    song..63
Zoogeographical regions..................123
Zugunruhe 44

Printed in Great Britain
by Amazon

51705997R00246